THE WHIRLIGIG MAKER'S BOOK

Full-Size Patterns and Step-by-Step Instructions for Making Fifteen Unique Animated Whirligigs

Jack Wiley

Copyright © 2013 by Jack Wiley

All Rights Reserved. No portion of this book may be reproduced or transmitted in any form whatsoever without express written permission from the author. WARNING—DISCLAIMER: The author and publisher shall have neither liability nor responsibility to any person or entity with respect to any loss or damage caused or alleged to be caused directly or indirectly by the information contained in this book.

For more information about the author, go to: **http://www.amazon.com/author/jackwileypublications**.

ISBN-13: 978-1508837206
ISBN-10: 1508837201

Printed by CreateSpace

CONTENTS

1. ANIMATED WHIRLIGIGS 5
2. MATERIALS, TOOLS, AND TECHNIQUES 11
3. DOVE 17
4. FOLK ROOSTER 25
5. FLYING UNICORN 33
6. GIRL GYMNAST 41
7. PENGUINS ON TEETER-TOTTER 57
8. DANCING MAN 71
9. UNICYCLING ROADRUNNER 85
10. CAROUSEL 105
11. KIDS ON TEETER-TOTTER 119
12. TRAMPOLINE 131
13. FERRIS WHEEL 149
14. UNICYCLIST 165
15. FLYING DUCK 183
16. ACROBATS 197
17. CLOWN 215

APPENDIX 229

Chapter 1

ANIMATED WHIRLIGIGS

There is presently a resurge of interest in animated whirligigs, both in building them and watching them perform their antics in the wind. The garage or basement workshop is one of the most popular recreational areas, with wood remaining the most popular construction material for hobbyist and do-it-yourselfers. This has created a need for interesting projects.

This book gives complete plans and instructions for making fifteen unique animated whirligigs, mainly from wood.

I first started making animated whirligigs in the 1980s, and have designed and built hundreds since then. From these, I have selected fifteen of my favorite original designs for inclusion in this book. These have all been built and tested, and are proven designs.

What level of skill is required to make the projects in covered in this book? First, I will give the bad news. Quite a bit of skill is required. The good news is that the fact you are reading this probably means that you have the necessary skill level.

It isn't necessary to have ever built a whirligig before, or any kind of action toy or decoration for that matter, but I do think you should have built something. As a minimum, you should know how to safely work with basic hand tools and whatever power tools you will be using.

With this in mind, the whirligigs shown in this book can be constructed to various quality levels, from crude to finely craft.

There are a variety of reasons for making the projects shown in this book. For many people, the fun and challenge is in the construction process. Others want to make them to use as displays or to give as gifts. Still others want to make them to sell.

Craft items that don't do anything can be difficult to sell (this may be the understatement of the year). Whirligigs sell themselves if you position them so that potential customers can see them in action, either outside in the wind or indoors in front of a fan.

The whirligigs detailed in this book perform a variety of actions, but each uses the power generated by the wind for turning one or more propellers.

The first four whirligigs in this book use the propellers themselves to provide the entire animation, and are often called "propeller-animated whirligigs." The Dove, Folk Rooster, and Flying Unicorn each have two propellers which simulate flying wings when they turn in the wind. The propellers are mounted so that one propeller turns clock-

The Dove whirligig uses propellers to simulate flying wings.

5

wise and the other counterclockwise. The entire whirligig is mounted on a pivot rod, which fits into a pivot socket on the bottom of the body of the whirligig. This allows the whirligig to turn on a vertical axis so that the whirligig can pivot. If everything is balanced properly, the propellers will always face the wind from one side or the other whenever the wind is at a threshold level or higher.

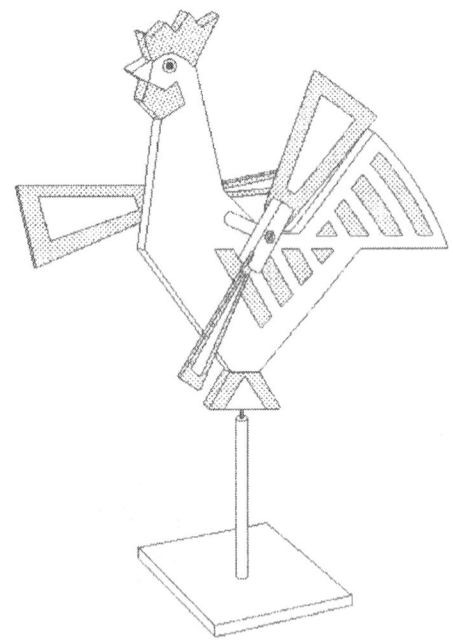

The Folk Rooster whirligig uses propellers to provide the animation.

The Flying Unicorn whirligig uses propellers to provide the action.

The Girl Gymnast also uses a propeller to provide the entire action of the whirligig. She twirls her legs while holding a handstand on the balance beam.

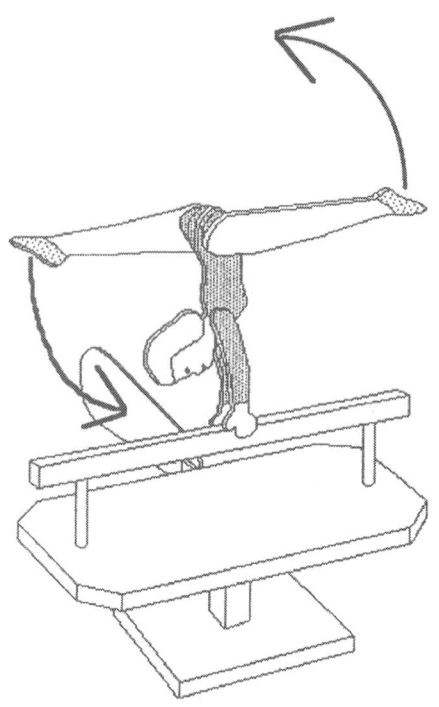

The action of Girl Gymnast whirligig.

The eleven other whirligigs featured in this book are of the action-mechanical type and share some common features. Each has a propeller mounted on a horizontal shaft. The entire whirligig is mounted on a pivot so that it can turn in a circle on a vertical axis by means of a wind vane.

The Penguins on Teeter-Totter whirligig features a crankshaft (fixed to the center of the propeller) that moves a connecting rod in a circular motion to provide the up and down movement of the teeter board. This is the basic mechanism that has been used on most of the traditional action-mechanical whirligigs.

The propeller on this whirligig provides the turning action of the crankshaft, but is not part of the animated action of the whirligig. The propeller can be replaced by a motor or crank, but the animated action remains the same provided that the crankshaft is turned at the same speed.

ANIMATED WHIRLIGIGS

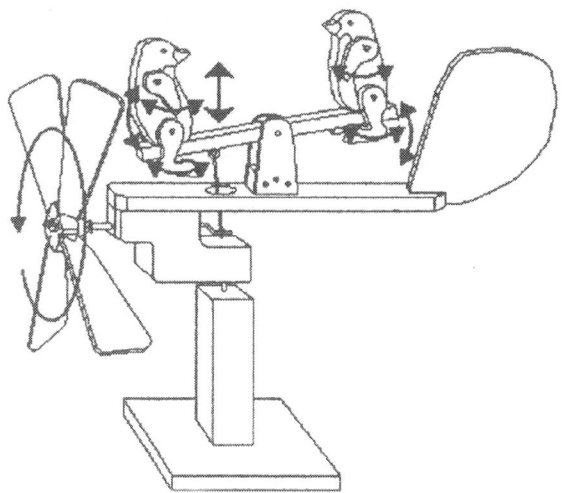

The Penguins on Teeter-Totter whirligig is an action-mechanical whirligig. The arrows show the action.

This whirligig also has wing and leg action. When the teeter-totter pivots at the center point, the ends of the teeter-totter move up and down, changing the penguin body angles, allowing the wings and legs to swing from the pivots.

The Dancing Man whirligig also has a crankshaft, but instead of having a connecting rod, the dancing figure pivots on the crank arm. The feet hang downward when the crankshaft turns, causing the feet to be moved up and down. The feet dance on the floor and, like the penguin wings, the arms swing. This whirligig is based on the popular folk toy, the "Limber Jack," which is worked by hand with a stick, with a thin board used as a dancing platform.

The Unicycling Roadrunner whirligig uses the propeller not only to turn the crankshaft, but also as part of the action as the wheel spokes. The cranks power the roadrunner leg action. This whirligig also features a second propeller that gives "flying" wing action.

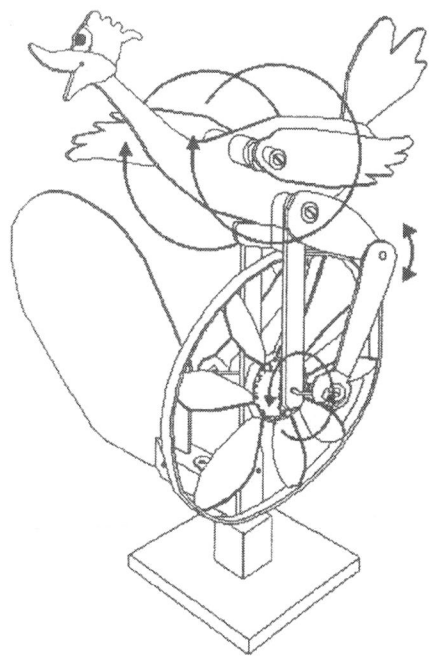

The Unicycling Roadrunner is a combination of the propeller-animated and action-mechanical types.

The Carousel whirligig works on a vertical shaft that is turned by the horizontal shaft fixed to the propeller. This whirligig also has a gear ratio. The horizontal propeller shaft turns faster than the vertical shaft that is used to turn the carousel platform.

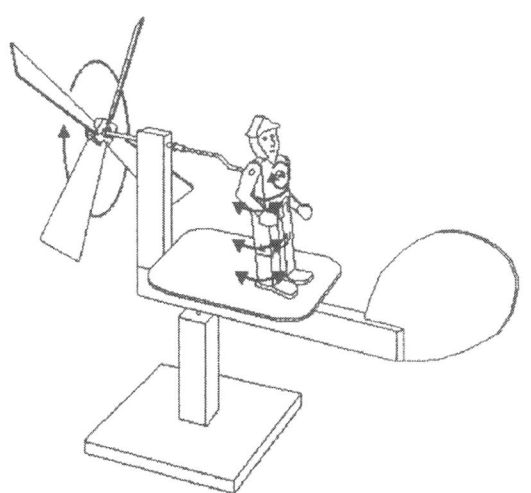

The crankshaft action causes the man to dance.

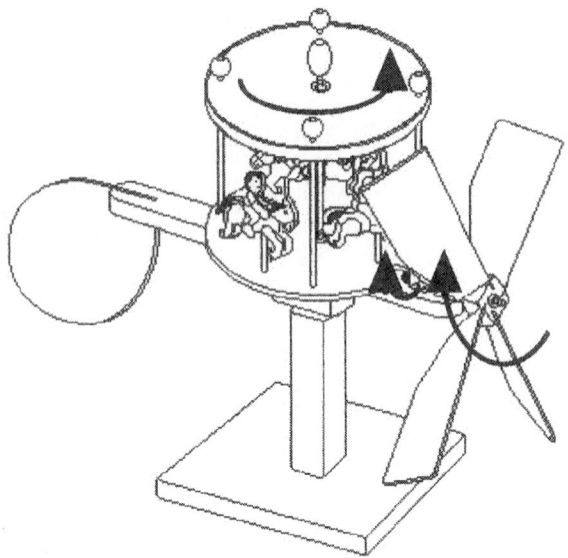

Mechanical action of Carousel whirligig.

The Kids on Teeter-Totter whirligig features a crankshaft (fixed to the center of the propeller) that moves a connecting rod in a circular motion to provide the up and down movement of the teeter board.

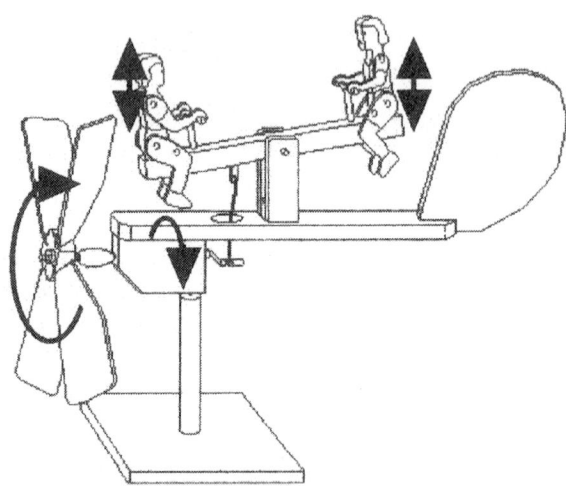

Mechanical action of Kids on Teeter-Totter whirligig.

The Trampoline whirligig is similar to the Dancing Man whirligig, except the performer is fixed to the crankshaft. The performer's body rotates in a somersaulting action as it is raised upward. The arms and legs are hanging on pivots when the performer is upright. The arms and legs change positions in relation to the body (rotate on the pivots) at various times during the somersaulting action. The feet contacting the trampoline bed add to the effect.

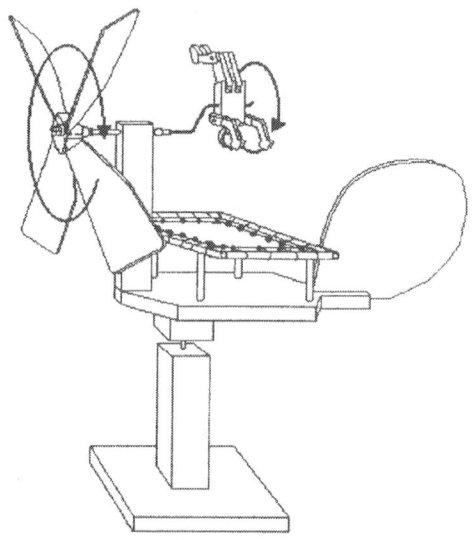

The trampoline performer is fixed to the crankshaft, which gives both jumping and somersaulting action.

The Ferris Wheel whirligig is turned by the horizontal shaft fixed to the propeller. A small wheel on this shaft turns the large wheel. This whirligig has a gear ratio. The small wheel turns faster than the large wheel.

ANIMATED WHIRLIGIGS

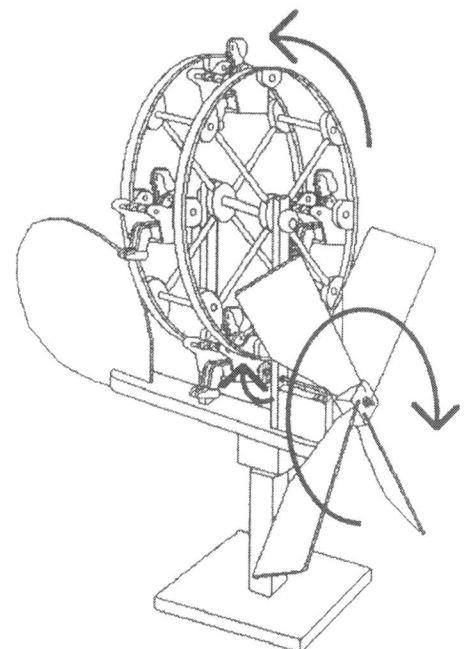

Mechanical action of Ferris Wheel whirligig.

The Flying Duck whirligig features a crankshaft (fixed to the center of the propeller) that moves a connecting rod in a circular motion to provide the up and down movement of the duck's body. The wings are attached to pivot wires. When the body moves up and down, the wings give a "flying" action.

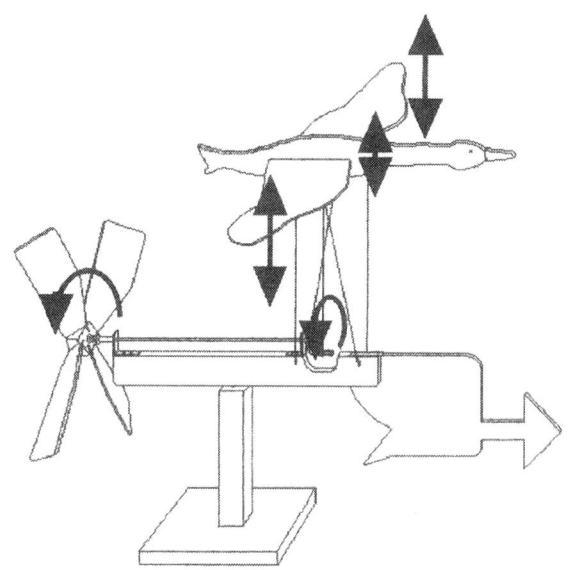

Mechanical action of Flying Duck whirligig.

The Unicyclist whirligig features a drive wheel on the propeller shaft that turns a larger driven wheel, which in turn moves a connecting rod that moves the unicycle back and forth. The turning wheel of the unicycle causes the unicyclist's legs to pedal. The unicyclist appears to keep balance while alternately riding the unicycle forward and backward!

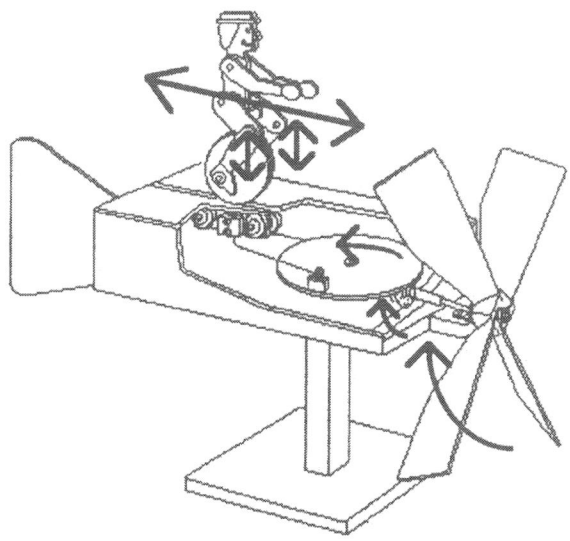

Mechanical action of Unicyclist whirligig.

The Acrobats whirligig has six clowns performing at the same time. Whirligigs with one or more acrobats with hands fixed to the propeller shaft have been designed and constructed previously. I decided to add additional acrobats to bars mounted on the ends of the propeller blades. The result gives the effect of a group of acrobats going crazy.

A unique feature of this whirligig is the attachment of figures directly to rods fixed to the propeller blades. Notice that the two clowns on the propeller shaft rotate by the hands, but the center of the rotation remains stationary. The acrobats on the propeller blades rotate by the hands, while at the same time circling with the rotating ends of the propeller blades. The clown bodies pivot from the arms at the shoulder joints, and the legs pivot from the clown bodies at the hip joints, providing a range of animated actions,

9

which vary depending on the speed of the rotating propeller and other factors. The propeller becomes part of the action like a Ferris wheel carrying passengers.

The Clown whirligig has a crankshaft that causes the clown's arms, tongue and eyes to pivot together to give a unique action.

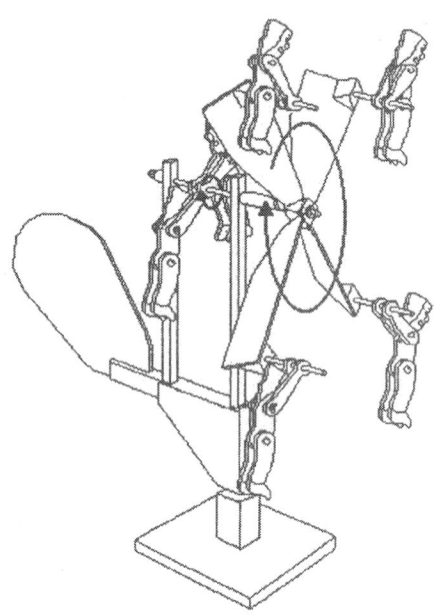

Acrobats perform not only on the propeller shaft, but also on rods on the tips of the propeller blades.

The Clown whirligig uses the turning propeller to give a unique action.

Chapter 2

MATERIALS, TOOLS, AND TECHNIQUES

For making quality whirligigs, materials, tools, and techniques are important considerations.

Wood is the primary material used in the construction of the projects detailed in this book, but metal crankshafts, connecting rods, fasteners, and other parts are also used. However, the metal work is quite elementary, and if you can do the wood work, no difficulty should be encountered with the metal work. The Trampoline whirligig also requires sewing the trampoline bed, but this is only a small part of the project, and if you can't do this yourself, you can probably find someone who can do it for you.

The plans that are shown feature simple construction methods using readily available materials. However, if desired, you can go beyond this. For example, figures cut from flat stock—silhouettes—are detailed, but you can use fully carved ones. More expensive woods and finishes can be substituted for those suggested.

The materials, tools, and construction methods actually used will depend on many factors, especially what you intend to do with the whirligigs, how many you intend to make, and what tools, materials, and workspace you have available. If you intend to make whirligigs to sell at a profit, you will also need to consider production methods, at least on a limited scale. Many people display their whirligigs on stands indoors, taking them outside only briefly to watch them work. This requires a less weatherproof construction than if the whirligigs are to remain outdoors for long periods of time.

MATERIALS

The primary material required is wood. Many kinds of wood can be used. You may have some suitable wood on hand; perhaps scrap pieces left over from previous construction jobs. The scrap bin at a local construction site or lumberyard should provide some suitable wood. While either soft or hard woods will work, soft woods, such as sugar or white pine, are usually easier to work with. Hardwoods are generally more durable, but also more expensive, often two to six times the price of soft woods.

Since whirligigs mainly require small pieces of wood, you can often use lower grades of wood by working around the knots and defects. This means laying out patterns on the wood so knots and defects will be in cutaway areas, ending up as scrap materials rather than as part of your project.

There are many other sources for wood for making whirligigs. Old chest of drawers, for example, can provide a variety of suitable woods. Garage sales and flea markets are another source. Look for items that have suitable wood. This also applies to other parts suitable for making whirligigs.

Plywood is specified for some whirligig parts. Even if you intend to keep the whirligig mainly indoors, I recommend that exterior grade plywood be used.

Hardwood dowels are required for some of the projects. These can be purchased from hardware stores, lumberyards, and craft and hobby stores. Prices and qualities vary so shop around.

Some of the projects require wire. In some cases, wire from a clothes hanger can be used. This has the necessary stiffness, yet is easy to bend to shape with pliers. Paper clips can be used for the small diameter wire used for some of the projects. Suitable wire is also available at hardware, craft, and hobby stores.

Brass tubing and rods are used for bearings and shafts. The sizes required are available from craft and hobby stores. The bolts and other fasteners required are readily available at hardware stores. A couple of the projects require brass strips. These are available at hobby and craft stores.

Ordinary white craft or carpenter glue is inexpensive and works well for most of the gluing required for the projects detailed, provided the whirligigs are kept mainly indoors. Epoxy glue or other waterproof types are recommended for whirligigs that are to be displayed outdoors.

A variety of paints can be used, but make certain that they are safe to apply and non-toxic, especially after they have dried. Small bottles of acrylic paint of the "waterproof" or "permanent" type (after they have dried) are available in sets, which provide all of the colors you will need for painting the figures used on the whirligigs. You will need at least one suitable paintbrush.

Paint pens, available at hobby stores, are also useful.

Clear plastic finishes can be added over some paints (after they have dried) to increase weather resistance.

For painting larger surfaces and production work, it is usually more economical to purchase paint in larger quantities. I use paints and finishes that do not have toxic fumes or unpleasant odors whenever possible.

TOOLS

For cutting wood parts to curved patterns, an ordinary coping saw can be used. A bench fork cut from a piece of wood, as shown, will allow you to move the piece of wood you are sawing around to cut curves and also keep the coping saw straight up and down.

Sawing in this fashion is quite tedious, however, and if you are going to make more than one or two whirligigs, you will probably want to use a power scroll or band saw.

A number of the projects detailed require cutting small parts from thin wood to curved patterns. I prefer a power scroll saw rather than a band saw for this work.

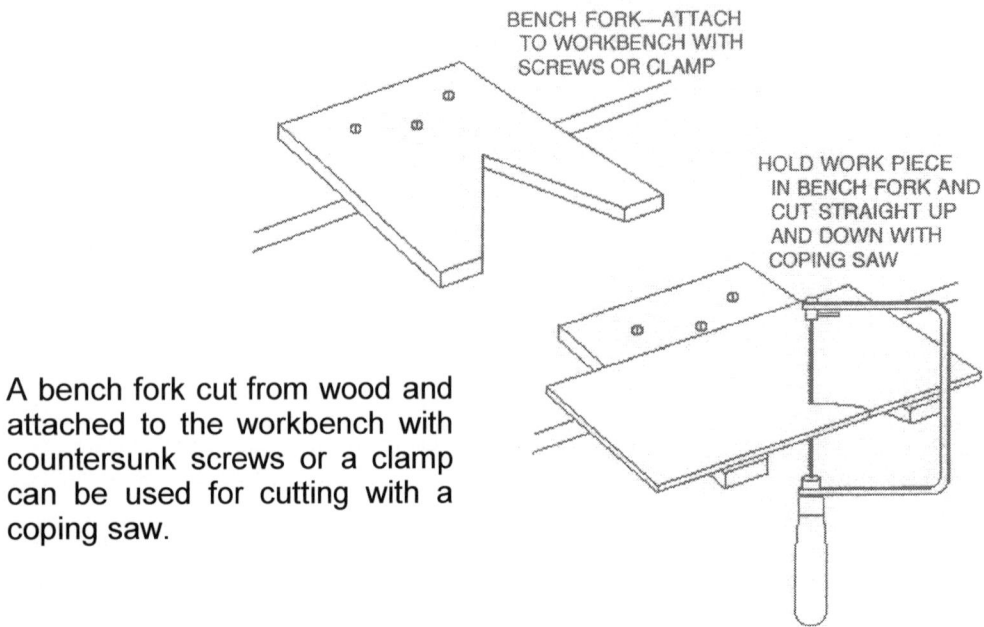

A bench fork cut from wood and attached to the workbench with countersunk screws or a clamp can be used for cutting with a coping saw.

MATERIALS, TOOLS, AND TECHNIQUES

Straight cuts can be made with hand or power saws, as desired.

Files and sandpaper are used for further shaping and smoothing of wood surfaces. Files are available in various shapes and sizes, and sandpaper in a variety of grits (coarse, medium, fine, etc.).

A bench mounted disk and/or belt sander will make sanding faster and easier, and is almost essential for profitable production work. These tools produce a lot of sanding dust, however, so you will need, as a minimum, a dust mask and eye protection. A special vacuum system for removing the dust is highly recommended.

Accurate drilling of holes is essential for making quality whirligigs. While the drilling can be done with a hand drill or portable power drill, it is difficult to make the holes perpendicular or accurately to a desired angle to the wood surface. Special guides are available for hand and portable power drills that permit more accurate drilling.

A drill press is ideal for accurate drilling. Along with a power scroll saw or band saw, I consider a drill press essential for production work. Without a drill press, it is extremely difficult to drill holes accurately enough to make quality whirligigs. The least expensive method is a drill press stand that holds a portable power drill. A regular bench or floor mounted drill press is better.

Regardless of the drill used, you will need a variety of bit sizes. For the same size axle, it is often necessary to make a hole for a tight fit and another so that the axle can turn freely. In order to do this, you will need bit sizes in 1/64" increments.

While all round parts required for these projects can be cut to shape with a coping saw or power scroll or band saw, a hole saw and/or circle cutter used with a drill press will make this work easier and more accurate.

A hammer and screwdriver are required for installing fasteners. Pliers and wire cutter are used for bending and cutting wire. Dies are required for threading the ends of brass rod.

A woodworker's bench vise is valuable (I don't see how you could get along without one) for holding materials. In addition to a vise especially designed for holding wood, a metal or general purpose vise is also useful, and for holding metal parts essential.

Other useful tools include a ruler for measuring and marking straight lines and a compass for making circle patterns.

TECHNIQUES

The construction steps for each project include marking the patterns on the wood, cutting and shaping the parts, and assembling and painting them.

Patterns

Full size patterns are provided for shaped figures and parts, making enlarging or reducing the drawings unnecessary. In order to protect this book, I suggest that you use a copier to make a copy of the patterns. Tracing paper can then be used to transfer the lines from the patterns to the wood. Special tracing paper is available from art and craft stores that give tracings that will not smear like those from carbon paper.

An alternate method is to use a copier to make a copy of the patterns on card stock as thick as the copier you are using can safely handle. These can then be cut out and used as templates for tracing the patterns onto the wood.

If you plan to make a number of whirligigs of the same plan, templates made from wood are useful.

Dimensions are given for rectangular and circle parts, and these can be marked on the wood with a straight edge, square, and compass using a pencil or other suitable marking tool.

Sawing

The wood parts are then sawn to shape. This means either straight or curved cutting. To minimize additional shaping and sanding, the cutting should be done as accurately as possible.

Safety is an important consideration when using a power scroll or band saw. Follow all safety guidelines recommended by the manufacturer of the particular tool. While dimensions are given in the material lists for wood the size of the finished parts or slightly larger, when cutting small parts you will want to use a larger piece of wood than this to give you space to hold the wood a safe distance from the cutting blade of the saw.

Cutting Circle Patterns

When making circle patterns, a compass will mark the exact center in addition to the circle pattern. The circle can then be cut from the wood by sawing along the line with a coping saw or a power scroll or band saw. If care is taken, a reasonably accurate wheel can be formed.

If available, a hole saw or wing circle cutter can be used, or the wheel can be turned on a lathe. Circle jigs are also available for sawing circles with a band saw.

Sanding and Assembly

In some cases, the sanding is best done before assembly; in other cases it is best to wait until the parts are together. Most of the assembly used for the projects in this book is by nails and gluing or gluing alone. Except for a few special cases, ordinary white carpenter glue can be used. In order for this glue to form a strong joint, it is essential to clamp the parts together until the glue sets. This can be accomplished by a tight fit of parts, nailing, or clamping the parts together.

Painting

The painting can be done after the parts have been shaped and sanded, but before assembly, or you can do the painting after assembly. Do not paint surfaces where glue is to be applied, however. For most projects, a combination of painting some parts before and others after assembly works best.

The two basic finishing methods are clear (with or without staining) and painted. In many cases, you can employ both methods in the same project. The figures are usually painted, but the amount of detail is a matter of personal choice.

Like working with wood, the painting can be a creative and rewarding part of the construction process, but it takes thought and practice to do a good job. While tips and suggestions are given for painting and finishing the projects, you can do this any way you like. In most cases, this will only affect the appearance of the whirligig and not how it works.

A PLACE TO WORK

Various types and sizes of workshops are used by experienced woodworkers. You won't need much to start with, though. Most people start out with whatever is readily available and then gradually improve on this over a period of time.

Ideal is to have a workshop that can be used just for woodworking; next best is to have a section of a garage or other suitable area that can be used just for woodworking.

In some cases, you may have to use the same work area that you use to repair the car for woodworking. This can also work if you can manage to keep the grease off your wood.

At the other extreme is the kitchen table, which is generally unsatisfactory because you must share it with eating, and who wants sawdust in their food?

To do quality woodwork, you need a work area that feels right. I know from experience that it is very difficult to do creative work in someone else's workshop.

You will probably want to strive for the best temperature, ventilation, and lighting conditions possible. In some cases, you will have considerable control over these factors. If conditions are not ideal, you may be able to improve the situation. Windows can be added for better ventilation and/or lighting. Artificial lights can be added and arranged to give good lighting where you need it.

After observing many woodshops and how they are used, I have noticed a range of orderliness and cleanliness, and this does not seem to have much bearing on the amount and quality of the work that they turn out. I have seen quality work come out of workshops that looked messy, and vice versa. While I prefer a clean and orderly shop, I must admit that mine does not always stay that way. Even though I try to have a specific storage place for every tool, they don't always get back there.

It doesn't take much woodworking to know that sawdust can be a problem, especially if you use power sanders. Frequent cleaning with a vacuum helps, especially if you rig the vacuum so that it collects the sawdust, or as much of it as possible, while it is being generated.

At the very least, you should wear a respirator (and get a good one that is approved for woodworking) and eye protection whenever you are generating sawdust.

Almost all experienced woodcrafters center most of their work on a good workbench. Size and height are important considerations. The bench top should be at least 2 feet wide and 3 feet long to be practical for most types of wood crafting, such as for making the whirligigs detailed in this book. A longer bench is usually even better. The height is usually from about 3 feet to 3 feet 3 inches for people of average height, but short and tall people may want to deviate somewhat from these standards.

The workbench should be sturdy. Any wobbling can make woodworking difficult.

Many existing shop benches will meet these requirements. You can purchase a shop bench especially with woodworking in mind. Many suitable workbenches are available. These can be purchased new in completed and kit form. Used workbenches are frequently available at lower prices than equivalent new ones. Still another possibility is to construct your own workbench.

GETTING STARTED

Before going on to the actual projects, a few words about this book are in order. The projects detailed have all been built and tested by me. For each project, the important construction steps have been illustrated so that you have not only patterns for cutting the wood parts to the proper shape, but also drawings of how they go together.

I have included full-size patterns for all wood parts that have curved shapes. Some rectangular shaped parts that were too large to fit the pages of this book have been reduced. However, you can easily lay out the patterns on the wood with a ruler and square.

In most cases, I have given my recommendations for specific materials and construction methods, but others can often be substituted. I have tried to use only readily available materials, but you may be able to improvise, such as by using a rare item that you find at a garage sale.

After you have built one or more of the whirligigs detailed in this book, you may want to go to original designs. This, I believe, is the real fun and challenge of making whirligigs, and the projects featured here will give you a foundation for doing this.

If you are new to woodworking, or it has been years since you have done any, I suggest that you build the Dove whirligig detailed in the next chapter. If you are already an active woodworker, you can start with any project you like, and build them in any order.

DISPLAY STANDS

The whirligigs are mounted on a pivot rod for display. Outdoors, the pivot rod can be driven into a fence post or other suitable support. For the whirligig to turn properly into the wind, the pivot rod should be vertical to a level surface. After the nail has been driven into the post, cut off the head and file smooth.

For indoor display, a stand can be constructed as shown. The stand is also useful for holding the whirligig during construction and testing.

You can also make the display stands more elaborate by using a round base, a round post, or by shaping these parts on a wood lathe.

THE WHIRLIGIG MAKER'S BOOK

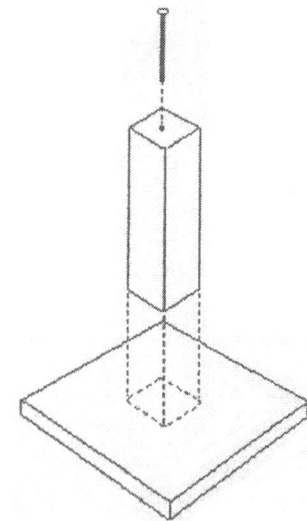

Assembly of display stand.

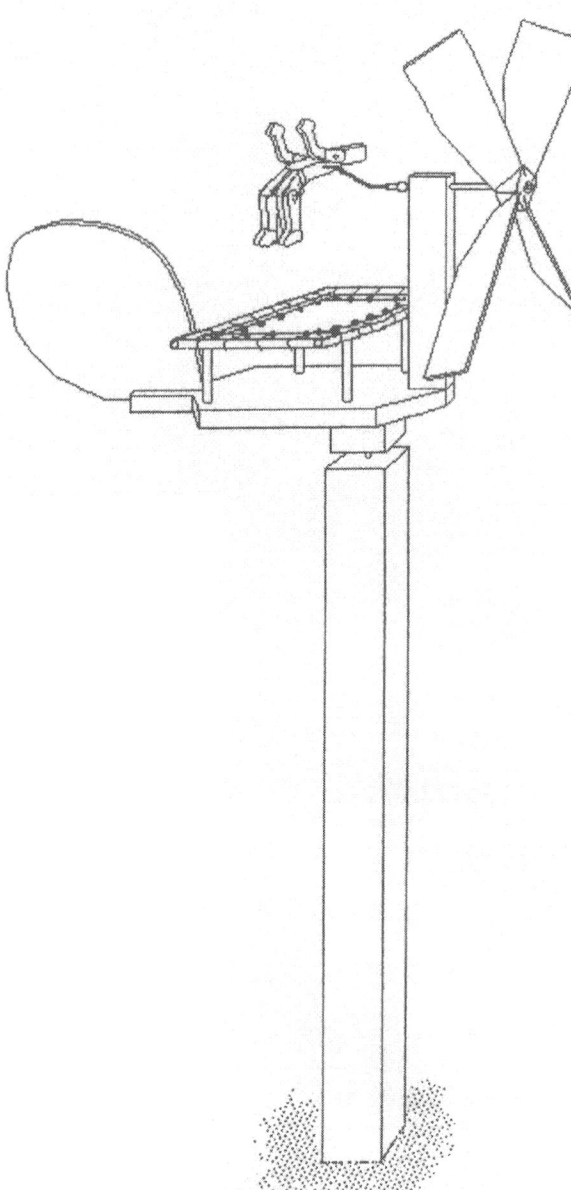

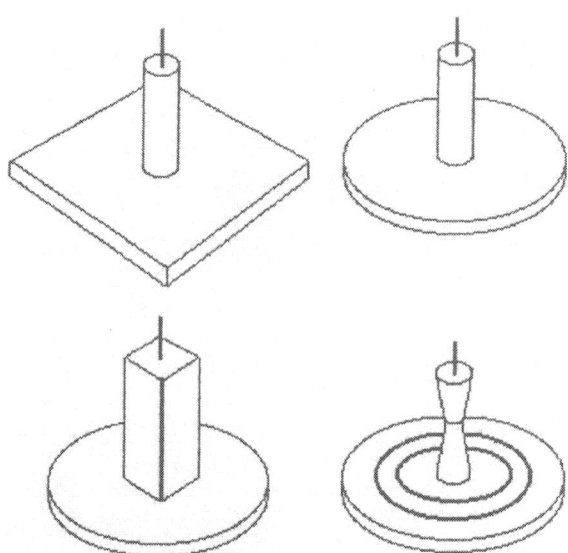

Whirligig mounted on post.

Display stands.

TESTING WHIRLIGIGS

It is difficult to test whirligigs during construction without a consistent source of wind. I use a small electric fan that has three speeds. All of the whirligigs detailed in this book will work five or six feet in front of the fan on the lowest setting. This requires having the shafts turn freely and no binding of moving parts.

Chapter 3

DOVE

The Dove whirligig is a fun project both to build and then watch perform after you have completed it. The propellers of this whirligig form the "flying" wings of the dove.

MATERIALS
- 5/8" diameter x 8" hardwood dowel for display stand post.
- 3/4" x 8" x 8" wood or plywood for display stand base.
- 5/32" diameter x 5" steel rod or nail for pivot rod for display stand.
- 3/4" x 5" x 13" wood for body.
- 1/8" x 3-1/2" x 28" wood or plywood for propeller blades.
- 3/4" x 3/4" x 6" wood for propeller hubs.
- 5/8" diameter x 5" hardwood dowel for axle for propellers.
- 1/4" outside diameter (11/64" inside diameter) x 3/4" copper or brass tube for propeller-hub bearing (two required).
- No. 9 x 2-1/2" round head wood screw (two required) for mounting propellers.
- No. 9 washer (four required).
- 1/4" outside diameter (11/64" inside diameter) x 2" copper or brass tube for pivot bearing.
- 1/4" diameter steel ball for pivot bearing.
- Glue.
- Finishing nails for attaching propeller blades to hubs (optional).
- Paint.

DISPLAY STAND
The display stand is useful not only for displaying the finished whirligig indoors, but also for holding the whirligig during construction and for testing it in front of a fan. Construction is easy. The base is 3/4" x 8" x 8" wood or plywood. Drill a 5/8" diameter hole in the center of the base. The 5/8" diameter x 8" hardwood dowel post is glued at one end inside the hole in the base. A 5/32" diameter x 5" steel rod or nail is driven 2" into the center of the top of the post for use as a pivot rod. First drill a pilot hole perpendicular to the top of the post and then drive the rod or nail into the hole. If a nail is used,

cut the head off of the nail with a hacksaw. File the upper end of the nail smooth, rounding the corners slightly.

Sand and paint the display stand. A clear or color finish can be used.

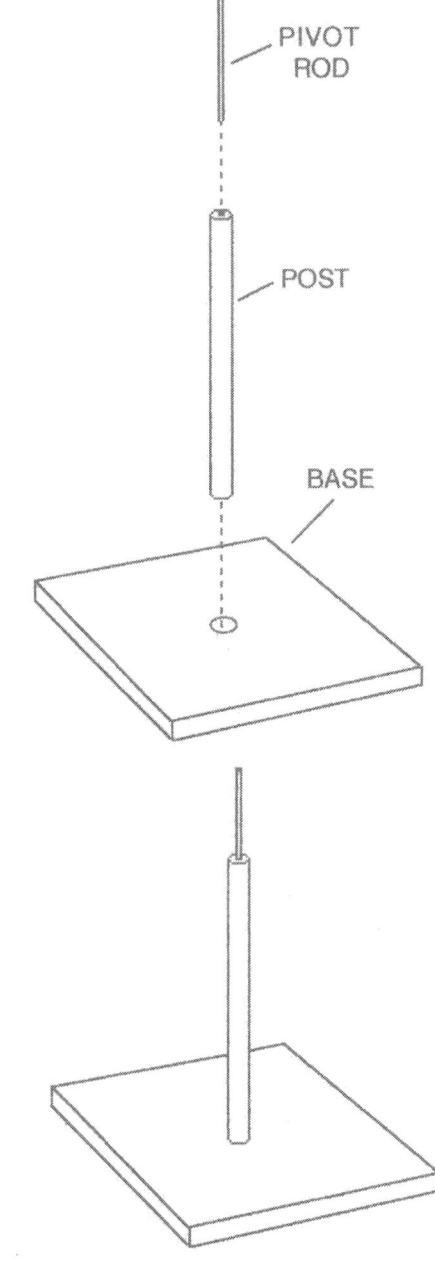

Assembly of display stand.

DOVE

BODY

The dove body is made of 3/4" x 5" x 13" wood. Mark the pattern for the body on the wood. Drill 5/8" diameter hole for hardwood dowel. Saw the dove body to the pattern. Drill a 1/4" diameter x 2-1/4" deep hole for the pivot tube in the position shown. The hole must be accurately centered and angled as shown in relation to the propeller axle hole. Then install the steel ball and copper or brass pivot tube in the hole. The tube should fit tightly in the hole so that it will not turn.

Sand the dove body and mark painting pattern. Make pilot holes for No. 9 wood screws in the ends of the 5/8" diameter X 5" hardwood dowel axle. Then glue the axle in the axle hole in the body, with the axle centered.

The dove body can be painted at this time, or you can wait until the assembly has been completed. However, it is best to remove the wing propellers before painting the body. Use the color scheme shown, or make up your own. The display base is handy for holding the dove body upright for painting.

PROPELLERS

The propeller hub is made from 3/4" x 3/4" x 3" wood. Two are required. Both have a 1/4" hole for the axle bearing. The holes must be centered and drilled perpendicular to the surface of the wood. Mark patterns for notches for propeller blades. Notice that one hub has the notches angled for a clockwise propeller and the other for counter-clockwise. The propellers on opposite sides of the whirligig will then turn in opposite directions to cancel each others thrust so the dove body is not spun around by the propeller action of the wings. Saw the notches in the hubs. Install the 1/4" diameter x 3/4" copper or brass bearing tubes in the holes. Use a punch to expand the ends of the tubing slightly.

Mark the patterns for the propeller blades on 1/8" wood or plywood. Cut the blades to shape and sand as necessary. Glue the blades in the notches with the blades facing as shown. Small finishing nails can be driven through the hub ends and propeller blades to reinforce the joint.

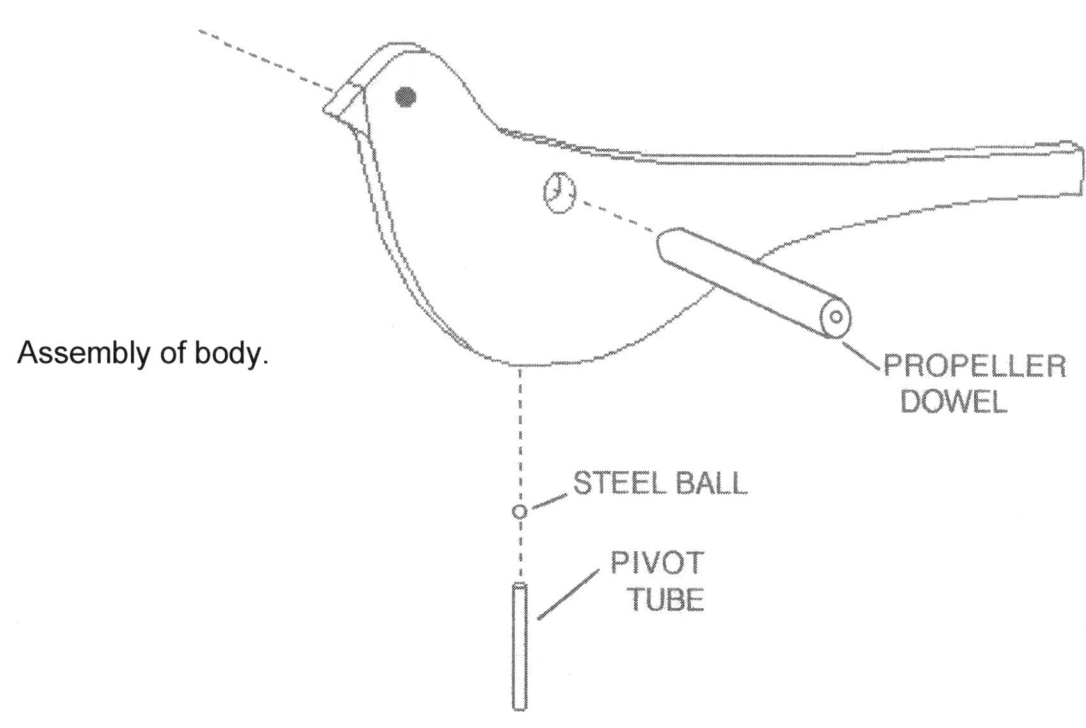

Assembly of body.

19

THE WHIRLIGIG MAKER'S BOOK

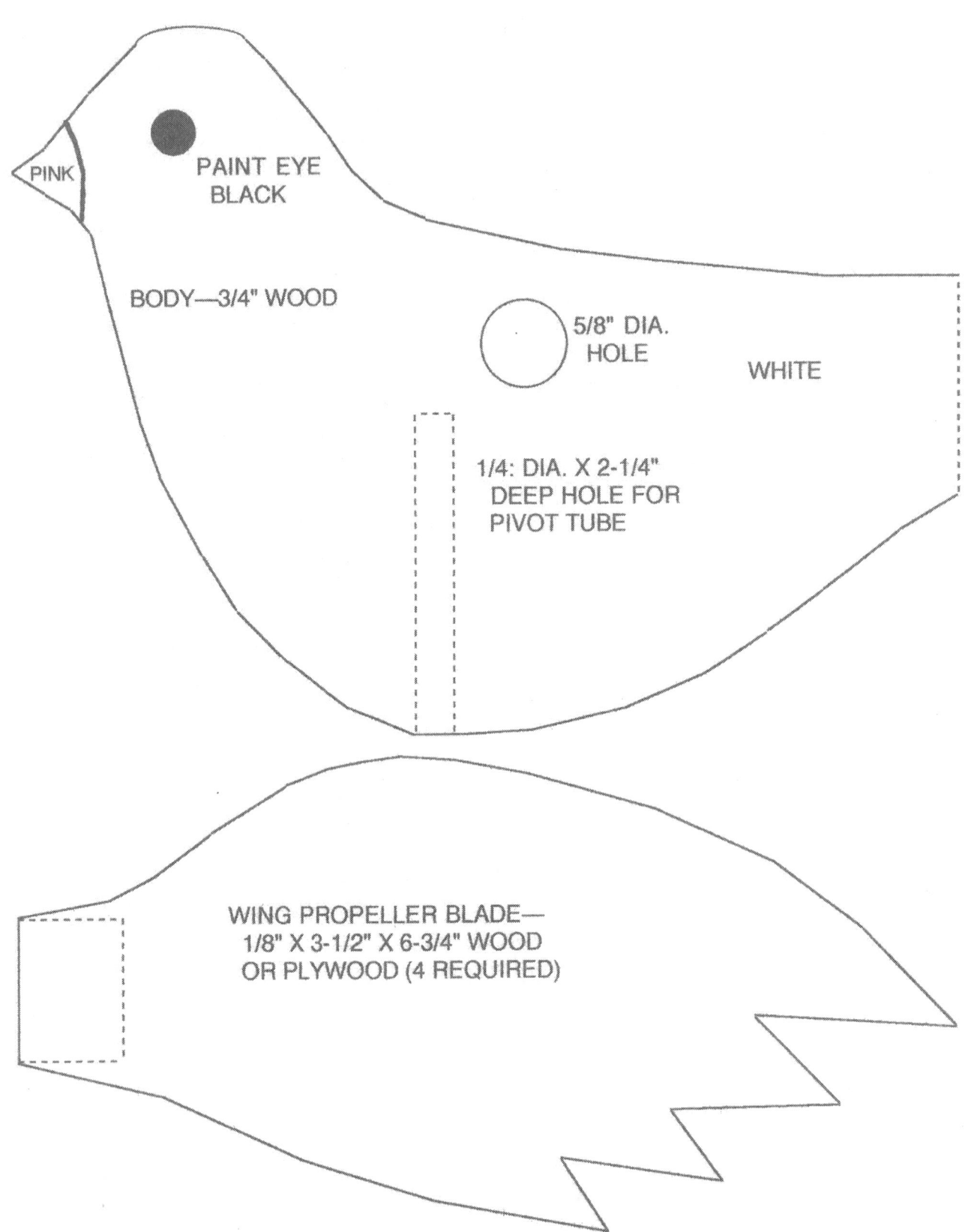

Full-size patterns for body, propeller blades, and hubs.

DOVE

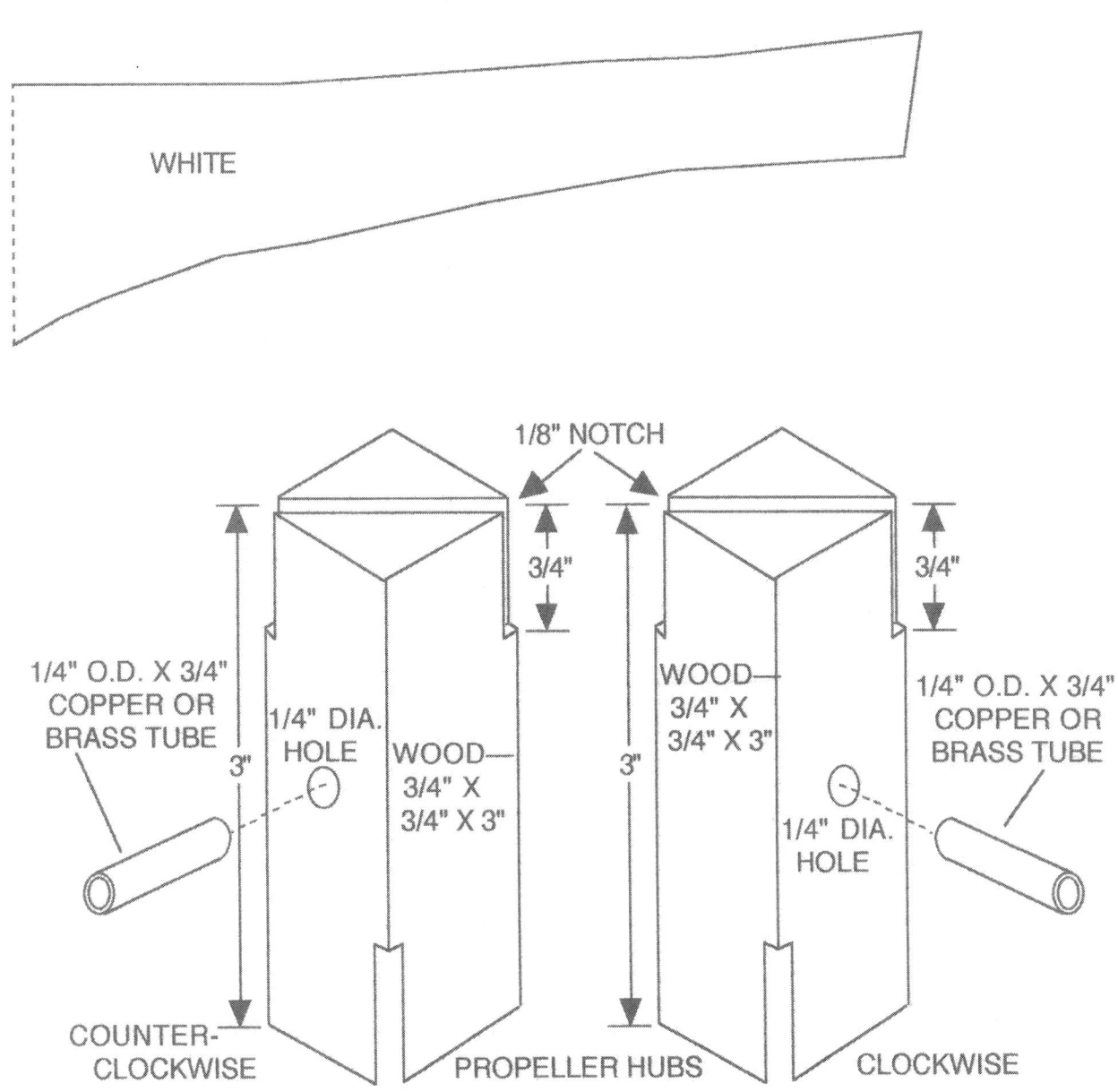

THE WHIRLIGIG MAKER'S BOOK

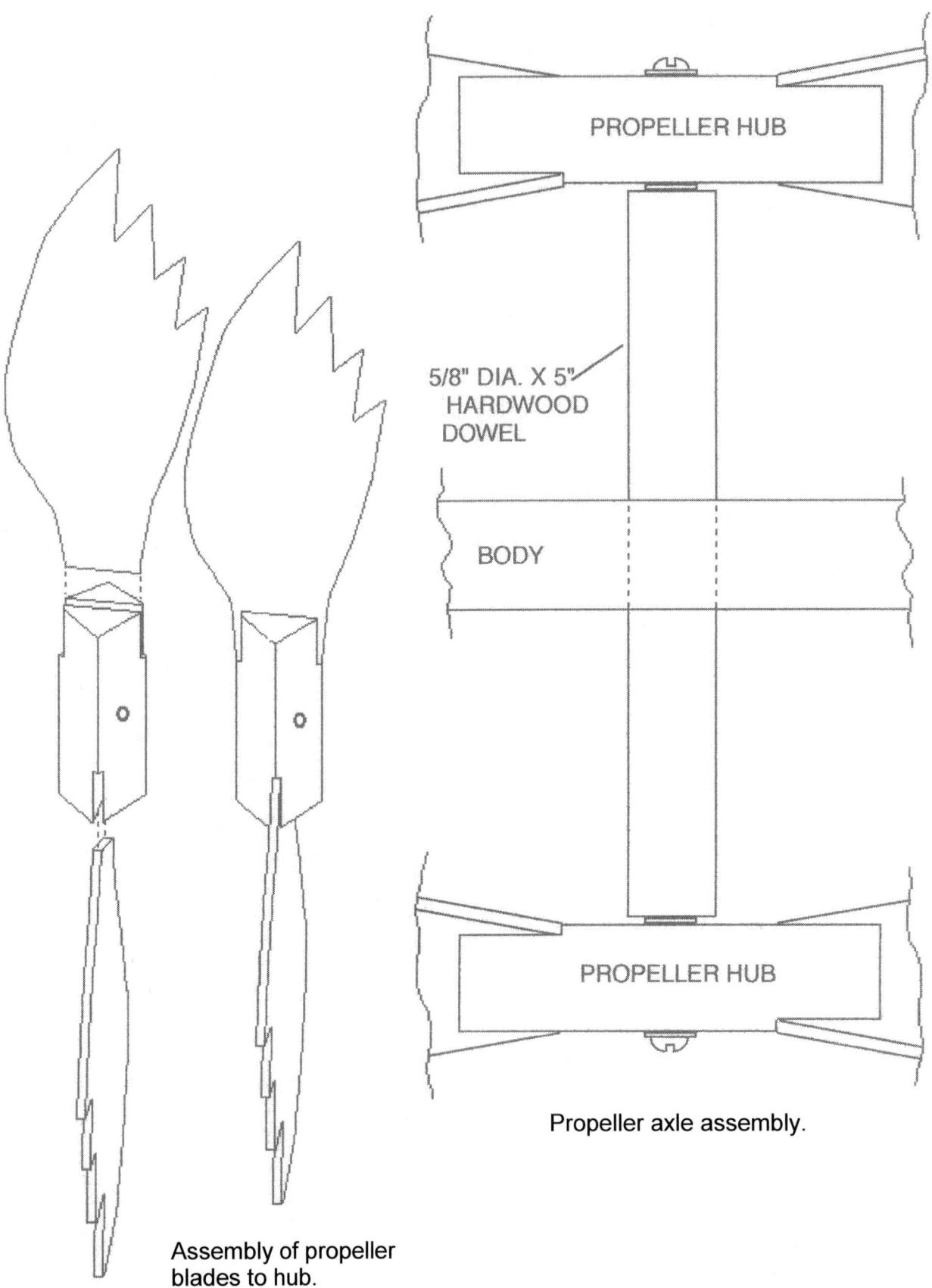

Assembly of propeller blades to hub.

Propeller axle assembly.

DOVE

In order for the whirligig to work properly, the propellers need to be balanced so that, when mounted, they balance in a horizontal position. When the blades stop in a no-wind condition, they should be in a horizontal position. If you find that one end of a propeller is heavier than the other, balance it be sanding the extra weight off the heavier blade.

Paint the propeller blades and hubs white. Or select your own colors and pattern.

Next, mount the propellers to the hardwood axle with No. 9 x 2-1/2" round head wood screws with a washer on each side of each hub. Leave the screws loose enough so that the propellers turn freely.

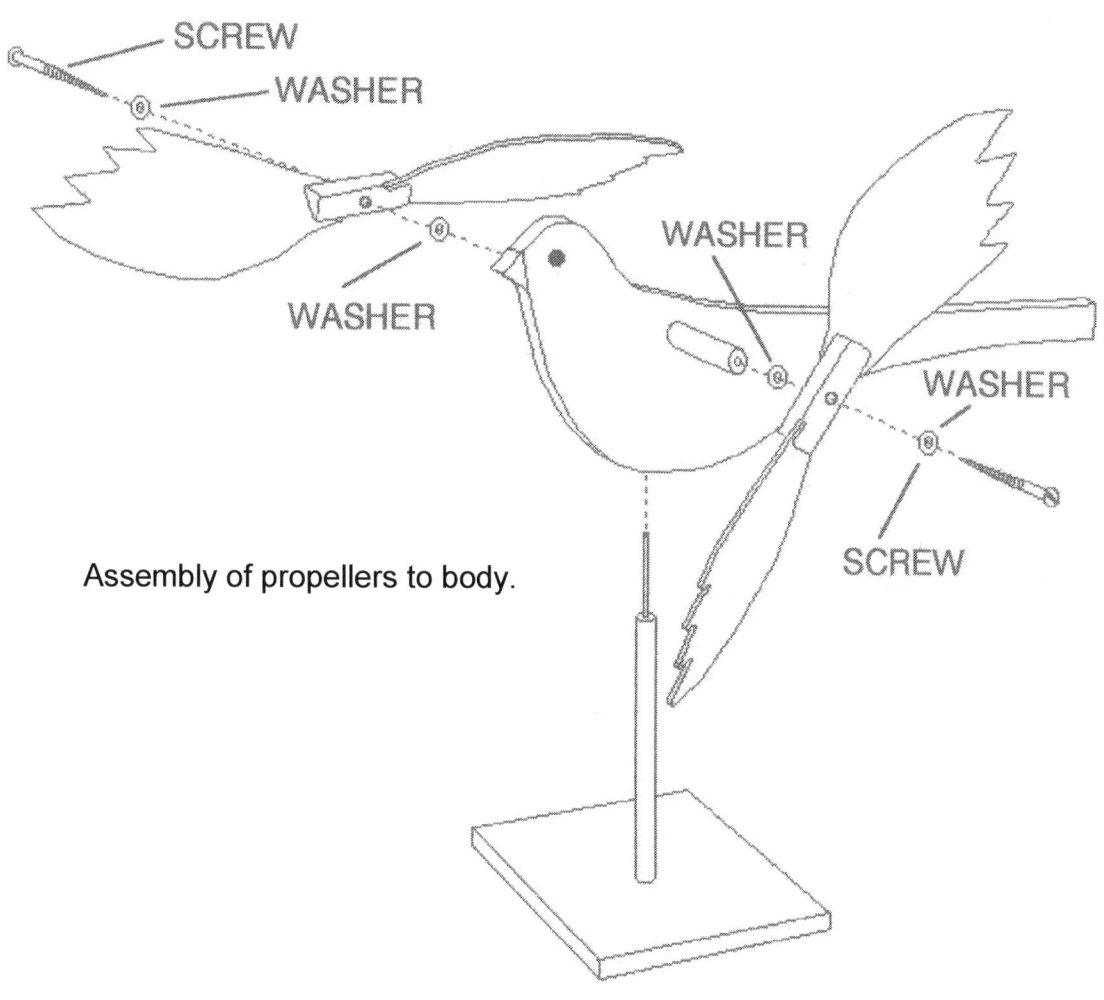

Assembly of propellers to body.

THE WHIRLIGIG MAKER'S BOOK

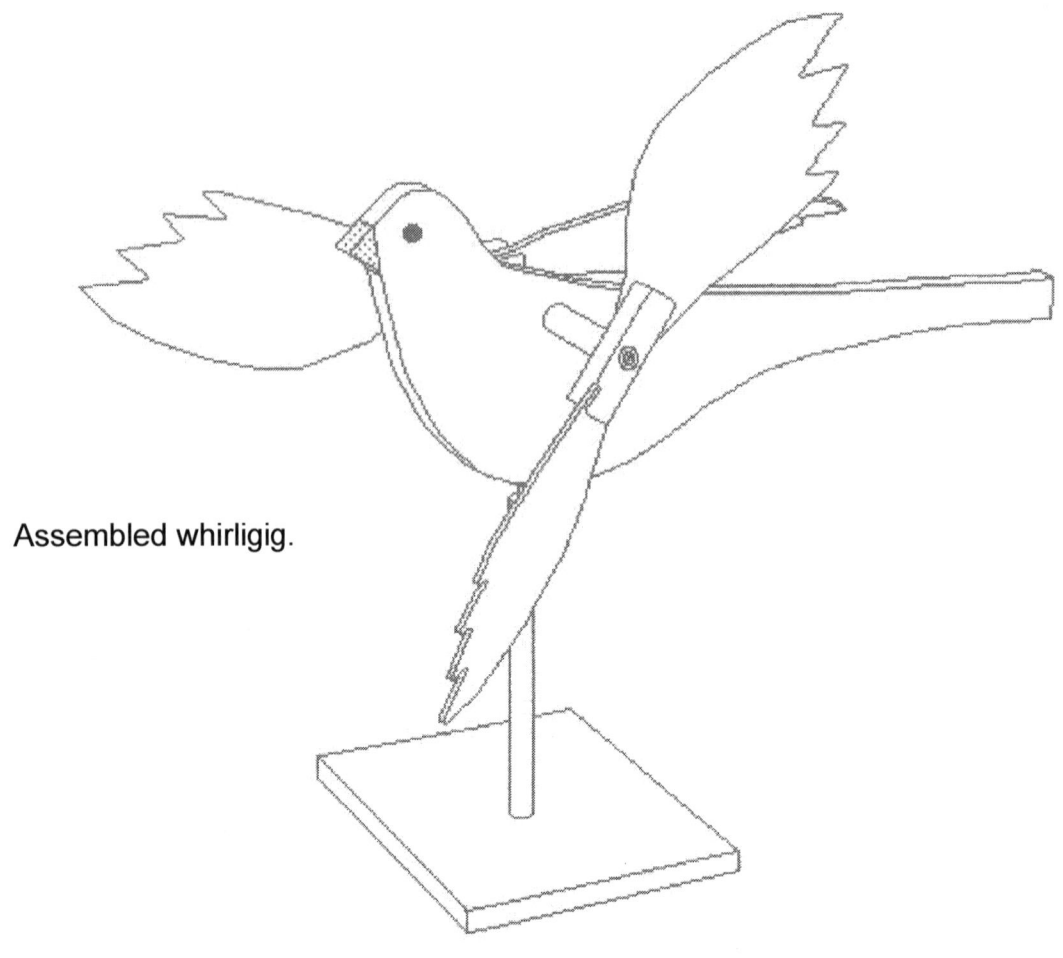

Assembled whirligig.

TESTING AND FINISHING

The whirligig is ready for testing. This can be inside with a fan or outdoors in a light wind. The whirligig should start easily if all of the parts turn properly.

Finish any painting that was not done previously.

Chapter 4

FOLK ROOSTER

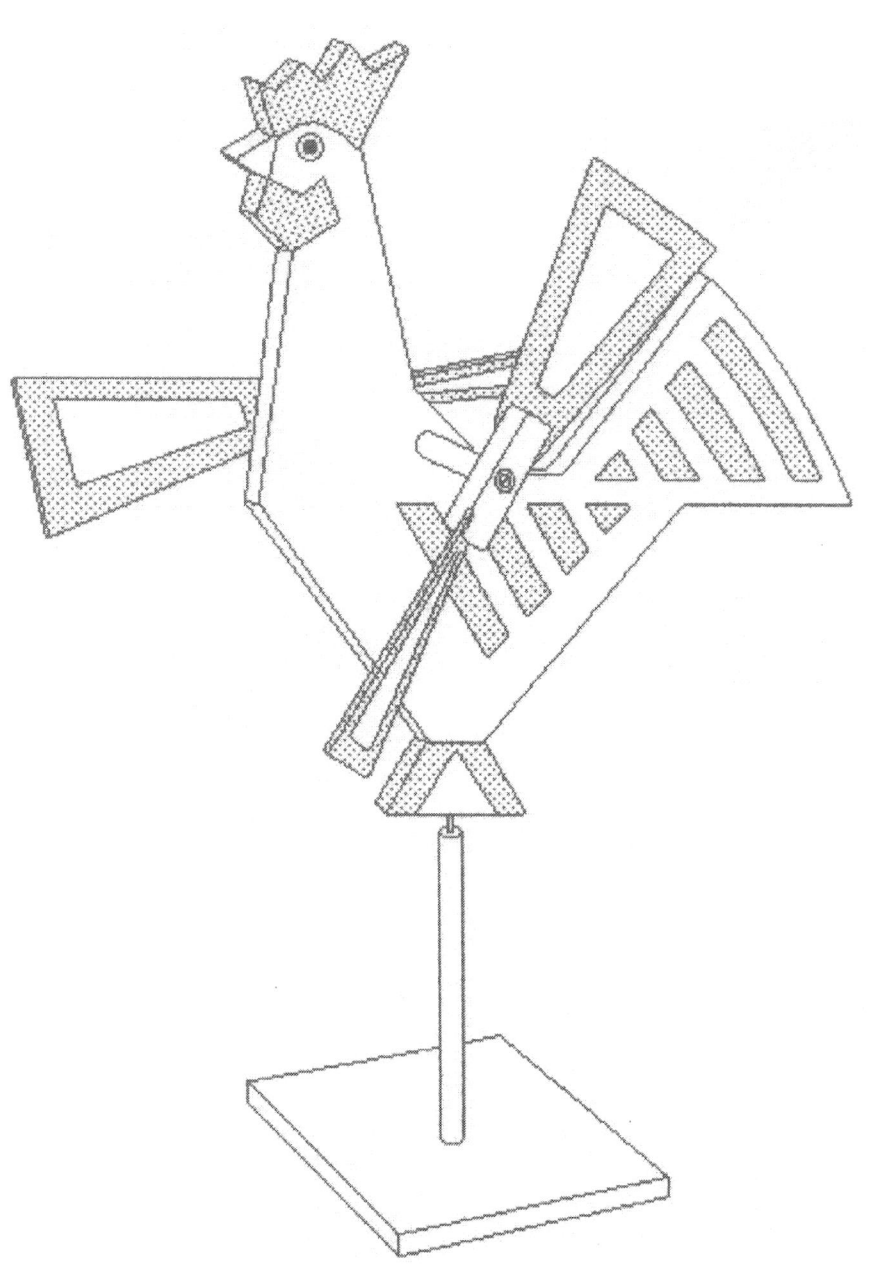

The Folk Rooster whirligig is a fun project both to build and then watch perform after you have completed it. The propellers of this whirligig form the "flying" wings of the rooster.

MATERIALS
- 5/8" diameter x 8" hardwood dowel for display stand post.
- 3/4" x 8" x 8" wood or plywood for display stand base.
- 5/32" diameter x 5" steel rod or nail for pivot rod for display stand.
- 3/4" x 10" x 12" wood or plywood for body.
- 1/8" x 3" x 20" wood or plywood for propeller blades.
- 3/4" x 3/4" x 6" wood for propeller hubs.
- 5/8" diameter x 5" hardwood dowel for axle for propellers.
- 1/4" outside diameter (11/64" inside diameter) x 3/4" copper or brass tube for propeller-hub bearing (two required).
- No. 9 x 2-1/2" round head wood screw (two required) for mounting propellers.
- No. 9 washer (four required).
- 1/4" outside diameter (11/64" inside diameter) x 2" copper or brass tube for pivot bearing.
- 1/4" diameter steel ball for pivot bearing.
- Glue.
- Finishing nails for attaching propeller blades to hubs (optional).
- Paint.

DISPLAY STAND
The display stand is useful not only for displaying the finished whirligig indoors, but also for holding the whirligig during construction and for testing it in front of a fan. Construction is easy. The base is 3/4" x 8" x 8" wood or plywood. Drill a 5/8" diameter hole in the center of the base. The 5/8" diameter x 8" hardwood dowel post is glued at one end inside the hole in the base. A 5/32" diameter x 5" steel rod or nail is driven 2" into the center of the top of the post for use as a pivot rod. First drill a pilot hole that is perpendicular to the top of the post and then drive the rod or nail into the hole. If a nail is used, cut the head off of the nail with a hacksaw. File the upper end of the nail smooth, rounding the corners slightly.

Sand and paint the display stand. A clear or color finish can be used.

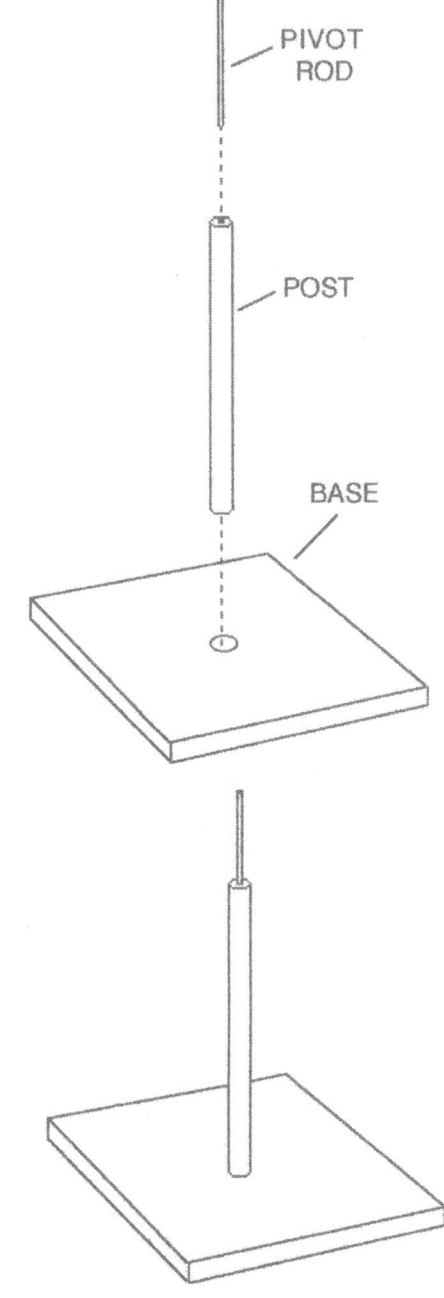

Assembly of display stand.

FOLK ROOSTER

BODY

The rooster body is made of 3/4" x 10" x 12" wood. Mark the pattern for the body on the wood. Drill 5/8" diameter hole for hardwood dowel. Saw the rooster body to the pattern. Drill a 1/4" diameter x 2-1/4" deep hole for the pivot tube in the position shown. The hole must be accurately centered and angled as shown in relation to the propeller axle hole. Then install the steel ball and copper or brass pivot tube in the hole. The tube should fit tightly in the hole so that it will not turn.

Sand the rooster body and mark painting pattern. Make pilot holes for No. 9 wood screws in the ends of the 5/8" diameter X 5" hardwood dowel axle. Then glue the axle in the axle hole in the body, with the axle centered.

The rooster body can be painted at this time, or you can wait until the assembly has been completed. However, it is best to remove the wing propellers before painting the body. Use the color scheme shown, or make up your own. The display base is handy for holding the rooster body upright for painting.

PROPELLERS

The propeller hub is made from 3/4" x 3/4" x 3" wood. Two are required. Both have a 1/4" hole for the axle bearing. The holes must be centered and drilled perpendicular to the surface of the wood. Mark patterns for notches for propeller blades. Notice that one hub has the notches angled for a clockwise propeller and the other for counter-clockwise. The propellers on opposite sides of the whirligig will then turn in opposite directions to cancel each others thrust so the rooster body is not spun around by the propeller action of the wings. Saw the notches in the hubs. Install the 1/4" diameter x 3/4" copper or brass bearing tubes in the holes. Use a punch to expand the ends of the tubing slightly.

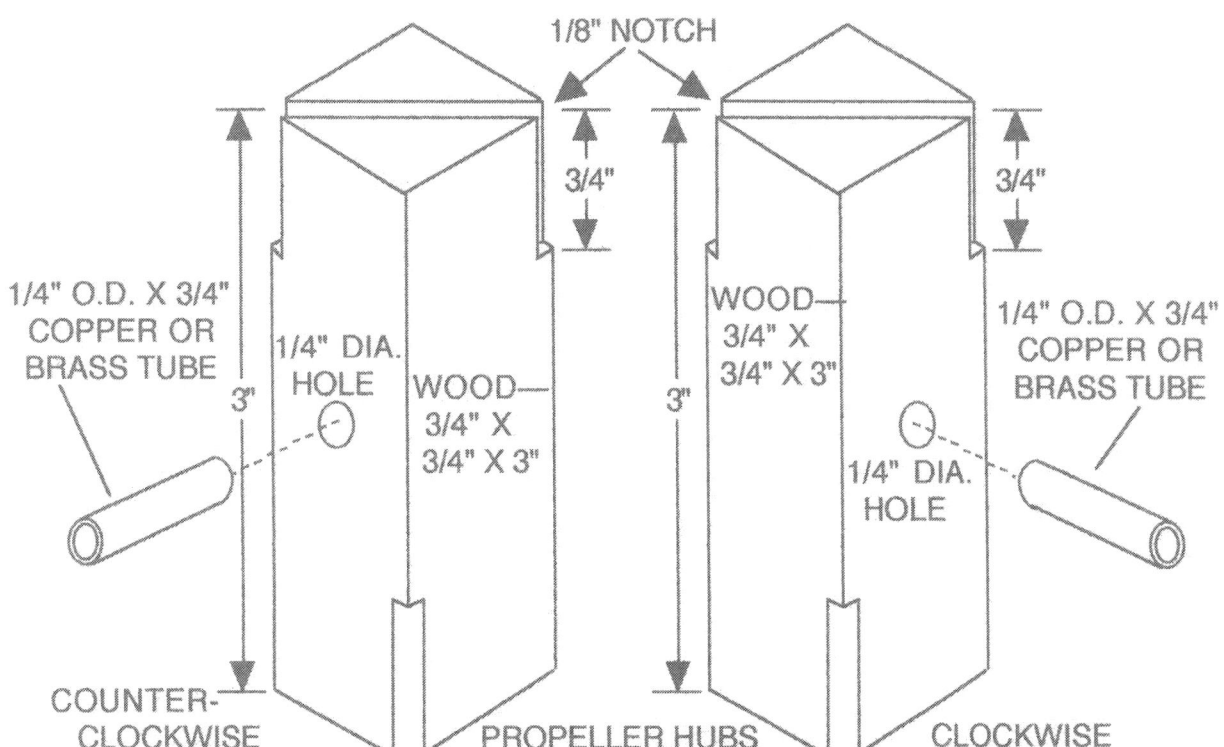

Full-size pattern for propeller hubs.

THE WHIRLIGIG MAKER'S BOOK

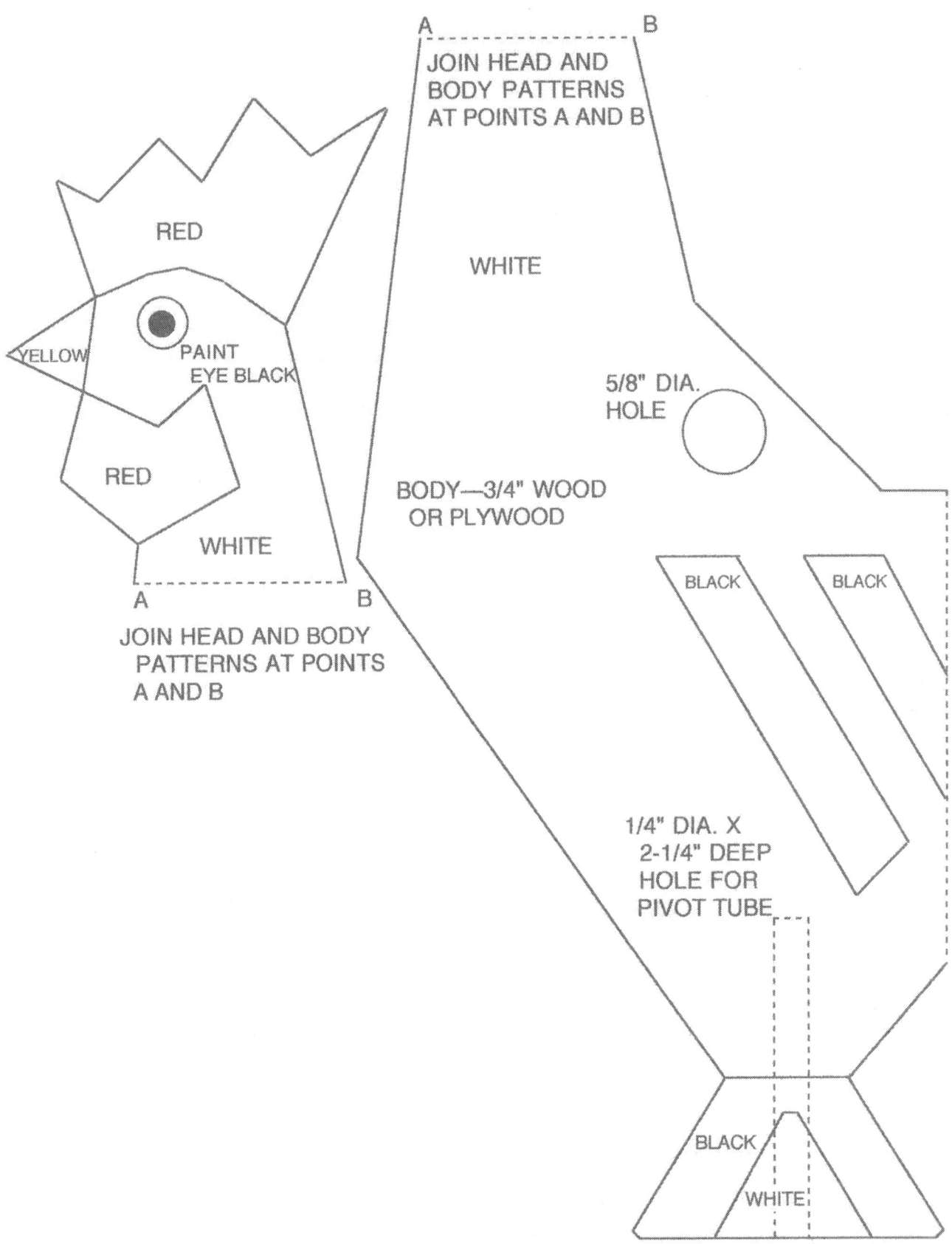

Full-size pattern for body and propeller blades.

FOLK ROOSTER

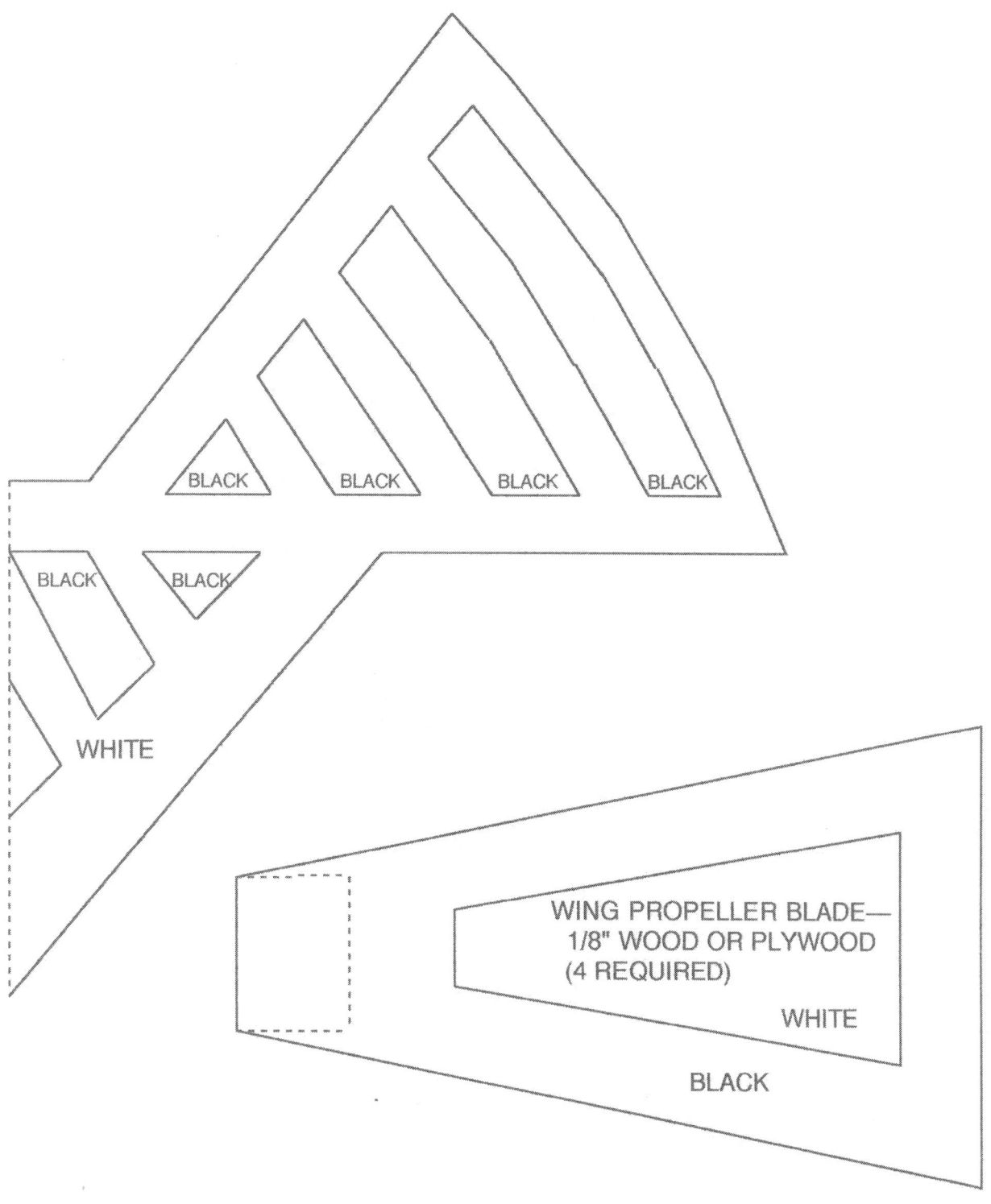

29

THE WHIRLIGIG MAKER'S BOOK

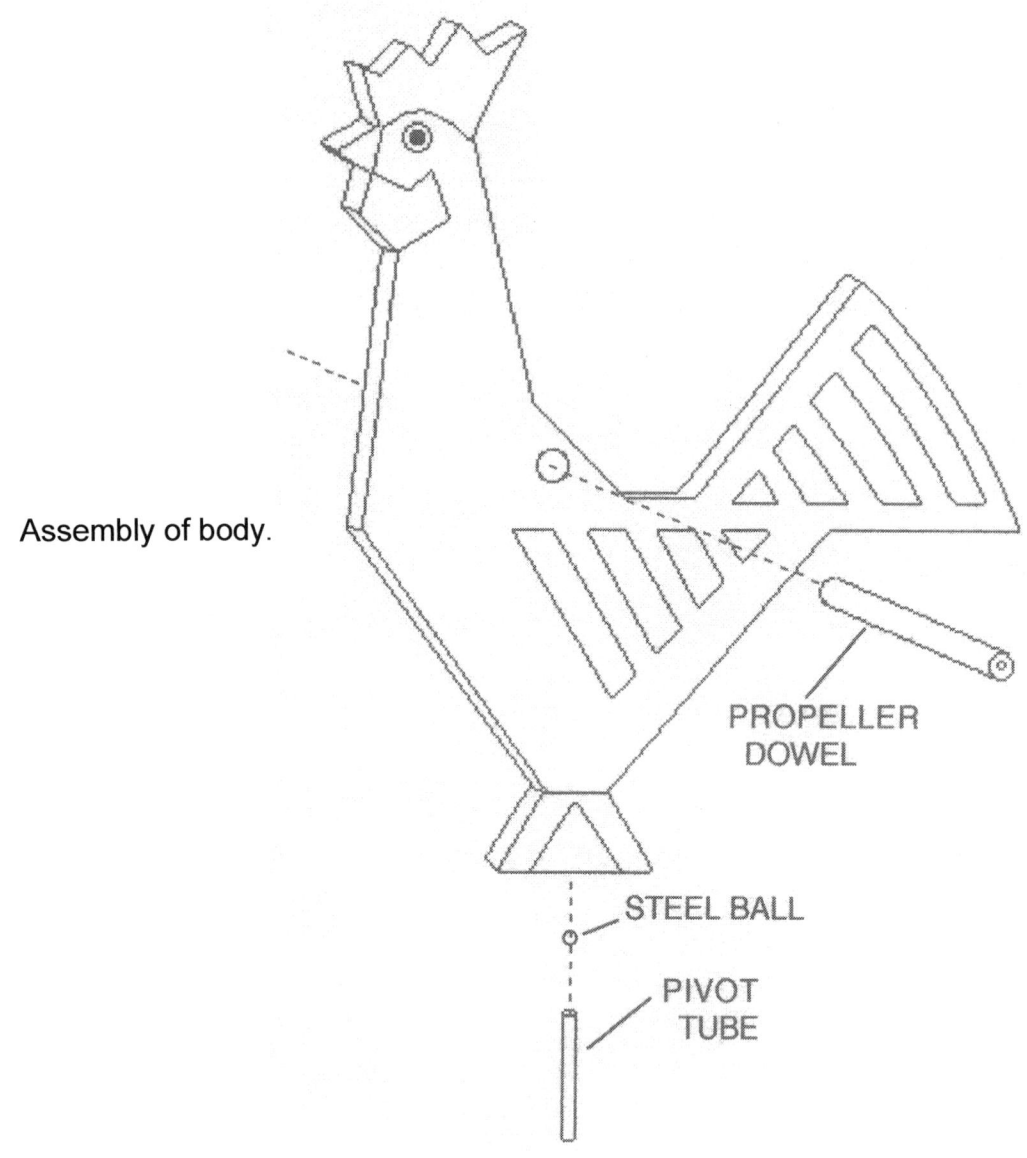

Assembly of body.

Mark the patterns for the propeller blades on 1/8" wood or plywood. Cut the blades to shape and sand as necessary. Glue the blades in the notches with the blades facing as shown. Small finishing nails can be driven through the hub ends and propeller blades to reinforce the joint.

In order for the whirligig to work properly, the propellers need to be balanced so that, when mounted, they balance in a horizontal position. When the blades stop in a no-wind condition, they should be in a horizontal position. If you find that one end of a propeller is heavier than the other, balance it be sanding the extra weight off the heavier blade.

Next, paint the propellers. Paint the white area on the blades first and then paint the remainder of the blades and hub black. Or select your own colors and pattern.

Mount the propellers to the hardwood axle with No. 9 x 2-1/2" round head wood screws with a washer on each side of each hub. Leave the screws loose enough so that the propellers turn freely.

FOLK ROOSTER

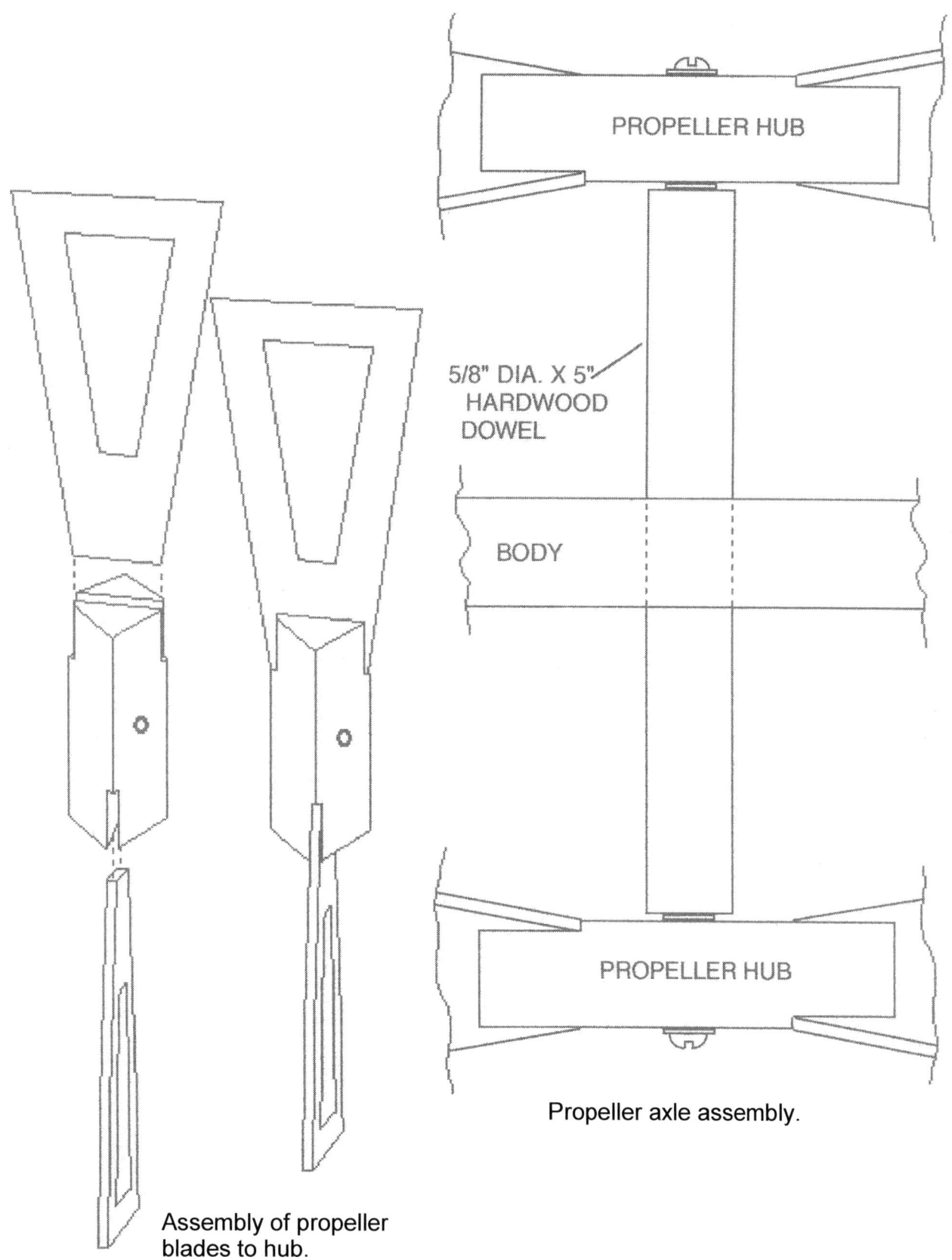

Assembly of propeller blades to hub.

Propeller axle assembly.

31

THE WHIRLIGIG MAKER'S BOOK

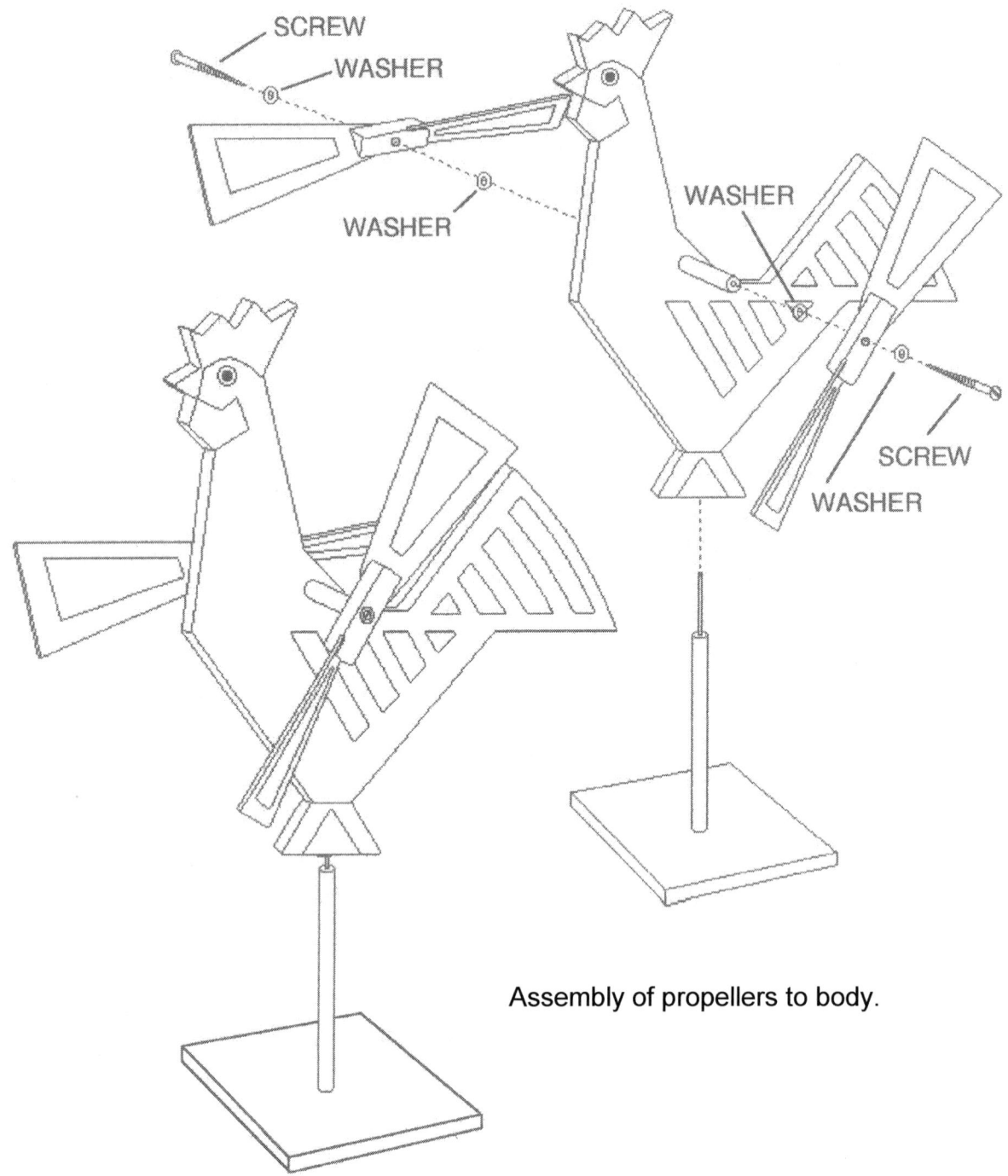

Assembly of propellers to body.

TESTING AND FINISHING

The whirligig is ready for testing. This can be inside with a fan or outdoors in a light wind. The whirligig should start easily if all of the parts turn properly.

Finish any painting that was not done previously.

Chapter 5

FLYING UNICORN

33

THE WHIRLIGIG MAKER'S BOOK

The Flying Unicorn whirligig is a fun project both to build and then watch perform after you have completed it. The propellers form the "flying" wings of the unicorn.

MATERIALS

- 5/8" diameter x 8" hardwood dowel for display stand post.
- 3/4" x 8" x 8" wood or plywood for display stand base.
- 5/32" diameter x 5" steel rod or nail for pivot rod for display stand.
- 3/4" x 9" x 12" wood or plywood for body.
- 3/8" diameter x 3" hardwood dowel for unicorn horn.
- 1/8" x 3-1/2" x 28" wood or plywood for propeller blades.
- 3/4" x 3/4" x 6" wood for propeller hubs.
- 5/8" diameter x 5" hardwood dowel for axle for propellers.
- 1/4" outside diameter (11/64" inside diameter) x 3/4" copper or brass tube for propeller-hub bearing (two required).
- No. 9 x 2-1/2" round head wood screw (two required) for mounting propellers.
- No. 9 washer (four required).
- 1/4" outside diameter (11/64" inside diameter) x 2" copper or brass tube for pivot bearing.
- 1/4" diameter steel ball for pivot bearing.
- Glue.
- Finishing nails for attaching propeller blades to hubs (optional).
- Paint.

DISPLAY STAND

The display stand is useful not only for displaying the finished whirligig indoors, but also for holding the whirligig during construction and for testing it in front of a fan. Construction is easy. The base is 3/4" x 8" x 8" wood or plywood. Drill a 5/8" diameter hole in the center of the base. The 5/8" diameter x 8" hardwood dowel post is glued at one end inside the hole in the base. A 5/32" diameter x 5" steel rod or nail is driven 2" into the center of the top of the post for use as a pivot rod. First drill a pilot hole perpendicular to the top of the post and then drive the rod or nail into the hole. If a nail is used, cut the head off of the nail with a hacksaw. File the upper end of the nail smooth, rounding the corners slightly.

Sand and paint the display stand. A clear or color finish can be used.

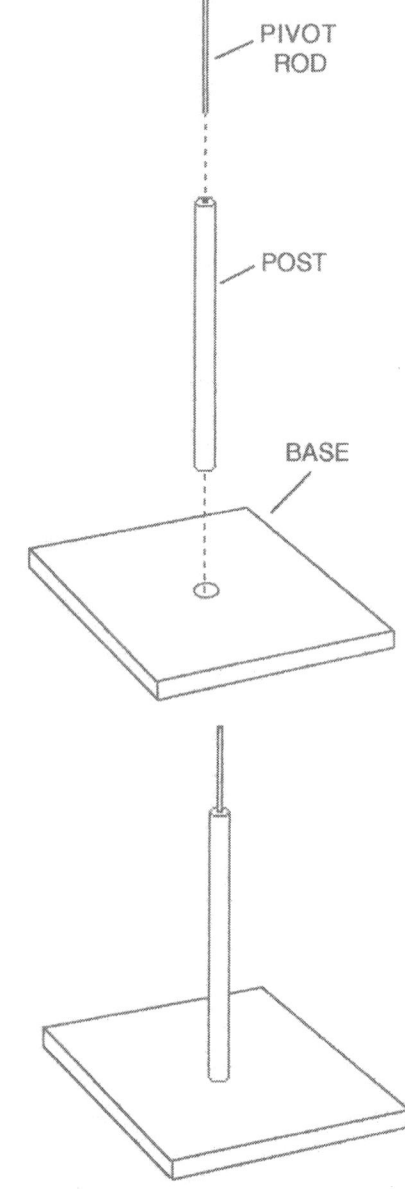

Assembly of display stand.

34

FLYING UNICORN

BODY

The unicorn body is made of 3/4" x 9" x 12" wood or plywood. Mark the pattern for the body on the wood. Drill 5/8" diameter hole for hardwood dowel. Saw the unicorn body to the pattern. Drill a 1/4" diameter x 2-1/4" deep hole for the pivot tube in the position shown. The hole must be accurately centered and angled as shown in relation to the propeller axle hole. Then install the steel ball and copper or brass pivot tube in the hole. The tube should fit tightly in the hole so that it will not turn.

Drill 3/8" diameter hole in body for mounting unicorn horn. Shape horn from 3/8" diameter x 3" wood dowel and glue in mounting hole in body.

Sand the unicorn body and mark painting pattern. Make pilot holes for No. 9 wood screws in the ends of the 5/8" diameter X 5" hardwood dowel axle. Then glue the axle in the axle hole in the body, with the axle centered.

The unicorn body can be painted at this time, or you can wait until the assembly has been completed. However, it is best to remove the wing propellers before painting the body. Use the color scheme shown, or make up your own. The display base is handy for holding the unicorn body upright for painting.

PROPELLERS

The propeller hub is made from 3/4" x 3/4" x 3" wood. Two are required. Both have a 1/4" hole for the axle bearing. The holes must be centered and drilled perpendicular to the surface of the wood. Mark patterns for notches for propeller blades. Notice that one hub has the notches angled for a clockwise propeller and the other for counter-clockwise. The propellers on opposite sides of the whirligig will then turn in opposite directions to cancel each others thrust so the unicorn body is not spun around by the propeller action of the wings. Saw the notches in the hubs. Install the 1/4" diameter x 3/4" copper or brass bearing tubes in the holes. Use a punch to expand the ends of the tubing slightly.

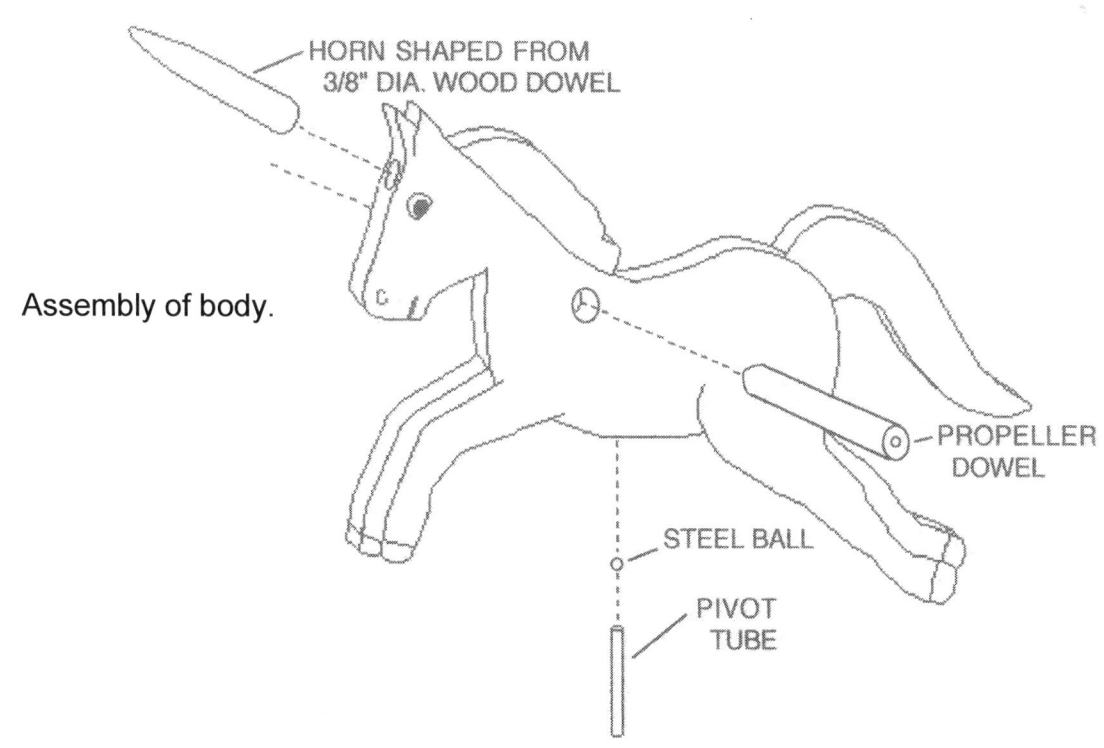

Assembly of body.

THE WHIRLIGIG MAKER'S BOOK

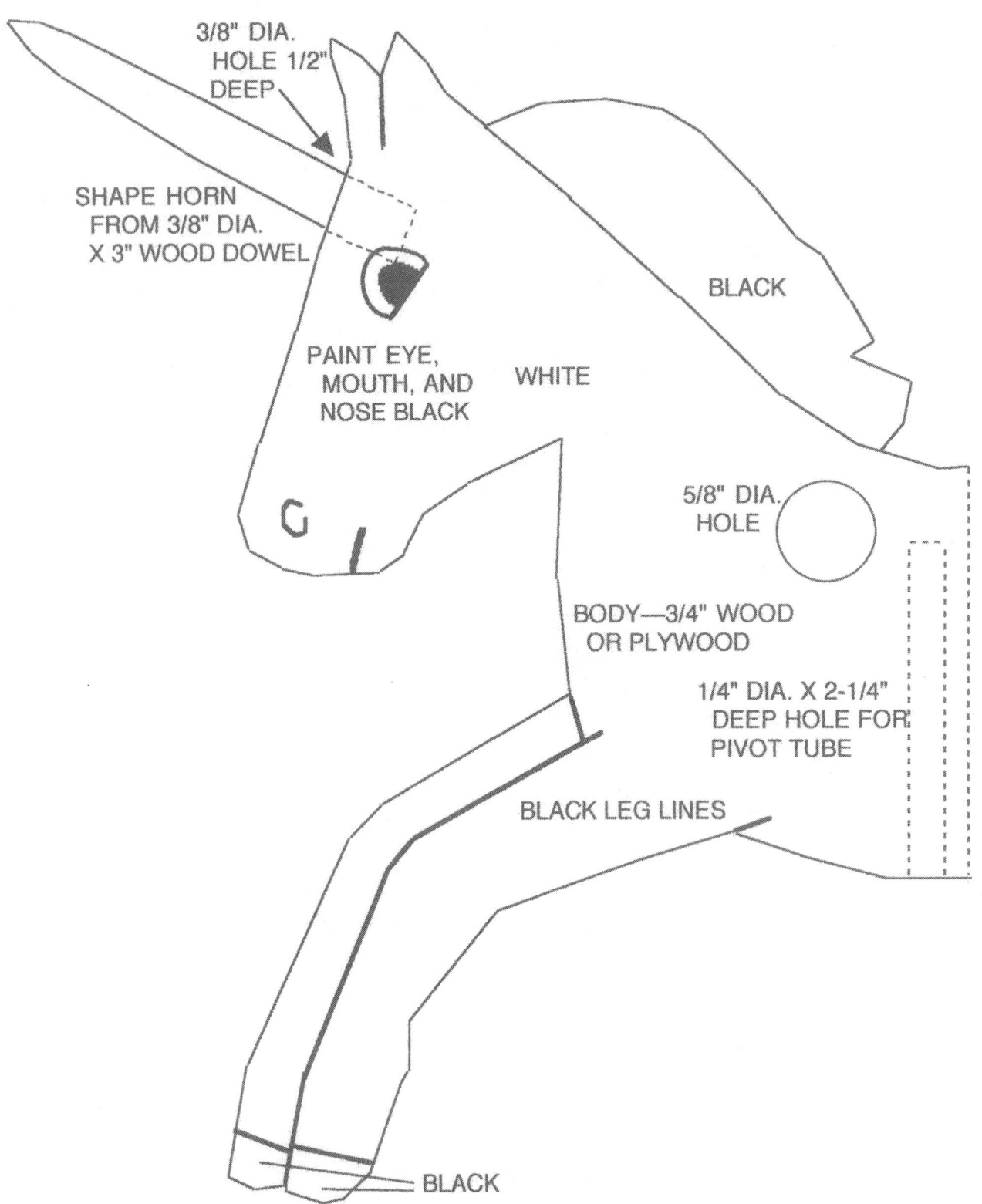

Full-size pattern for body.

FLYING UNICORN

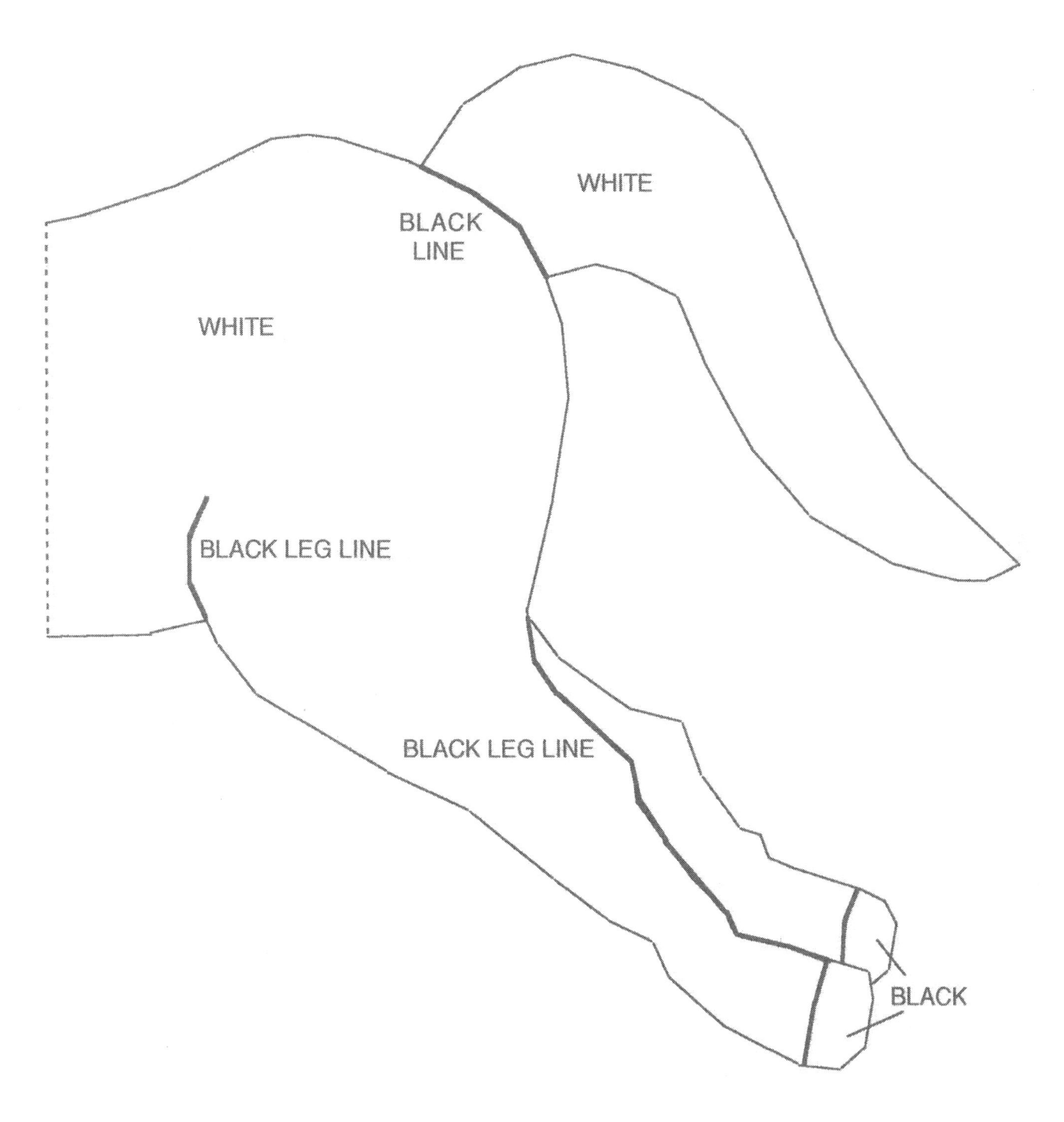

WHITE

BLACK
LINE

WHITE

BLACK LEG LINE

BLACK LEG LINE

BLACK

37

THE WHIRLIGIG MAKER'S BOOK

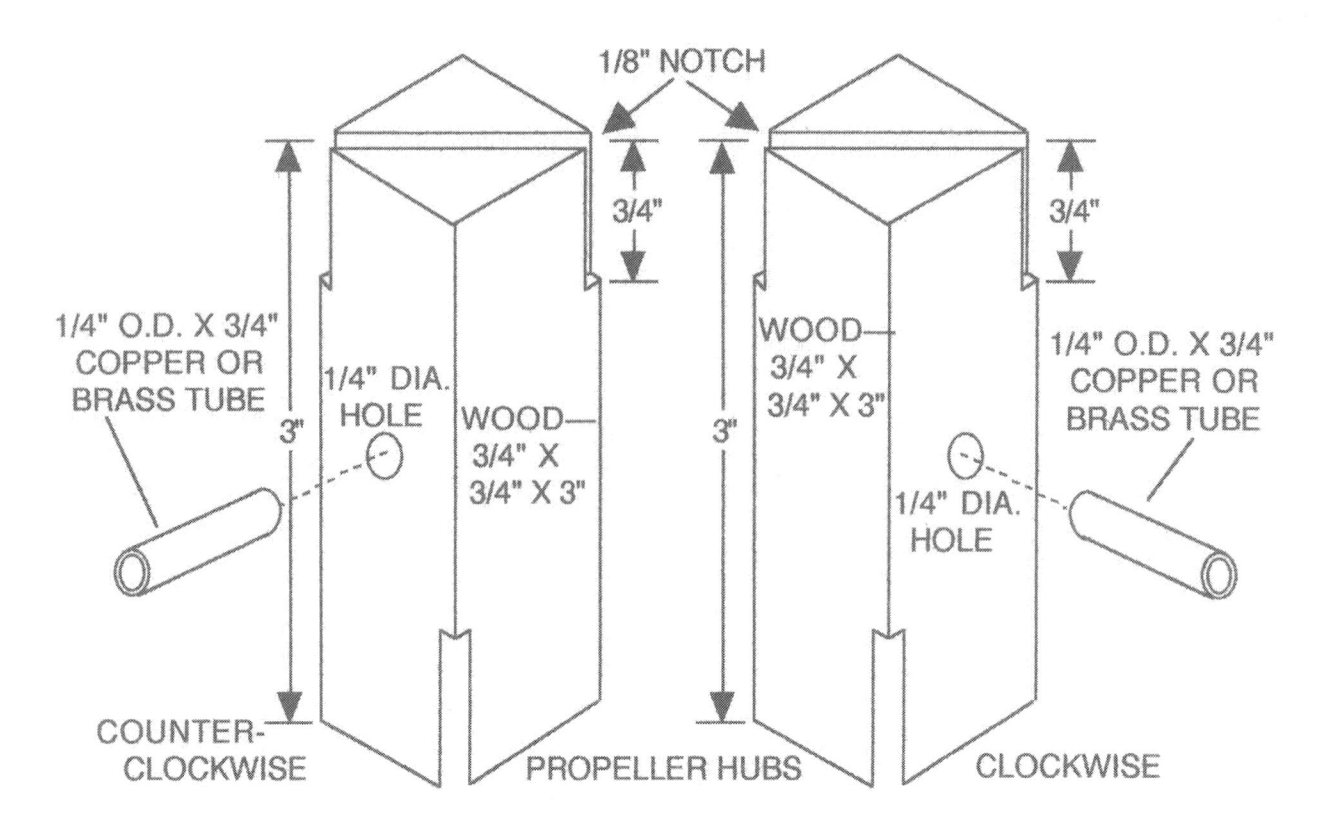

Full-size pattern for propeller hubs.

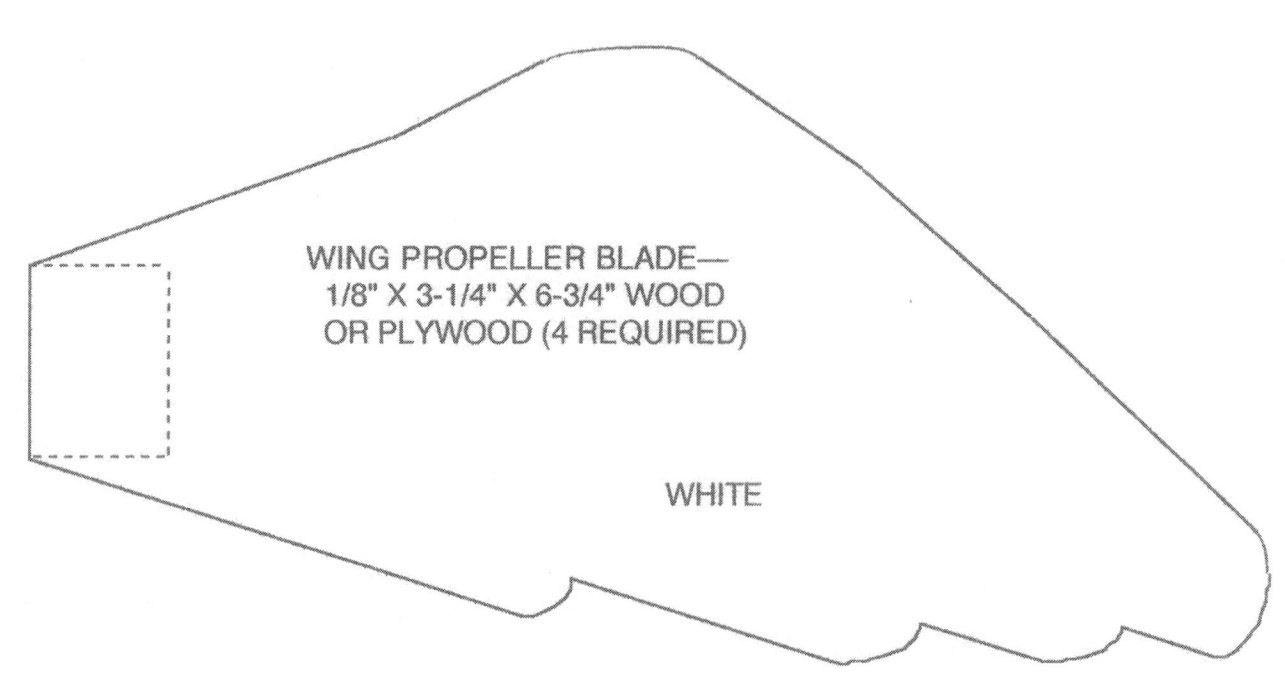

Full-size pattern for propeller blades.

38

FLYING UNICORN

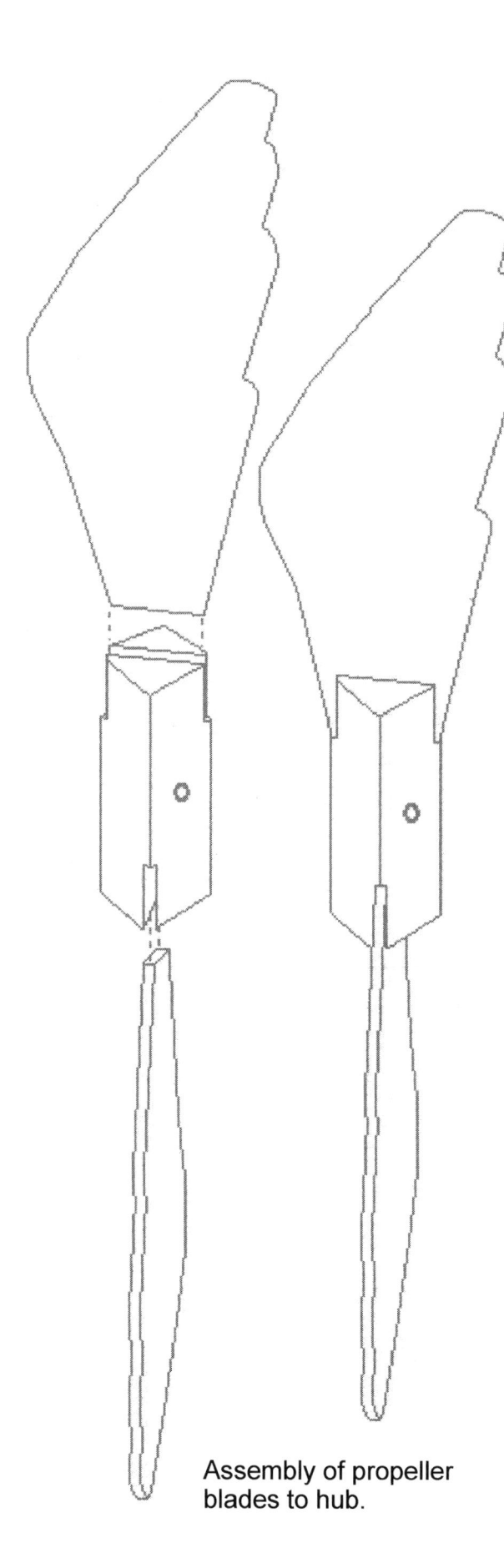

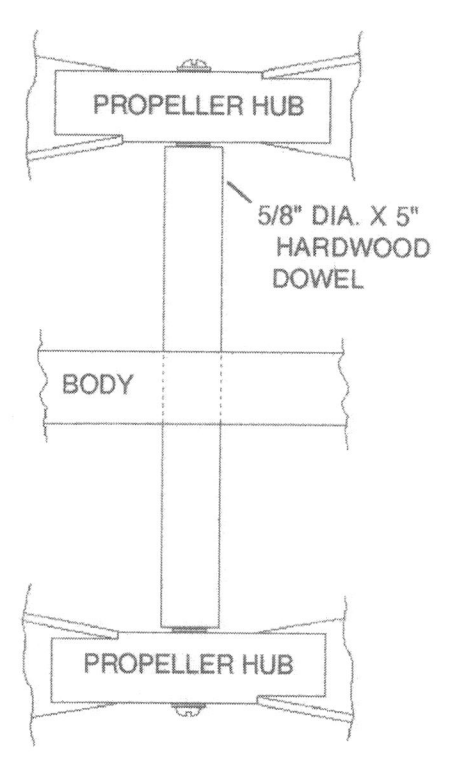

Propeller axle assembly.

Assembly of propeller blades to hub.

Mark the patterns for the propeller blades on 1/8" wood or plywood. Cut the blades to shape and sand as necessary. Glue the blades in the notches with the blades facing as shown. Small finishing nails can be driven through the hub ends and propeller blades to reinforce the joint.

In order for the whirligig to work properly, the propellers need to be balanced so that, when mounted, they balance in a horizontal position. When the blades stop in a no-wind condition, they should be in a horizontal position. If you find that one end of a propeller is heavier than the other, balance it be sanding the extra weight off the heavier blade.

Paint the propeller blades and hubs white. Or select your own colors and pattern.

Mount the propellers to the hardwood axle with No. 9 x 2-1/2" round head wood screws with a washer on each side of each hub. Leave the screws loose enough so that the propellers turn freely.

THE WHIRLIGIG MAKER'S BOOK

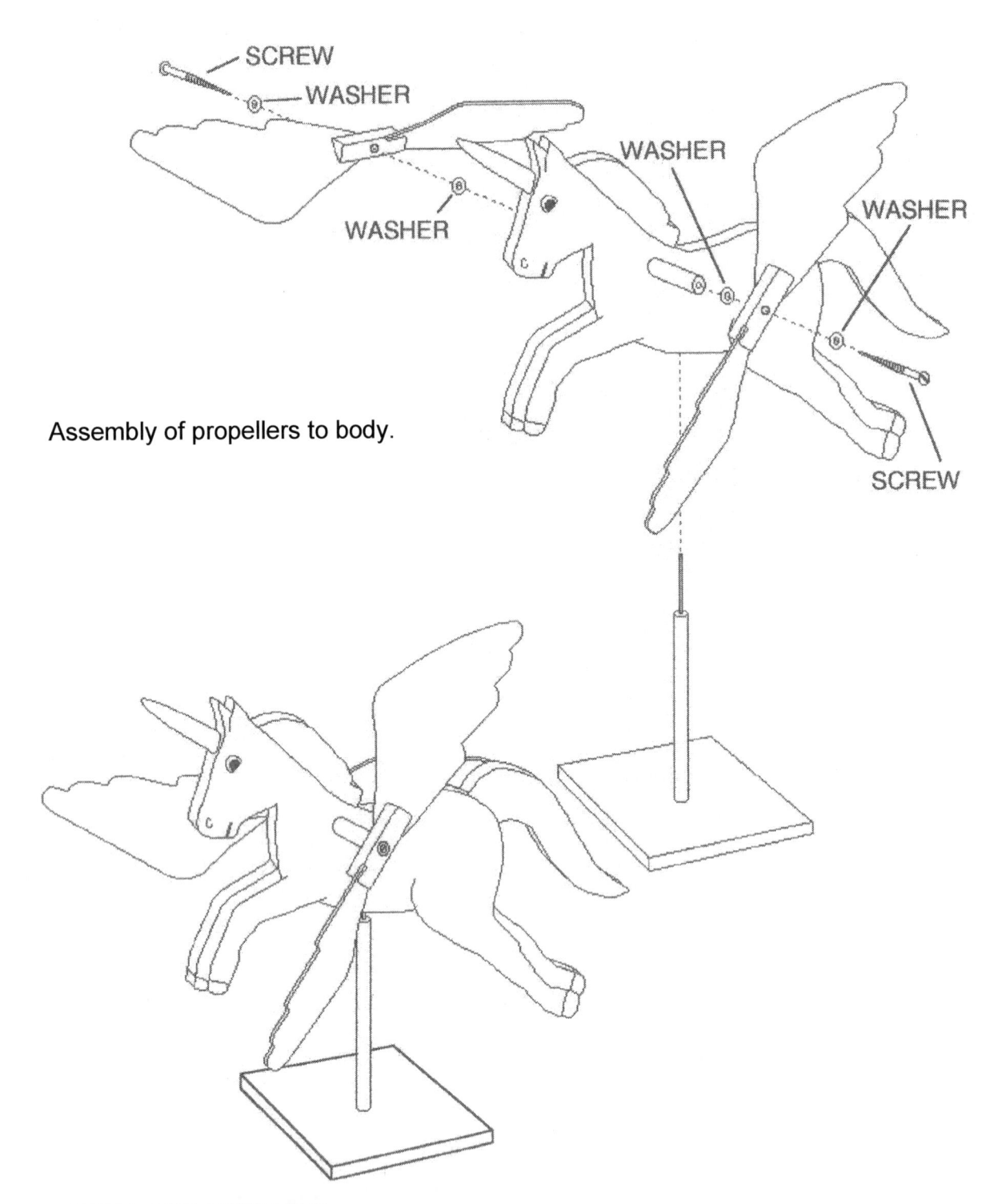

Assembly of propellers to body.

TESTING AND FINISHING

The whirligig is ready for testing. This can be inside with a fan or outdoors in a light wind. The whirligig should start easily if all of the parts turn properly.

Finish any painting that was not done previously.

Chapter 6

GIRL GYMNAST

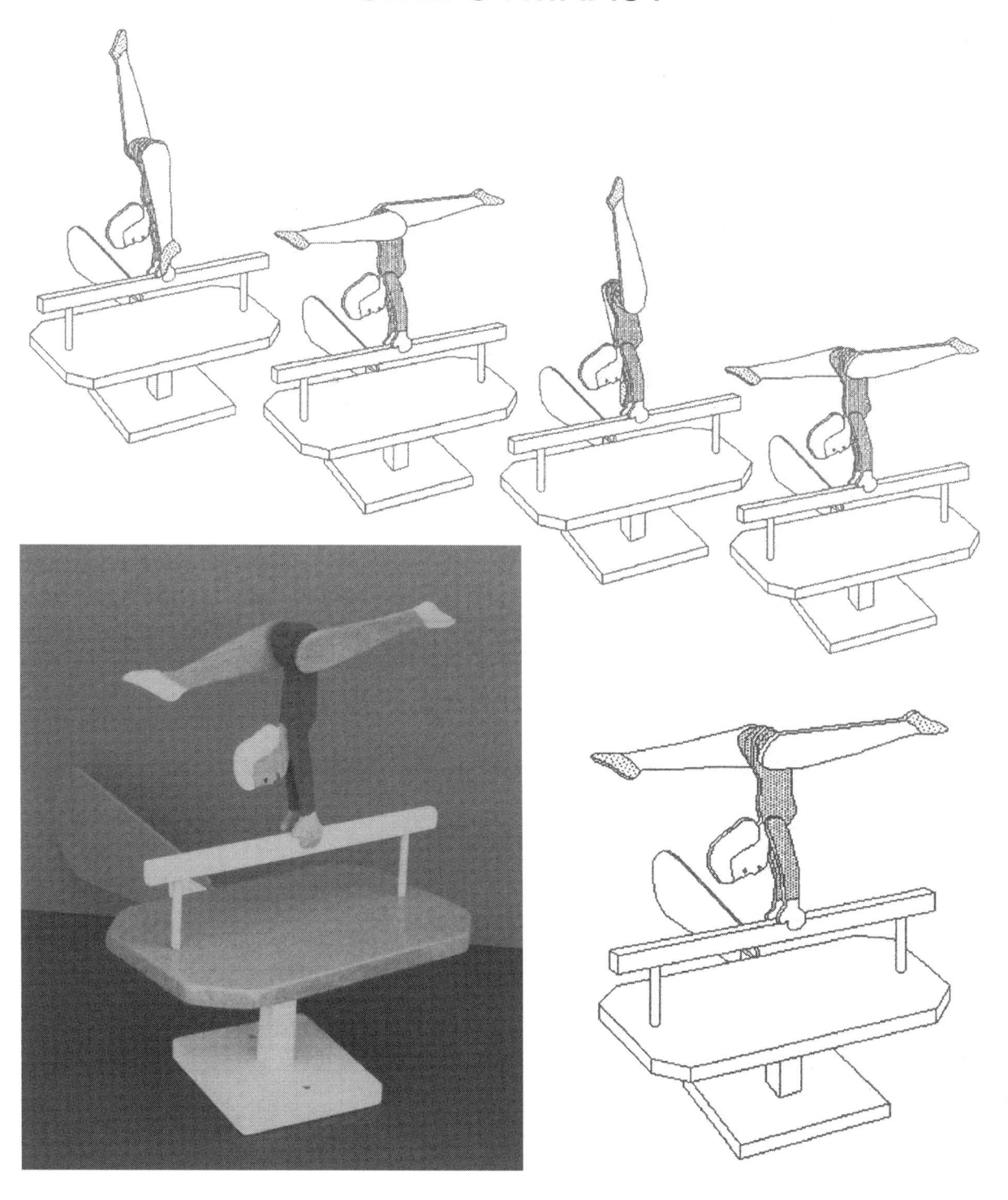

The Girl Gymnast whirligig is a fun project both to build and then watch perform after you have completed it. The propeller of this whirligig, like traditional arm and wing circling designs, forms the twirling legs of the girl in a handstand.

MATERIALS

- 3/4" x 6" x 6" wood or plywood for display base.
- 1" x 1" x 3" wood for display post.
- 3/4" x 1" x 8-1/2" wood for platform.
- 3/4" x 8" x 12" wood for floor.
- 1/2" x 7/8" x 12" wood for beam.
- 1/4" x 5" x 12-1/2" plywood for vane.
- 3/16" x 6" x 12" wood or plywood for girl's body and arms and legs.
- 1/4" x 1-1/2" x 3" wood or plywood for leg spacers.
- 1-1/2" x 1-1/2" x 3" wood for angle blocks.
- 1/4" diameter x 12" hardwood dowel for beam posts and leg axle.
- Metal or plastic washer with 17/64" diameter hole (2 required) for use on leg axle.
- 1/4" outside diameter (9/64" inside diameter) x 1-1/2" brass tubing for pivot bearing.
- 1/4" diameter steel ball for pivot bearing.
- 1/8" diameter x 4" nail for pivot rod for display base.
- Glue.
- Finishing nails.
- Small felt pad for display base (4 required).
- Paint.

DISPLAY STAND

The display stand is useful not only for displaying the finished whirligig indoors, but also for holding the whirligig during construction and for testing it in front of a fan. Construction is easy. The base is 3/4" x 6" x 6" wood or plywood. The 1" x 1" x 3" wood post is glued and nailed to the center of the base. A 1/8" diameter x 4" nail is driven 2" into the center of the top of the post for use as a pivot rod. First drill a pilot hole perpendicular to the top of the post and then drive the nail into the hole. Cut the head off of the nail with a hacksaw. File the upper end of the nail smooth, rounding the corners slightly.

Sand and paint the display stand. A clear or color finish can be used.

Attach felt pads to the corners of the underside of the base.

PLATFORM

The platform is made of 3/4" x 1" x 8-1/2" wood. Make a 1/4" x 2-1/2" slot for the vane. Round the corners of the platform by the vane slot, as shown. Drill a 1/4" diameter hole for the pivot tube in the position shown. The hole must be accurately centered and perpendicular to the wood surface for the whirligig to work properly. I use a drill press and drill press vise for drilling this hole.

The floor is 3/4" x 8" x 12" wood shaped to the pattern shown. Drill 1/4" diameter holes for the beam posts in the positions shown.

Glue and nail the floor to the platform. Then install the steel ball and brass pivot tube in the hole in the platform. The tube should fit tightly in the hole so that it will not turn.

Cut the vane from 1/4" plywood to the pattern shown. Glue the vane in the platform slot, as shown.

The beam is 1/2" x 7/8" x 12" wood. Drill 1/4" diameter holes 5/8" into the beam for the posts in the positions shown.

Assemble the posts and beam together and to the floor with glue joints.

Sand the platform. The platform can be painted at this time, or you can wait until the assembly has been completed. The color scheme can be as desired. Leave the hand-placement areas unpainted for gluing the girl's hands to the beam.

GIRL GYMNAST

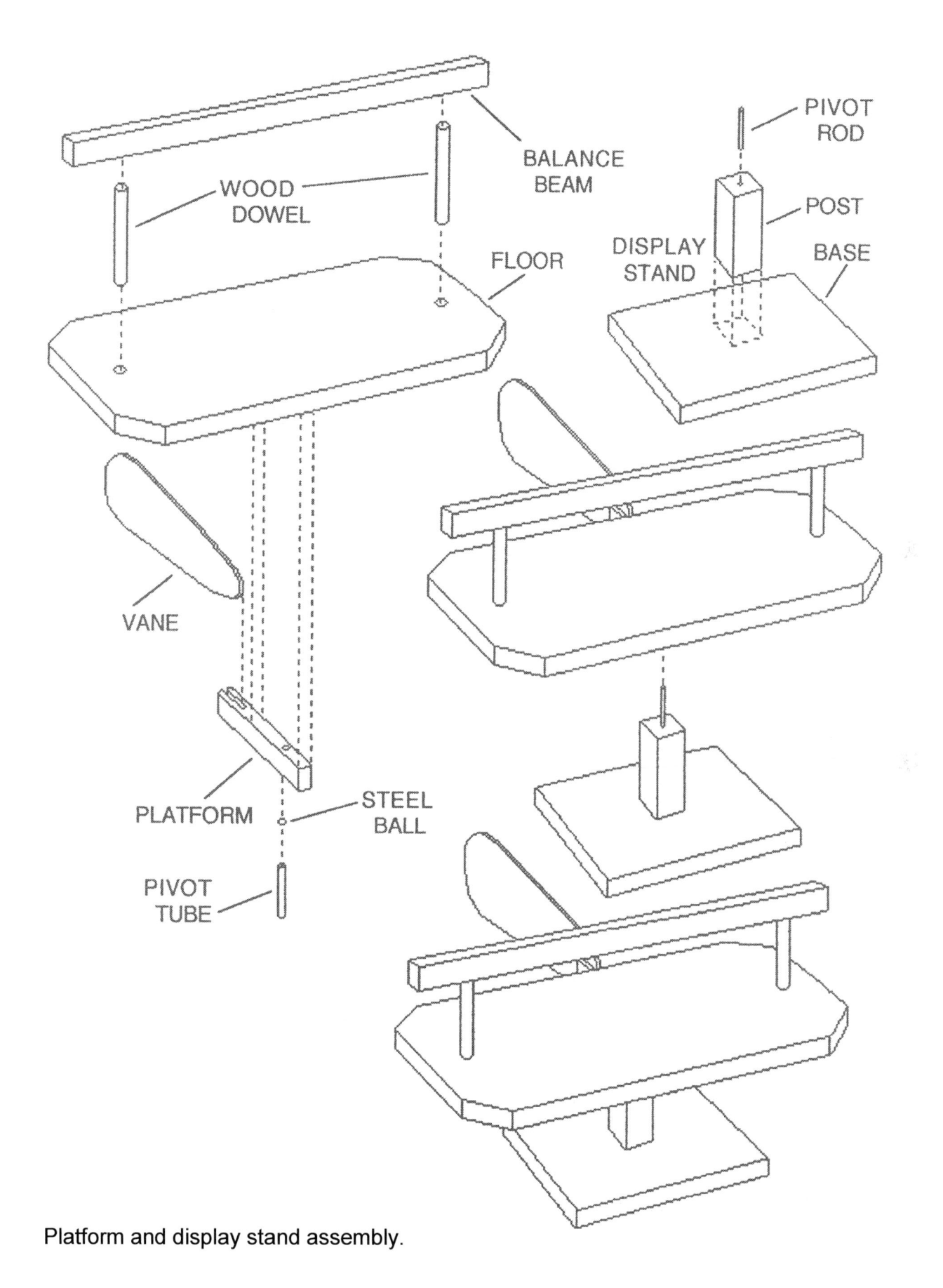

Platform and display stand assembly.

43

THE WHIRLIGIG MAKER'S BOOK

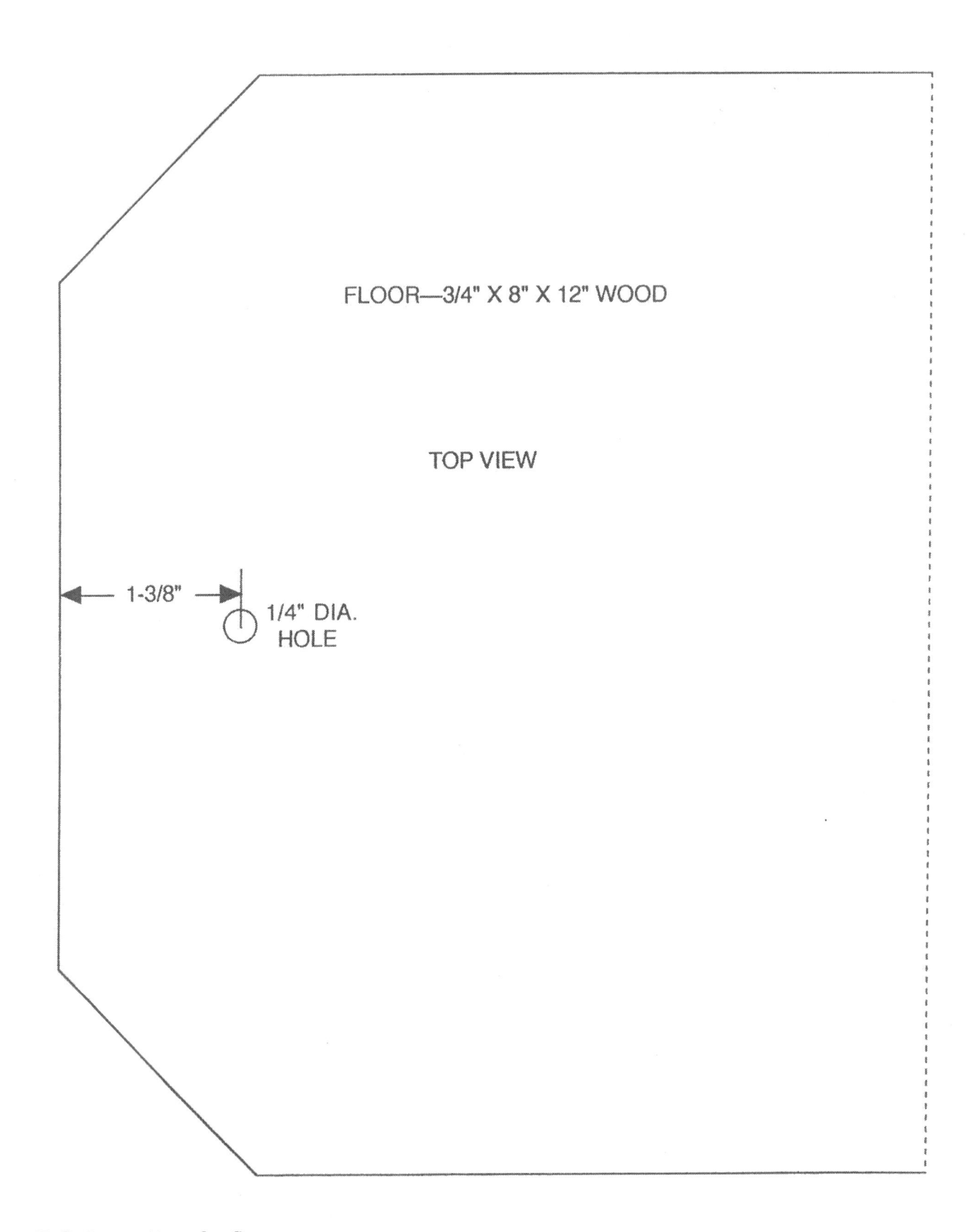

FLOOR—3/4" X 8" X 12" WOOD

TOP VIEW

1-3/8"

1/4" DIA. HOLE

Full-size pattern for floor.

44

GIRL GYMNAST

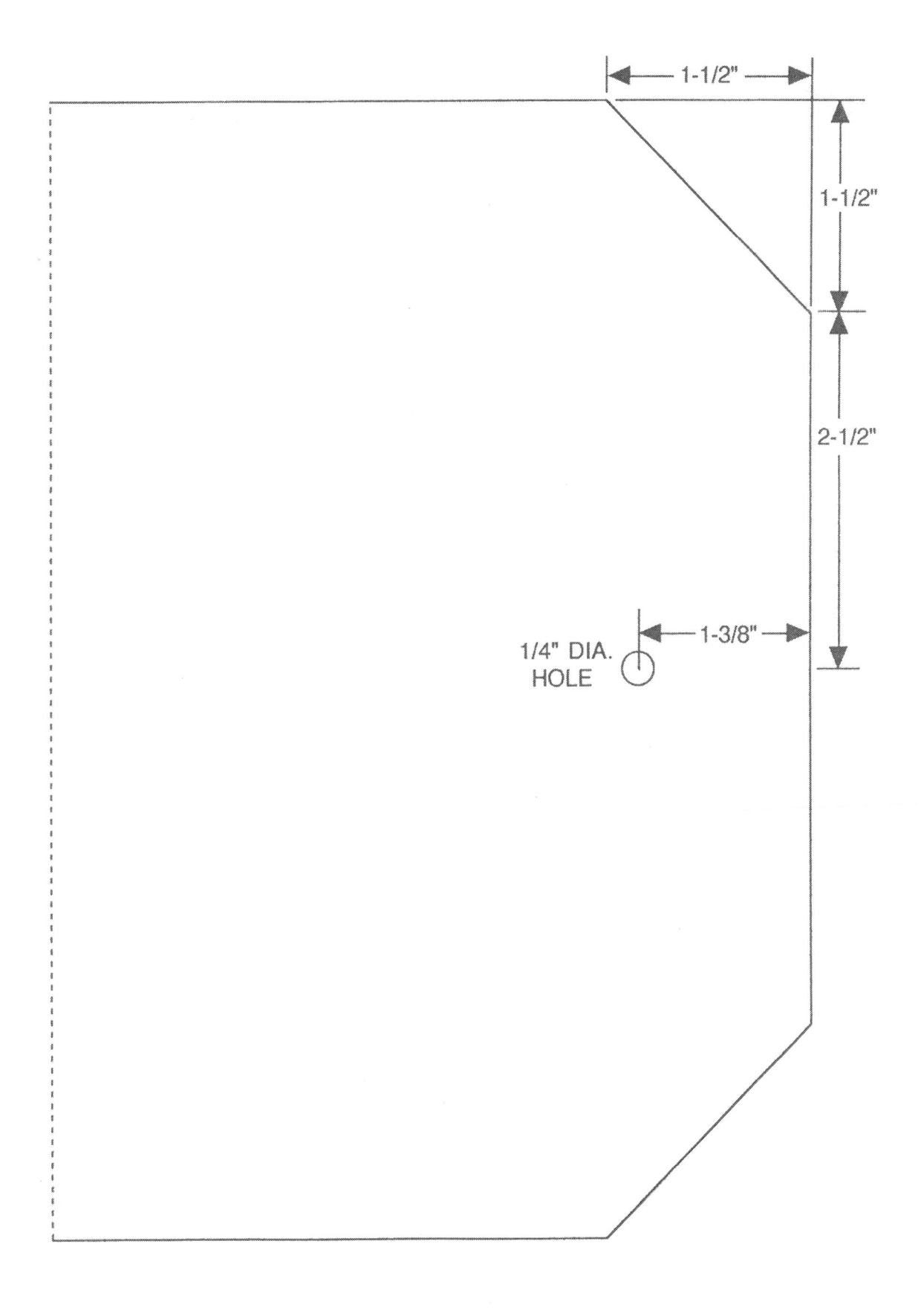

1-1/2"

1-1/2"

2-1/2"

1/4" DIA. HOLE

1-3/8"

45

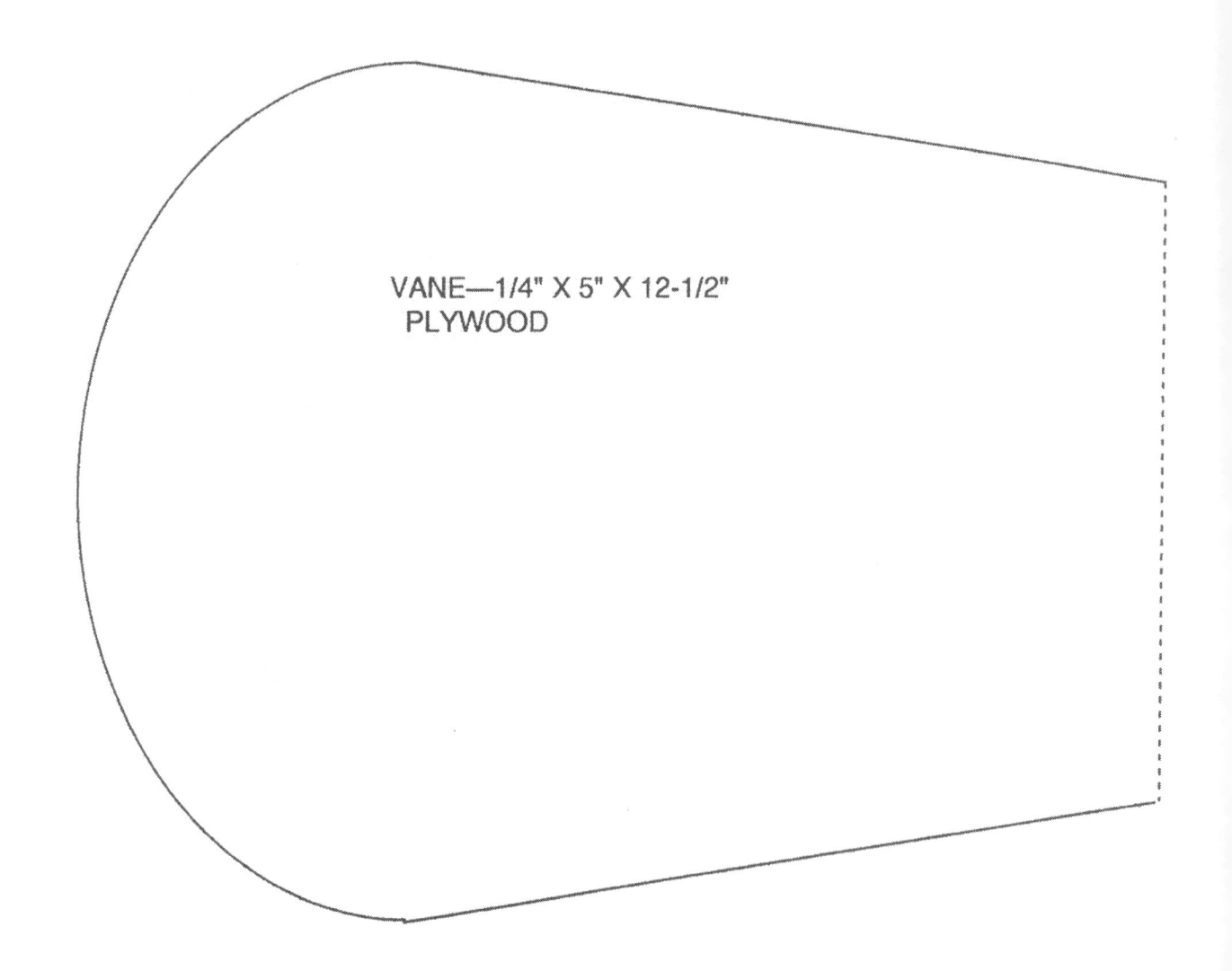

THE WHIRLIGIG MAKER'S BOOK

VANE—1/4" X 5" X 12-1/2"
PLYWOOD

Full-size pattern for vane.

GIRL GYMNAST

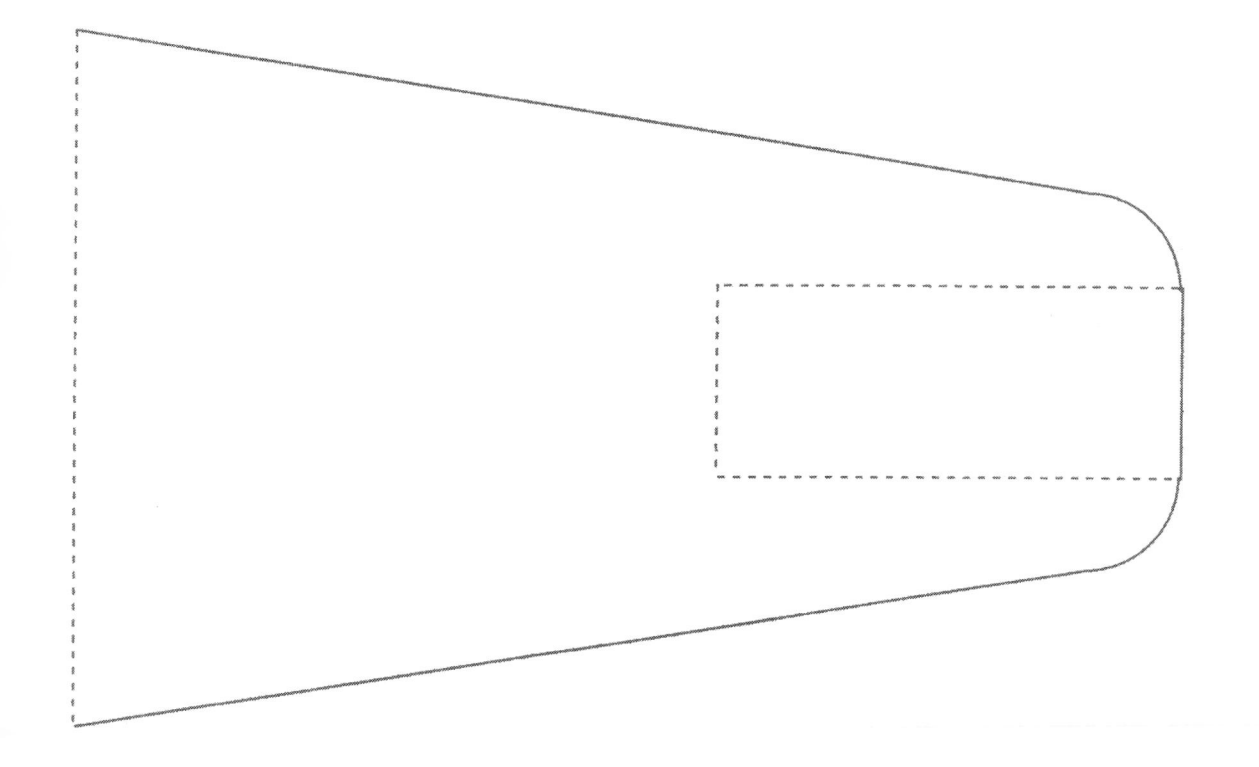

THE WHIRLIGIG MAKER'S BOOK

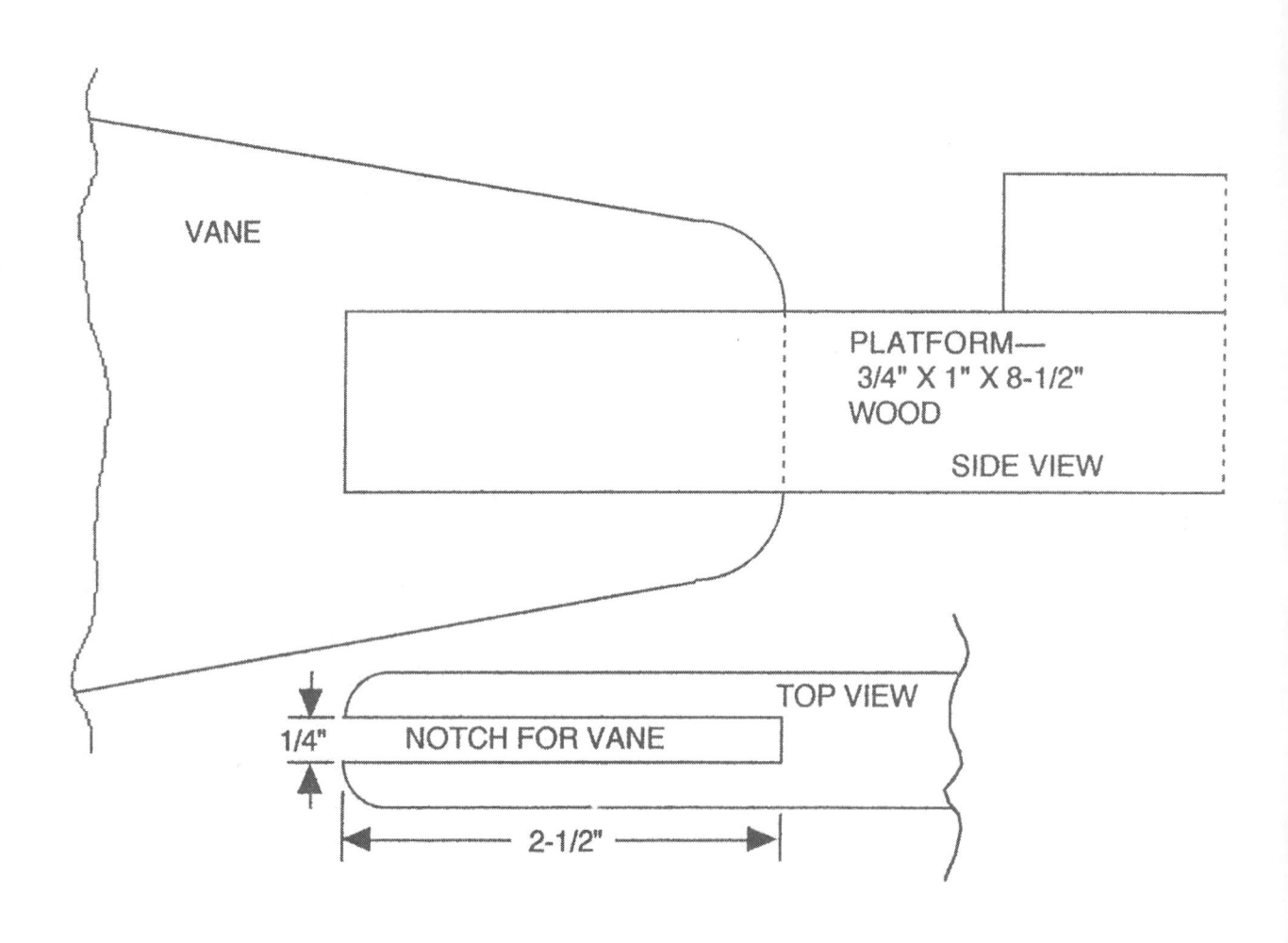

VANE

PLATFORM—
3/4" X 1" X 8-1/2"
WOOD

SIDE VIEW

TOP VIEW

1/4"

NOTCH FOR VANE

2-1/2"

Full-size plan and patterns for display stand and platform.

GIRL GYMNAST

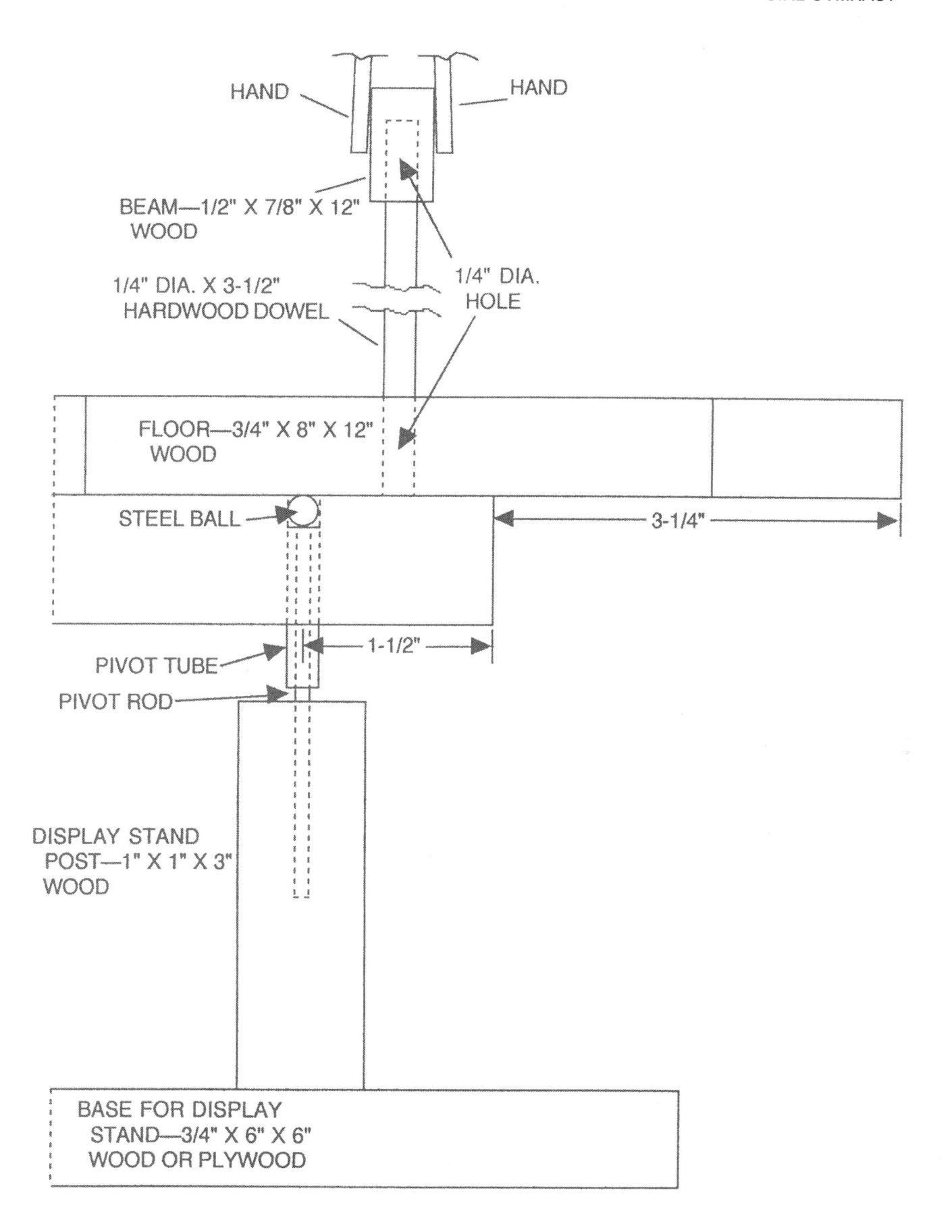

HAND HAND

BEAM—1/2" X 7/8" X 12" WOOD

1/4" DIA. X 3-1/2" HARDWOOD DOWEL

1/4" DIA. HOLE

FLOOR—3/4" X 8" X 12" WOOD

STEEL BALL

3-1/4"

PIVOT TUBE

1-1/2"

PIVOT ROD

DISPLAY STAND POST—1" X 1" X 3" WOOD

BASE FOR DISPLAY STAND—3/4" X 6" X 6" WOOD OR PLYWOOD

49

THE WHIRLIGIG MAKER'S BOOK

BEAM—1/2" X 7/8" X 12" WOOD

HAND PLACEMENT

1/4" DIA. HOLE

1/4" DIA. X 3-1/2" HARDWOOD DOWEL

VANE NOT SHOWN

FLOOR—3/4" X 8" X 12" WOOD

FRONT VIEW

1-3/8"

STEEL BALL

PLATFORM—3/4" X 1" X 8-1/2" WOOD

PIVOT TUBE

PIVOT ROD

Full-size plan and patterns for display stand and platform and balance beam.

DISPLAY STAND POST—1" X 1" X 3" WOOD

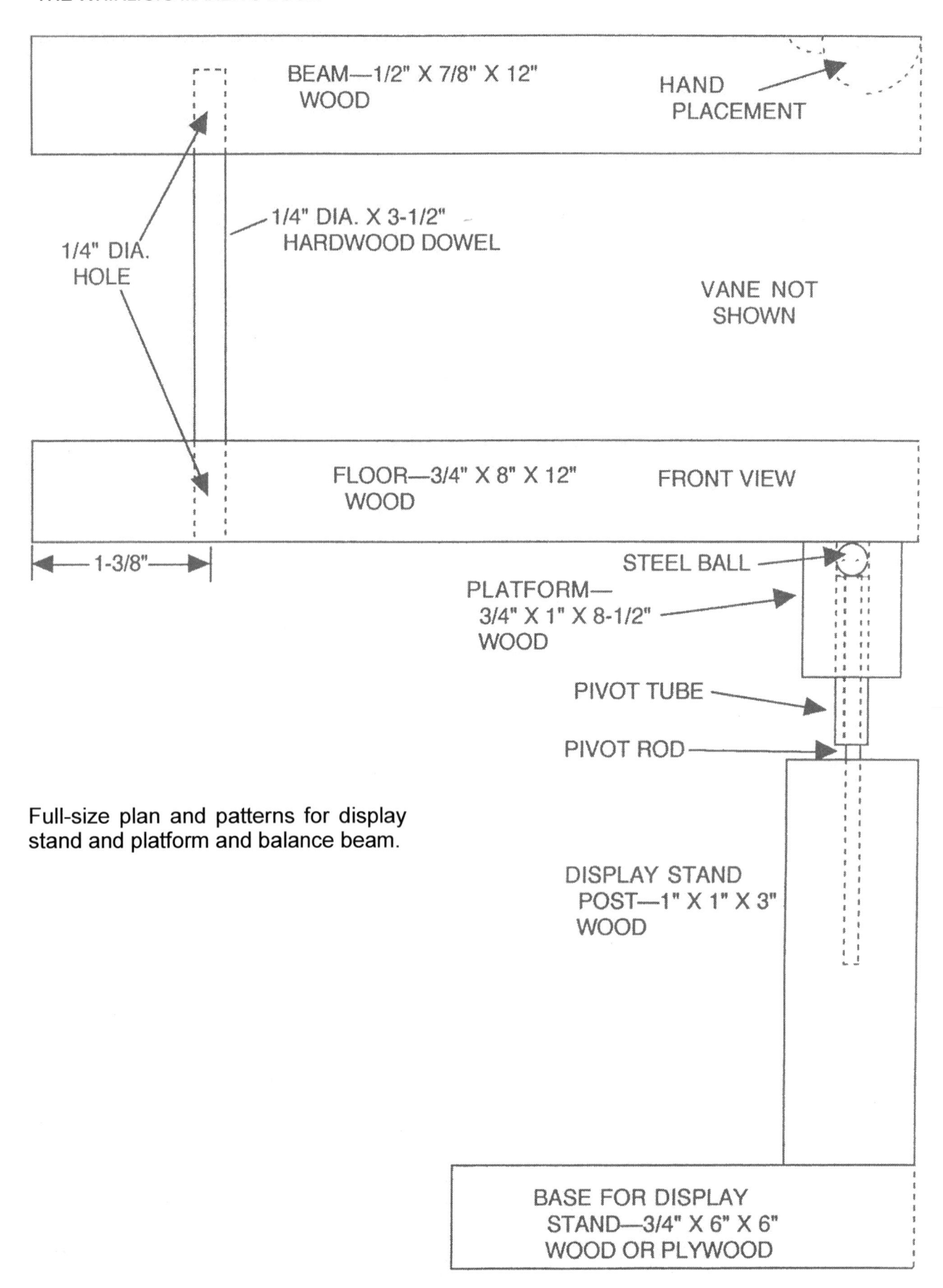

BASE FOR DISPLAY STAND—3/4" X 6" X 6" WOOD OR PLYWOOD

GIRL GYMNAST

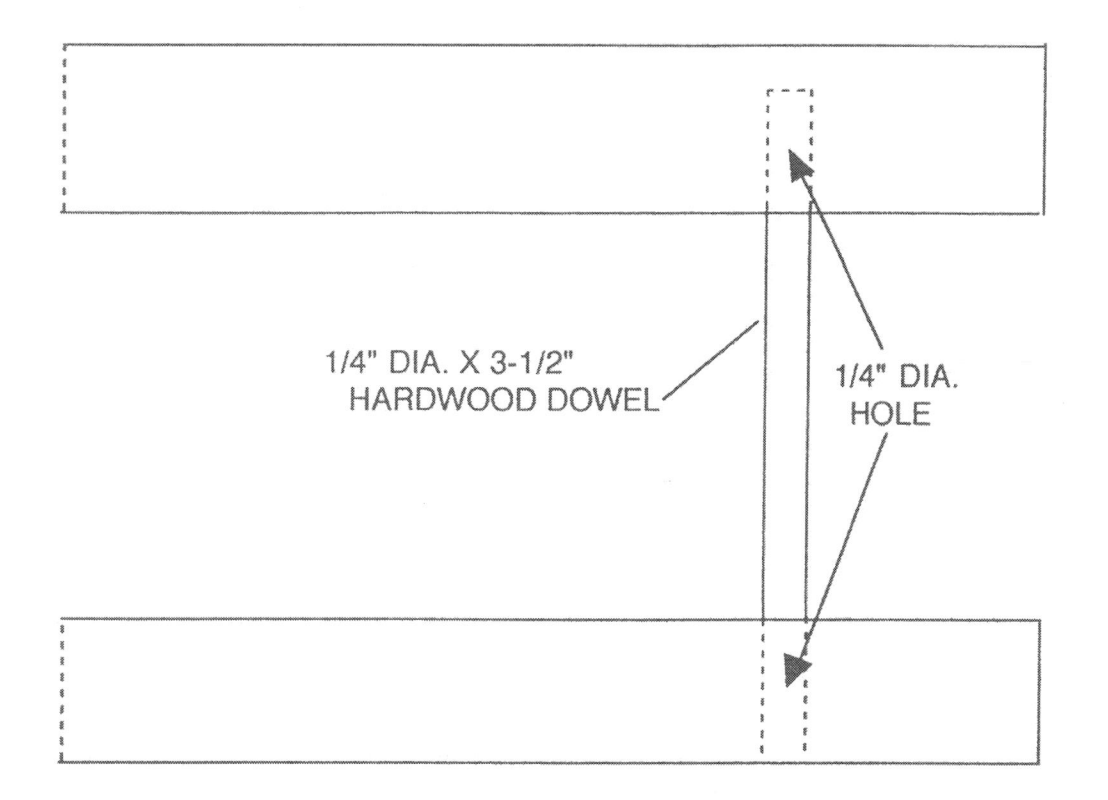

1/4" DIA. X 3-1/2"
HARDWOOD DOWEL

1/4" DIA.
HOLE

Assembly of girl.

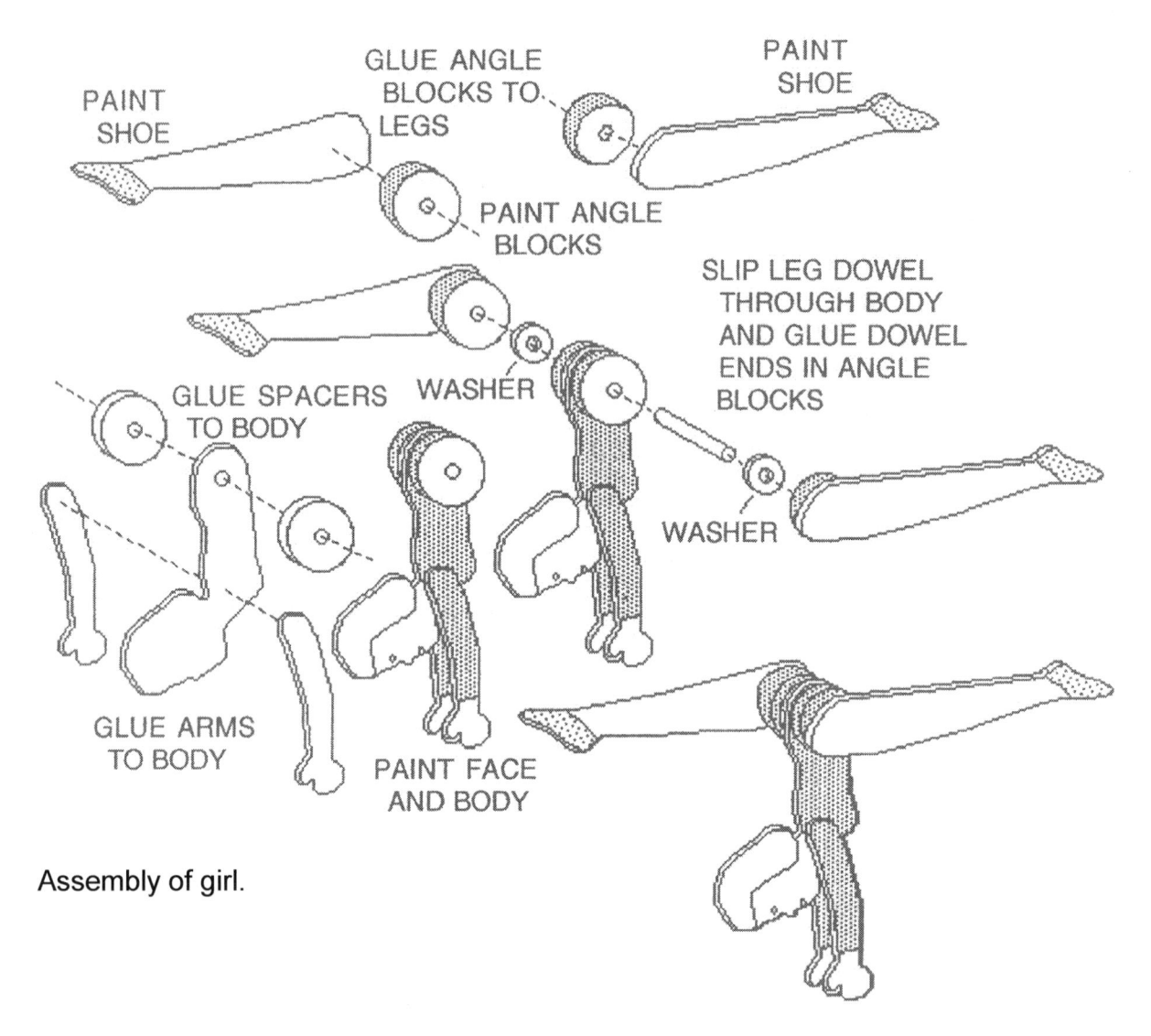

HANDSTAND GIRL

The girl's legs form a split propeller, which turns on a shaft. With the girl facing as shown, a counterclockwise propeller is used.

Cut and shape the parts for the handstand girl to the patterns shown. Drill leg axle holes, in the girl's body and through the spacers and angle blocks.

Glue the legs to the angle blocks in the positions shown. This must be done accurately if the whirligig is to work properly. Paint the angle blocks and shoes.

Glue the spacers and arms to the girl's body, with the hands angled to 1/2" apart. Allow the glue to set, then paint the face and body.

Slip leg dowel through body. The dowel must turn freely. Apply paraffin wax or wood lubricant to the dowel, taking care not to get any on the areas where the dowel will be glued to the angle blocks. Next, glue dowel ends in angle blocks, using washers over dowel as shown.

Glue the girl's hands to the beam in the position shown.

TESTING AND FINISHING

The whirligig is ready for testing. This can be inside with a fan or outdoors in a light wind. The whirligig should start easily if all of the parts turn properly.

Finish any painting that was not done previously.

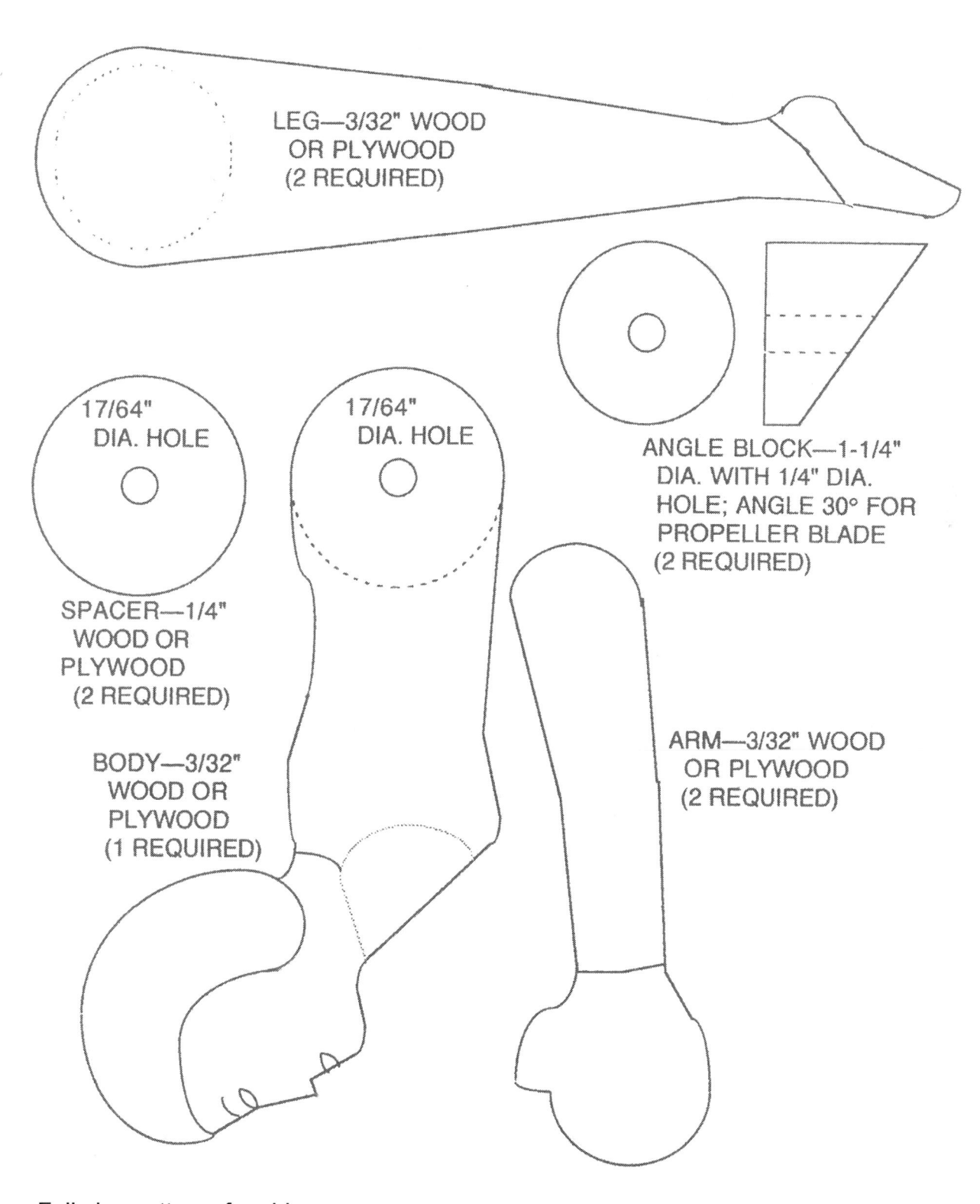

GIRL GYMNAST

LEG—3/32" WOOD OR PLYWOOD (2 REQUIRED)

17/64" DIA. HOLE

17/64" DIA. HOLE

ANGLE BLOCK—1-1/4" DIA. WITH 1/4" DIA. HOLE; ANGLE 30° FOR PROPELLER BLADE (2 REQUIRED)

SPACER—1/4" WOOD OR PLYWOOD (2 REQUIRED)

BODY—3/32" WOOD OR PLYWOOD (1 REQUIRED)

ARM—3/32" WOOD OR PLYWOOD (2 REQUIRED)

Full-size patterns for girl.

53

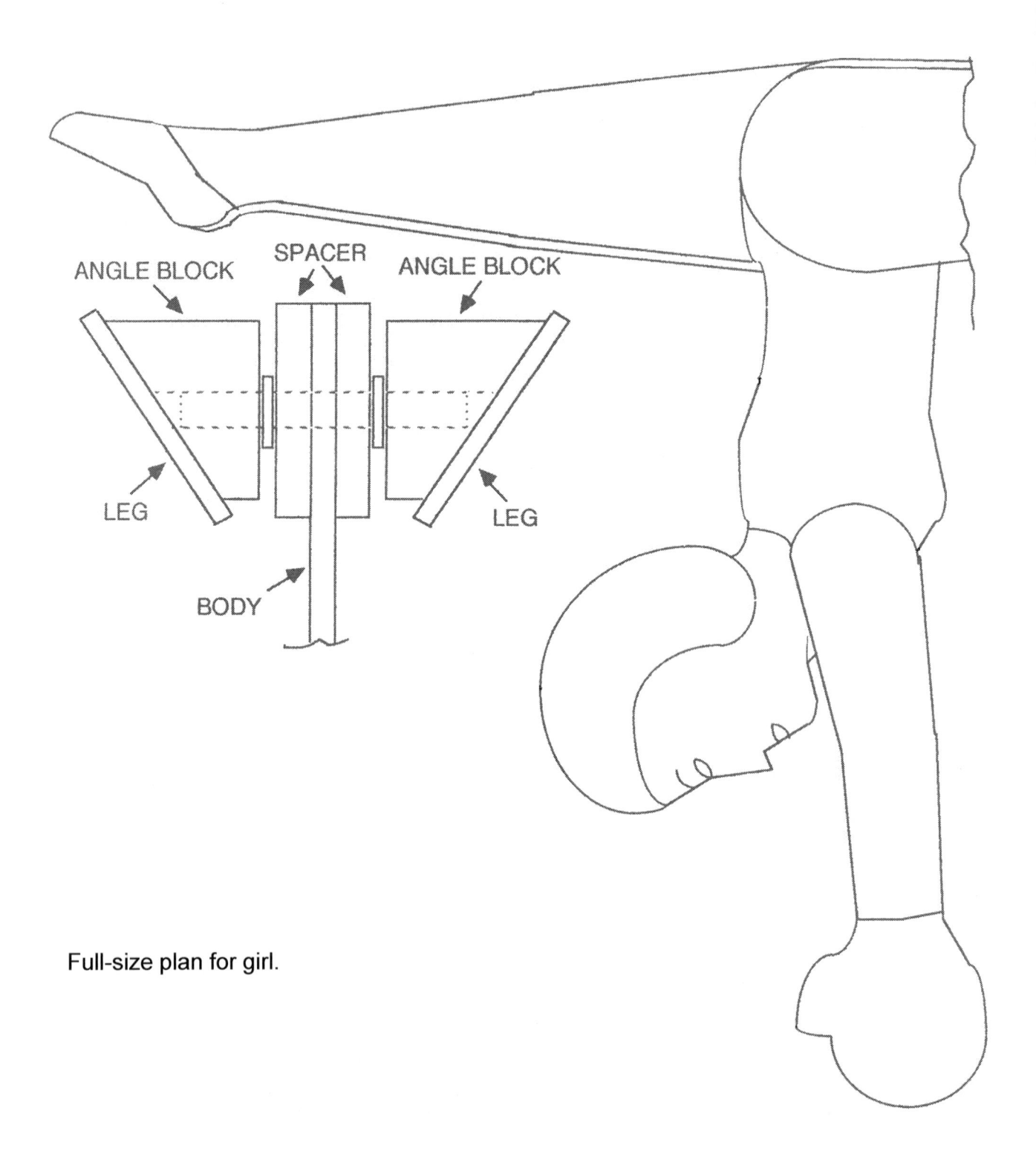

THE WHIRLIGIG MAKER'S BOOK

ANGLE BLOCK SPACER ANGLE BLOCK

LEG LEG

BODY

Full-size plan for girl.

GIRL GYMNAST

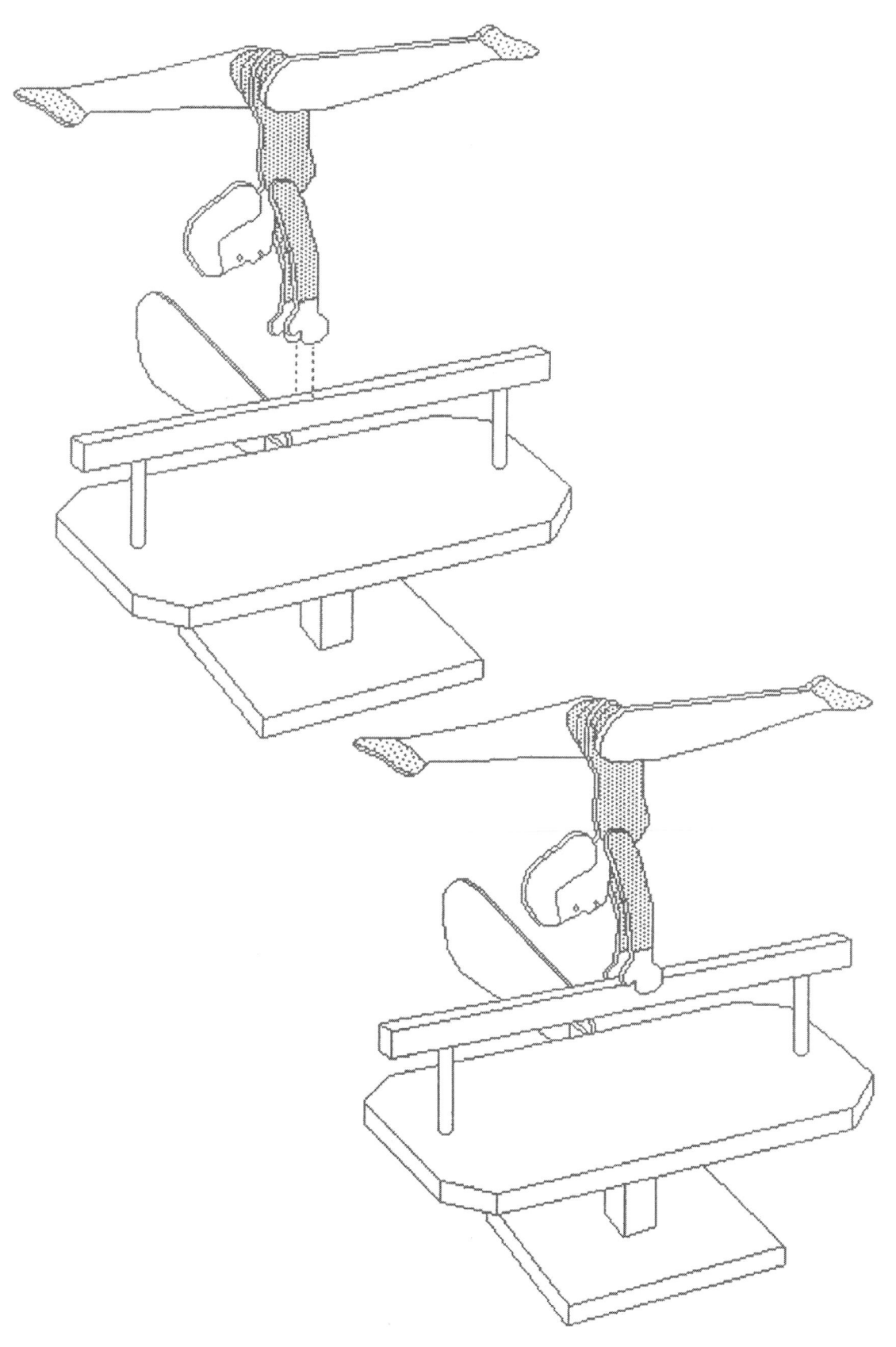

Assembly of girl to balance beam.

55

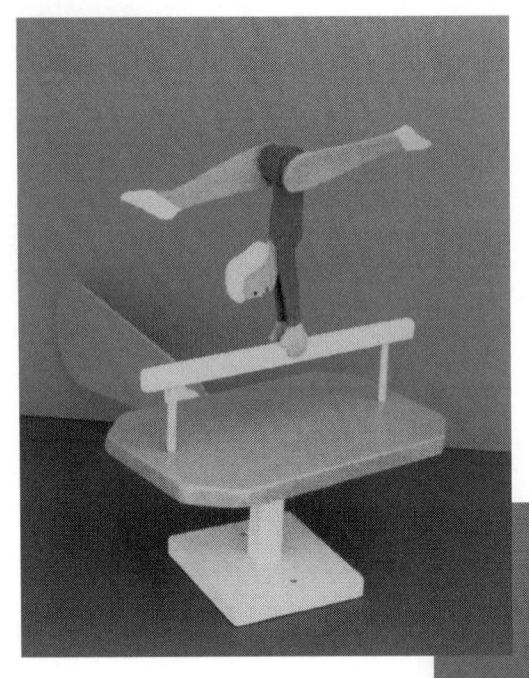

The Girl Gymnast whirligig in action.

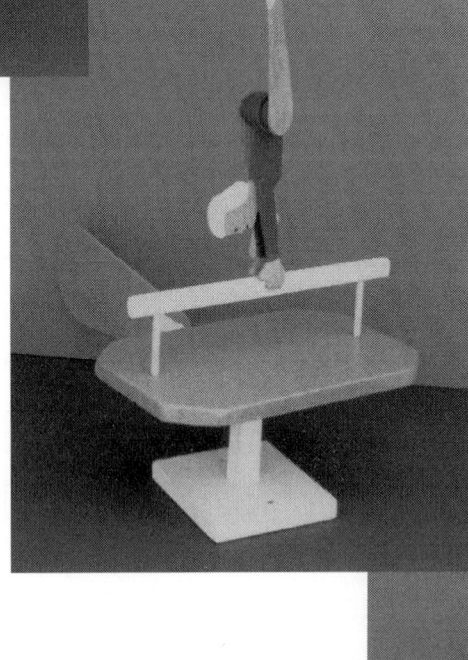

Chapter 7

PENGUINS ON TEETER-TOTTER

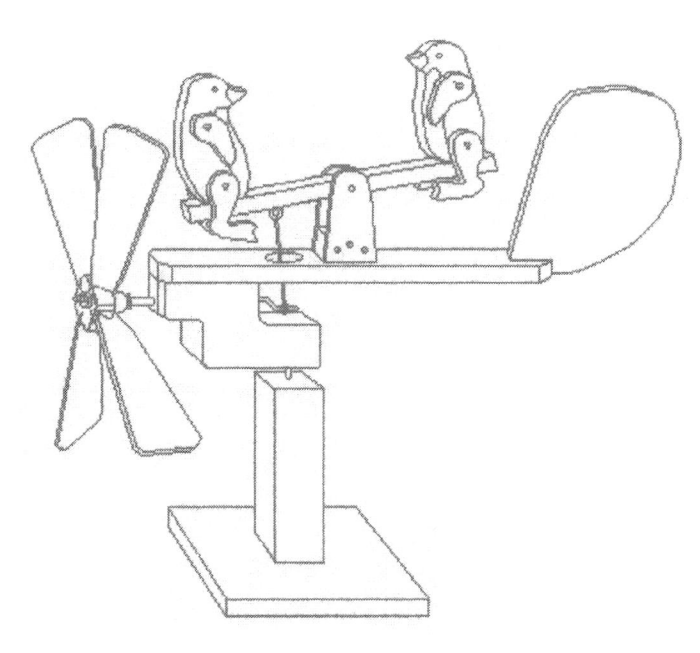

The Penguins on Teeter-Totter whirligig has a unique action. Not only do the penguins ride up and down, but also swing their wings and legs back and forth.

MATERIALS

- 3/4" x 8" x 8" wood or plywood for display base.
- 1-1/2" x 1-1/2" x 6" wood for display post.
- 3/4" x 2-1/4" x 14" wood for platform.
- 3/4" x 1" x 1-1/2" wood for teeter-totter base block.
- 1-1/2" x 3-1/2" x 5" wood for propeller shaft and pivot block.
- 1/2" x 5-1/2" x 10" wood for teeter-totter plank and penguin bodies.
- 1/8" x 2" x 4" plywood for spacers.
- 1/4" x 7" x 8" plywood for vane.
- 1/4" x 6" x 6" wood or plywood for penguin wings and legs.
- 1/4" x 1-1/2" x 7-1/2" wood for teeter-totter posts.
- 3/16" x 3-3/4" x 14" wood or plywood for propeller blades.
- 3/4" x 1-1/2" x 1-1/2" wood for propeller hub.
- 1/4" diameter x 1-1/4" hardwood dowel for teeter-totter pivot.
- 1/2" diameter wood ball with 1/8" diameter hole for propeller shaft spacer.
- 1/4" outside diameter (9/64" inside diameter) x 5-1/4" brass tubing for shaft and pivot bearings.
- 1/8" diameter x 7-1/2" brass rod for crank shaft.
- 1/16" diameter x 6" stiff wire for connecting rod.
- 1/32" diameter x 10" stiff wire for attaching wings and legs to penguin bodies.
- 1/4" diameter steel ball for pivot bearing.
- 6-32 nut (2 required) for attaching propeller hub to shaft.
- Washer (3 required) for use on propeller shaft.
- 1/8" diameter x 4" nail for pivot rod for display base.
- 4-40 x 1-1/2" bolt (3 required) for attaching teeter-totter posts to mounting block.
- Small plastic washer (8 required) for wing and leg spacers.
- 4-40 nut (3 required) for attaching teeter totter posts to mounting block.
- Glue.
- Finishing nails.
- Small felt pad for display base (4 required).
- Paint.

DISPLAY STAND

The display stand is useful not only for displaying the finished whirligig indoors, but also for holding the whirligig during construction and for testing it in front of a fan. Construction is easy. The base is 3/4" x 8" x 8" wood or plywood. The 1-1/2" x 1-1/2" x 6" post is glued and nailed (use finishing nails from underside) to the center of one side of the base. A 1/8" diameter x 4" nail is driven 2" into the center of the top of the post for use as a pivot rod. Make certain that the nail is driven perpendicular to the top of the post. Cut the head off of the nail with a hacksaw. File the upper end of the nail smooth, rounding the corners slightly.

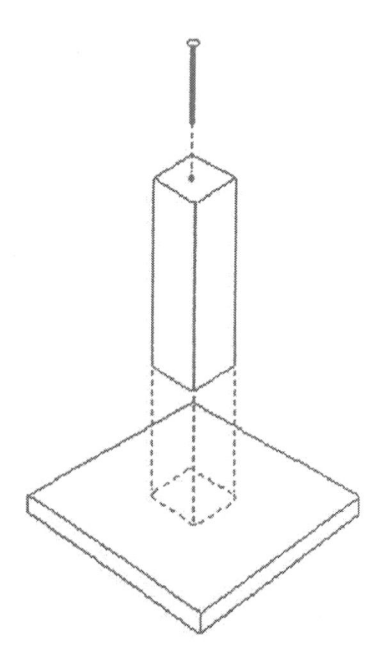

Assembly of display stand.

Sand and paint the display stand. A clear or color finish can be used. A white finish will add a feeling of snow or ice to the penguin whirligig.

Attach felt pads to the corners of the underside of the base.

PLATFORM

The platform is made of 3/4" x 2-1/4" x 14" wood. Shape the ends, as shown. Drill a 1-1/4" hole for the connecting rod and make a 1/4" x 2" slot for the vane. Attach a 3/4" x 1" x 1-1/2" base block for the teeter-totter posts to the platform in the position shown with glue and finishing nails.

The propeller shaft and pivot block is shaped from 1-1/2" x 3-1/2" x 5" wood to the pattern shown. Drill 1/4" holes for the propeller shaft tube and the pivot tube, as shown. The holes must be accurately centered and perpendicular to the wood surfaces for the whirligig to work properly. I use a drill press and drill press vise for drilling these holes.

Glue and nail the wood propeller shaft and pivot block to the platform. Then install the brass shaft tube. The tube should fit tightly in the hole so that it will not turn. Next, install a 1/4" diameter steel ball in the pivot hole. Then install the brass pivot tube, as shown.

Cut the vane from 1/4" plywood to the pattern shown. Glue the vane in the platform slot, as shown.

Sand the platform. The platform can be painted at this time, or you can wait until the assembly has been completed.

PROPELLER AND CRANKSHAFT

The crankshaft is made from 1/8" diameter x 7-1/2" brass rod. Make threads for 2" on one end of the rod using a 6-32 die. Bend the crank on the other end of the rod to the pattern shown. Then carefully file a notch evenly around the shaft for the connecting rod. Slip the crankshaft into the shaft tube. The shaft should turn freely in the tube with no binding. Apply light oil to the shaft to further decrease friction.

The propeller hub is made from 3/4" x 1-1/2" x 1-1/2" wood. Drill a 1/8" shaft hole. Cut the 3/16" wide x 1/2" deep notches for the propeller blades at 45 degree angles to the face of the hub. A counterclockwise propeller is shown, but you can reverse the notches for a clockwise rotation if desired. The slots need to be made accurately for the whirligig to work properly.

Cut the propeller blades from 3/16" wood or plywood to the pattern shown. Then glue them in the slots in the hub. Place the hub on a flat surface with the forward side down. The blades are then installed with the forward side flush with the flat surface.

Install a washer, nut, and wood ball over the threaded end of the shaft, as shown. Then thread the propeller hub onto the shaft. Secure the propeller with a washer and nut.

Test the assembly in front of a fan to make certain that the propeller and shaft assembly works properly.

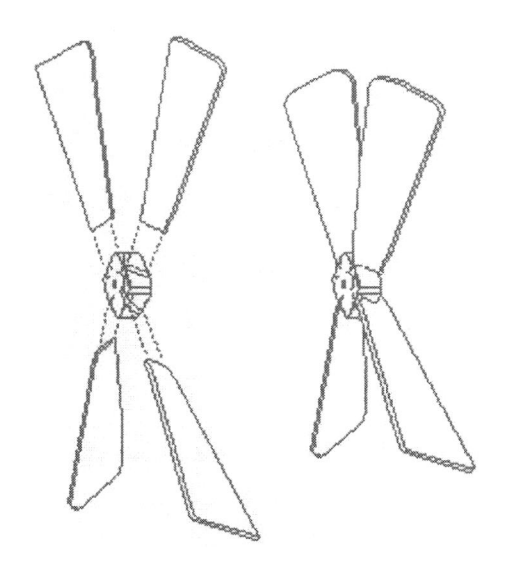

Assembly of propeller blades to hub.

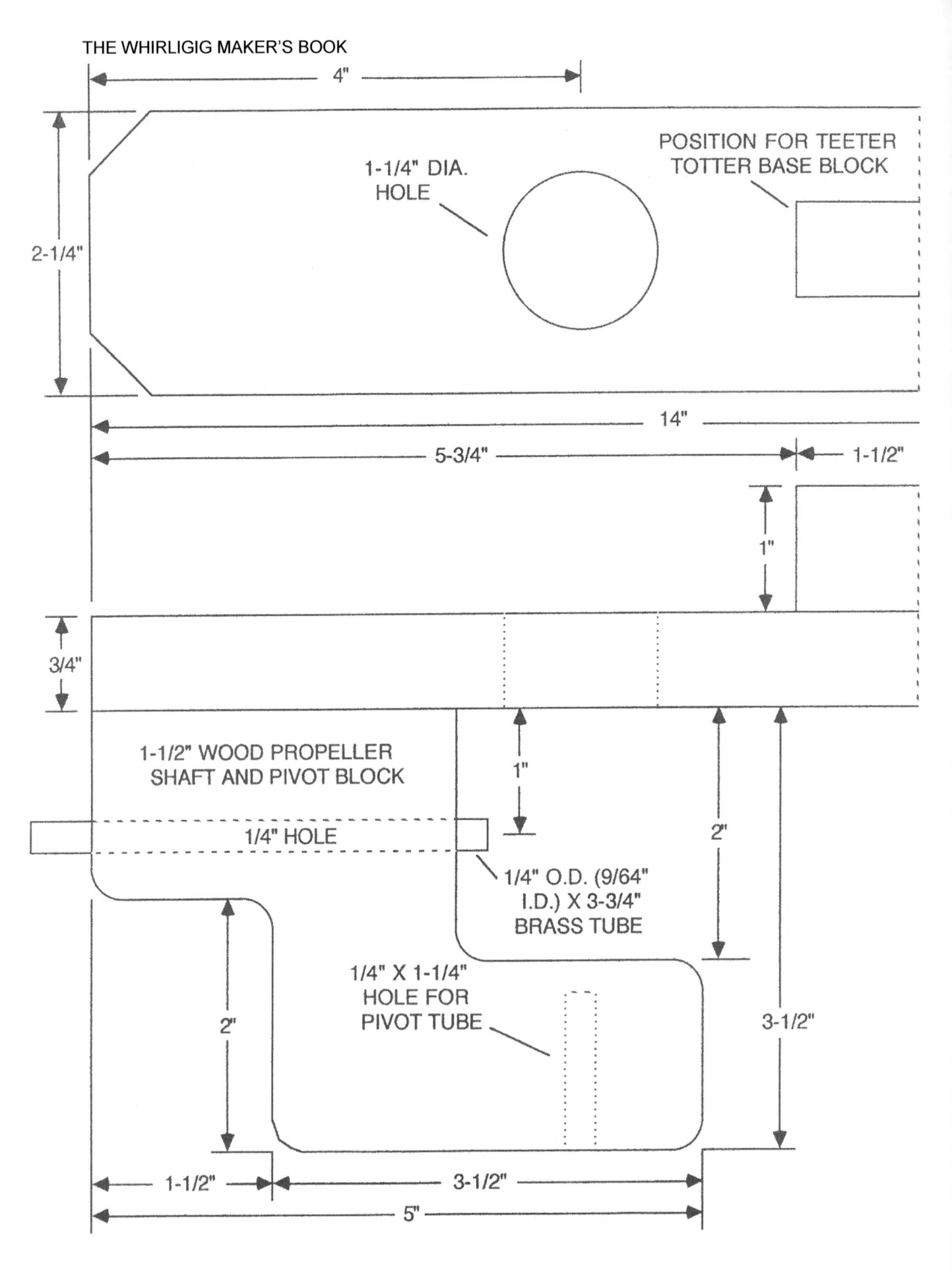

THE WHIRLIGIG MAKER'S BOOK

60

PENGUINS ON TEETER-TOTTER

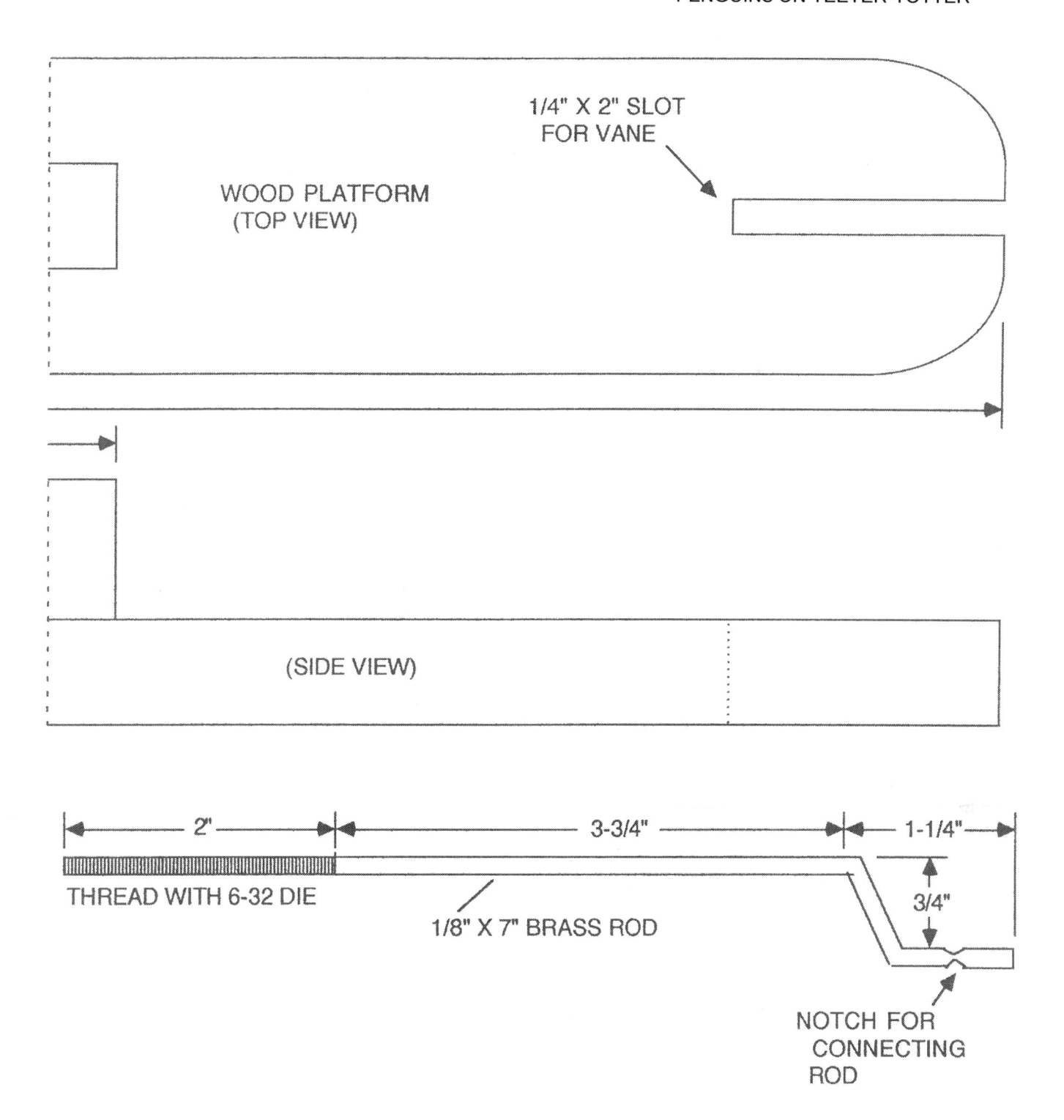

WOOD PLATFORM (TOP VIEW)

1/4" X 2" SLOT FOR VANE

(SIDE VIEW)

2" — THREAD WITH 6-32 DIE

3-3/4" — 1/8" X 7" BRASS ROD

1-1/4"

3/4"

NOTCH FOR CONNECTING ROD

Full-size plan and patterns for platform and crankshaft.

THE WHIRLIGIG MAKER'S BOOK

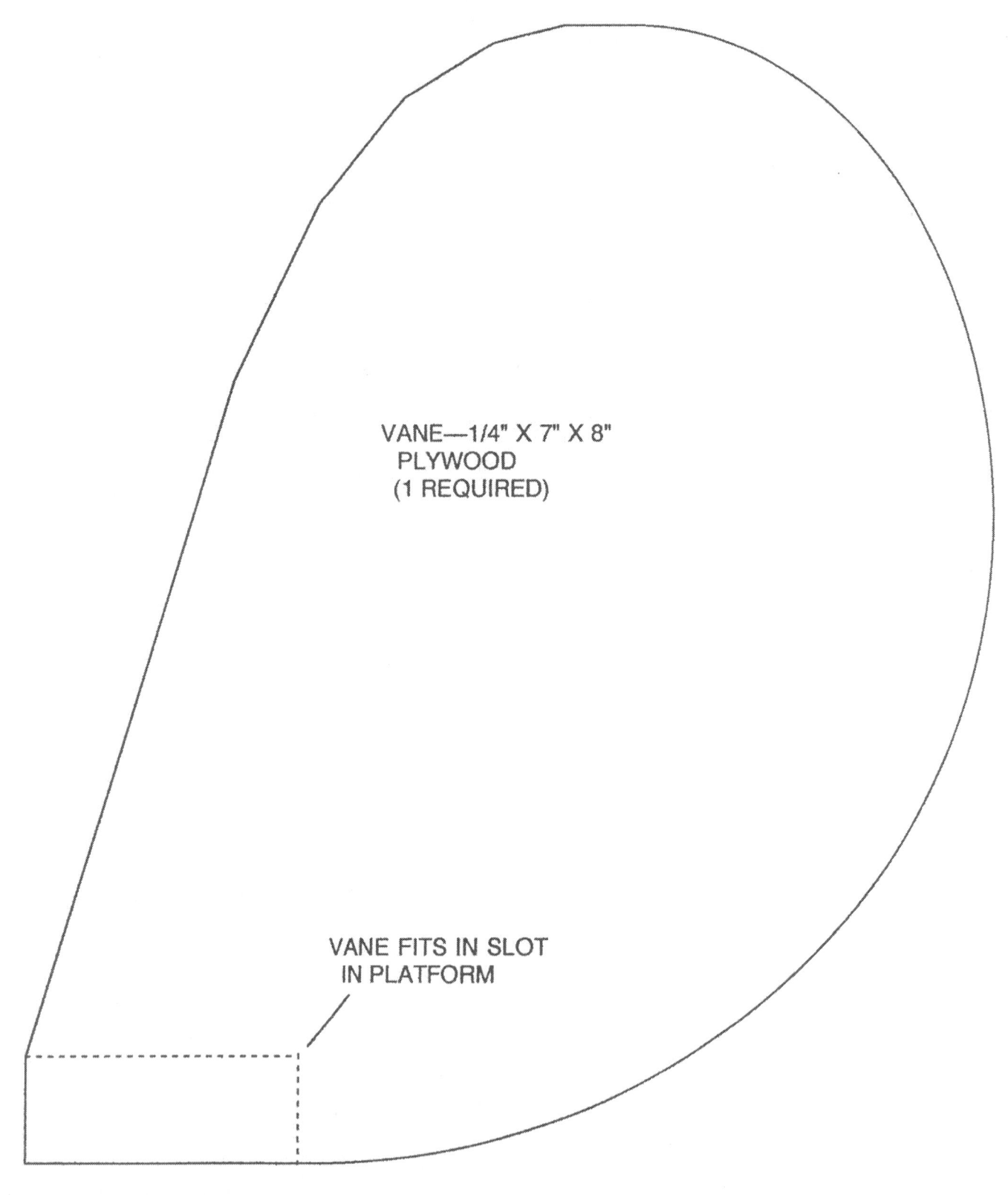

VANE—1/4" X 7" X 8"
PLYWOOD
(1 REQUIRED)

VANE FITS IN SLOT
IN PLATFORM

Full-size pattern for vane.

PENGUINS ON TEETER-TOTTER

2-1/2"

PROPELLER BLADE—
3/16" WOOD OR
PLYWOOD
(4 REQUIRED)

7"

1-1/4"

PROPELLER HUB—3/4" WOOD
(1 REQUIRED)

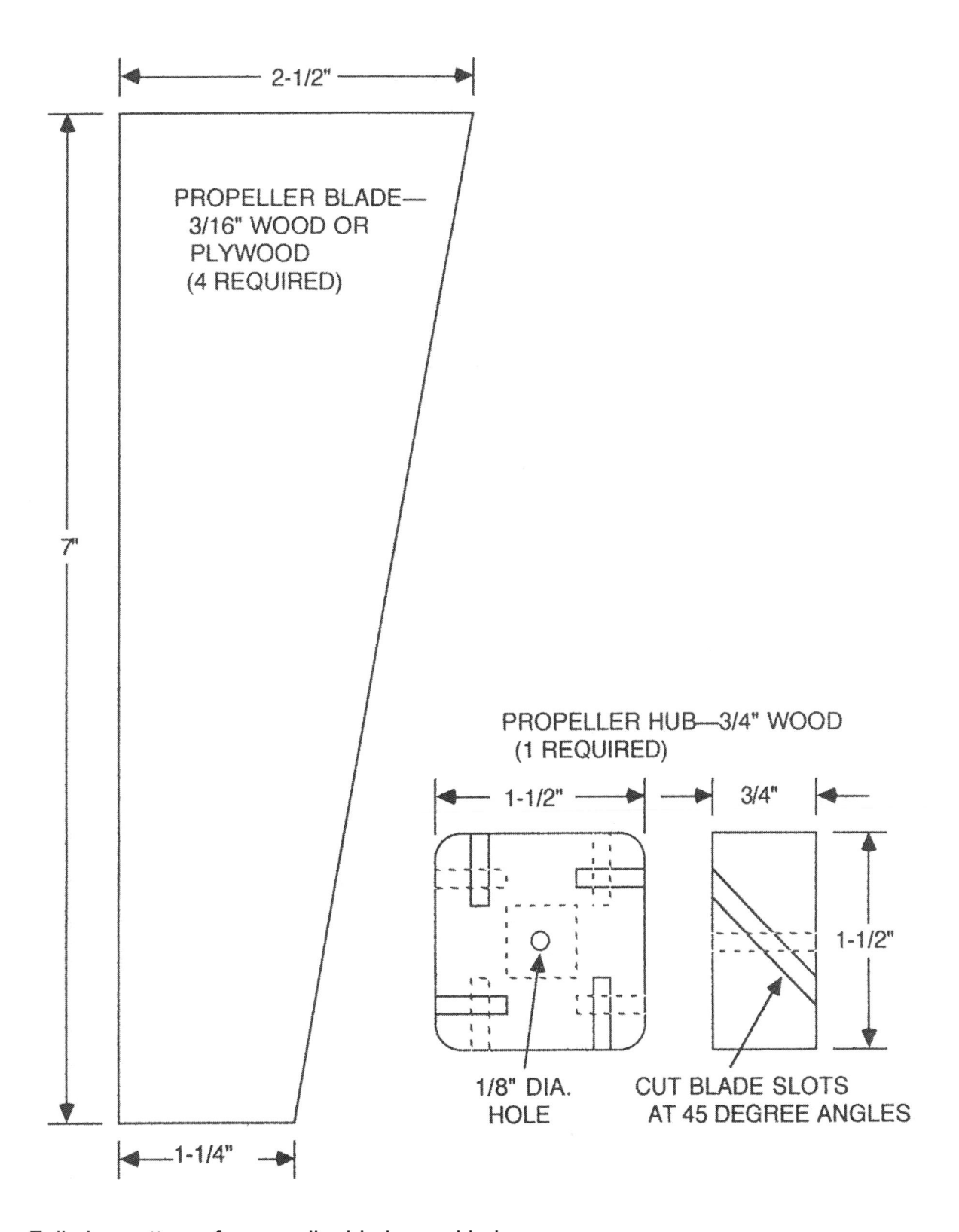

1-1/2"

3/4"

1-1/2"

1/8" DIA. HOLE

CUT BLADE SLOTS
AT 45 DEGREE ANGLES

Full-size patterns for propeller blades and hub.

THE WHIRLIGIG MAKER'S BOOK

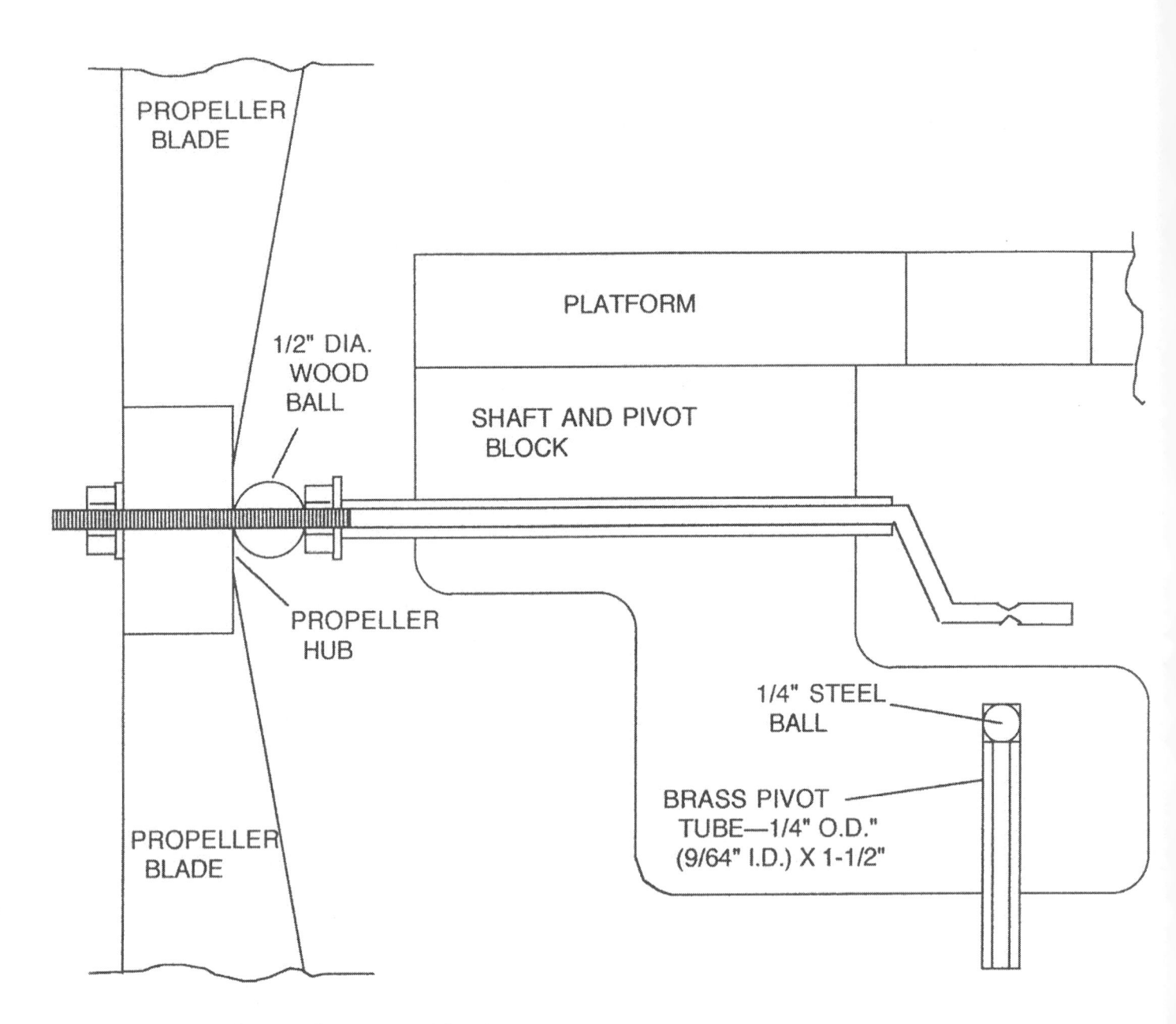

Crankshaft and pivot assembly plan.

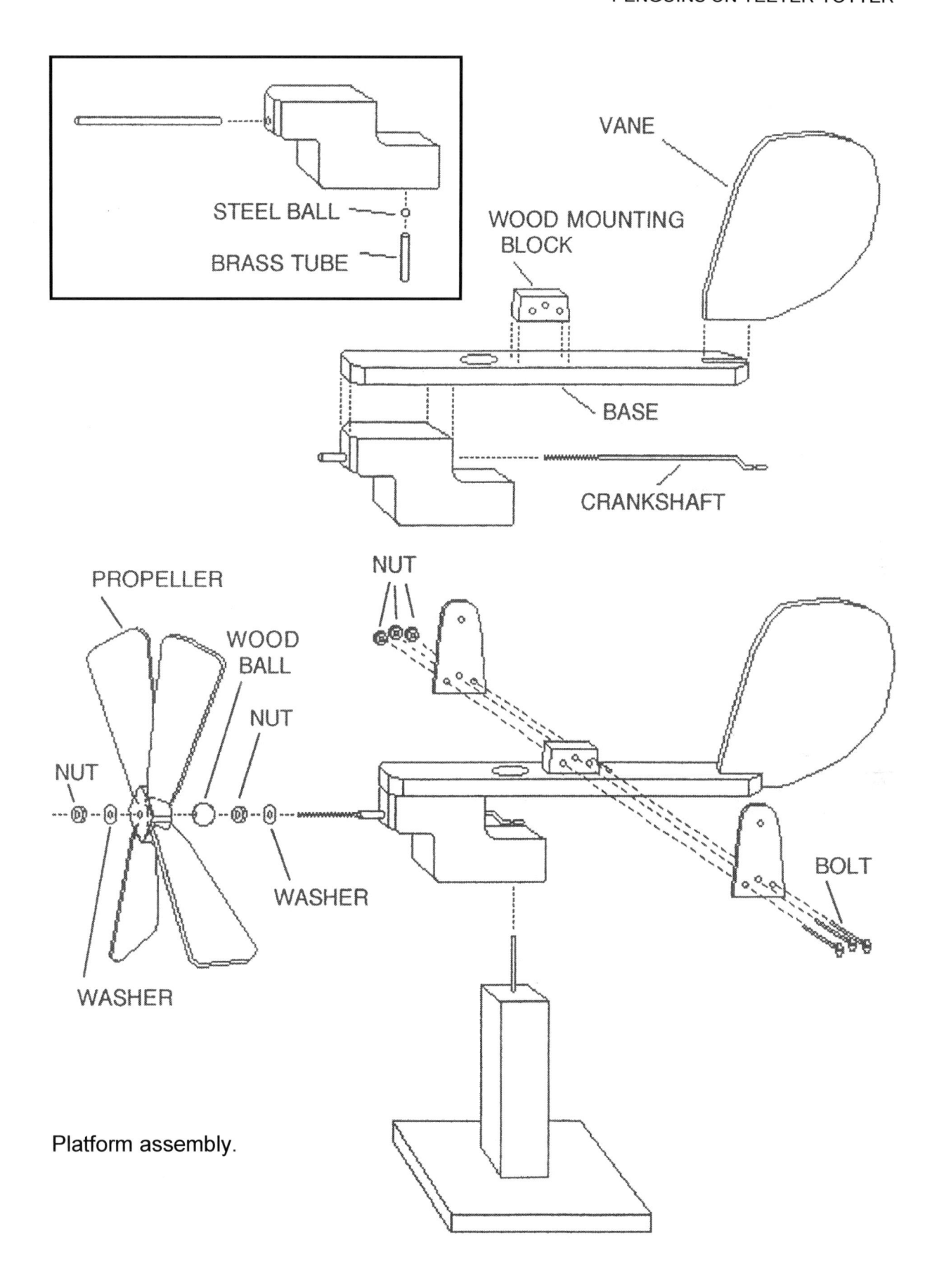

PENGUINS ON TEETER-TOTTER

STEEL BALL
BRASS TUBE

VANE
WOOD MOUNTING BLOCK
BASE
CRANKSHAFT

PROPELLER
WOOD BALL
NUT
NUT
WASHER
WASHER
NUT
BOLT

Platform assembly.

65

THE WHIRLIGIG MAKER'S BOOK

TEETER-TOTTER AND PENGUINS

Cut the teeter-totter posts and spacers to the patterns shown. Attach the posts to the mounting block by drilling three holes through the mounting block and posts and fastening the posts in place with three bolts and nuts. An alternate method is to attach the posts to the mounting block with glue and finishing nails.

The teeter-totter plank and penguin bodies are cut from 1/2" x 5-1/2" x 10" wood. Trace the pattern onto the wood. An alternate method is to use a 3/4" x 1/2" x 10" piece of wood for the plank. Then cut the penguins separately and attach to the plank with glue and wood dowel pegs. Regardless of the method used, drill 1/16" wire holes in the penguin bodies in the positions shown. Drill a 1/4" hole in the center of the plank for the pivot dowel. File this hole slightly larger so that a 1/4" wood dowel will turn freely in the hole. An alternate method is to drill a 17/64" hole.

Glue the 1/8" thick plywood spacers to the sides of the plank, using a 1/4" dowel to line up the holes.

Install an eye screw in the underside of the plank in the position shown for the connecting rod attachment. Then connect the teeter-totter plank to the posts with the wood dowel. The teeter-totter plank should pivot freely. If not, remove the wood dowel and sand areas that cause the binding. Apply paraffin wax to the center section of the hardwood dowel.

Cut the penguin wings and legs to the patterns shown. The painting can be done at this time, or you can do a trial assembly and then disassemble for painting later. The wings and legs are then attached to the penguin bodies with wires. Use small plastic washers between the bodies and wings and legs. Bend loop rings in the ends of the wires.

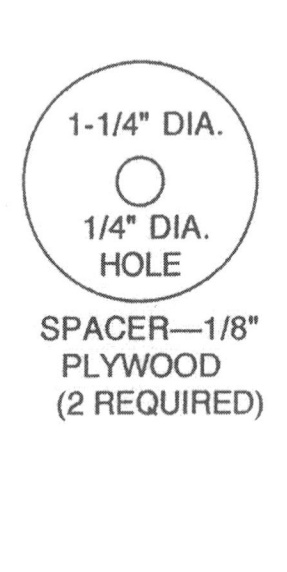

Patterns for teeter-totter posts and spacers.

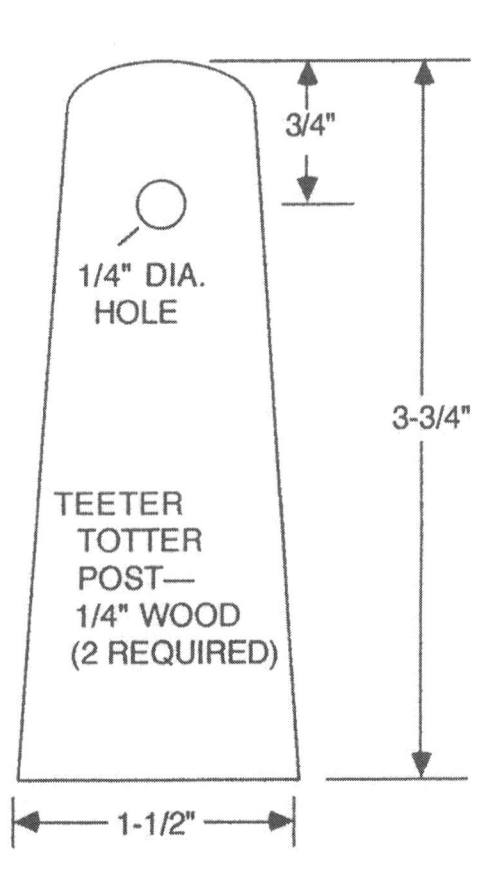

PENGUINS ON TEETER-TOTTER

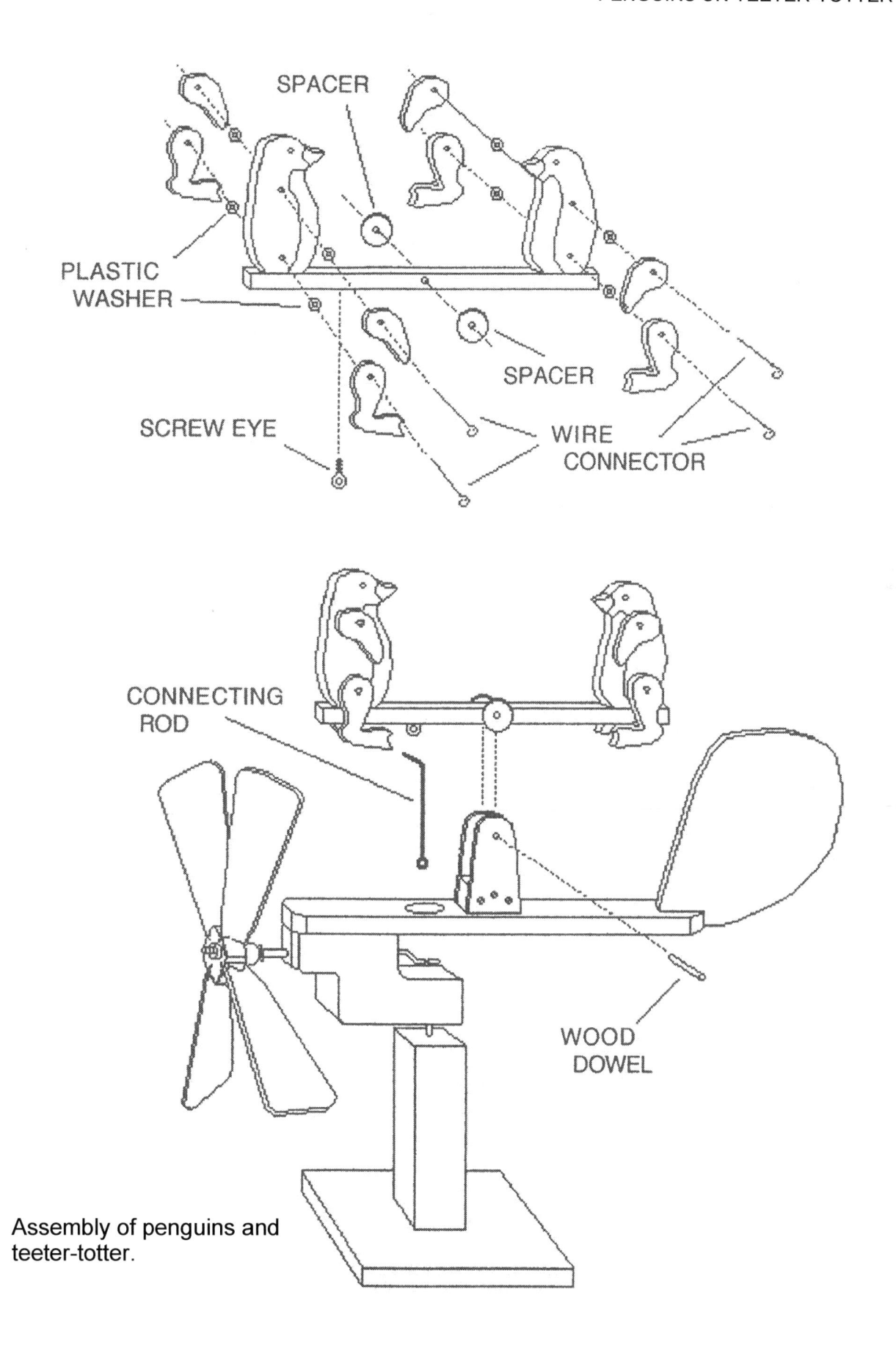

Assembly of penguins and teeter-totter.

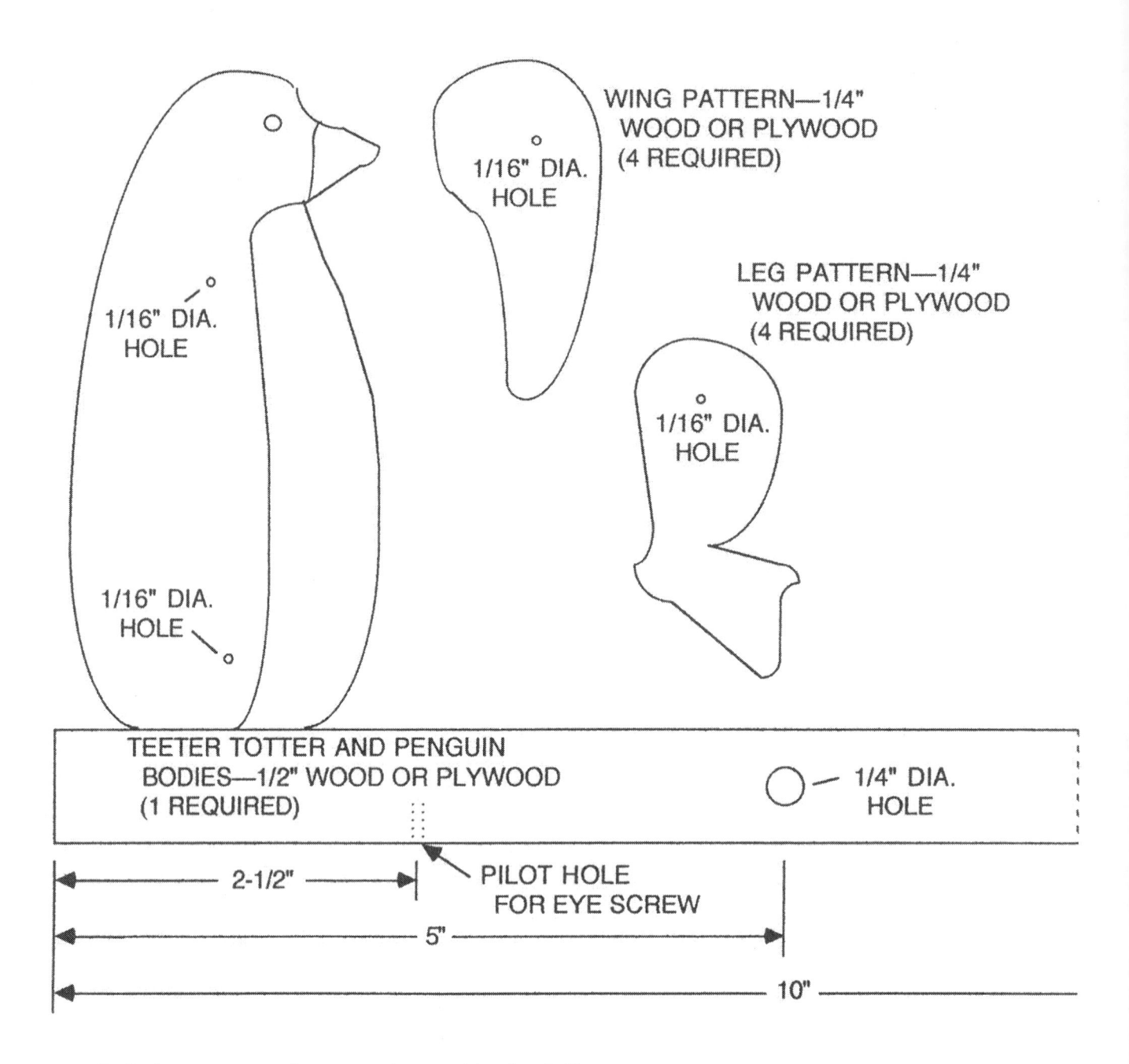

THE WHIRLIGIG MAKER'S BOOK

1/16" DIA. HOLE

1/16" DIA. HOLE

1/16" DIA. HOLE

WING PATTERN—1/4" WOOD OR PLYWOOD (4 REQUIRED)

1/16" DIA. HOLE

LEG PATTERN—1/4" WOOD OR PLYWOOD (4 REQUIRED)

1/16" DIA. HOLE

TEETER TOTTER AND PENGUIN BODIES—1/2" WOOD OR PLYWOOD (1 REQUIRED)

1/4" DIA. HOLE

2-1/2"

PILOT HOLE FOR EYE SCREW

5"

10"

Full-size patterns for penguins and teeter-totter.

PENGUINS ON TEETER-TOTTER

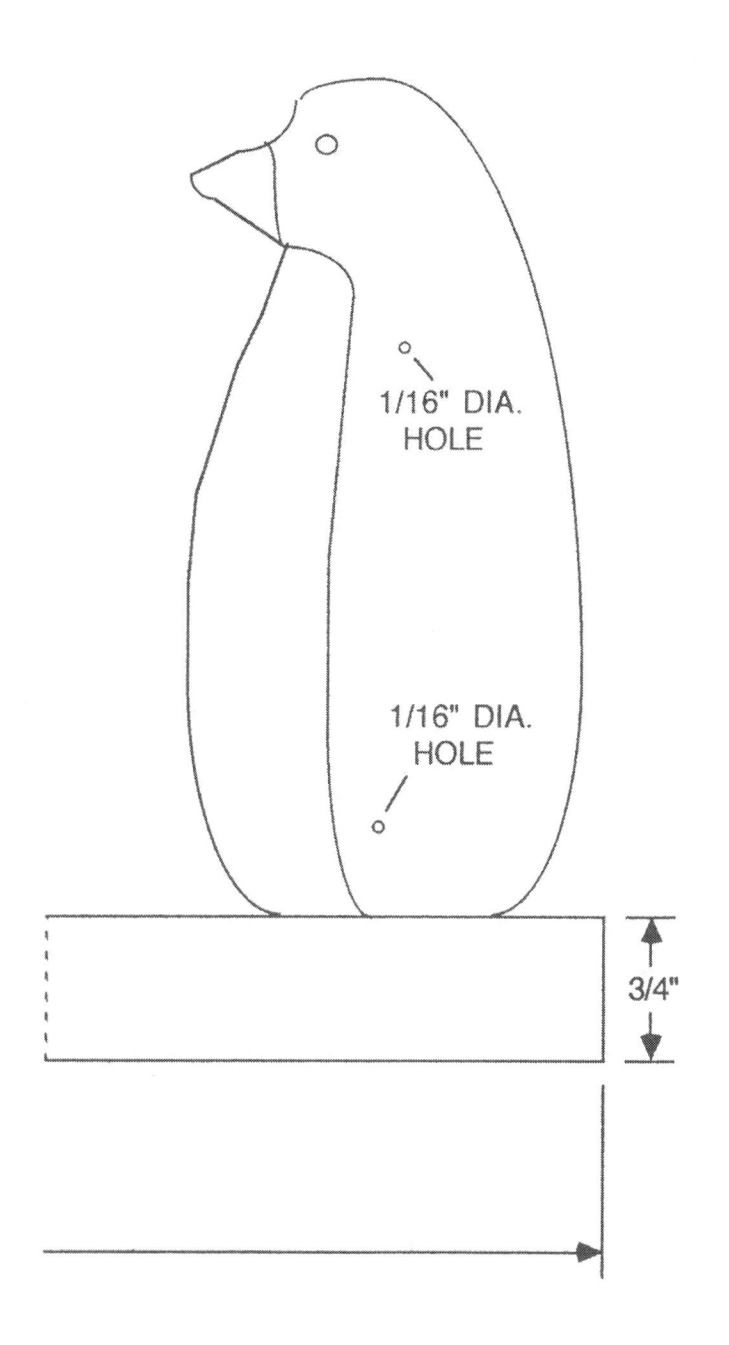

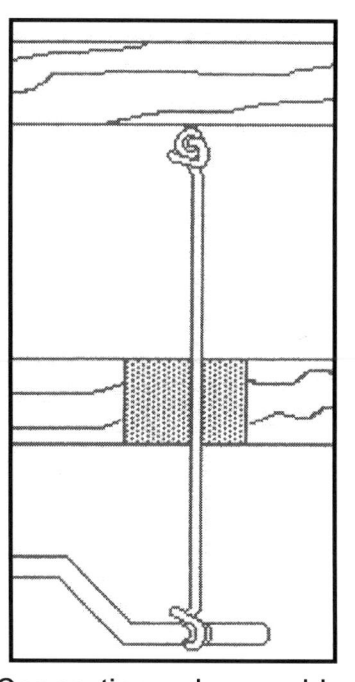

1/16" DIA. HOLE

1/16" DIA. HOLE

3/4"

Connecting rod assembly.

69

The connecting rod is shaped from 1/16" diameter x 6" stiff wire. Bend a wire loop around the groove in the crank shaft, as shown. The wire passes through the hole in the platform and is connected to the eye screw on the teeter-totter plank. Bend the wire so that the teeter-totter plank will be level when the crank is in a horizontal position to one side. Pass the wire through the eye and then bend a loop, as shown. The loops must be a fairly close fit, but not so tight that binding will occur.

TESTING AND FINISHING

The whirligig is ready for testing. This can be inside with a fan or outdoors in a light wind. The whirligig should start easily if all of the parts turn properly. Make any necessary adjustments and add oil to friction areas of metal parts.

This whirligig is slightly out of balance. The crankshaft is more difficult to turn when the crank is downward than when it is upward. This can be corrected by adding a small weight to the tip of one or more propeller blades until the system is balanced. However, I have found that this whirligig works well even without balancing weights, so this is optional.

If sanding and painting was not done previously, disassemble as necessary and do the sanding and painting. I paint the entire display stand, platform and vane assembly, and propeller white; the wood ball on the propeller shaft and the teeter-totter posts and plank red; the penguin bodies black and white with yellow beaks, the legs yellow, and the wings black with white edges.

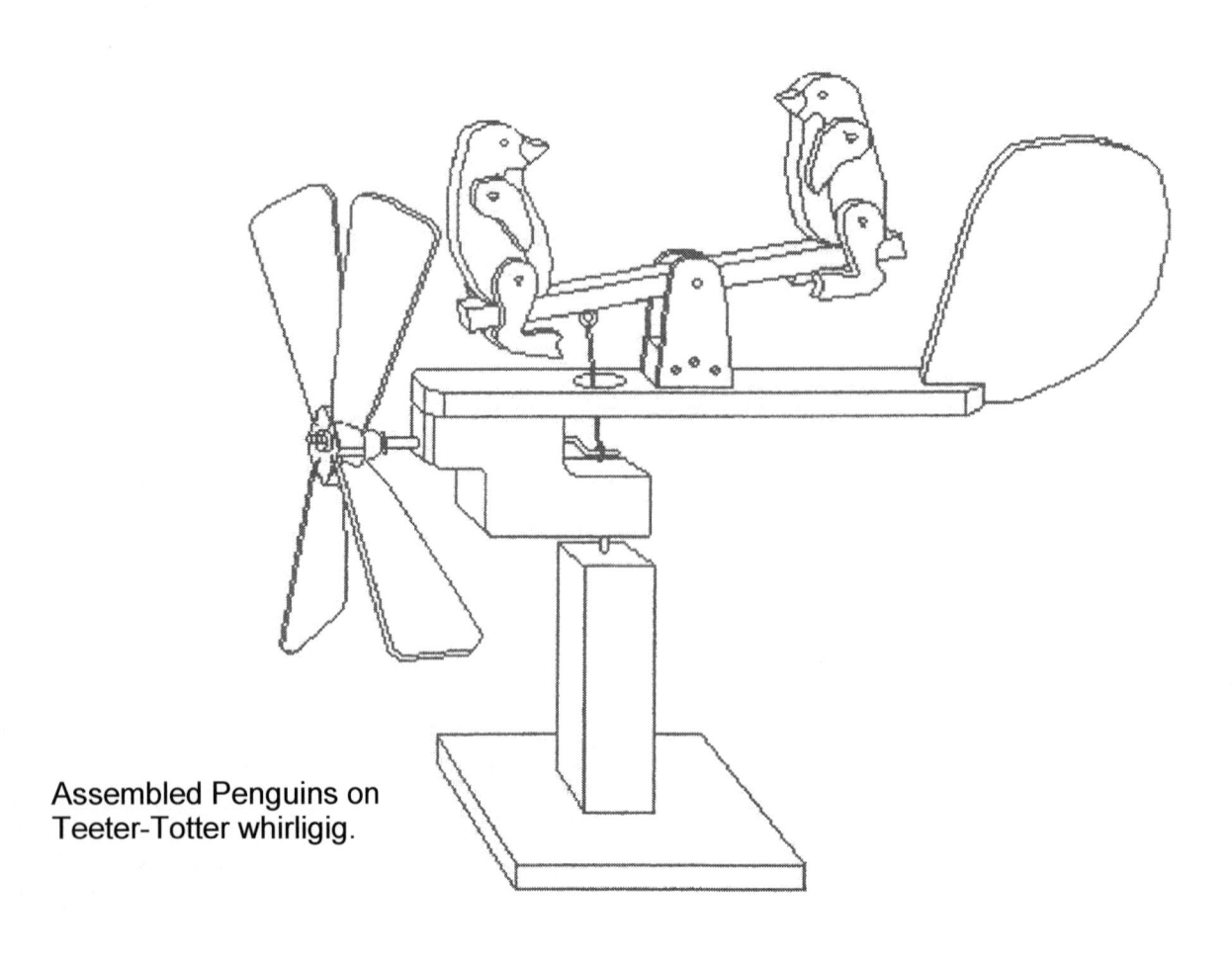

Assembled Penguins on Teeter-Totter whirligig.

Chapter 8

DANCING MAN

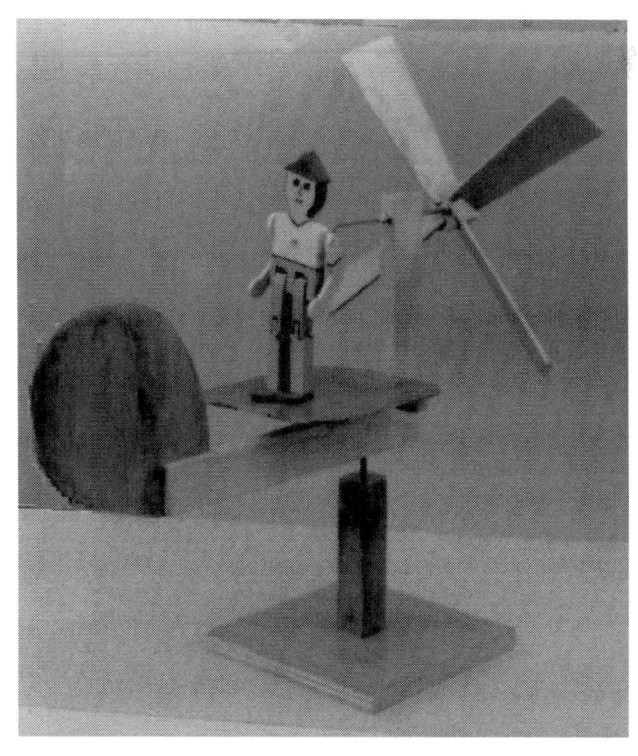

The Dancing Man whirligig has a unique action. The turning action of the crankshaft creates not only leg movement, with the feet clicking on the dance floor, but also arm swinging.

MATERIALS

- 3/4" x 8" x 8" wood or plywood for display base.
- 1-1/2" x 1-1/2" x 6" wood for display post.
- 3/4" x 1-1/2" x 21-1/2" wood for main platform and propeller shaft post.
- 1/4" x 8" x 8" plywood for vane.
- 1/8" x 6-1/2" x 8" plywood for dance floor.
- 3/4" x 3/4" x 6-1/2" wood for dance floor mounting blocks.
- 3/16" x 3-3/4" x 14" wood or plywood for propeller blades.
- 3/4" x 1-1/2" x 1-1/2" wood for propeller hub.
- 1/2" x 2" x 10" wood for dancing man body and legs.
- 3/16" x 3" x 8" wood for arms and feet.
- 1/4" outside diameter (7/64" inside diameter) x 3-3/4" brass tubing for shaft bearing.
- 3/32" diameter x 12" brass rod for crank shaft.
- 1/4" outside diameter (9/64" inside diameter) x 1-1/2" brass tube for pivot bearing.
- 3/16" O.D. (7/64" I.D.) x 1/2" brass tube crankshaft bearing on dancing man's body.
- 3/32" diameter x 2" brass rod for connecting upper legs to dancing man's body.
- 1/32" diameter x 8" stiff wire for attaching arms to body and upper and lower legs together.
- 1/4" diameter steel ball for pivot bearing.
- 4-40 nut (2 required) for attaching propeller hub to shaft.
- Washer (4 required) for use on propeller shaft.
- 1/8" diameter x 4" nail for pivot rod for display base.
- 3/32" inside diameter x 1" plastic tubing for crankshaft spacers.
- Small plastic washer (2 required) for use on arm wires.
- Glue.
- Finishing nails.
- Small felt pad for display base (4 required).
- Paint.

DISPLAY STAND

The display stand is useful not only for displaying the finished whirligig indoors, but also for holding the whirligig during construction and for testing it in front of a fan. Construction is easy. The base is 3/4" x 8" x 8" wood or plywood. The 1-1/2" x 1-1/2" x 6" post is glued and nailed (use finishing nails from underside) to the center of one side of the base. A 1/8" diameter x 4" nail is driven 2" into the center of the top of the post for use as a pivot rod. Make certain that the nail is driven perpendicular to the top of the post. Cut the head off of the nail with a hacksaw. File the upper end of the nail smooth, rounding the corners slightly.

Sand and paint the display stand. A clear or color finish can be used.

Attach felt pads to the corners of the underside of the base.

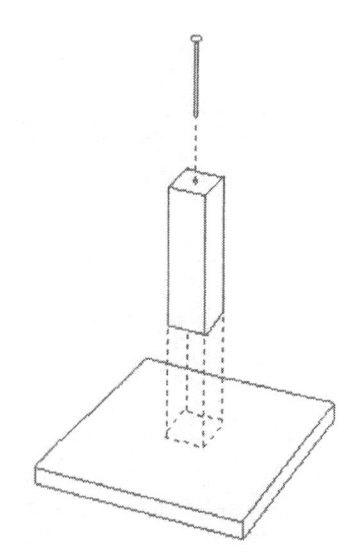

Assembly of display stand.

PLATFORM

The platform is made of 3/4" x 1-1/2" x 14" wood. Make a 1/4" x 2-1/2" slot for the vane. Drill a 1/4" diameter x 1-1/4" hole for the pivot bearing in the position shown. The hole must be accurately centered and perpendicular to the wood surface for the whirligig to work properly.

The propeller shaft post is made from 3/4" x 1-1/2" x 7-1/2" wood. Drill a 1/4" diameter hole for the propeller shaft tube, as shown. The hole must be accurately centered and perpendicular to the wood surface for the whirligig to work properly.

Glue and nail the wood propeller shaft post to the platform. Then install the brass shaft tube. The tube should fit tightly in the hole so that it will not turn. Next, install a 1/4" diameter steel ball in the pivot hole. Then install the brass pivot tube, as shown.

Cut the vane from 1/4" plywood to the pattern shown. Glue the vane in the platform slot, as shown.

Glue and nail the dance floor mounting blocks to the platform. The dance floor is 1/8" plywood cut to the pattern shown. Glue and nail it to the mounting blocks, making certain that it is centered and the forward edge is flush against the shaft post.

Sand the platform. The platform can be painted at this time, or you can wait until the assembly has been completed.

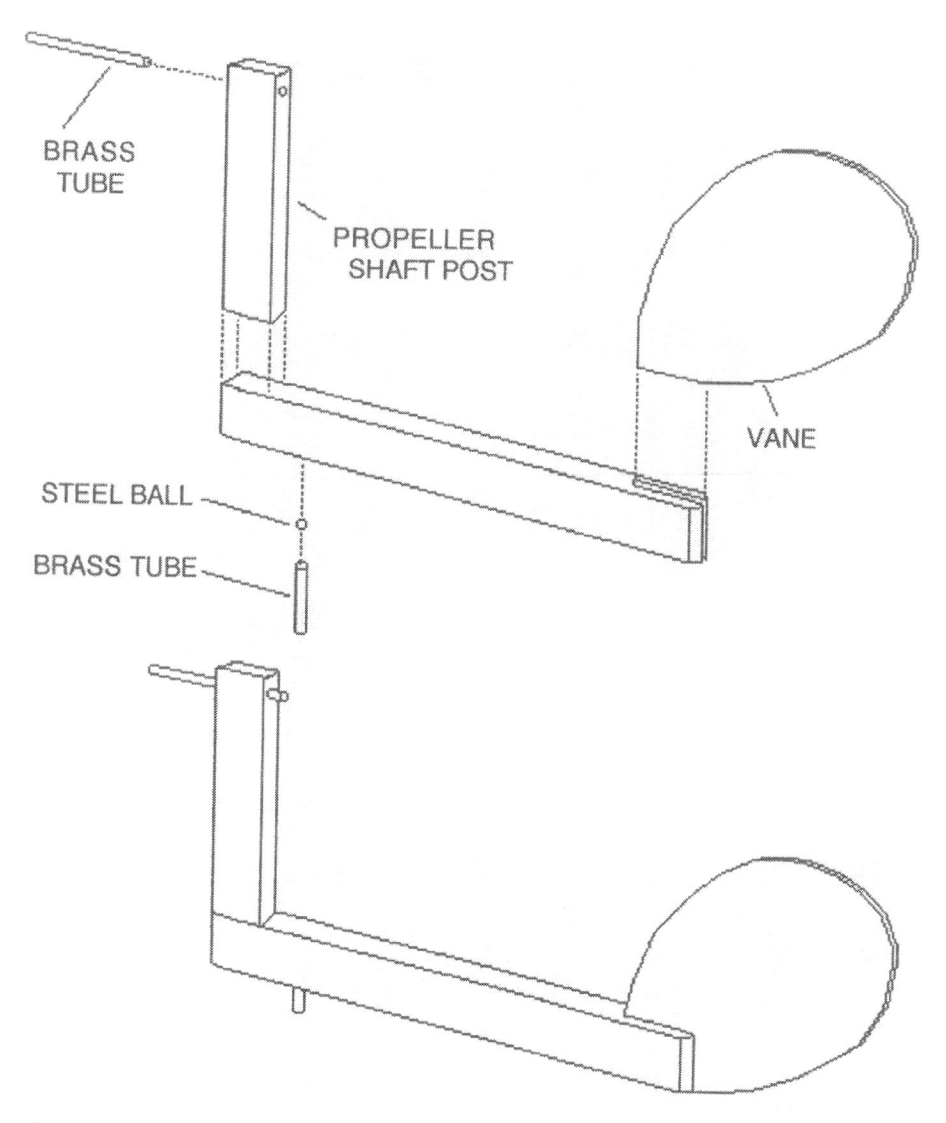

Assembly of platform.

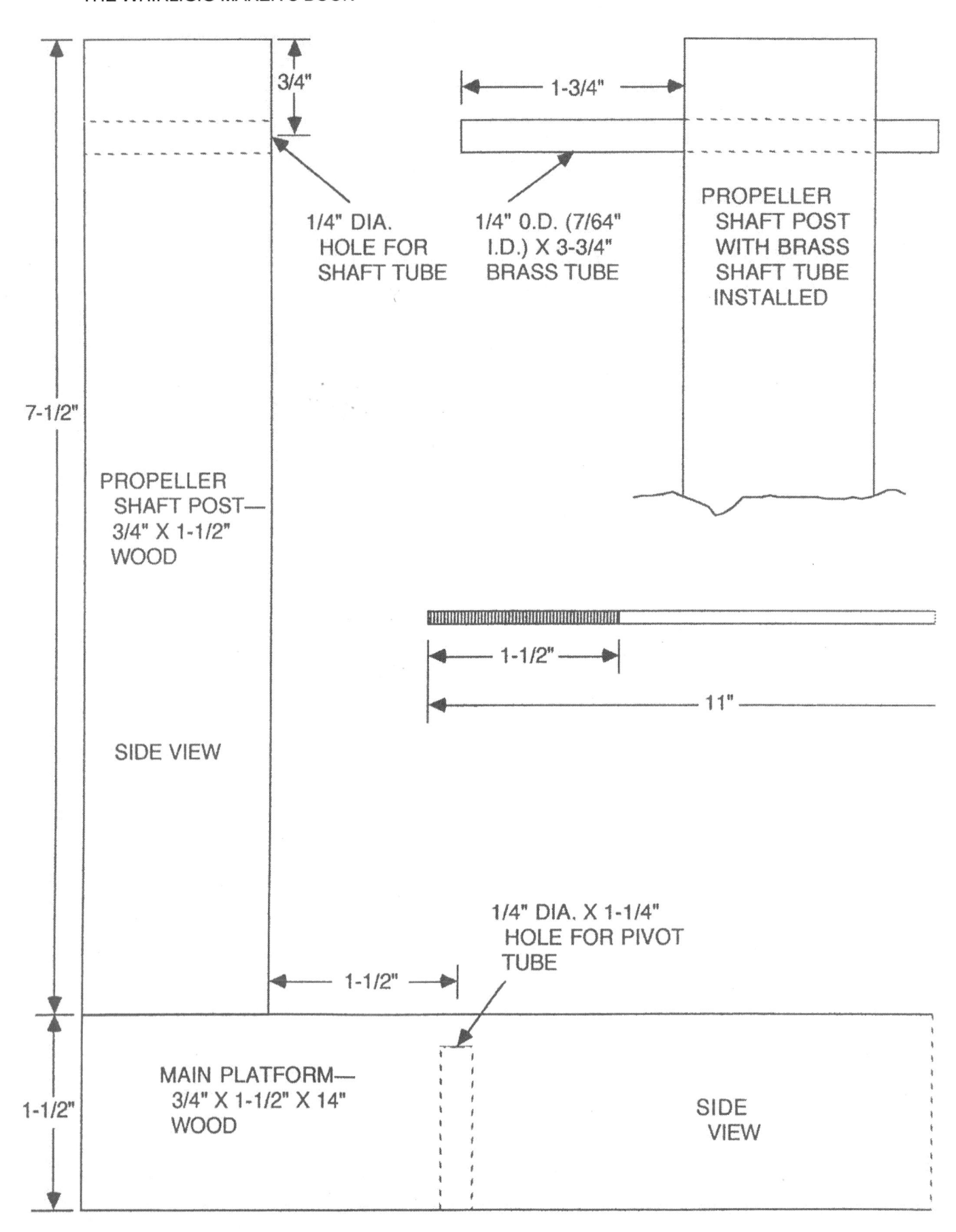

THE WHIRLIGIG MAKER'S BOOK

3/4"

1-3/4"

1/4" DIA. HOLE FOR SHAFT TUBE

1/4" O.D. (7/64" I.D.) X 3-3/4" BRASS TUBE

PROPELLER SHAFT POST WITH BRASS SHAFT TUBE INSTALLED

7-1/2"

PROPELLER SHAFT POST— 3/4" X 1-1/2" WOOD

SIDE VIEW

1-1/2"

11"

1/4" DIA. X 1-1/4" HOLE FOR PIVOT TUBE

1-1/2"

MAIN PLATFORM— 3/4" X 1-1/2" X 14" WOOD

1-1/2"

SIDE VIEW

74

DANCING MAN

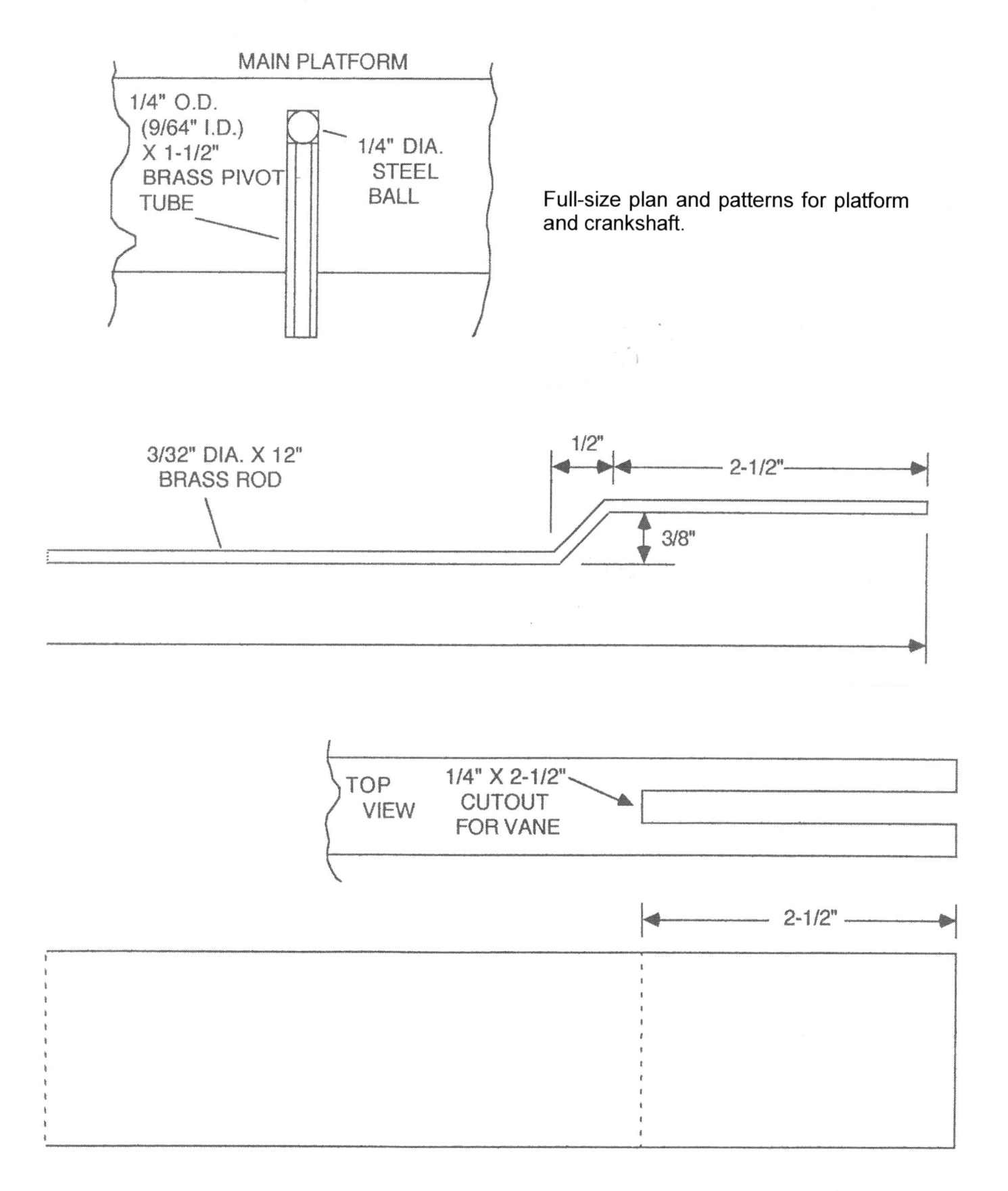

MAIN PLATFORM

1/4" O.D. (9/64" I.D.) X 1-1/2" BRASS PIVOT TUBE

1/4" DIA. STEEL BALL

Full-size plan and patterns for platform and crankshaft.

3/32" DIA. X 12" BRASS ROD

1/2"

2-1/2"

3/8"

TOP VIEW

1/4" X 2-1/2" CUTOUT FOR VANE

2-1/2"

75

THE WHIRLIGIG MAKER'S BOOK

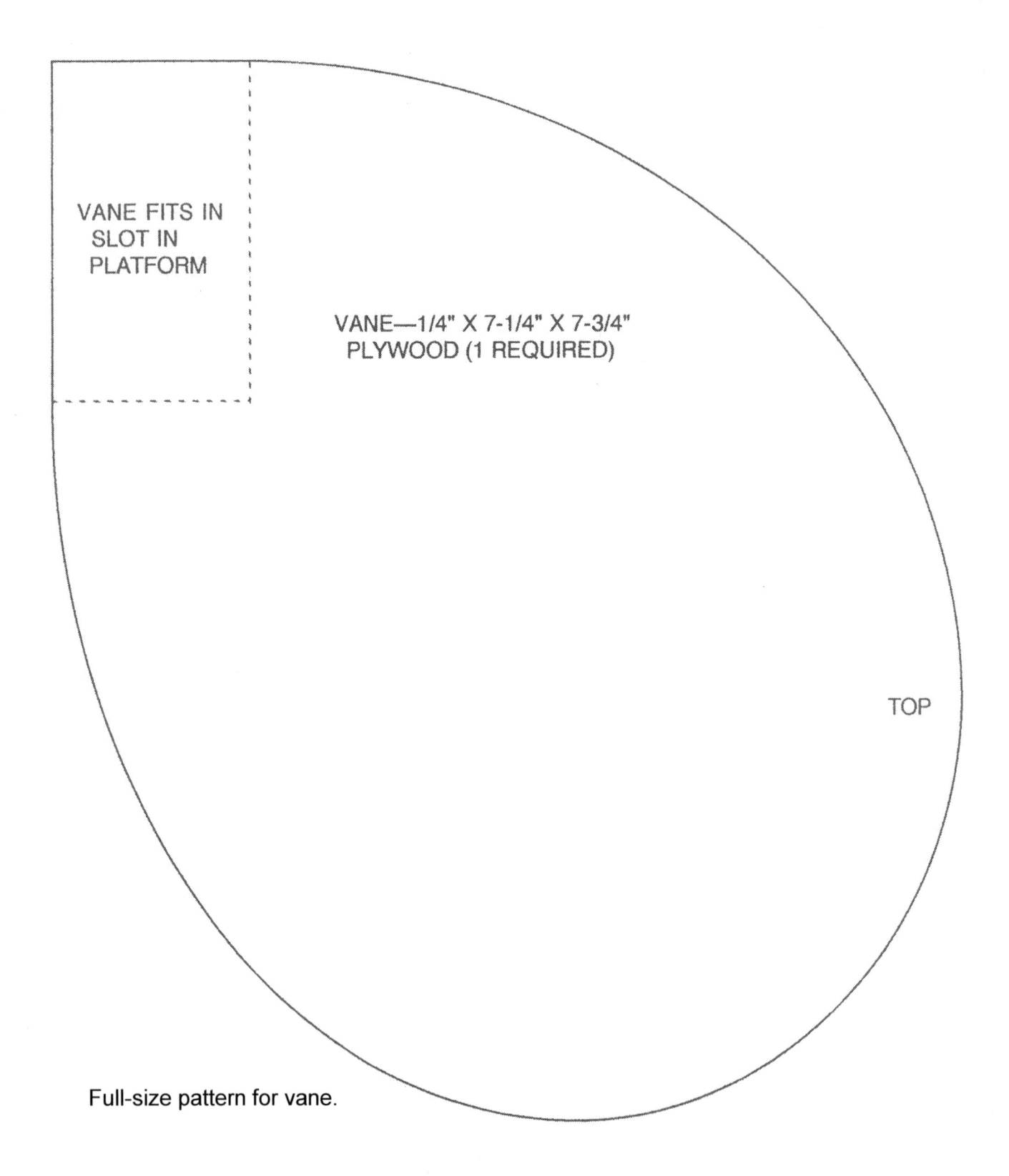

VANE FITS IN
SLOT IN
PLATFORM

VANE—1/4" X 7-1/4" X 7-3/4"
PLYWOOD (1 REQUIRED)

TOP

Full-size pattern for vane.

DANCING MAN

3/4"

MOUNTING
BLOCK—
3/4" X 3/4" X 4"
WOOD

3/4"

MOUNTING BLOCK—
3/4" X 3/4" X 2-1/2"
WOOD

DANCE FLOOR—1/8" X 6-1/2" X 8"
PLYWOOD (1 REQUIRED)

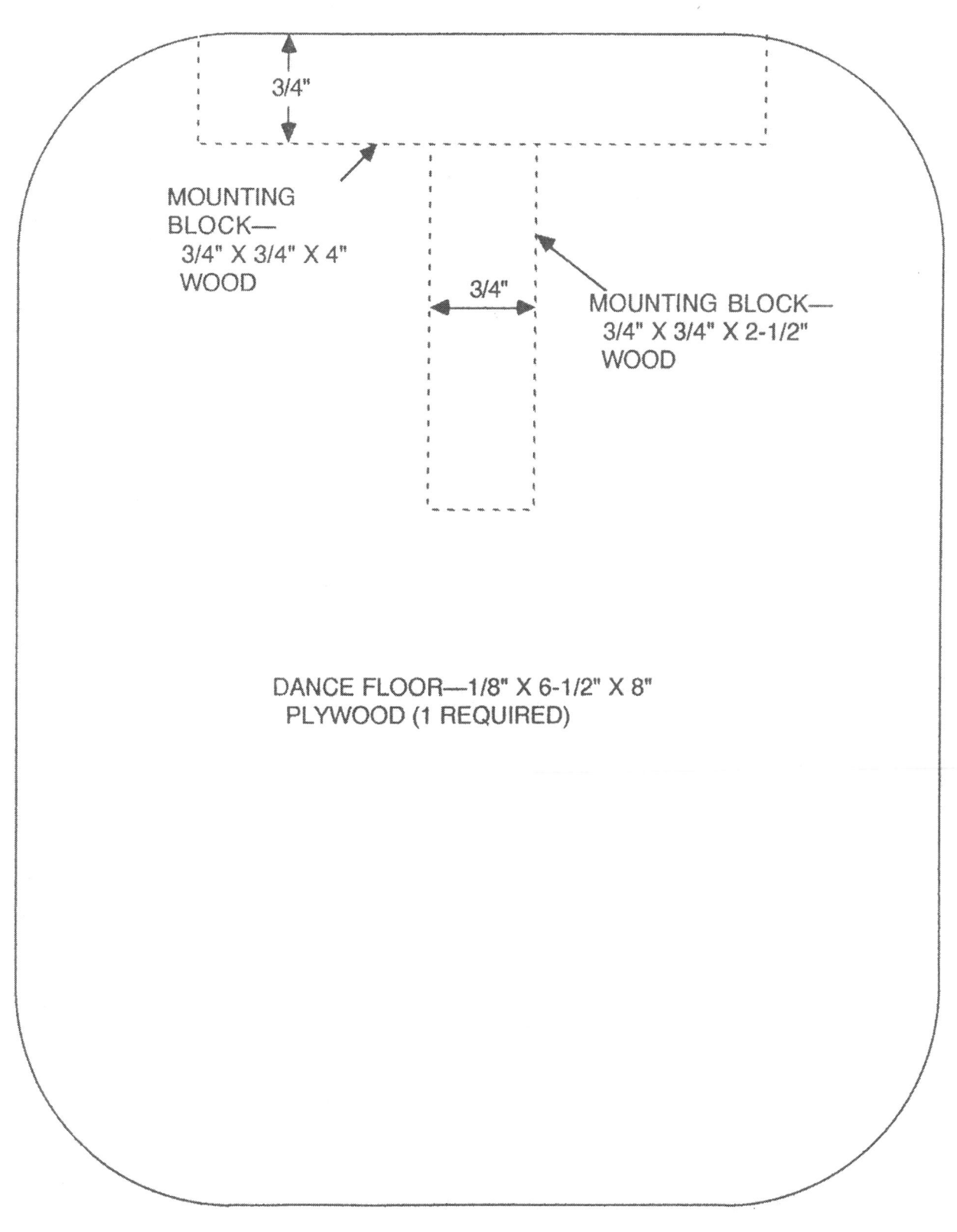

Full-size pattern for dance floor.

77

THE WHIRLIGIG MAKER'S BOOK

PROPELLER AND CRANKSHAFT

The crankshaft is made from 3/32" diameter x 12" brass rod. Make threads for 1-1/2" on one end of the rod using a 4-40 die. Bend the crank on the other end of the rod to the pattern shown. Install a washer and 1/4" long plastic spacer over the shaft 3-3/4" from the threads. The plastic spacer must fit tightly over the shaft to keep the shaft in position in the brass tube. Slip the crankshaft into the

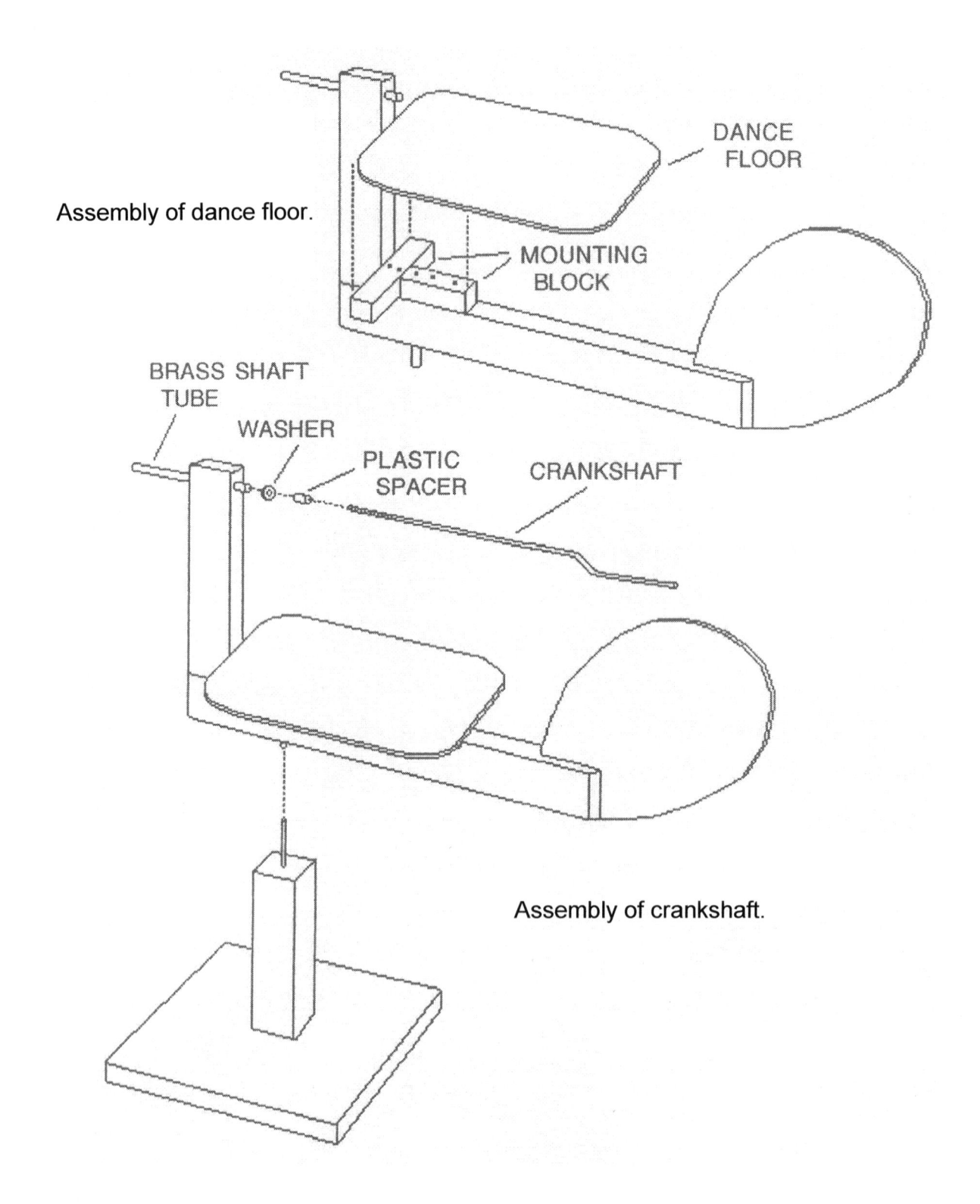

Assembly of dance floor.

Assembly of crankshaft.

DANCING MAN

PROPELLER BLADE—
3/16" WOOD OR PLYWOOD
(4 REQUIRED)

2-1/2"
7"
1-1/4"

PROPELLER HUB—3/4" WOOD
(1 REQUIRED)

1-1/2"
3/4"
1-1/2"

3/32" DIA. HOLE

CUT BLADE SLOTS AT 45 DEGREE ANGLES

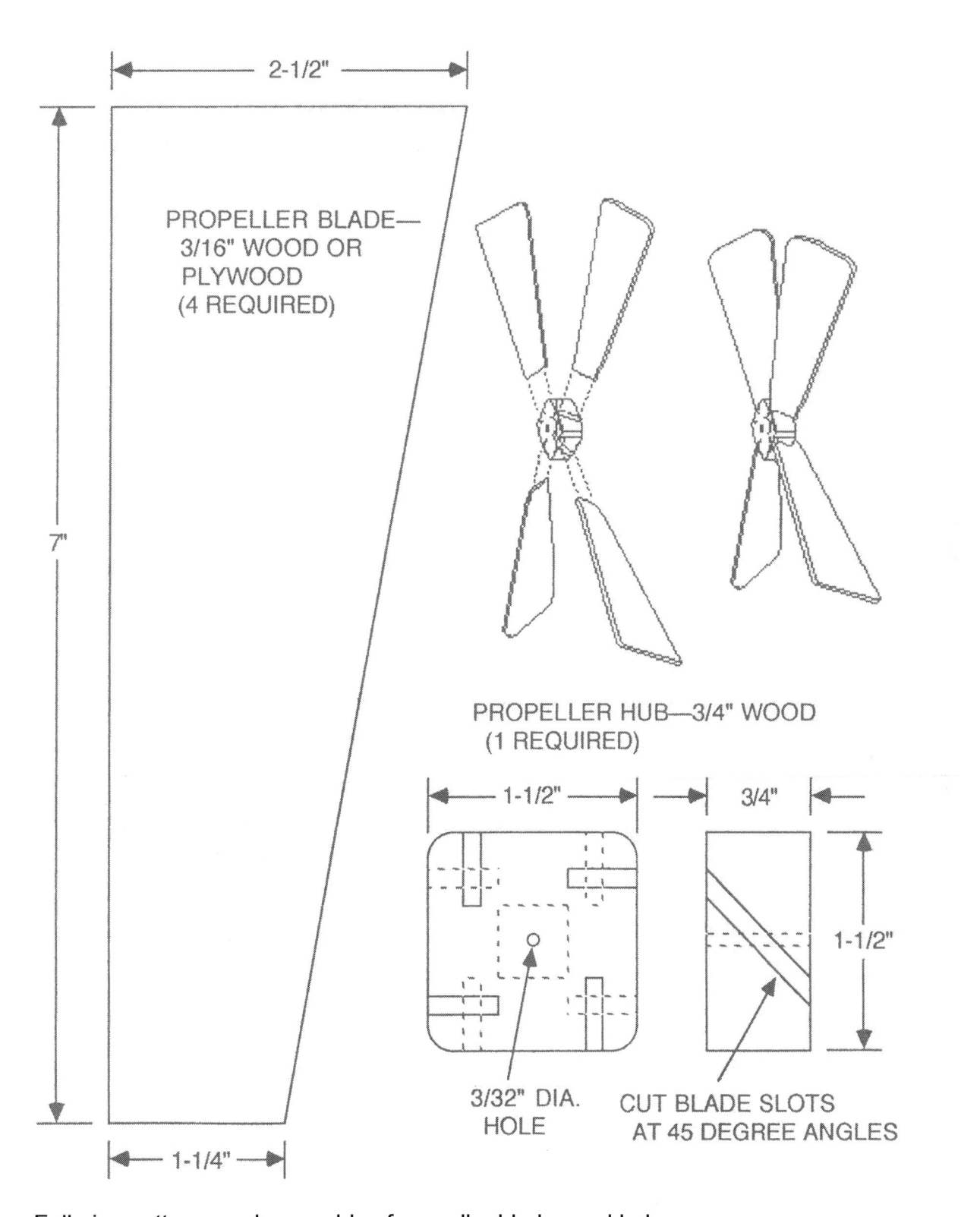

Full-size patterns and assembly of propeller blades and hub.

THE WHIRLIGIG MAKER'S BOOK

Crankshaft assembly plan.

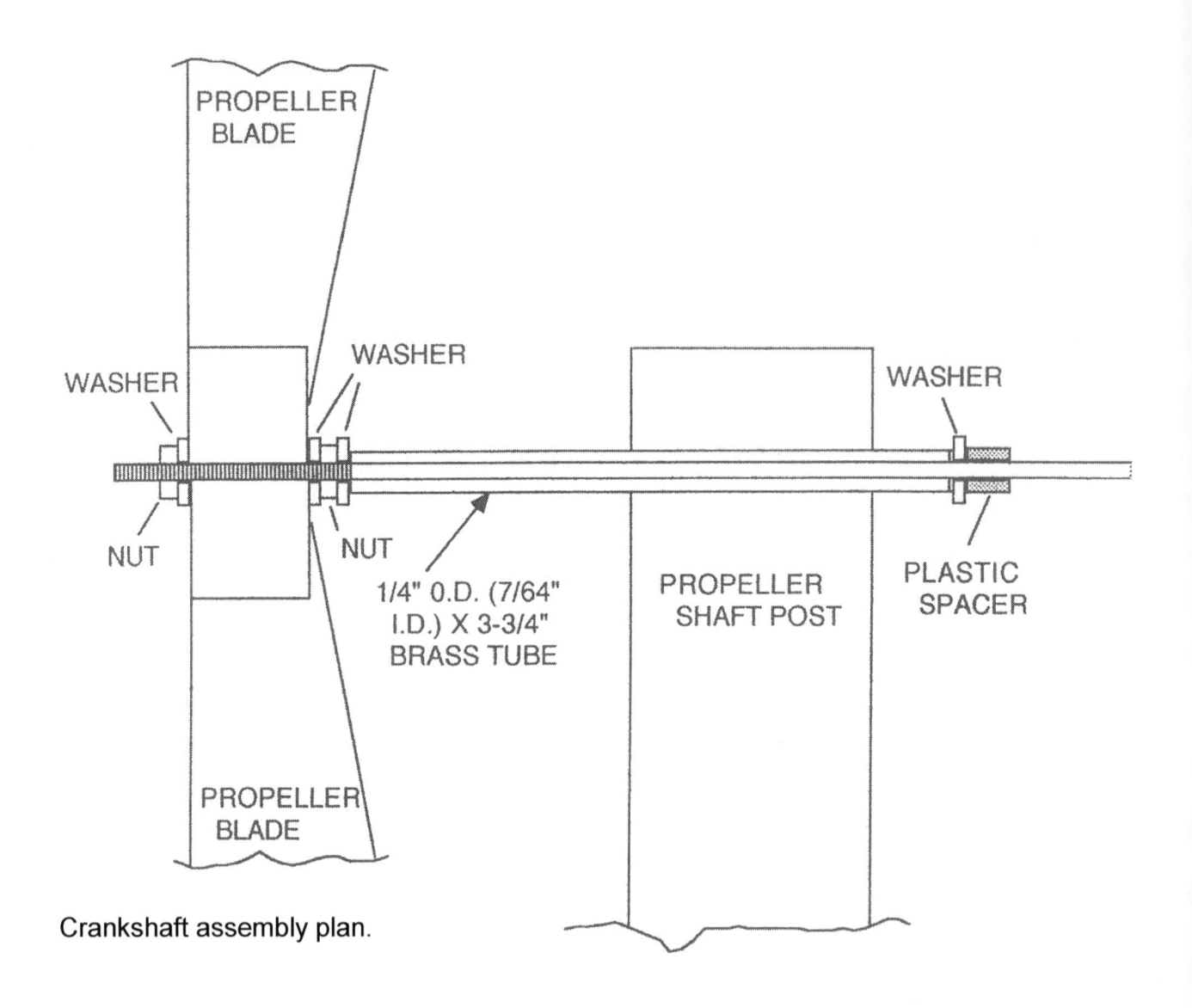

shaft tube. The shaft should turn freely in the tube with no binding. Apply light oil to the shaft to further decrease friction.

The propeller hub is made from 3/4" x 1-1/2" x 1-1/2" wood. Drill a 3/32" shaft hole. Cut the 3/16" wide x 1/2" deep notches for the propeller blades at 45 degree angles to the face of the hub. A counterclockwise propeller is shown, but you can reverse the notches for a clockwise rotation if desired. The slots need to be made accurately for the whirligig to work properly.

Cut the propeller blades from 3/16" wood or plywood to the pattern shown. Then glue them in the slots in the hub. Place the hub on a flat surface with the forward side down.

The blades are then installed with the forward side flush with the flat surface.

Install a washer, nut, and washer over the threaded end of the shaft, as shown. Then thread the propeller hub onto the shaft. Secure the propeller with a washer and nut.

Test the assembly in front of a fan to make certain that the propeller and shaft assembly works properly.

DANCING MAN

3/32" DIA. BRASS CRANK SHAFT

PLASTIC SPACER

PLASTIC SPACER

3/16" O.D. (7/64" I.D.) X 1/2" BRASS TUBE

WOOD DANCER BODY

NUT

WASHER

WASHER

WASHER

NUT

PLASTIC SPACER

CRANKSHAFT

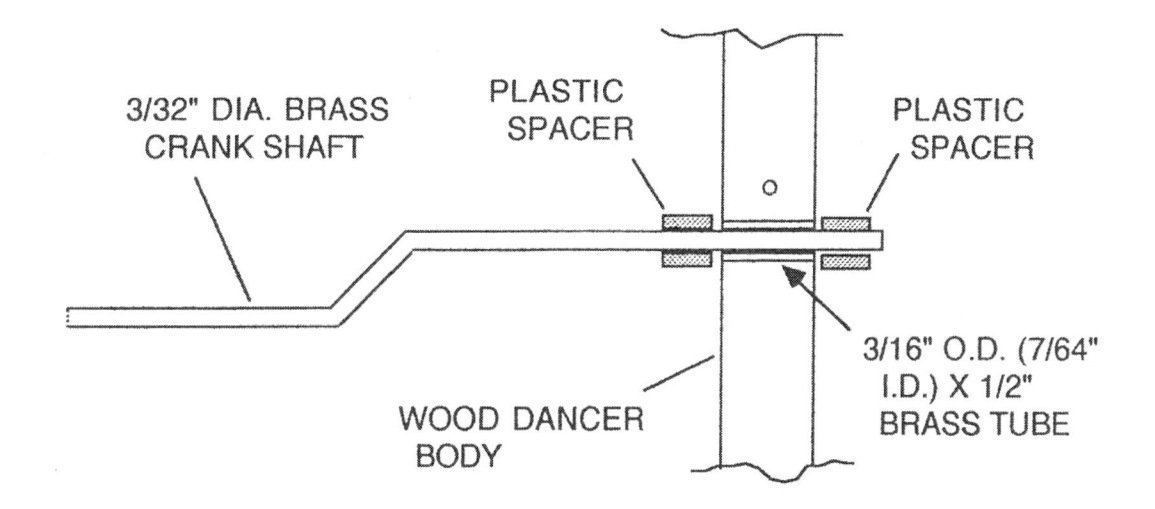

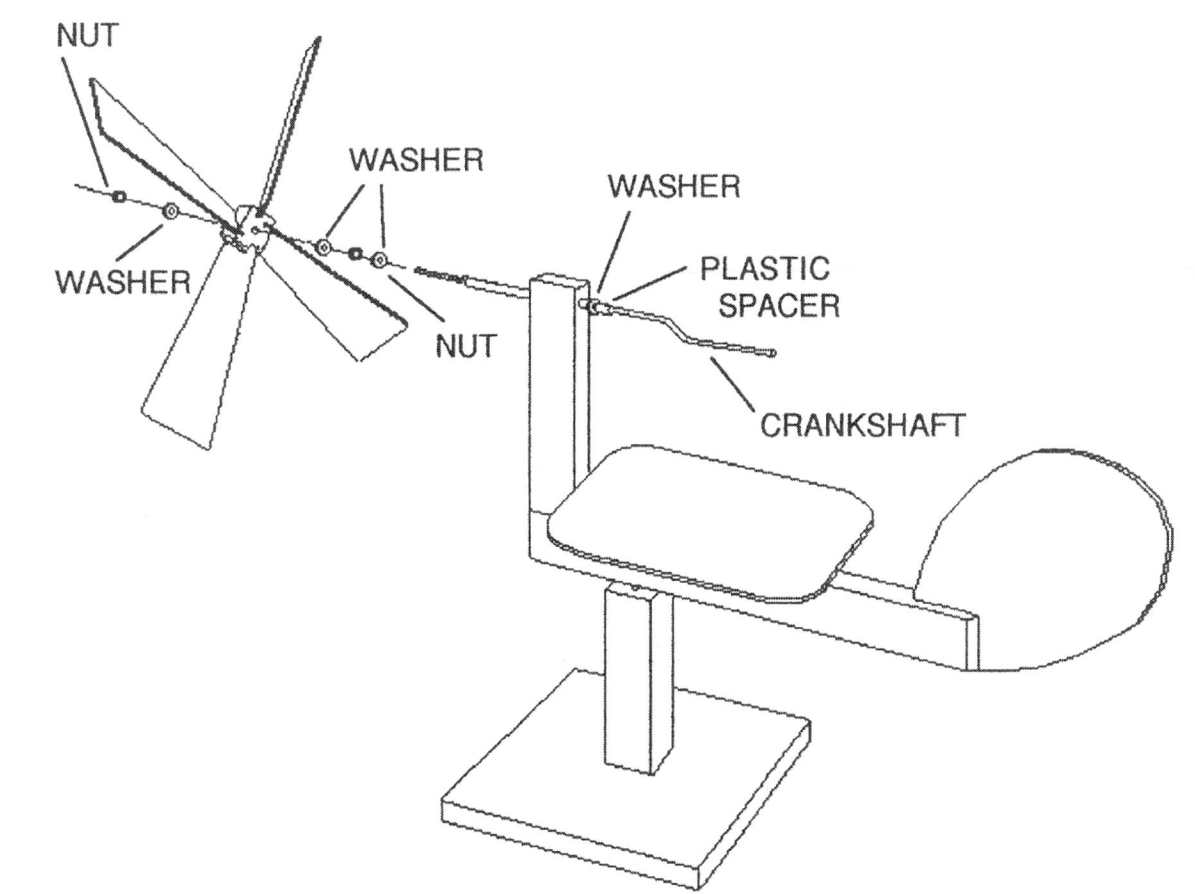

Assembly of propeller to crankshaft.

81

DANCING MAN

Cut the dancing man parts to the patterns shown. Drill holes before sawing the parts to shape. The feet are glued and nailed to the bottom ends of the lower legs.

Install a 3/16" outside diameter, 7/64" inside diameter x 1/2" brass tube in the crankshaft hole in the dancing man's body. The tube should fit tightly in the wood so that it will not turn.

The dancing man parts are best sanded and painted before assembly. If desired, however, you can do a trial assembly for testing the whirligig and then disassemble later for painting.

The upper legs are attached to the body with a 3/32" diameter x 2" brass rod. The arms are attached to the body with 1/32" diameter stiff wire, using plastic washers between the arms and the body. Bend and loop one end of the wire. Pass the other end through the holes in the parts. Bend and loop the other end of the wire and cut off excess wire. The arms should swing freely from the body.

Attach the upper and lower leg parts together with wires in a similar manner.

Assemble the dancing man on the crankshaft between two plastic spacers, as shown. This completes the assembly of the Dancing Man whirligig.

TESTING AND FINISHING

The whirligig is ready for testing. This can be inside with a fan or outdoors in a light wind. The whirligig should start easily if all of the parts turn properly. Make any necessary adjustments and add oil to friction areas of metal parts. The dancing man's feet should make noisy clapping contact with the dance floor. Make necessary adjustments in crankshaft to achieve desired dancing.

This whirligig is slightly out of balance. The crankshaft is more difficult to turn when the crank is downward than when it is upward. This can be corrected by adding small weights to the end outer end of one or more propeller blades until the system is balanced. However, I have found that this whirligig works well even without balancing weights, so this is optional.

If sanding and painting was not done previously, disassemble as necessary and do the sanding and painting.

You can create your own original whirligigs using this same mechanism. As a starter, you may want to replace the dancing man with a dancing woman, clown, frog, or other figure.

Assembly of dancing man.

DANCING MAN

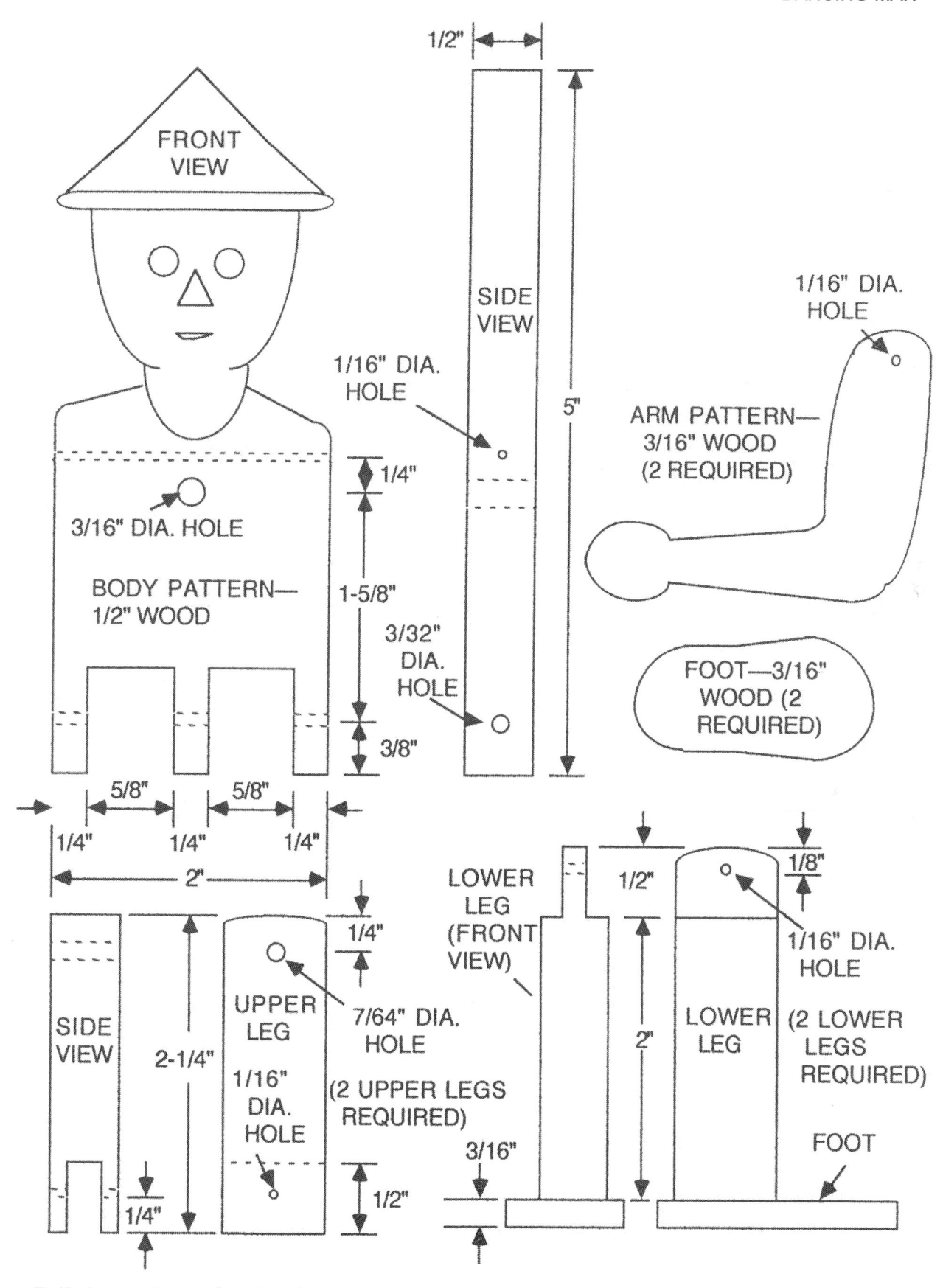

Full-size patterns for dancing man.

83

THE WHIRLIGIG MAKER'S BOOK

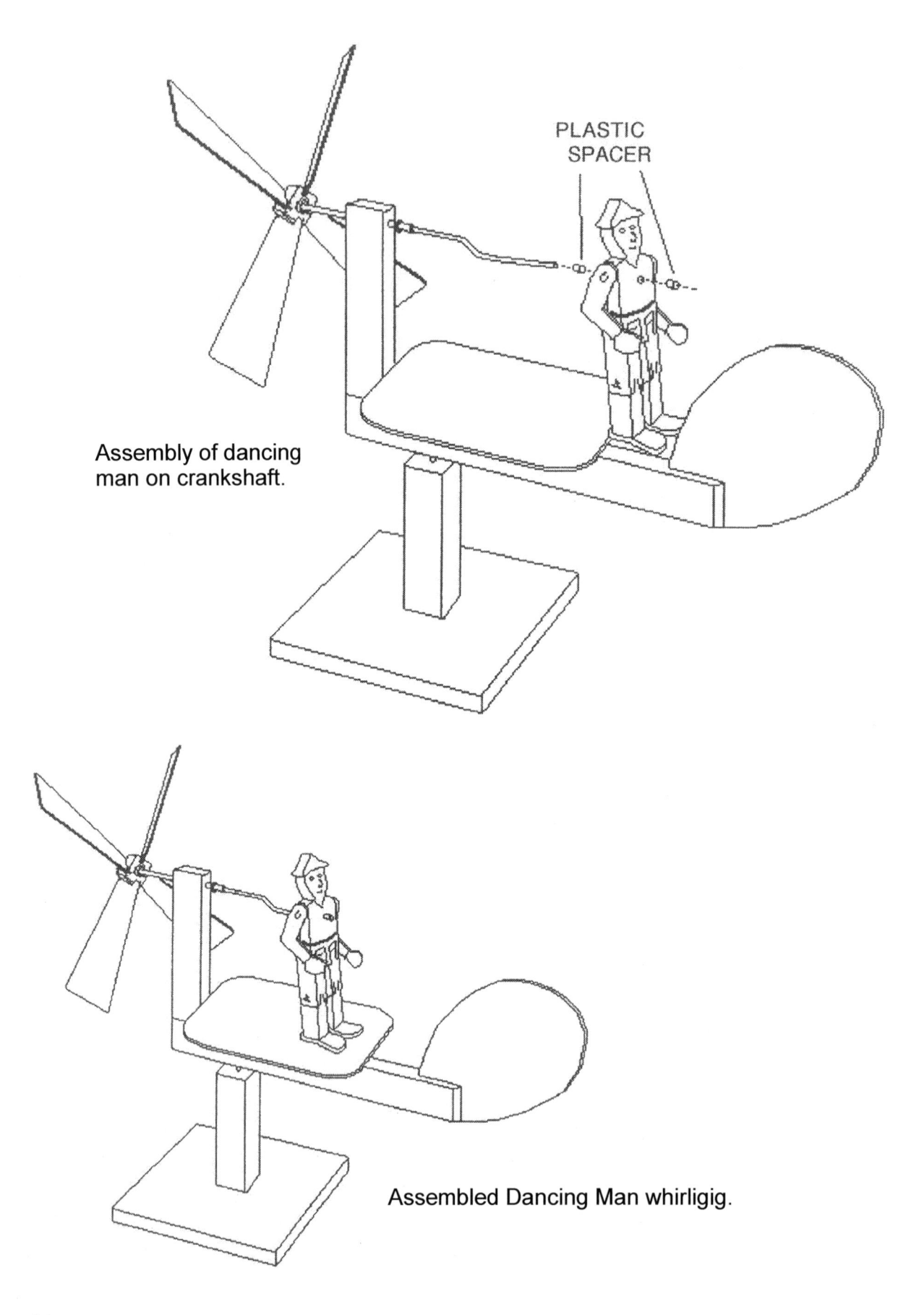

PLASTIC SPACER

Assembly of dancing man on crankshaft.

Assembled Dancing Man whirligig.

Chapter 9

UNICYCLING ROADRUNNER

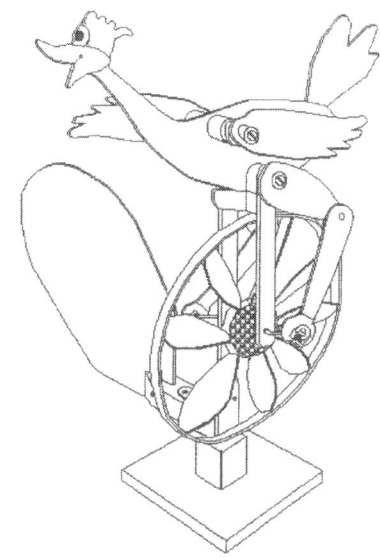

The Unicycling Roadrunner whirligig is of my own original design. It has a 12-inch diameter wind spinner. When placed in the wind outdoors or in the path of an indoor fan, the roadrunner not only pedals the unicycle, but also gives a "flying" wing action. This whirligig is unique. Unlike most standard whirligigs, the wind spinner is part of the action, forming the unicycle wheel, rather than being simply a power source.

Complete instructions and full-size patterns are given for making this whirligig, using either a standard plastic daisy wheel or constructing your own wind spinner from wood.

MATERIALS

- 3/4" x 8" x 8" wood or plywood for display base.
- 1-1/2" x 1-1/2" x 4" wood for display post.
- 1-1/2" x 1-1/2" x 6" wood for platform.
- 5/16" x 1-1/2" x 15" wood for inside fork.
- 5/16" x 3/4" x 9" wood for outside fork.
- 3/4" x 7/8" x 4" wood for fork stem spacers.
- 3/16" x 1" x 2" plywood for leg spacers.
- 1/4" x 12" x 20" plywood for roadrunner body and wing blocks.
- 1/4" x 9" x 12" plywood for vane.
- 1" x 1" x 4" wood for wing mount blocks.
- 3/4" x 3/4" x 2" wood for wing blocks.
- 3/16" x 3" x 15" wood or plywood for wing blades.
- 1/8" x 8" x 9" plywood for roadrunner legs.
- 12" diameter wood embroidery hoop.
- Either a 12-inch plastic daisy wheel or a wooden Tinkertoy spool for propeller hub and 1/8" x 5" x 24" wood or plywood for propeller blades.
- 3/32" diameter x 10" stiff wire for axle.
- 7/32" outside diameter (5/64" inside diameter) x 2" plastic tubing for axle adapter.
- 3" x 5" shelf bracket (available at hardware stores).
- 1/8" diameter x 4" nail for pivot rod for display base.
- Bolts, nuts, washers, and screws for attaching vane and inside fork to platform (see assembly drawings).
- 5/16" outside diameter (17/64" inside diameter) x 2-1/4" brass tubing wing shaft bearing.
- 1/4" outside diameter (3/16" inside diameter) x 2-3/8" brass tube for wing shaft.
- 3/16" diameter x 5-1/4" bolt for mounting wing blades.
- 3/16" diameter x 3-1/2" bolt for mounting wing blades.
- 3/16" washer (6 required) for leg and wing bolts.
- 3/16" nut (4 required) for leg and wing bolts.
- Plastic tubing for spacers on 3/32" wire (must fit tightly over wire).
- 1/2" tack (2 required) for joining upper and lower leg parts.
- Glue.
- Finishing nails.
- Thread for sewing propeller blades to wood hoop.
- Small felt pad for display base (4 required).
- Paint.

DISPLAY STAND

The display stand is useful not only for displaying the finished whirligig indoors, but also for holding the whirligig during construction and for testing it in front of fan. Construction is easy. The base is 3/4" x 8" x 8" wood or plywood. The 1-1/2" x 1-1/2" x 4" post is glued and nailed (use finishing nails from underside) to the center of one side of the base. A 1/8" diameter x 4" nail is driven 2" into the center of the top of the post for use as a pivot rod. Make certain that the nail is driven perpendicular to the top of the post. Cut the head off of the nail with a hacksaw. File the upper end of the nail smooth, rounding the corners slightly.

Sand and paint the display stand. A clear or color finish can be used.

Attach felt pads to the corners of the underside of the base.

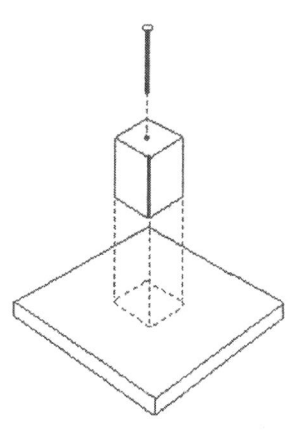

Assembly of display stand.

WIND SPINNER WHEEL

The unique wind spinner wheel, which is both the power source and an action component of the whirligig, is made either by fitting a manufactured plastic daisy wheel or a wooden hub and propeller blades to a 12-inch diameter embroidery hoop.

Plastic Daisy Wheel

A 12-inch diameter manufactured plastic daisy wheel with a 2-1/2 inch diameter center and 1-3/4 inch wide propeller blades were used to make the whirligig shown. A 12-inch diameter wooden embroidery ring (only the solid inside ring is used) forms the wheel tire.

Two different suitable daisy wheels are available in the area where I live, but there may be others. One of these is made in Canada, the other in the United States. Regardless of which one is used, the blades must fit exactly inside the hoop. When I use one of the daisy wheels made in Canada, I have to trim a short section from the tip of each blade. In order to have the hub centered in the hoop, the same amount must be trimmed from each blade. The daisy wheels made in the United States that I have used require small wood spacers between the tip of each propeller blade and the hoop.

Mark the hoop into eight sections equal distance apart around the hoop. This can be done by marking a circle on a piece of cardboard the same diameter as the outside of the hoop. Draw a line across the hoop that passes through the center point. Then make three additional lines that pass through the center point 45 degrees, 90 degrees, and 135 degrees from the first line. Place the hoop over the pattern and, using a pencil, mark the eight divisions on the hoop. Along the centerline outside the hoop, mark points 1/8-inch on each side of each of the eight divisions around the hoop for drilling 1/16-inch diameter holes.

After the holes have been drilled, lightly sand the hoop to remove all pencil marks.

Drill a 1/16-inch diameter hole in the center of the tip of each blade 1/8 inch from the blade tip. If small wood spacers are required for the blades to reach the hoop, these should be fitted and glued in place before drilling the holes, which should go through both the hoop and the spacers.

Next, sew the blade tips to the hoop, making six loops for each blade through the matching pair of hoop holes and the blade hole. Tie the thread ends inside the hoop by the blade hole.

After all blades have been sewn, check for alignment and then apply glue to the thread. Allow to dry.

Wooden Wind spinner

Construction of a wooden wind spinner is more difficult. A Tinkertoy spool with the standard eight holes around the outside and an axle hole through the center is used for the hub. The blades (eight are required) are cut from 1/8-inch thick wood or plywood to the pattern shown. You may have to change the blade length shown on the pattern slightly so that the blades will fit the hoop exactly with the hub axle hole in the exact center of the wheel. All eight blades are cut to the exact same pattern and the blade tip hole drilled through all blades at the same point.

The hub ends of the blades should fit the hub mounting holes tightly. The blades are glued to the hub with each blade at a 45 degree angle. All blades must be angled the same amount and direction. Notice that if the edges of the blades toward the counterclockwise direction are toward the front of the wheel, the wheel will rotate in the wind in a

THE WHIRLIGIG MAKER'S BOOK

counterclockwise direction, and vice versa. For a counterclockwise rotation, the roadrunner must face the direction shown for the correct pedaling direction. If you make a clockwise wind spinner, you need to reverse the direction the roadrunner is facing.

The blade tips are sewn and glued to the wooden embroidery hoop in the same manner as detailed previously for the plastic daisy wheel. Make certain the hub is centered and the hoop aligned before applying glue to the thread.

Installing Wire Axle

A 10-inch length of 3/32-inch diameter clothes hanger wire or other suitable wire is used for the axle. A plastic adapter 2 inches long that fits tightly over the wire axle and inside the daisy wheel or wood spool hub is used. If the adapter is exactly the right inside and outside diameter, the wire axle can be installed without glue. If the axle can still be turned, it can be glued in place with epoxy or other suitable glue. It is important that the axle wire be centered in the adapter and the adapter centered in relation to the wheel

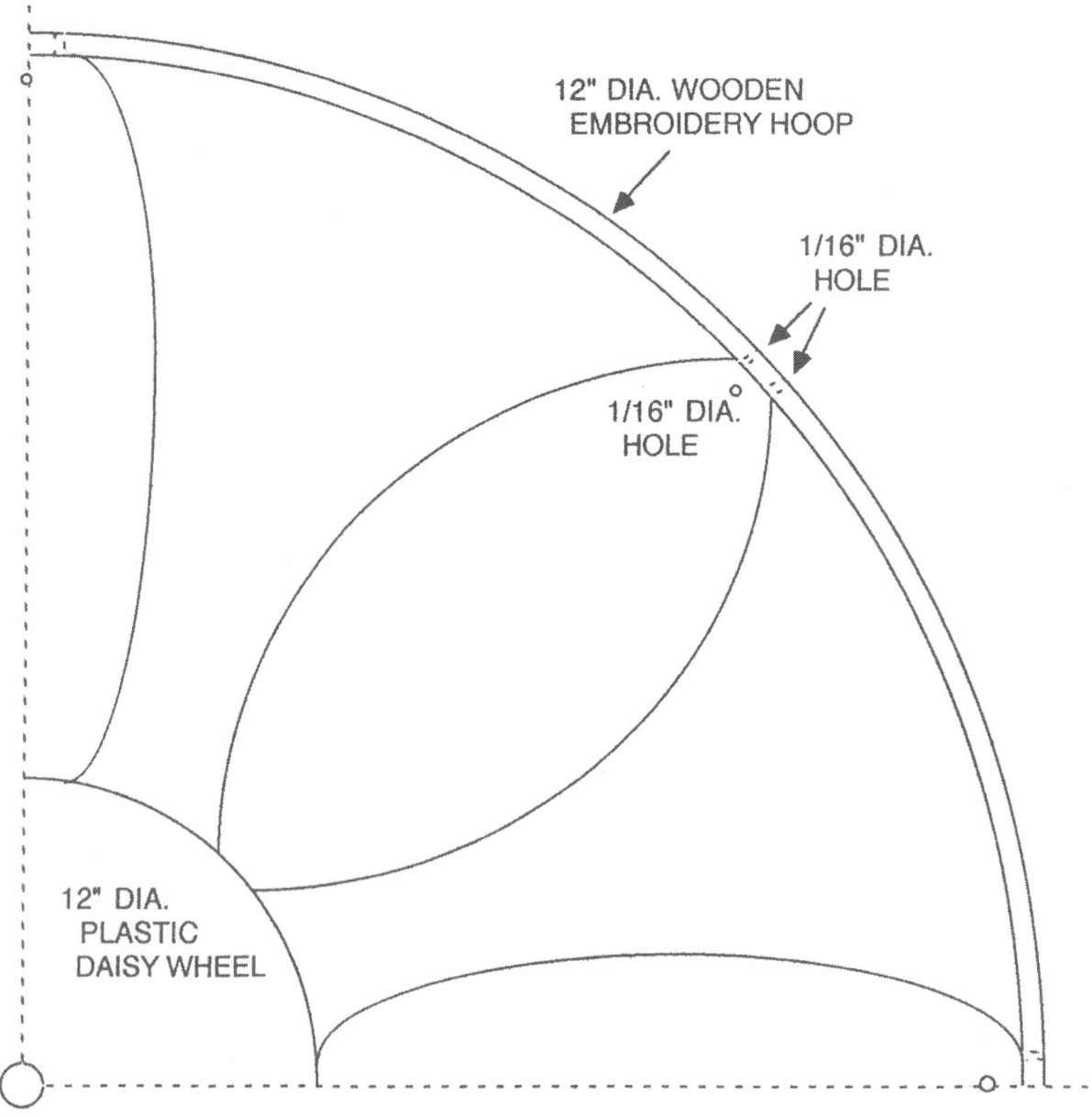

Assembly of daisy wheel to hoop.

UNICYCLING ROADRUNNER

12" DIA. WOODEN EMBROIDERY HOOP

1/16" DIA. HOLE

1/16" DIA. HOLE

WOODEN PROPELLER BLADE

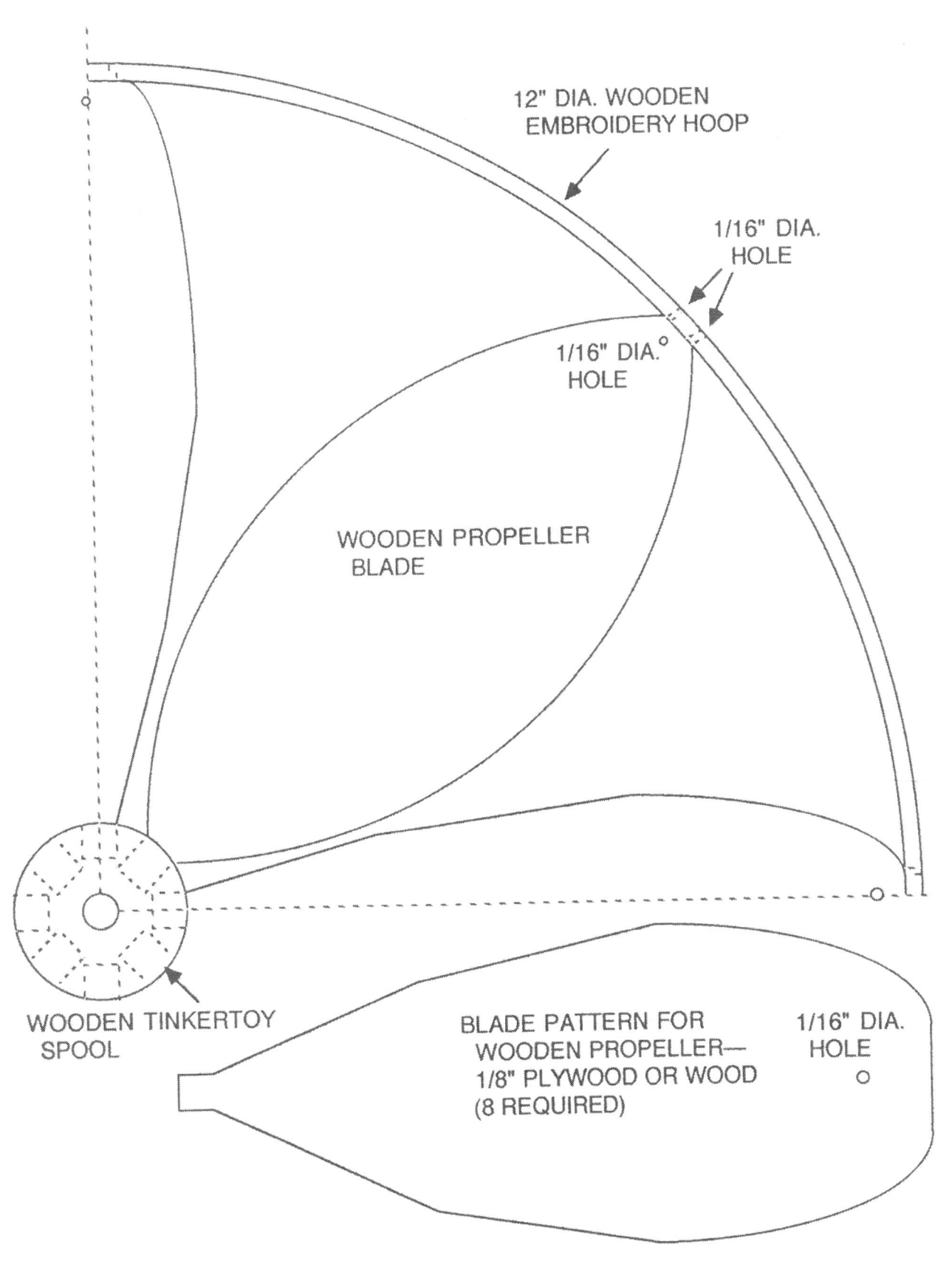

WOODEN TINKERTOY SPOOL

BLADE PATTERN FOR WOODEN PROPELLER—
1/8" PLYWOOD OR WOOD
(8 REQUIRED)

1/16" DIA. HOLE

Assembly and pattern for propeller blade for wooden wind spinner.

89

hoop, and that the axle remains fixed inside the wind spinner. The whirligig will not work properly if the wire axle can turn inside the hub.

If everything was done properly, the wheel should be in alignment when held by the axle at each side of the hub and spun. If the axle is not in the center of the wheel or the wheel is out of alignment, the whirligig will not work properly, and corrections should be made before continuing the construction.

PLATFORM

The platform is made of 1-1/2" x 1-1/2" x 6" wood. Make a 1/4" x 2-1/2" slot for the vane. Drill a 1/4" diameter x 1-1/4" hole for the pivot bearing in the position shown. The hole must be accurately centered and perpendicular to the wood surface for the whirligig to work properly.

Shape the leg spacers, fork stem spacers, inside and outside fork prongs, roadrunner body, wing mount blocks, and vane to the patterns shown.

Assemble the platform to the inside fork prong using a 3-inch by 5-inch shelf mounting bracket, as shown. If desired, a 1-1/2-inch square block cut in half from corner to corner can be used instead of the shelf mounting bracket. The fork prong is glued and nailed to the platform.

The shelf bracket is screwed and bolted to the platform and inside fork prong. Notice that no fastener is used at the axle hole. If the bracket does not pull tight against the fork prong, drill two 1/16-inch holes in the fork prong at the neck of shelf bracket and sew the bracket to the prong with five or six loops of thread. Tie a tight knot and apply glue to the thread.

Attach a fork stem spacer to the roadrunner's body (on the right side for a counterclockwise wind spinner, and on the left side if a clockwise wind spinner) with glue and brads or small finishing nails.

Then attach the spacer to the upper end of the inside fork prong with glue and nails. A 3/16-inch diameter bolt can be used to align the holes.

The vane is mounted to the platform with two 1/8-inch diameter round-head bolts, as

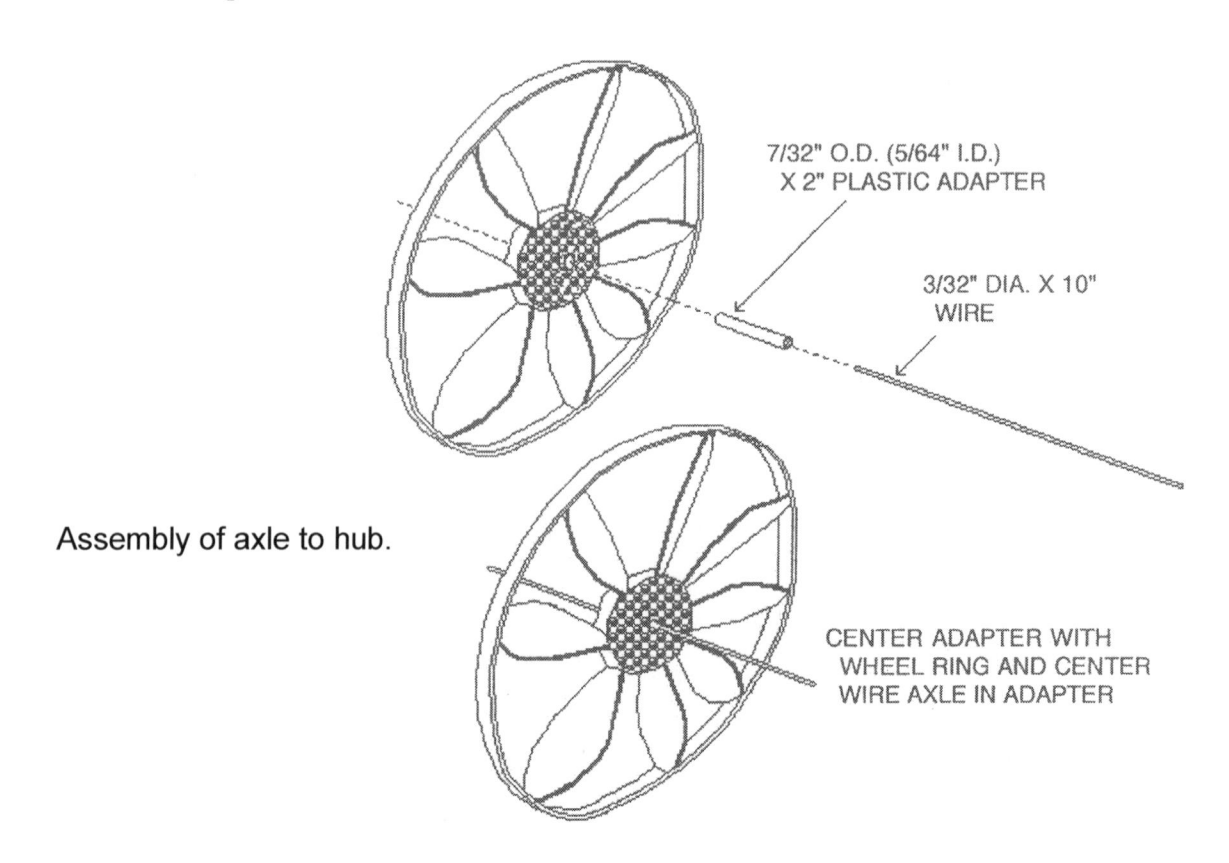

Assembly of axle to hub.

shown. This allows the vane to be removed for shipping and transporting of the whirligig. An alternate method is to permanently mount the vane with glue and/or nails.

Sand the platform assembly. The platform assembly can be painted at this time, or you can wait until assembly has been completed. Also paint the outside fork prong except for the glue contact area. It is much easier to paint the inside areas of the fork prongs before the wheel has been installed. The roadrunner's body can also be painted at this time, except for areas where wing mounting blocks will be glued in place.

WHEEL AND WING AND LEG ASSEMBLY

Install the wheel axle through the inside fork prong, as shown. Then install the outside fork prong over axle. With the outside fork stem spacer in position, bolt the parts together with 3/16-inch diameter leg mounting bolt. Check to make certain that the wind spinner wheel rotates easily and that there is a small space between the fork prongs and the wheel hub adapter so that the adapter will not be pinched between the fork prongs.

When everything looks okay, remove leg mounting bolt and apply glue for mounting spacer and the inside fork prong to roadrunner's body. Use bolt for lining up holes and clamping joint for glue to dry. Reinforce joint with finishing nails.

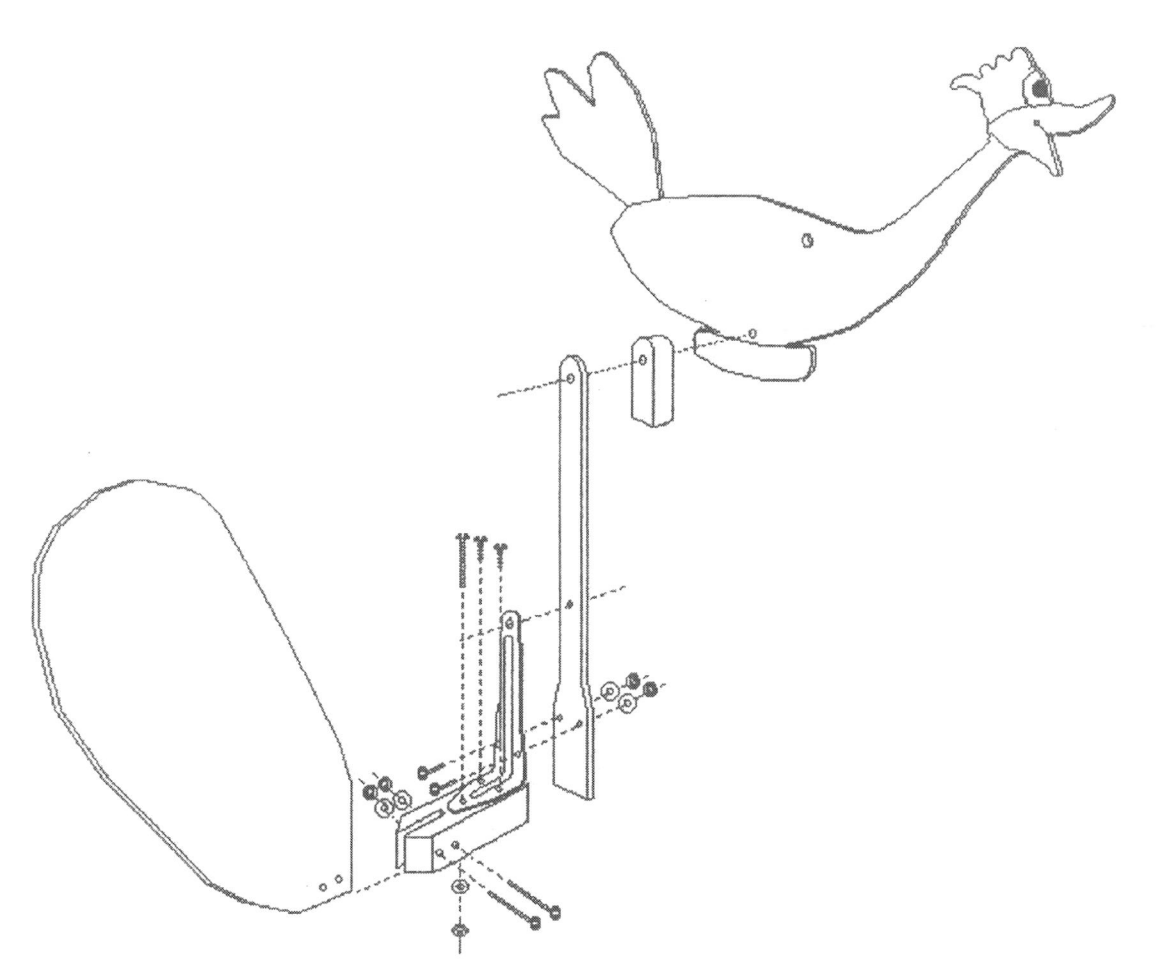

Assembly of platform.

THE WHIRLIGIG MAKER'S BOOK

3/4" DIA. 3/16" PLYWOOD LEG SPACERS (2 required)

13/64" DIA. HOLE

1-7/8" 13/64" DIA. HOLE 3/8"

FORK STEM SPACER— 7/8" WOOD (2 REQUIRED)

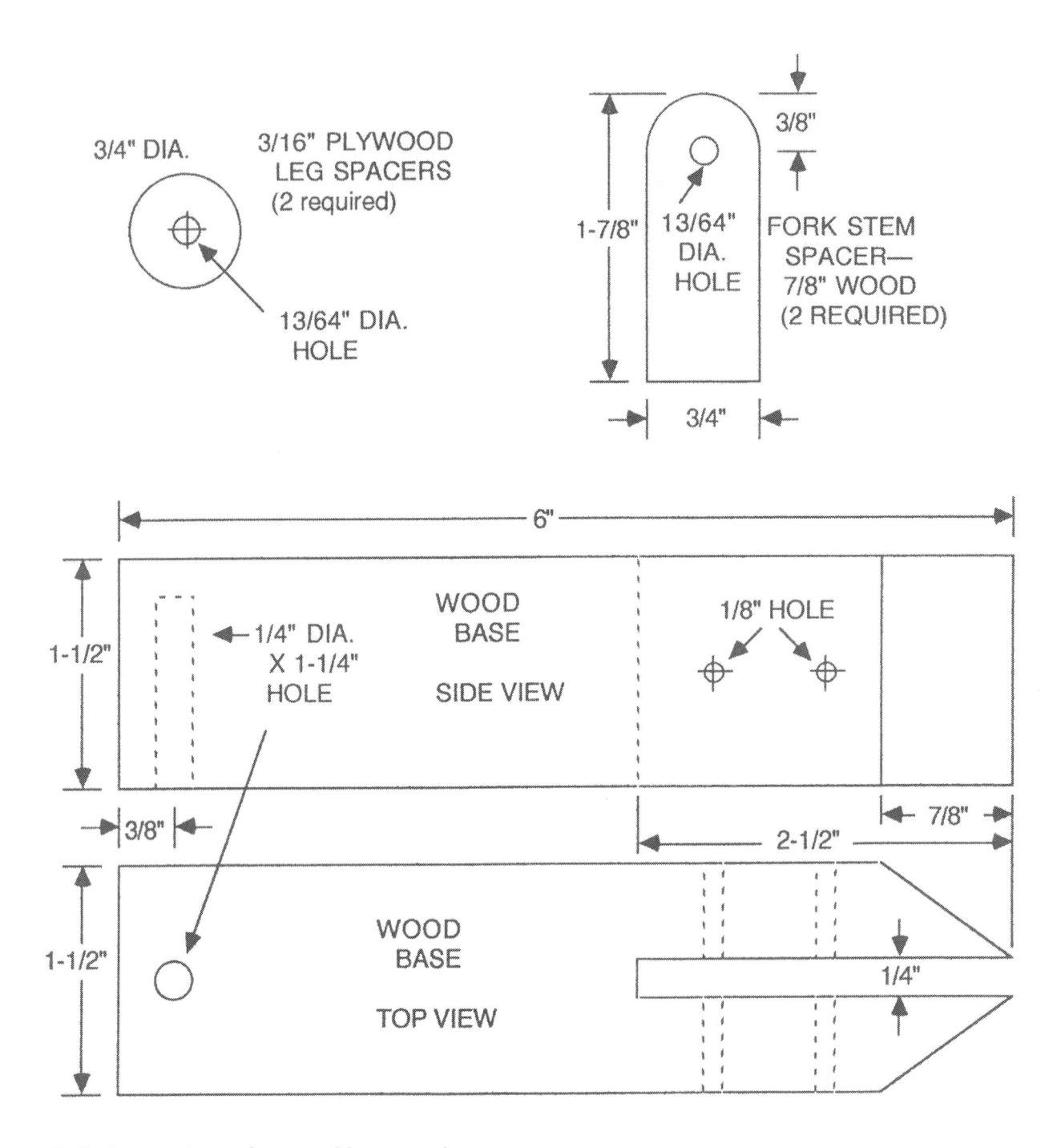

3/4"

6"

1-1/2"

1/4" DIA. X 1-1/4" HOLE

WOOD BASE SIDE VIEW

1/8" HOLE

3/8"

2-1/2"

7/8"

1-1/2"

WOOD BASE TOP VIEW

1/4"

Full-size patterns for wood base and spacers.

92

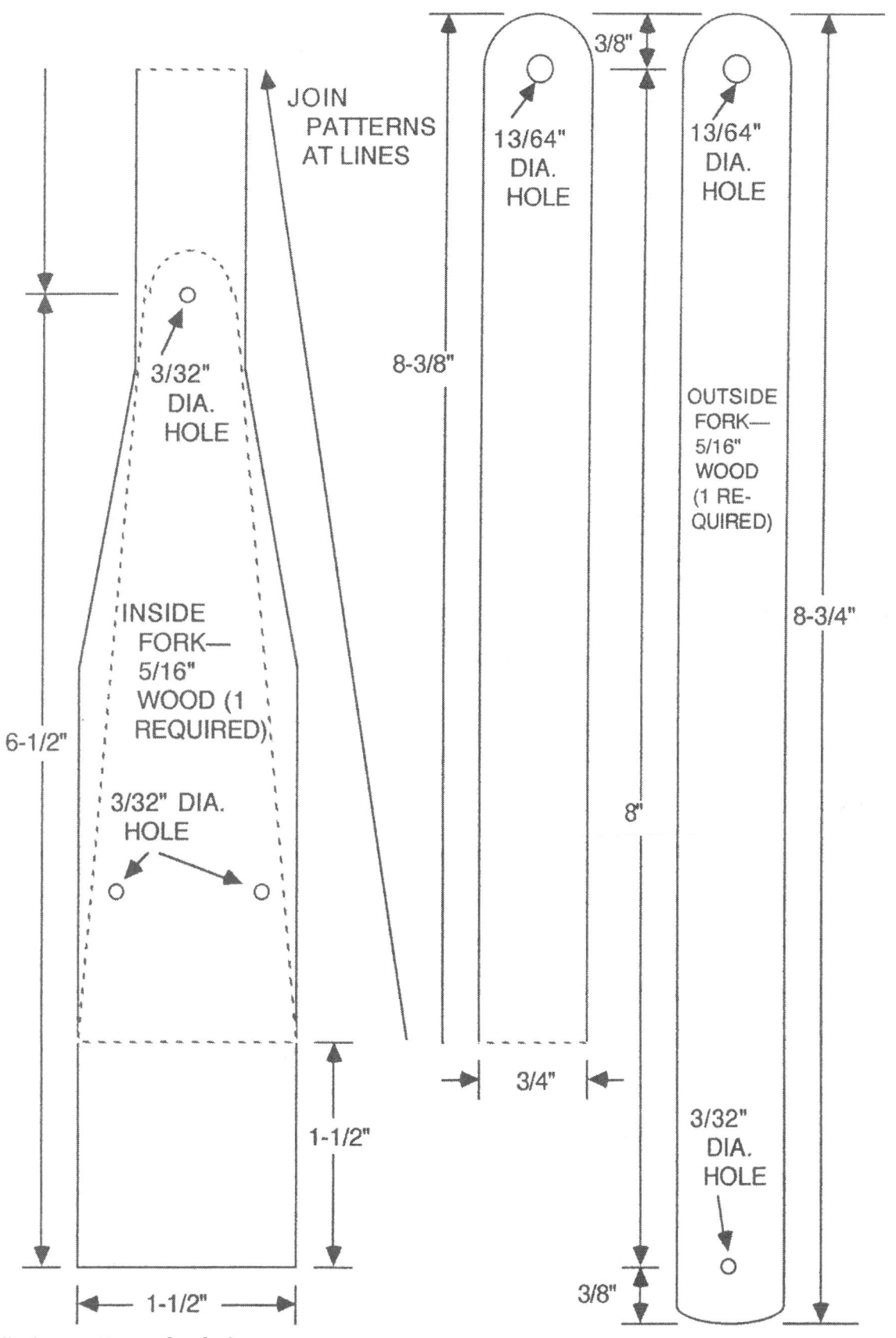

UNICYCLING ROADRUNNER

Full-size patterns for fork prongs.

THE WHIRLIGIG MAKER'S BOOK

JOIN PATTERNS AT LINES

WING MOUNT BLOCK—1" WOOD (2 REQUIRED)

1" DIA. WITH 5/16" HOLE IN CENTER

5/16" DIA. HOLE

ROADRUNNER PATTERN— 1/4" X 12" X 20" PLYWOOD

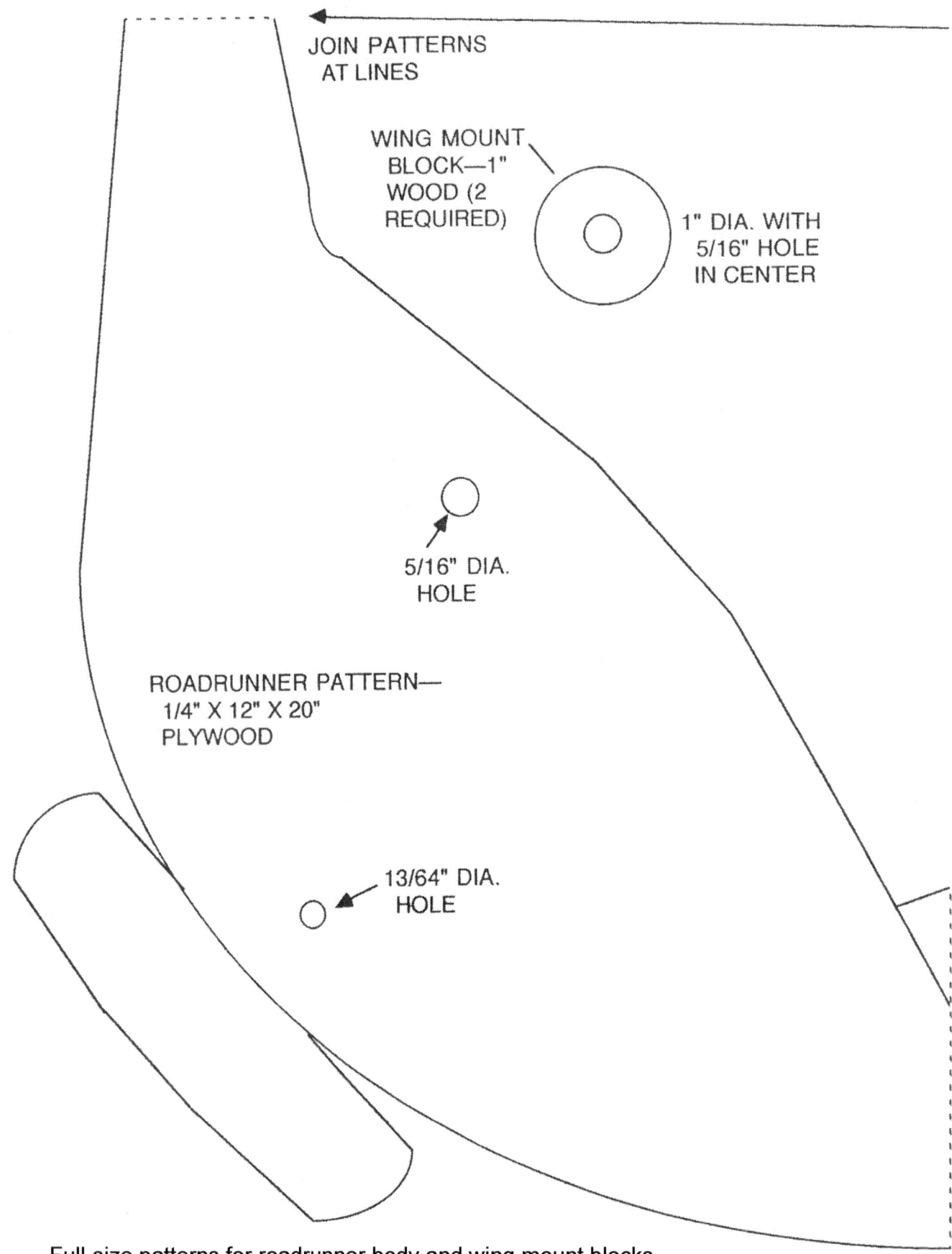

13/64" DIA. HOLE

Full-size patterns for roadrunner body and wing mount blocks.

UNICYCLING ROADRUNNER

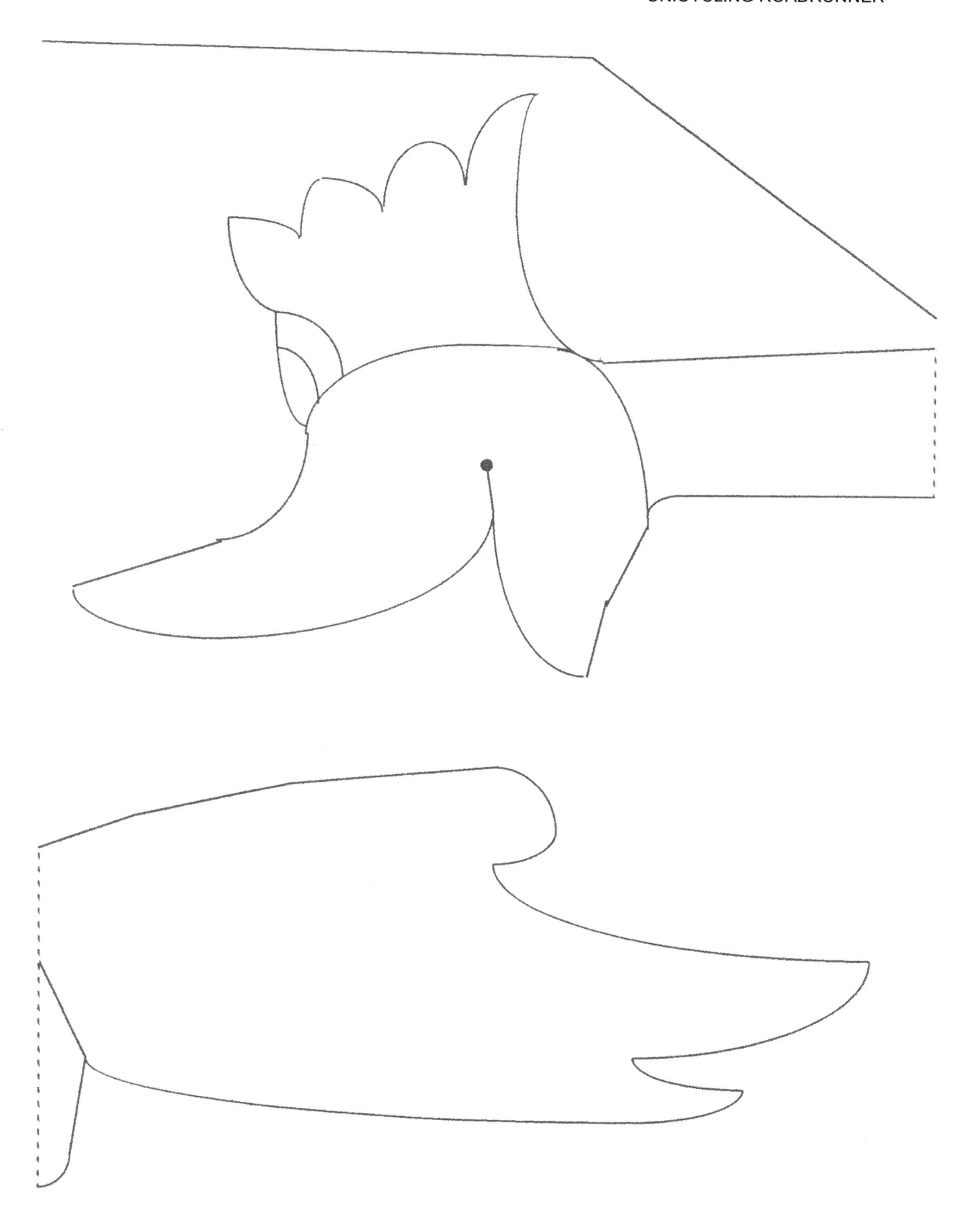

95

THE WHIRLIGIG MAKER'S BOOK

Full-size pattern for vane.

VANE—1/4" X 9" X 12"
PLYWOOD (1 REQUIRED)

1/8" DIA.
HOLE

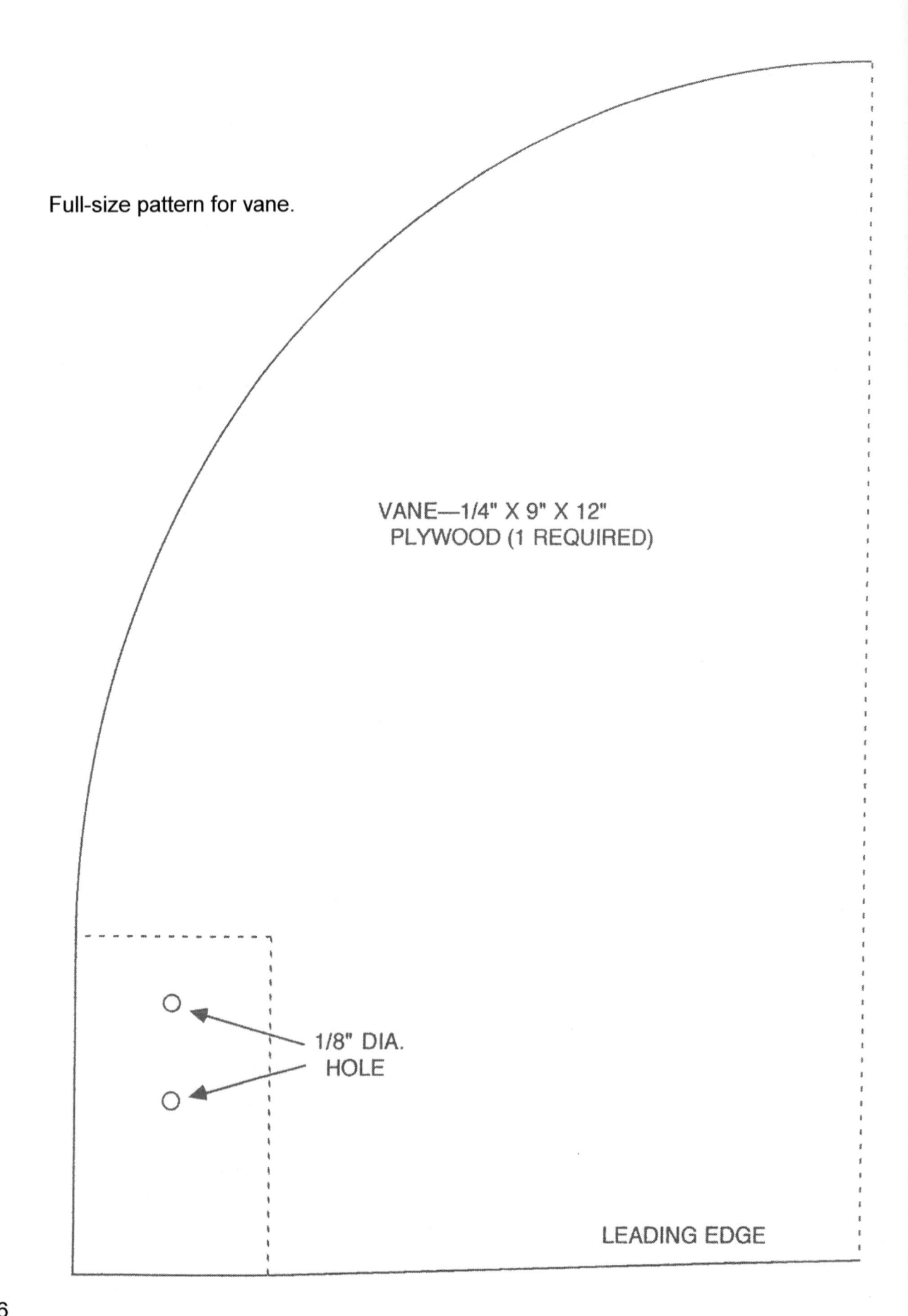

LEADING EDGE

UNICYCLING ROADRUNNER

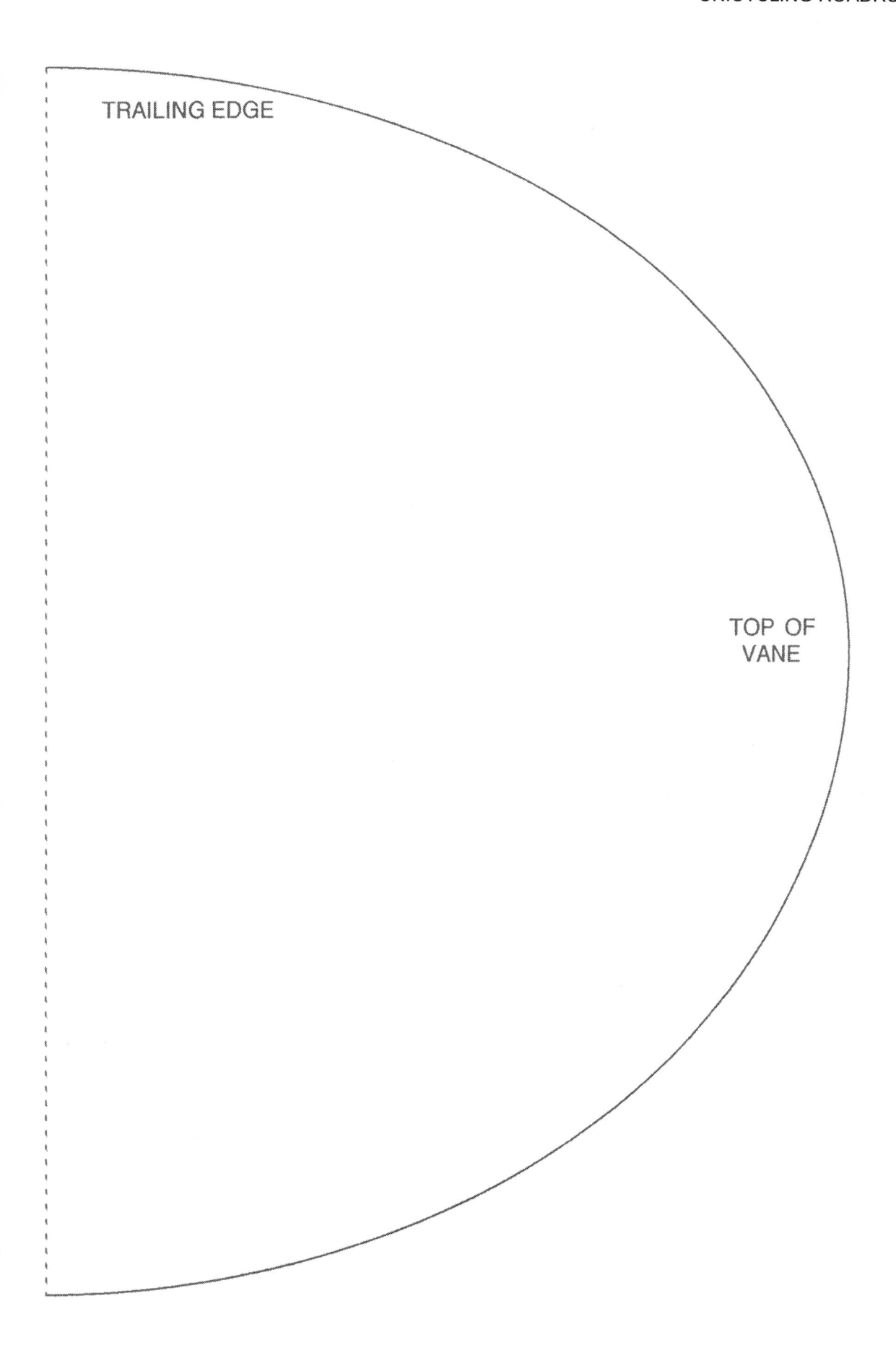

TRAILING EDGE

TOP OF
VANE

Completed first stage of assembly.

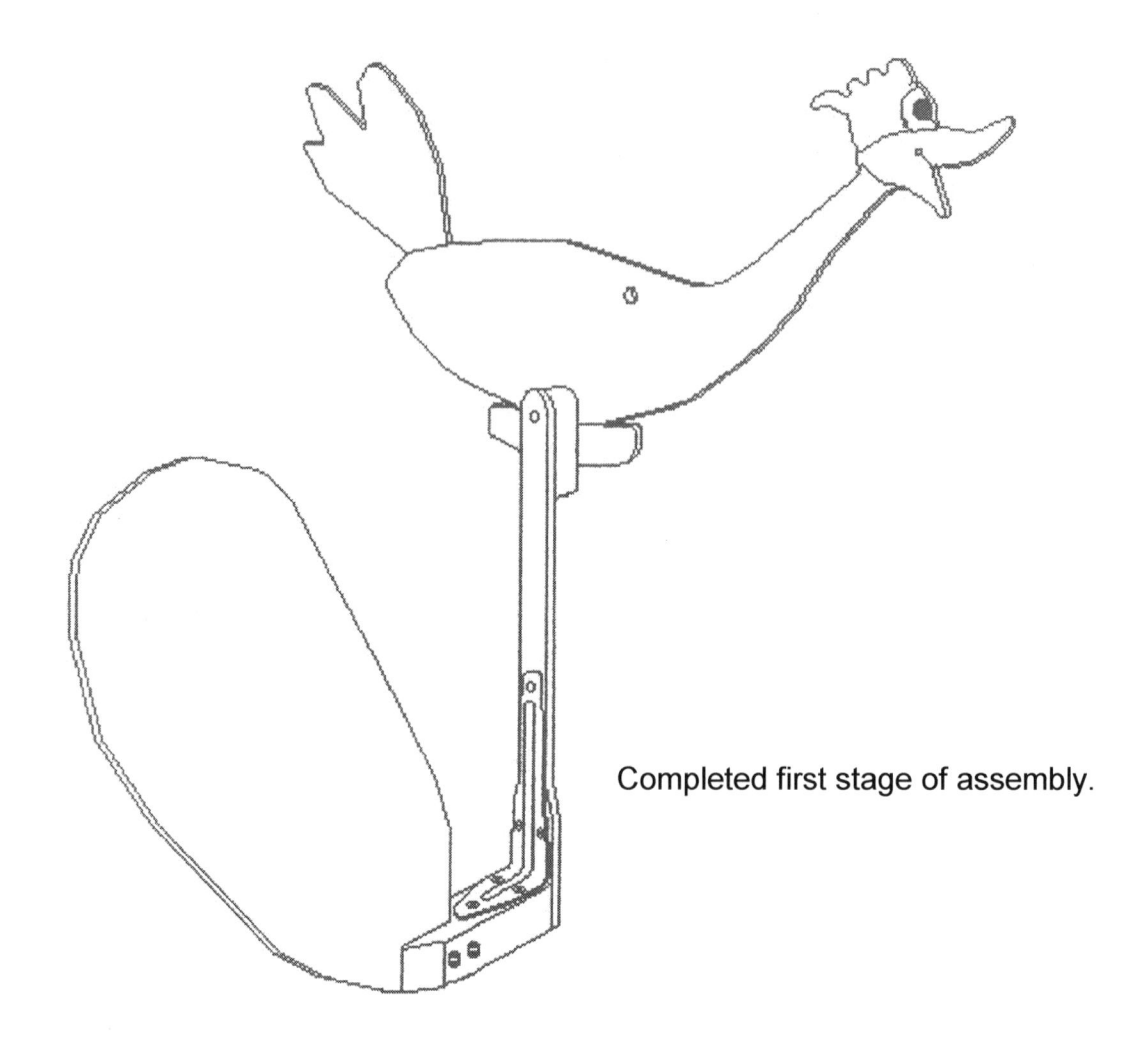

Check to make certain that wheel is lined up properly and spins freely. Allow glue to set.

The leg spacers and wing mounting blocks are then glued in place. Use bolts to hold the spacers in place until the glue sets.

The remainder of the painting of the platform and wheel assembly can be done at this time.

Bend the ends of the axle wire 1/8 inch from the outside of the fork prongs to form diametrically opposite crank arms. Grip the wire with the tip of needle nose pliers against the fork prong and bend the extended wire. Repeat on the opposite side.

Next, bend the pedal axles 1-1/4-inch from the wheel axle, as shown.

Install 5/16" outside diameter (17/6" inside diameter) x 2-1/4" brass tubing in wing mounting blocks. The tubing must fit tightly so that it will not turn.

Cut the upper and lower legs to the patterns shown. I recommend sanding and painting leg parts before assembly. The upper and lower legs are attached together with 1/2-inch tacks, with the lower leg outward on each side. Bend the end of the tacks back toward the wood and tap point into wood. Work the joints until they turn easily. Apply paraffin wax to the contact areas of the joint.

Spacers are made from the plastic covering from 12-gauge copper electrical wire. These are cut to 1/8-inch lengths. Four are required. Slip a spacer over each pedal axle and position against crank bend. The spacers should fit snuggly over the wire so that they will not slip around the bend in the wire.

The roadrunner claws are then installed on the pedal axles. A plastic spacer is slipped over the wires and positioned about 1/8 inch

UNICYCLING ROADRUNNER

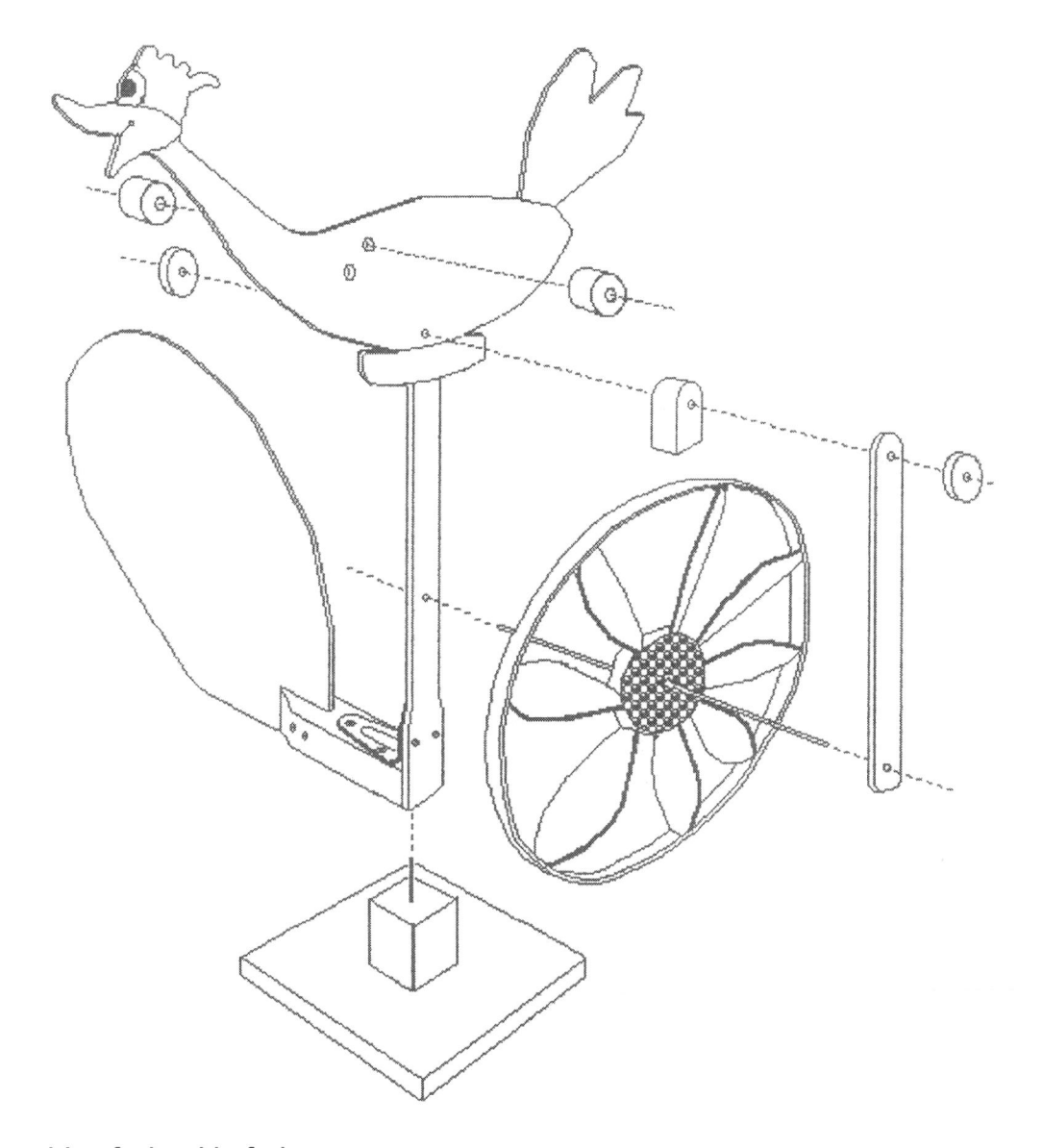

Assembly of wheel in fork prongs.

from the pedal axle hole so that the foot can still turn freely when the pedal axle rotates.

Bolt the legs to the roadrunner's body, using 3/16-inch diameter x 3-1/2" round head stove bolt. Notice that the joint between the upper and lower legs bends backwards. A washer is used on each side. Secure the bolt with a hex-head nut. Tighten the nut to the point where the legs can still rotate freely. Cut off any excess threads. Tap threads with a sharp punch between the bolt and nut to prevent the nut from working loose. File the end of the bolt smooth.

Bend and loop the ends of the pedal wires, as shown. Cut off excess wire and file the ends smooth.

Cut the wing and wing angle spacers to the patterns shown. Glue the spacers to the wings so that the wings form propeller blades at 45 degree angles to the mounting axle. Notice that the blades for the two wings are at opposite angles to each other.

99

THE WHIRLIGIG MAKER'S BOOK

I recommend painting the wings before further assembly.

The wing blades are assembled to the roadrunner's body with a 3/16" diameter x 5-1/4" bolt, as shown. A 1/4" outside diameter (3/16" inside diameter) brass tube is used as a shaft to cover the threads. The wing blades are bolted to the threaded shaft in diametrically opposite directions so that they are fixed to the shaft. Apply light oil between the inside and outside brass tubes so that the wings spin freely on the shaft.

This completes the assembly. Paint as desired and the project is complete. If painting was done before assembly, some touch up painting may be required.

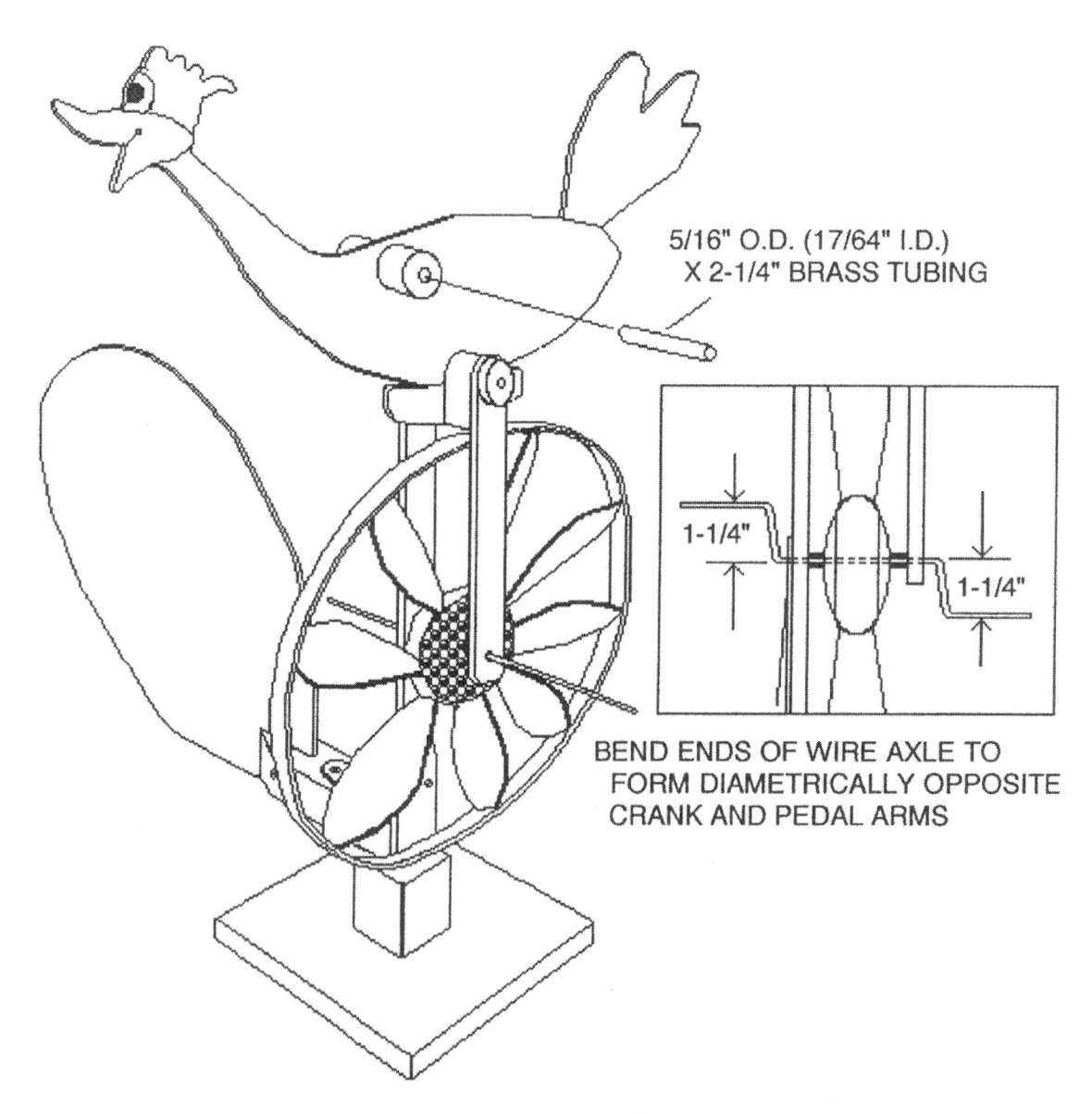

5/16" O.D. (17/64" I.D.) X 2-1/4" BRASS TUBING

1-1/4"

1-1/4"

BEND ENDS OF WIRE AXLE TO FORM DIAMETRICALLY OPPOSITE CRANK AND PEDAL ARMS

Crank and brass tubing assembly.

UNICYCLING ROADRUNNER

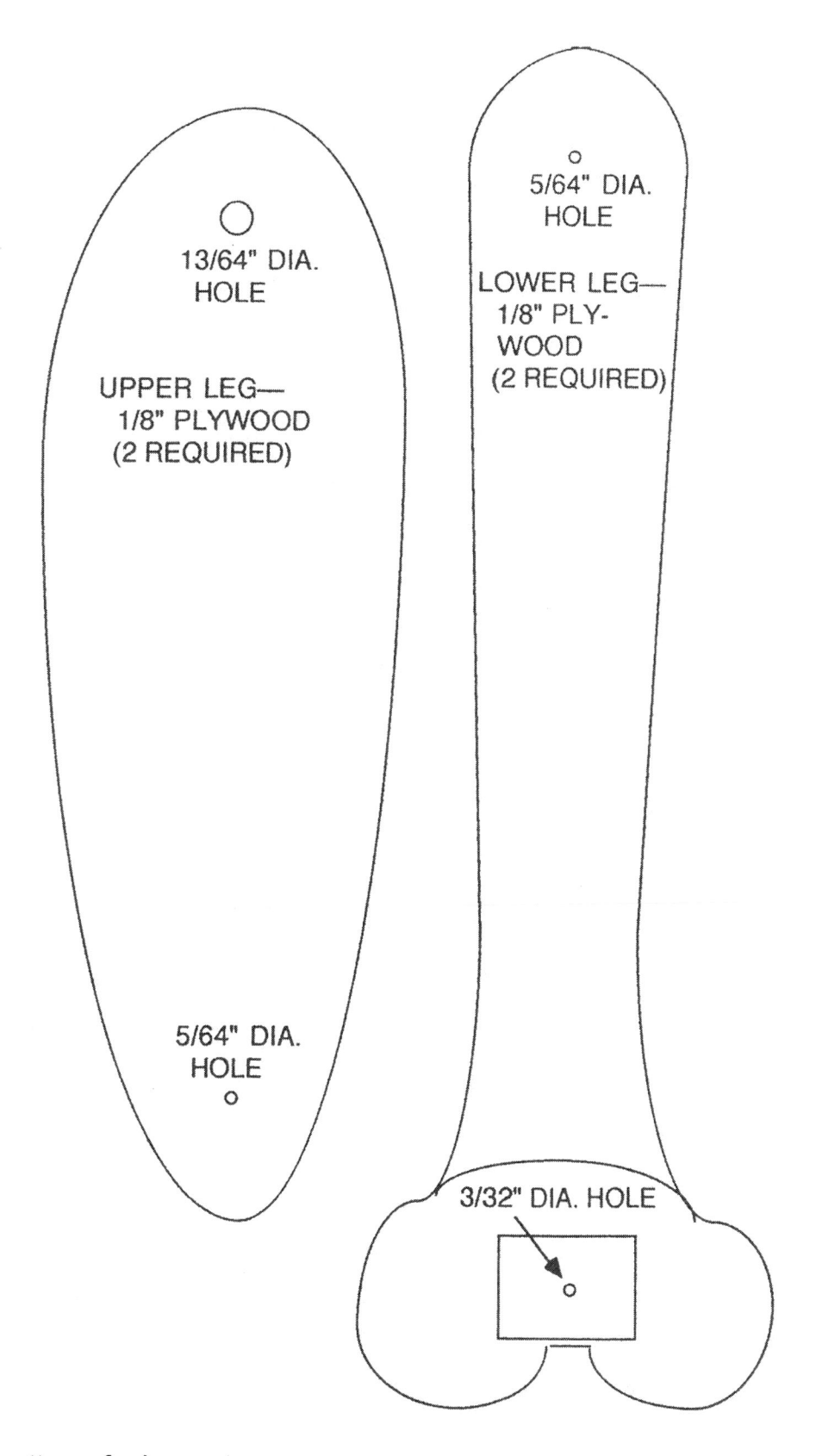

13/64" DIA. HOLE

UPPER LEG—
1/8" PLYWOOD
(2 REQUIRED)

5/64" DIA. HOLE

5/64" DIA. HOLE

LOWER LEG—
1/8" PLY-
WOOD
(2 REQUIRED)

3/32" DIA. HOLE

Full-size patterns for leg parts.

THE WHIRLIGIG MAKER'S BOOK

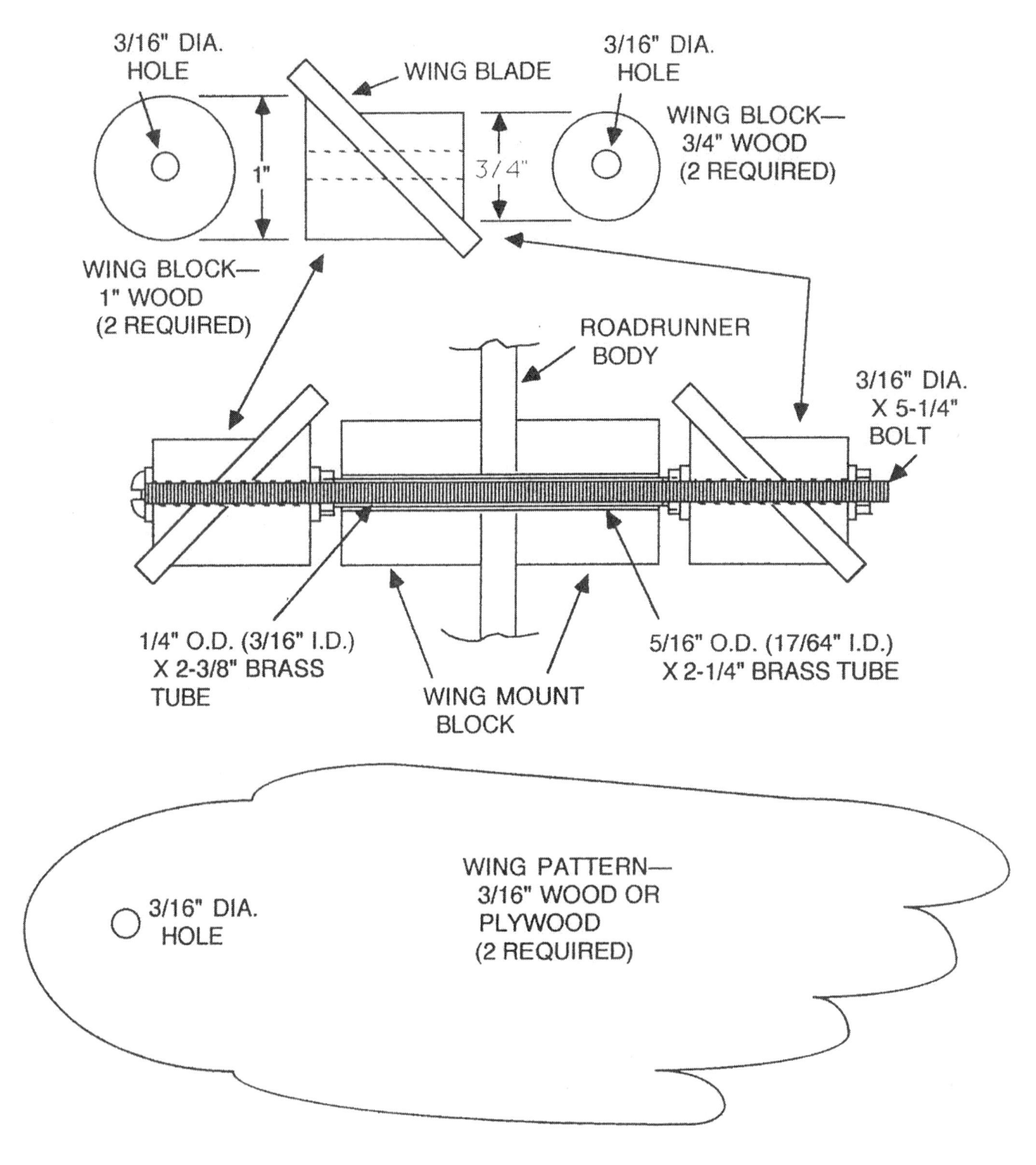

Assembly and patterns for wings.

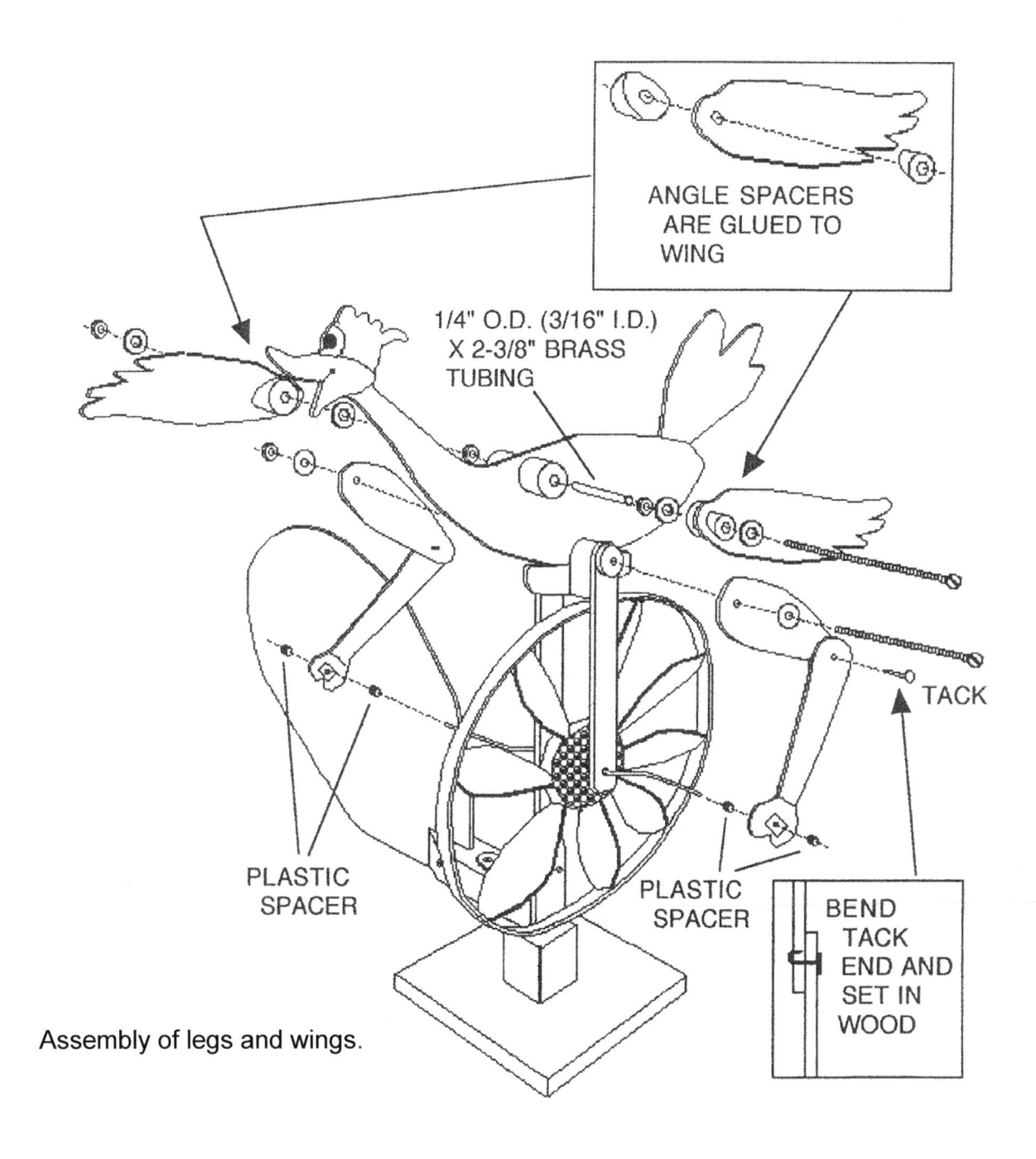

UNICYCLING ROADRUNNER

ANGLE SPACERS ARE GLUED TO WING

1/4" O.D. (3/16" I.D.) X 2-3/8" BRASS TUBING

TACK

PLASTIC SPACER

PLASTIC SPACER

BEND TACK END AND SET IN WOOD

Assembly of legs and wings.

103

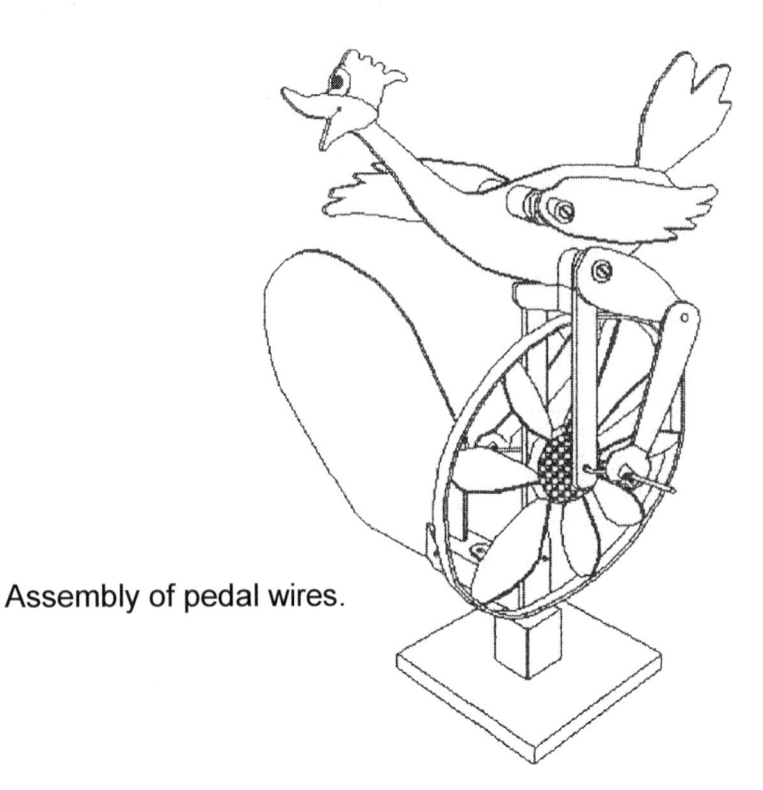

THE WHIRLIGIG MAKER'S BOOK

Assembly of pedal wires.

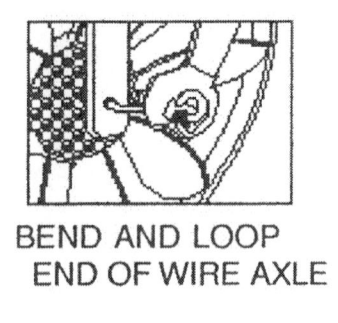

BEND AND LOOP
END OF WIRE AXLE

TESTING

The whirligig is ready for testing. This can be inside with a fan or outdoors in a light wind. The whirligig should start easily if all of the parts turn properly. Make any necessary adjustments and add oil to friction areas of metal parts and paraffin wax to wood and wood and metal friction areas.

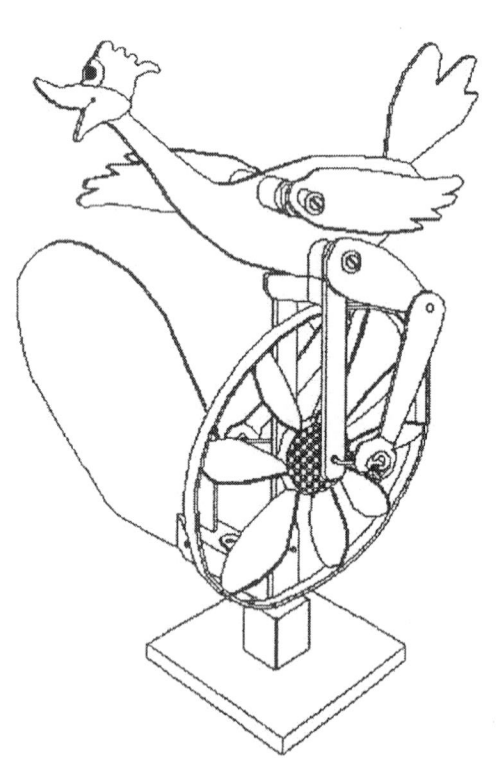

Assembled Unicycling Roadrunner whirligig.

Chapter 10

CAROUSEL

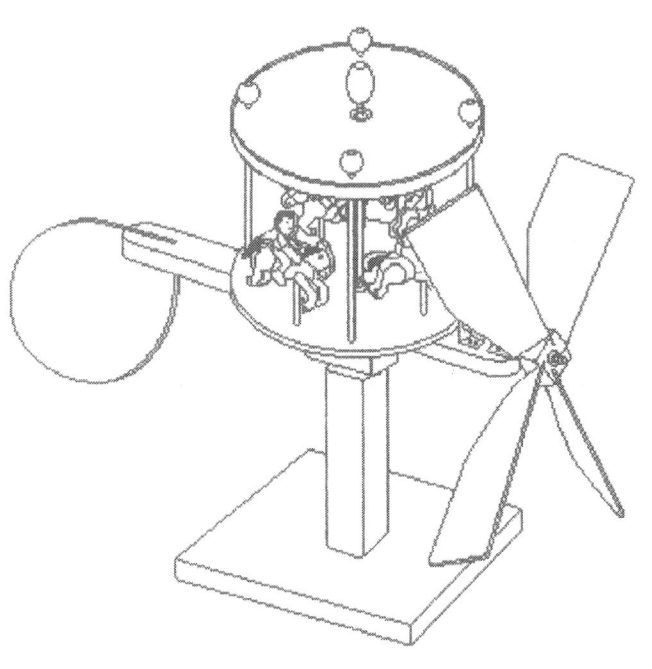

The Carousel whirligig is a fun project both to build and then watch perform after you have completed it.

MATERIALS

- 3/4" x 8-1/2" x 8-1/2" wood or plywood for display base.
- 1-1/2" x 1-1/2" x 7-1/2" wood for display post.
- 3/4" x 1-3/4" x 16" wood for platform.
- 1-3/4" x 2" x 2-1/2" wood for pivot block.
- 1/4" x 7" x 8" plywood for vane.
- 3/16" x 3" x 30" wood or plywood for propeller blades.
- 3/4" x 1-1/2" x 1-1/2" wood for propeller hub.
- 1/4" outside diameter (9/64" inside diameter) x 2" brass tubing for pivot bearing.
- 1/4" diameter steel ball for pivot bearing.
- 1/8" diameter x 6-1/4" brass rod for propeller shaft.
- 6-32 nut (8 required) for attaching propeller hub and drive wheel to shaft.
- Washer (6 required) for use on propeller shaft.
- 1/8" diameter x 4" nail for pivot rod for display base.
- 1/2" x 1" x 1" brass L-bracket (2 required) for mounting propeller shaft.
- Screw (4 required) for attaching brackets to platform.
- 3/8" outside diameter (1/8" inside diameter) x 1-1/2" plastic tube for propeller shaft spacers.
- 3/4" diameter rubber wheel with 1/8" diameter shaft hole for drive wheel.
- 1/4" diameter x 10" brass rod threaded 1-1/2" on ends and two nuts and two washers for platform shaft.
- 7/8" diameter x 1-1/2" macramé bead with 1/4" diameter hole for platform shaft cap.
- 1/4" x 8" x 16" plywood for platform floor and roof.
- 1/4" diameter x 28" hardwood dowel for platform posts.
- 3/16" x 12" hardwood dowel for horse poles.
- Brass lamp fitting with 3/8" diameter threaded shaft and 17/64" hole with washer and nut (2 of each required).
- 5/8" diameter wood ball 1/4" diameter hole (4 required) post decorations.
- 1/2" x 2-1/2" x 12" wood for horse and rider bodies.
- 1/8" x 10" x 10" plywood for arms and legs of riders and horse legs.
- Glue.
- Finishing nails.
- Small felt pad for display base (4 required).
- Paint.

DISPLAY STAND

The display stand is useful not only for displaying the finished whirligig indoors, but also for holding the whirligig during construction and for testing it in front of a fan. Construction is easy. The base is 3/4" x 8-1/2" x 8-1/2" wood or plywood. The 1-1/2" x 1-1/2" x 7-1/2" post is glued and nailed to the center of the base. A 1/8" diameter x 4" nail is driven 2" into the center of the top of the post for use as a pivot rod. Drill a pilot hole that is perpendicular to the top of the post before driving the nail into the hole. Cut the head off of the nail with a hacksaw. File the upper end of the nail smooth, rounding the corners slightly.

Sand and paint the display stand. A clear or color finish can be used.

Attach felt pads to the corners of the underside of the base.

PLATFORM

The platform is made of 3/4" x 1-3/4" x 16" wood. Shape the ends, as shown. Make a 1/4" x 2-1/2" slot for the vane. Drill a 1/4" diameter hole for the platform shaft and attach the brass rod to the platform, as shown.

Use 1/2" x 1" x 1" brass L-brackets with 9/64" holes for the propeller shaft. Fasten the brass L-brackets to the platform with screws. Depending on the brackets selected, it may be necessary to expand the sizes of the holes and/or drill additional holes.

The pivot block is shaped from 1-3/4" x 2" x 2-1/2" wood to the pattern shown. Drill a 1/4" hole for the pivot tube, as shown. The hole must be accurately centered and perpendicular to the wood surfaces for the whirligig

VANE—1/4" X 6-3/4" X 8"
PLYWOOD (1 REQUIRED)

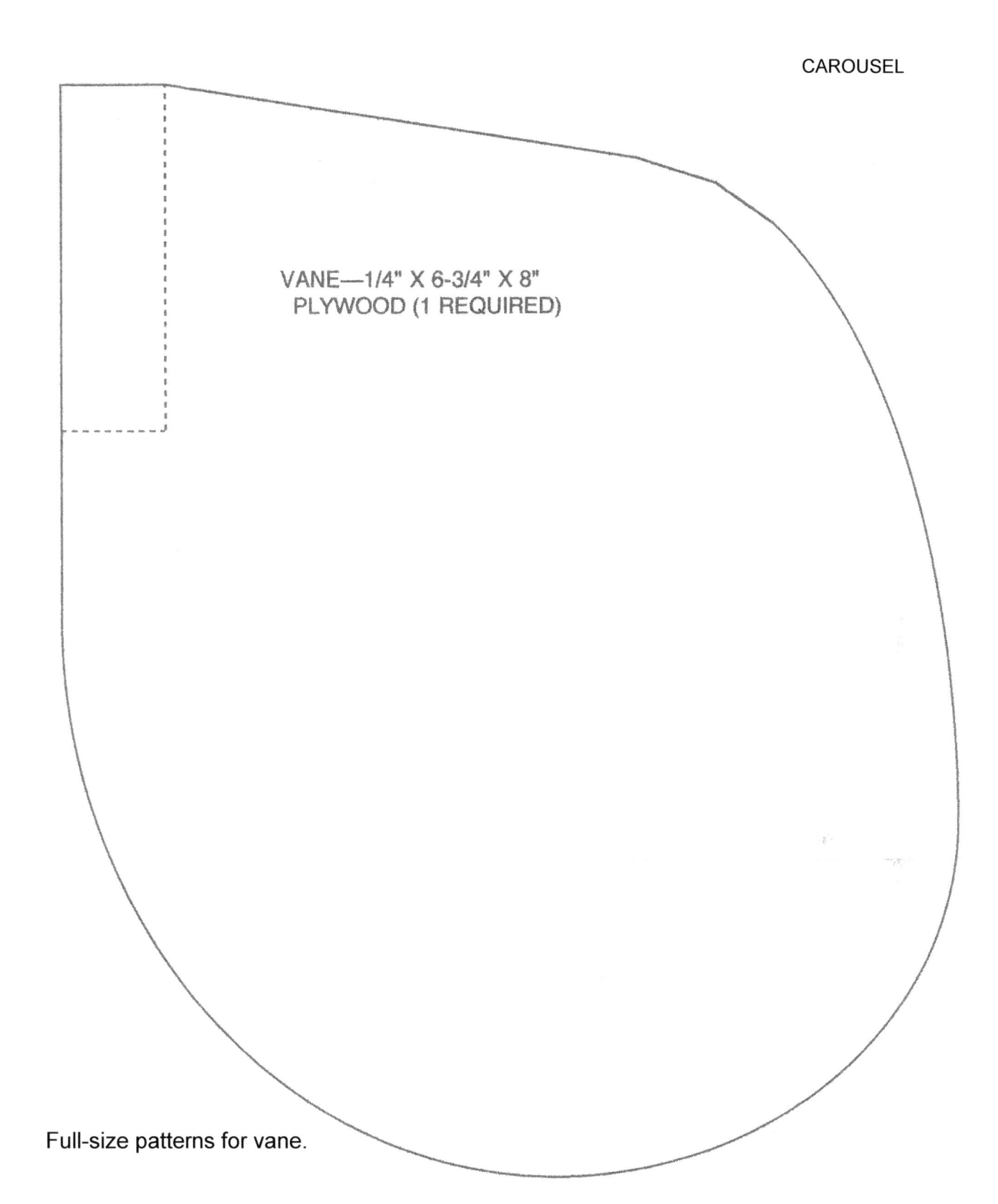

Full-size patterns for vane.

to work properly. Also drill a 5/8" diameter hole so that the block will fit over the platform shaft mounting. I use a drill press and drill press vise for drilling these holes.

THE WHIRLIGIG MAKER'S BOOK

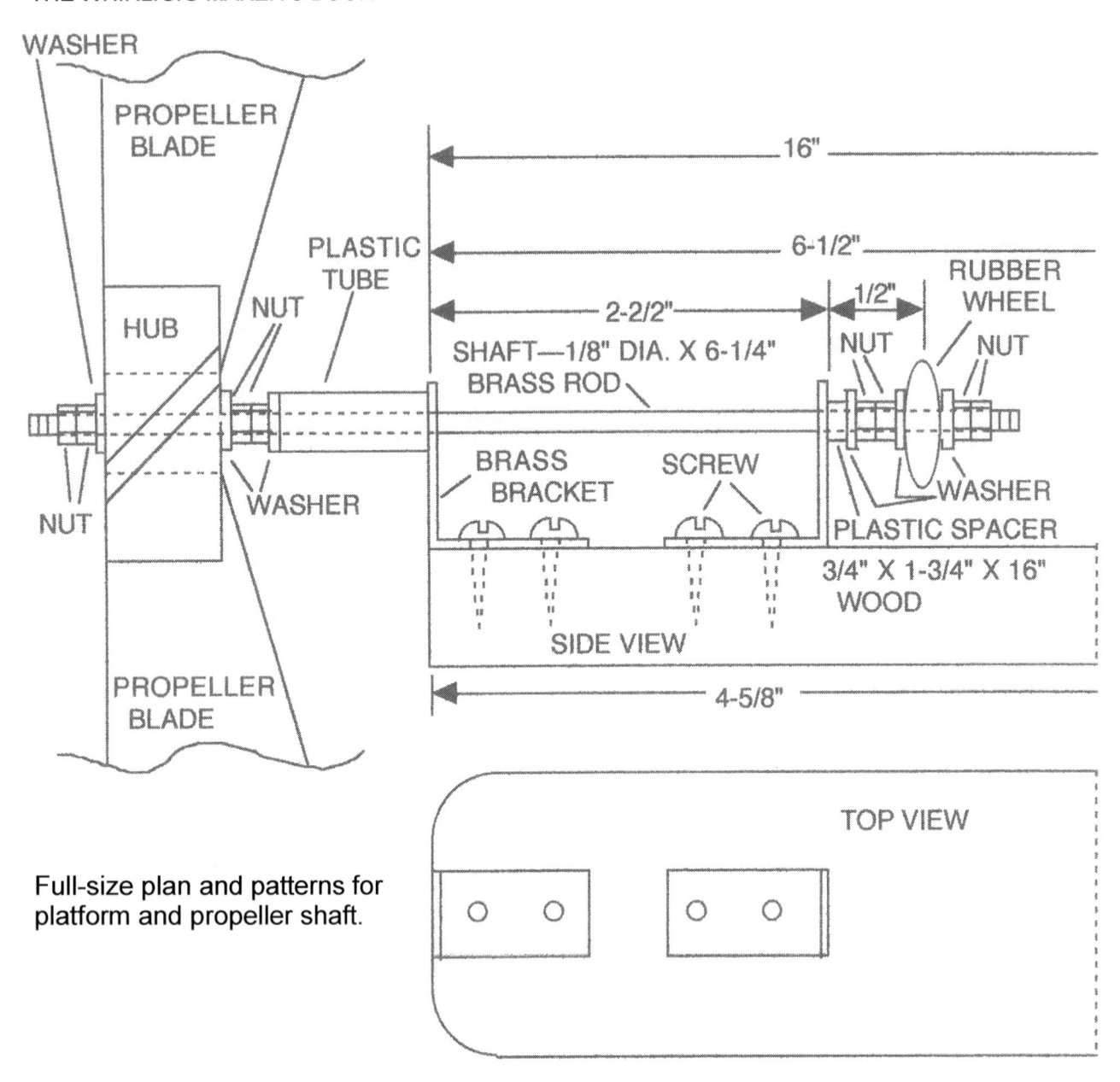

Full-size plan and patterns for platform and propeller shaft.

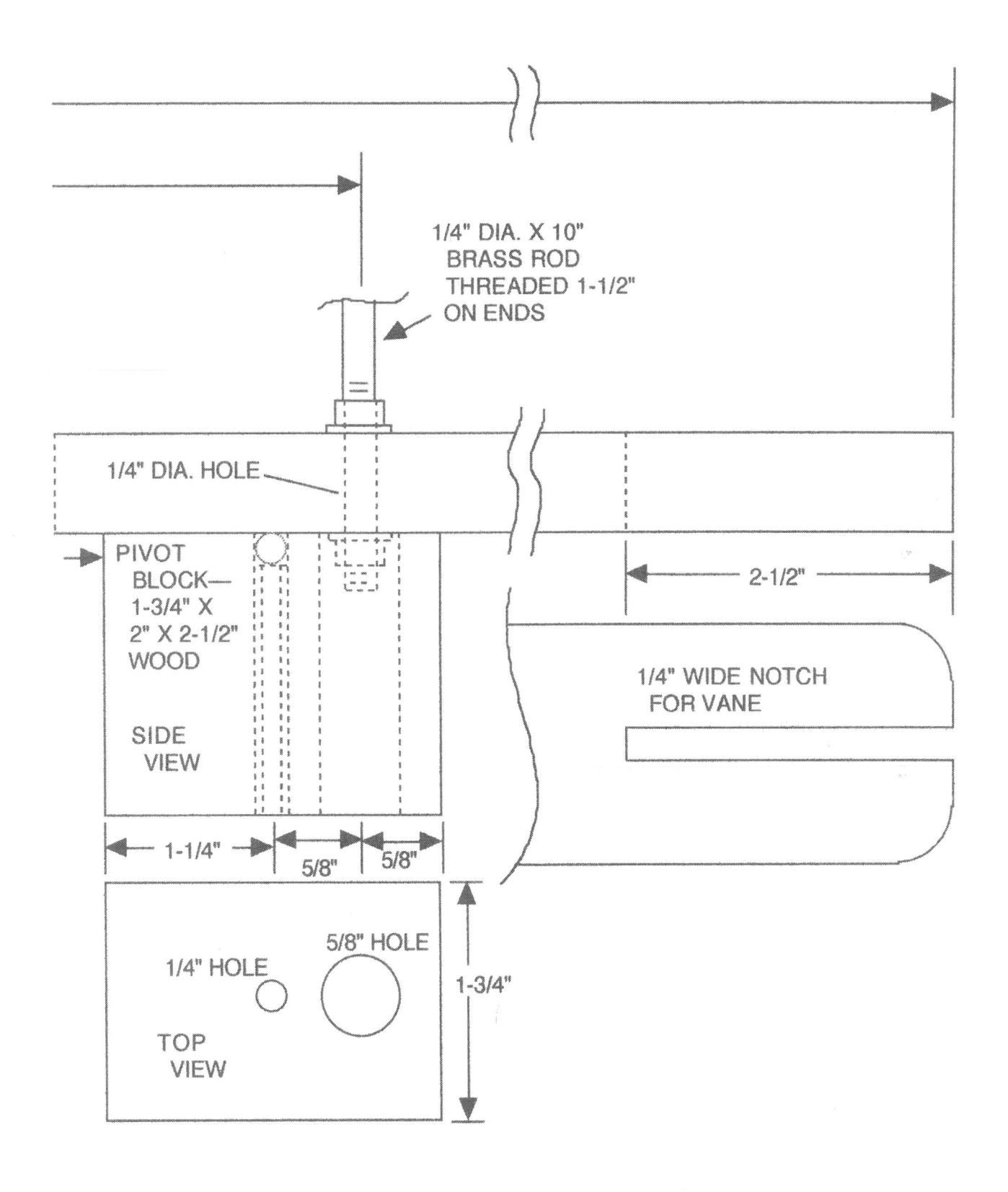

CAROUSEL

1/4" DIA. X 10"
BRASS ROD
THREADED 1-1/2"
ON ENDS

1/4" DIA. HOLE

PIVOT
BLOCK—
1-3/4" X
2" X 2-1/2"
WOOD

SIDE
VIEW

2-1/2"

1/4" WIDE NOTCH
FOR VANE

1-1/4"   5/8"   5/8"

1/4" HOLE   5/8" HOLE

1-3/4"

TOP
VIEW

109

THE WHIRLIGIG MAKER'S BOOK

Glue and nail the wood pivot block to the platform. Next, install a 1/4" diameter steel ball in the pivot hole. Then install the brass pivot tube, as shown.

Cut the vane from 1/4" plywood to the pattern shown. Glue the vane in the platform slot, as shown.

Sand the platform. The platform can be painted at this time, or you can wait until the assembly has been completed. The color scheme can be as desired.

PROPELLER AND SHAFT

The propeller shaft is made from 1/8" diameter x 6-1/4" brass rod. Make threads for 1-3/4" on one end of the rod and 1" on the other end using a 6-32 die. Slip the crankshaft into the holes in the mounting brackets. Install spacers, washers, nuts and drive wheel on shaft. The shaft should turn freely in the tube with no binding. Apply light oil to the shaft to further decrease friction.

The propeller hub is made from 3/4" x 1-1/2" x 1-1/2" wood. Drill a 1/8" shaft hole. Cut the 3/16" wide x 1/2" deep notches for the propeller blades at 45 degree angles to the face of the hub. Notice that a clockwise propeller is used so that the horses and riders will circle forward.

Cut the propeller blades from 3/16" wood or plywood to the pattern shown. Then glue the blades in the slots in the hub. Place the hub on a flat surface with the forward side down. The blades are then installed with the forward side flush with the flat surface.

Install the propeller on the shaft, as shown. Secure the propeller with a washer and two nuts.

Test the assembly in front of a fan to make certain that the propeller and shaft assembly works properly.

PLATFORM WHEEL ASSEMBLY

The platform wheel has a floor and roof connected by posts. The floor and roof are 8" diameter circles cut from 1/4" plywood. They can be cut out with a hand coping saw or power scroll or band saw, or a fly circle cutter or other circle cutting device can be used.

A 3/8" diameter hole is drilled through the exact centers for the brass lamp fittings. Matching 1/4" holes are drilled in the floor and roof, as shown on the pattern. Four 3/16" diameter holes are made in the floor only.

Four 1/4" diameter x 6-1/2" hardwood dowels are then installed and glued in place in the floor and roof holes, as shown. Decorative 5/8" diameter wood balls are glued to the tops of the posts.

The 8" inside diameter embroidery hoop is glued in place to the upper platform, as shown.

Brass lamp fittings with 17/64" diameter holes are installed in the floor and roof, as shown. The platform wheel can then be painted or a clear finish applied, as desired.

HORSES AND RIDERS

The patterns for the horses and riders for the carousel are shown. The bodies for the horses and riders are cut from 1/2" thick wood. Make two with boy riders and two with girl riders. Mark the patterns on the wood. Then drill the 3/16" diameter holes for the poles in the wood before doing the cutting. The drilling must be done accurately to avoid splitting the wood and to have the holes exactly vertical.

Cut the bodies of the horses and riders to the patterns. Sand the figures. Saw the arms and legs from 1/8" plywood to the patterns shown. then glue the arms and legs to the bodies. If desired the legs of the horses can be placed in different positions on each side of the same horse and in different positions on each horse.

The horses and riders can be painted as desired. As a general rule, use bright and contrasting colors and keep the details simple.

Glue the 3/16" diameter hardwood dowel poles in the horses so that they extend 1-3/4" below the horse bodies. Then glue the lower ends of the poles in the platform wheel floor with the horses and riders facing forward in the direction of rotation of the wheel.

Install the platform wheel over the vertical shaft. Thread the macramé bead over the threads on the upper end of the shaft.

CAROUSEL

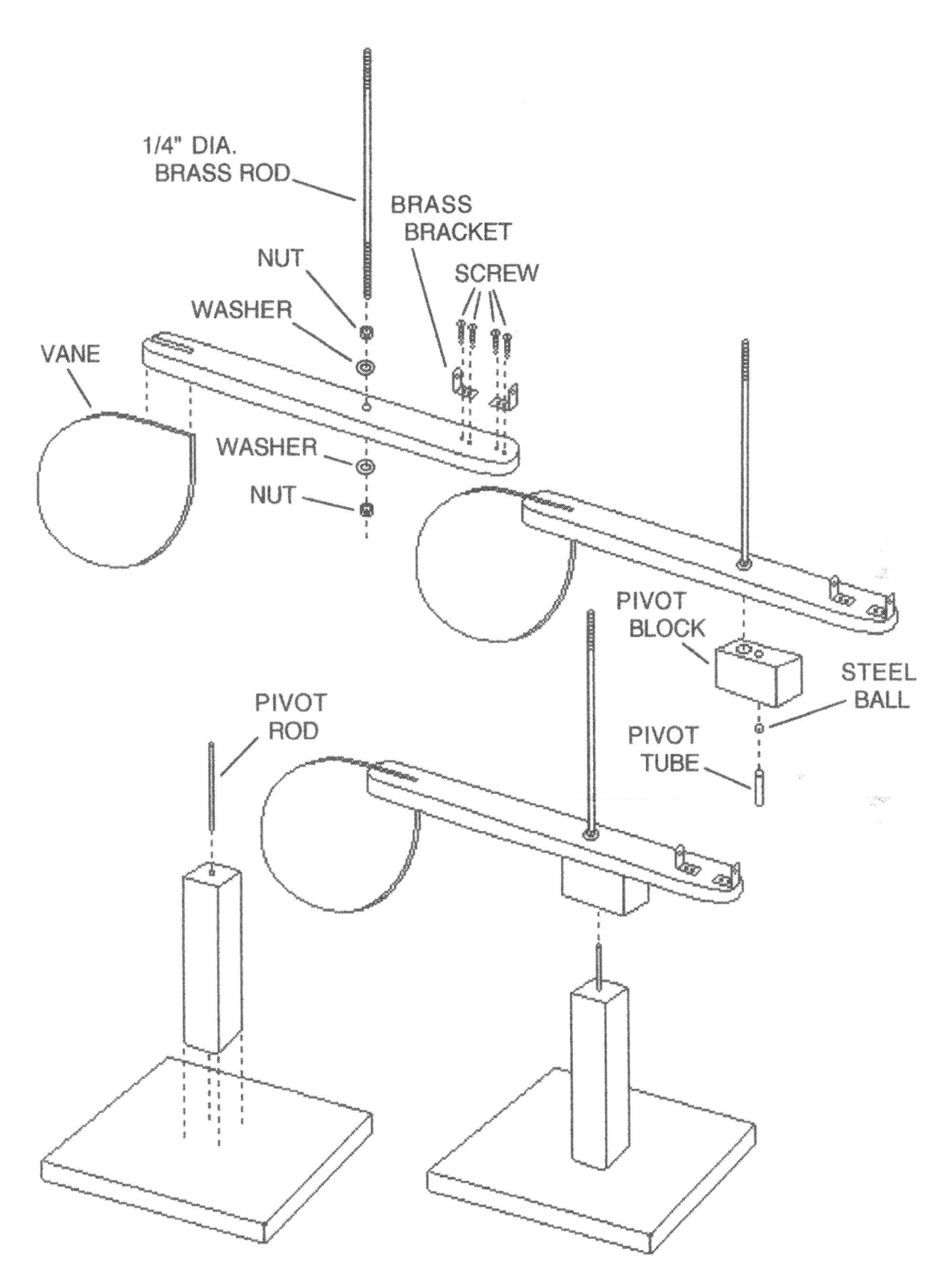

Assembly of base and platform.

111

THE WHIRLIGIG MAKER'S BOOK

ASSEMBLY OF PROPELLER

PROPELLER BLADE—
3/16" WOOD OR PLYWOOD
(4 REQUIRED)

3"

3"

7-1/2"

1-1/4"

PROPELLER HUB—3/4" WOOD (1 REQUIRED)

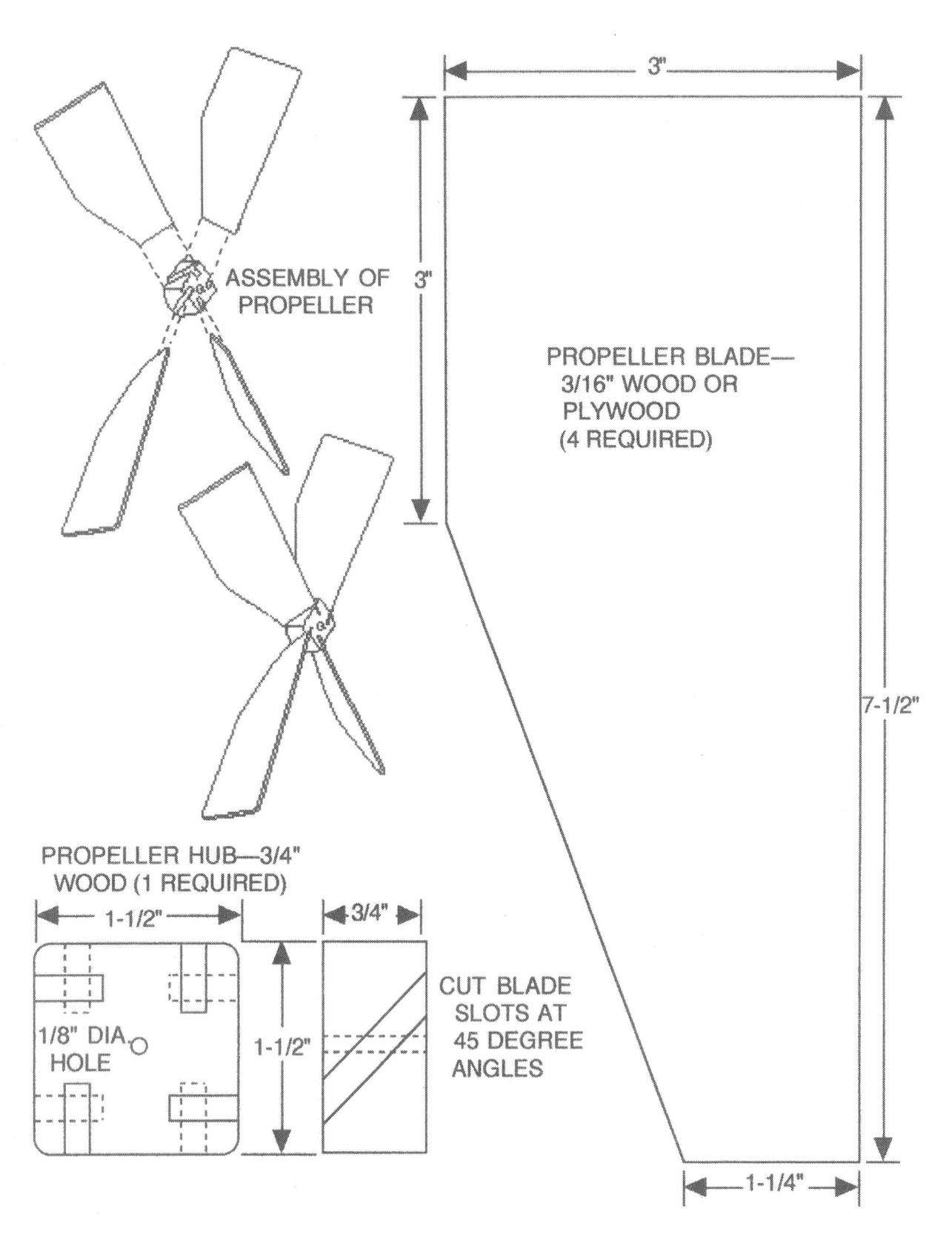

1-1/2"

1/8" DIA HOLE

3/4"

1-1/2"

CUT BLADE SLOTS AT 45 DEGREE ANGLES

Full-size patterns for propeller blades and hub.

112

CAROUSEL

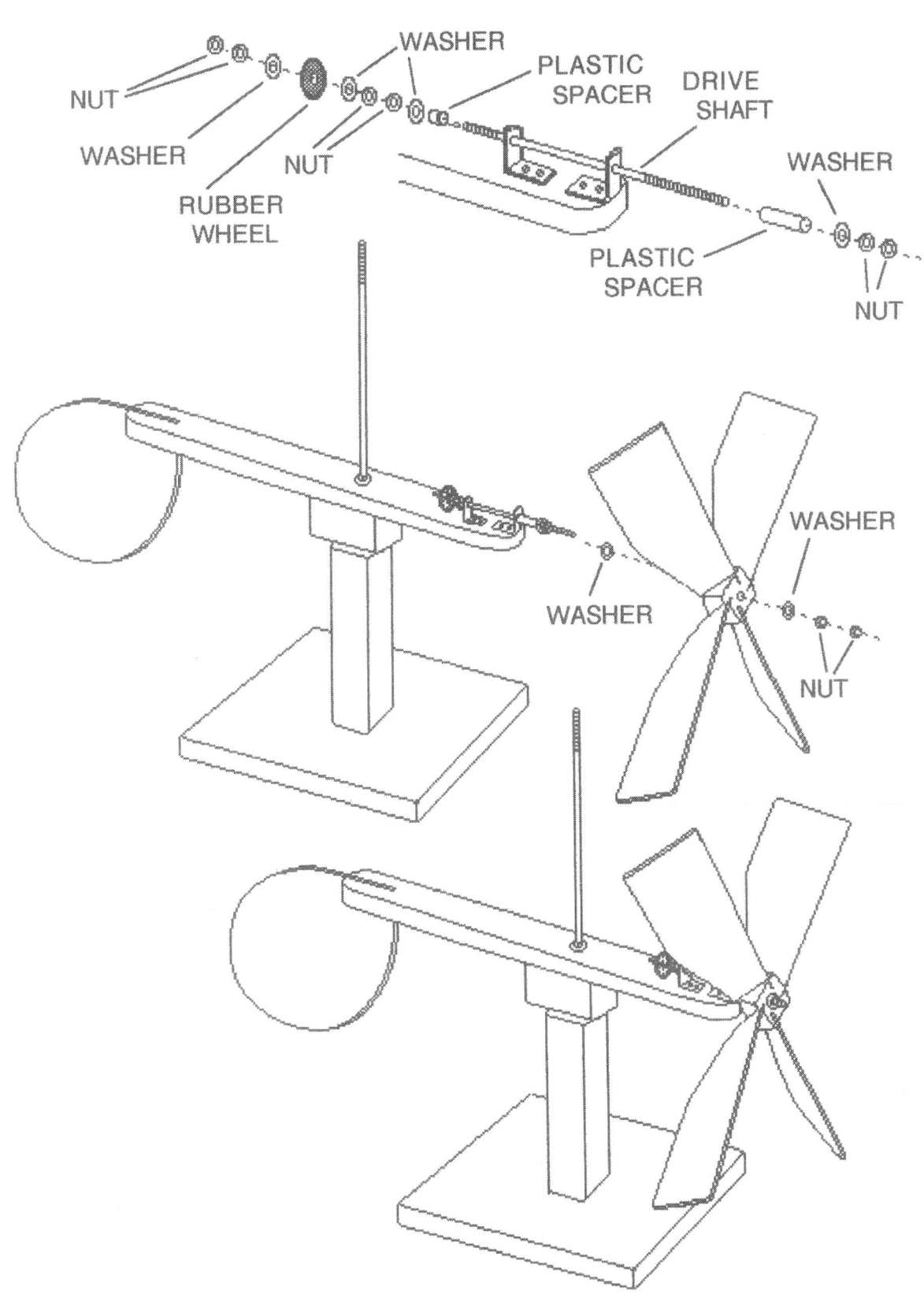

Assembly of propeller shaft.

113

THE WHIRLIGIG MAKER'S BOOK

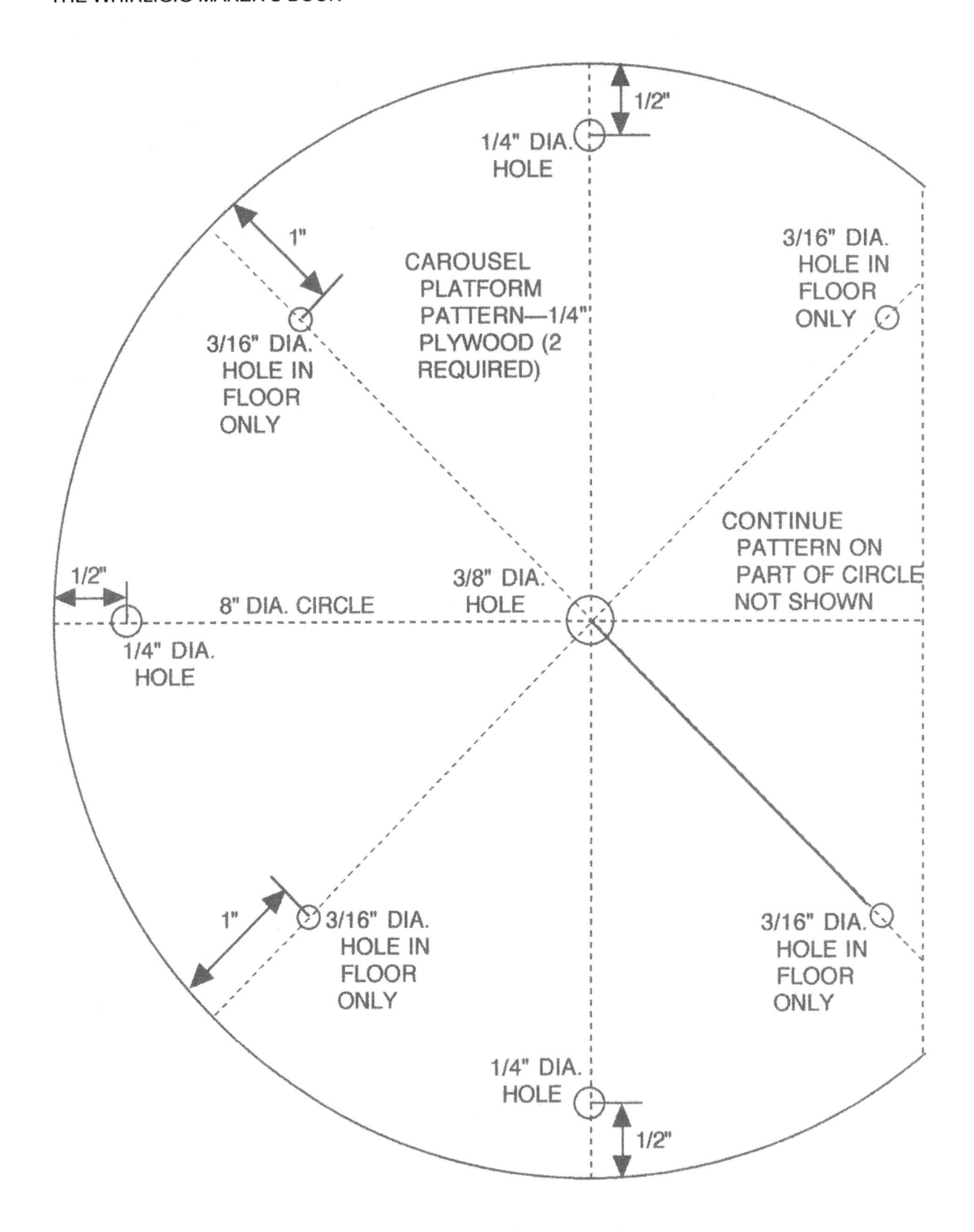

Full-size pattern for floor and roof.

CAROUSEL

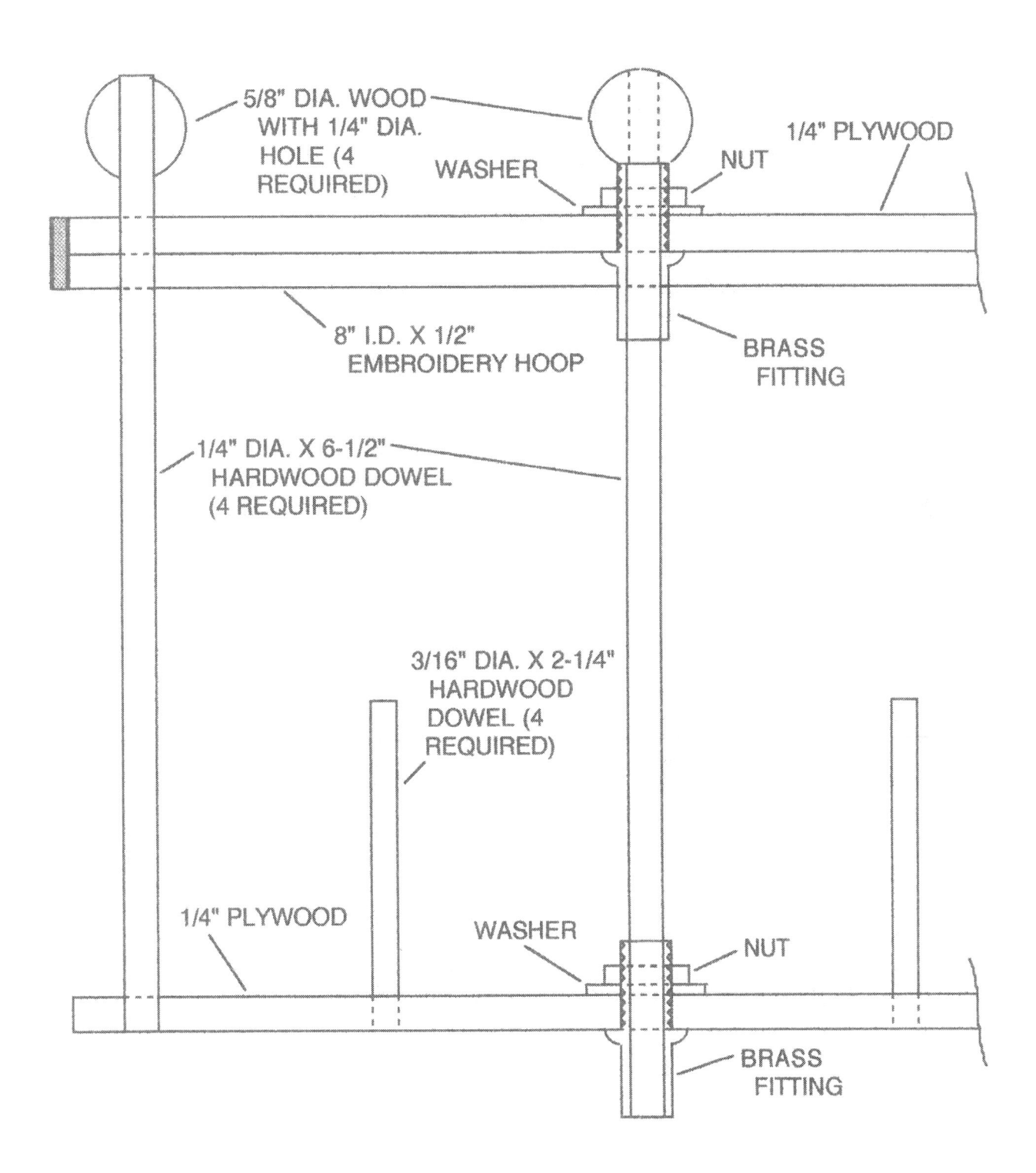

- 5/8" DIA. WOOD WITH 1/4" DIA. HOLE (4 REQUIRED)
- WASHER
- NUT
- 1/4" PLYWOOD
- 8" I.D. X 1/2" EMBROIDERY HOOP
- BRASS FITTING
- 1/4" DIA. X 6-1/2" HARDWOOD DOWEL (4 REQUIRED)
- 3/16" DIA. X 2-1/4" HARDWOOD DOWEL (4 REQUIRED)
- 1/4" PLYWOOD
- WASHER
- NUT
- BRASS FITTING

Assembly plan for platform wheel.

115

THE WHIRLIGIG MAKER'S BOOK

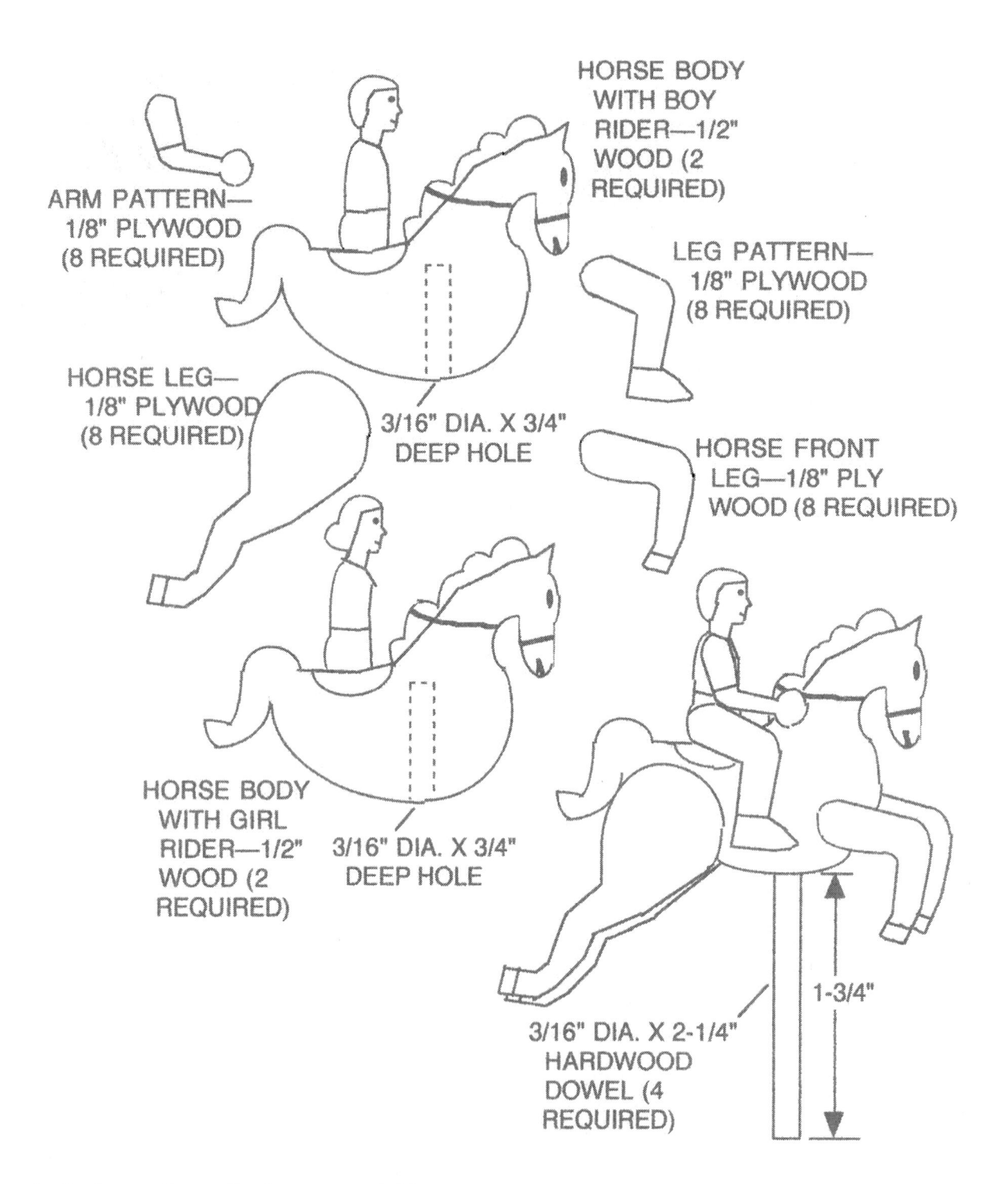

ARM PATTERN—
1/8" PLYWOOD
(8 REQUIRED)

HORSE BODY
WITH BOY
RIDER—1/2"
WOOD (2
REQUIRED)

LEG PATTERN—
1/8" PLYWOOD
(8 REQUIRED)

HORSE LEG—
1/8" PLYWOOD
(8 REQUIRED)

3/16" DIA. X 3/4"
DEEP HOLE

HORSE FRONT
LEG—1/8" PLY
WOOD (8 REQUIRED)

HORSE BODY
WITH GIRL
RIDER—1/2"
WOOD (2
REQUIRED)

3/16" DIA. X 3/4"
DEEP HOLE

3/16" DIA. X 2-1/4"
HARDWOOD
DOWEL (4
REQUIRED)

1-3/4"

Full-size patterns for horses and riders.

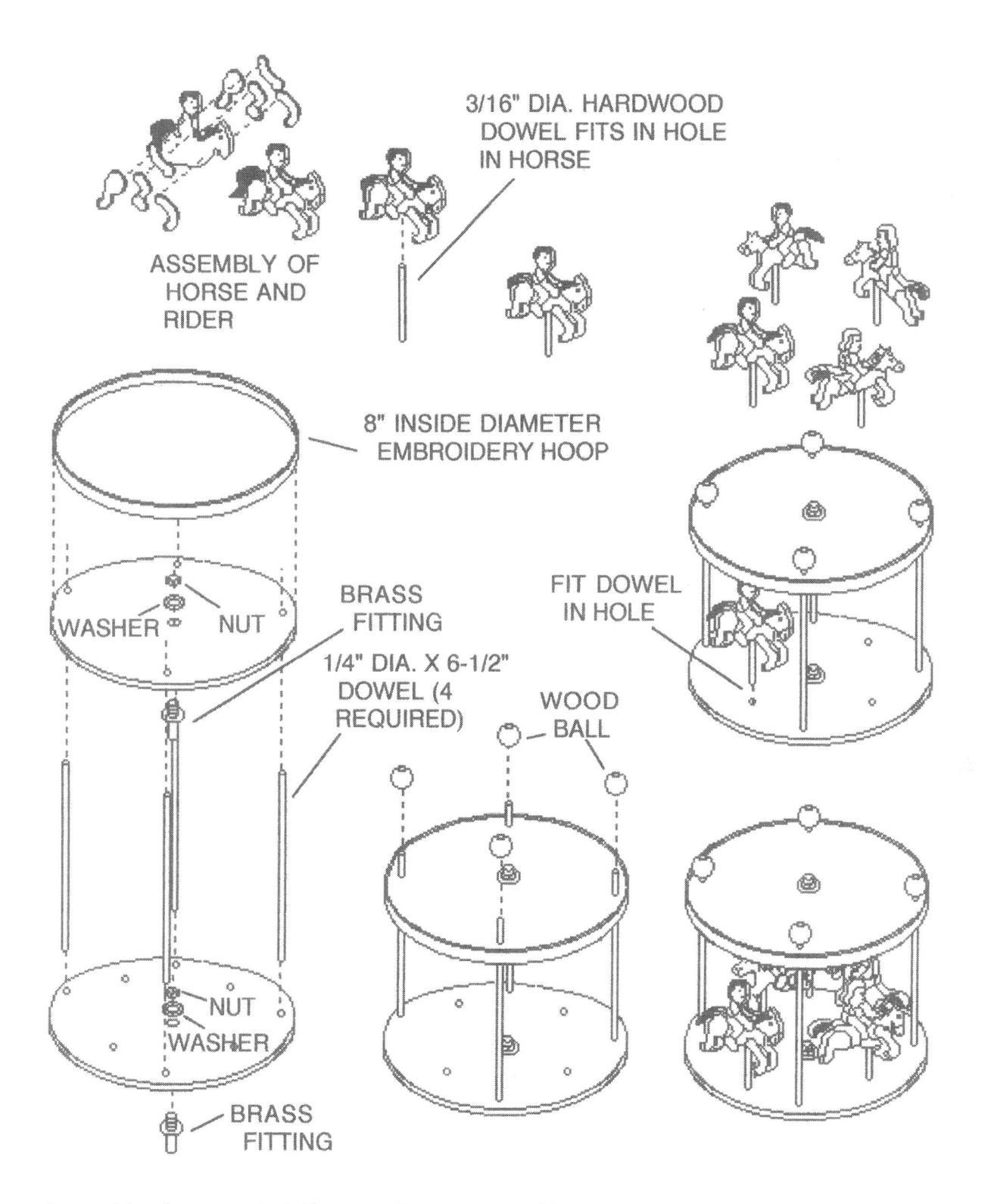

CAROUSEL

3/16" DIA. HARDWOOD DOWEL FITS IN HOLE IN HORSE

ASSEMBLY OF HORSE AND RIDER

8" INSIDE DIAMETER EMBROIDERY HOOP

WASHER NUT

BRASS FITTING

1/4" DIA. X 6-1/2" DOWEL (4 REQUIRED)

WOOD BALL

FIT DOWEL IN HOLE

NUT
WASHER

BRASS FITTING

Assembly of carousel platform and horses and riders.

117

MACRAME BEAD

Assembly of carousel to platform.

TESTING AND FINISHING

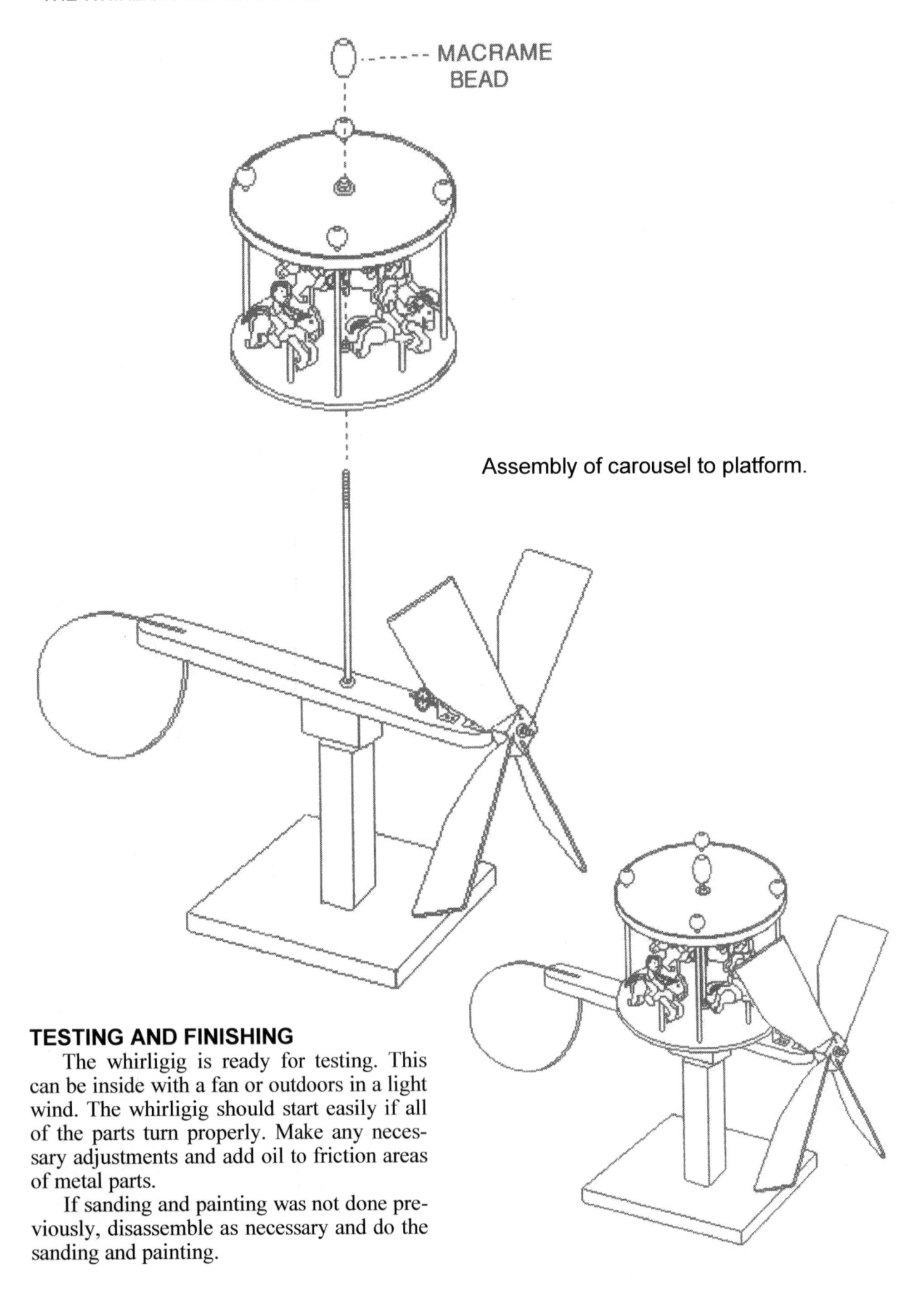

The whirligig is ready for testing. This can be inside with a fan or outdoors in a light wind. The whirligig should start easily if all of the parts turn properly. Make any necessary adjustments and add oil to friction areas of metal parts.

If sanding and painting was not done previously, disassemble as necessary and do the sanding and painting.

Chapter 11

KIDS ON TEETER-TOTTER

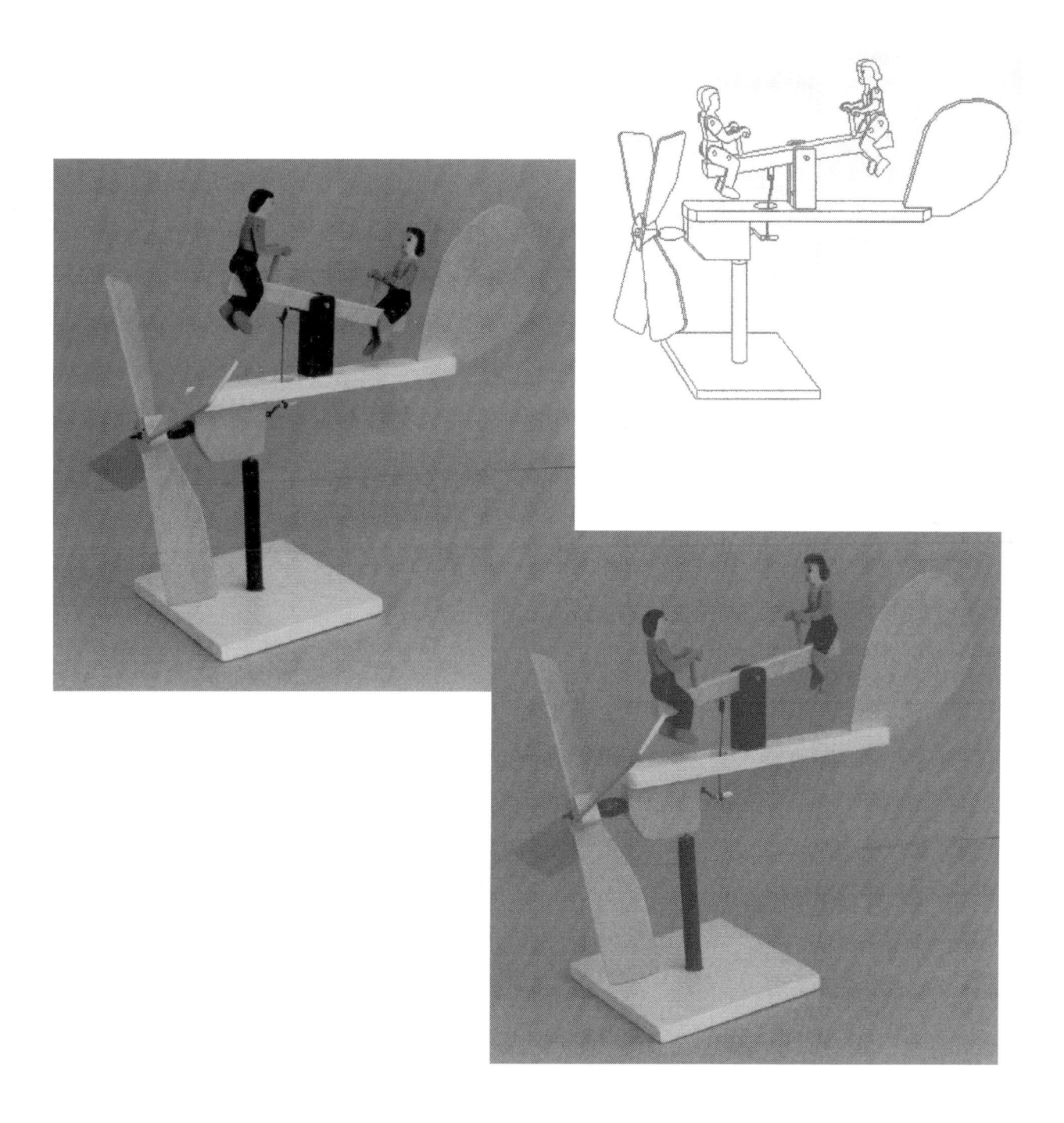

THE WHIRLIGIG MAKER'S BOOK

The Kids on Teeter-Totter whirligig is a fun project both to build and then watch perform after you have completed it.

MATERIALS

- 3/4" x 8-1/2" x 8-1/2" wood or plywood for display base.
- 3/4" diameter x 7" hardwood dowel for display post.
- 3/4" x 2" x 14" wood for platform.
- 1/2" x 3/4" x 1-1/4" wood for teeter-totter base block.
- 3/4" x 2-1/2" x 3-1/2" wood for propeller shaft and pivot block.
- 1/2" x 4-1/2" x 10" wood for teeter-totter plank and children's bodies.
- 1/4" x 7" x 8" plywood for vane.
- 3/16" x 4" x 12" wood or plywood for children's arms and legs.
- 1/4" x 1-1/4" x 8" wood for teeter-totter posts.
- 3/16" x 2-1/2" x 28" wood or plywood for propeller blades.
- 3/4" x 1-1/2" x 1-1/2" wood for propeller hub.
- 1/4" diameter x 6" hardwood dowel for teeter-totter pivot and hand posts.
- 3/16" diameter x 3" hardwood dowel for hand-hold rods.
- 7/8" diameter x 1-1/2" macramé bead with 1/4" diameter hole for propeller shaft tube.
- 1/4" outside diameter (9/64" inside diameter) x 7-1/2" brass tubing for shaft and pivot bearings.
- 1/8" diameter x 9-3/4" brass rod for crank shaft.
- 5/64" diameter x 6" stiff wire for connecting rod.
- 1/32" diameter x 18" stiff wire for attaching arms and legs to children's bodies.
- 1/4" diameter steel ball for pivot bearing.
- 6-32 nut (4 required) for attaching propeller hub to shaft.
- Washer (4 required) for use on propeller shaft.
- 1/8" diameter x 4" nail for pivot rod for display base.
- 1/16" x 1/4" x 1-1/2" brass strip for connecting rod bracket.
- Short lengths of plastic tubing for crank shaft and connecting rod spacers.
- Glue.
- Finishing nails.
- Small felt pad for display base (4 required).
- Paint.

DISPLAY STAND

The display stand is useful not only for displaying the finished whirligig indoors, but also for holding the whirligig during construction and for testing it in front of a fan. Construction is easy. The base is 3/4" x 8-1/2" x 8-1/2" wood or plywood. The 3/4" diameter x 7" hardwood dowel post is glued in a 3/4" diameter hole drilled in the center of the base. A 1/8" diameter x 4" nail is driven 2" into the center of the top of the post for use as a pivot rod. Drill a pilot hole that is perpendicular to the top of the post. Cut the head off of the nail with a hacksaw. File the upper end of the nail smooth, rounding the corners slightly.

Sand and paint the display stand. A clear or color finish can be used.

Attach felt pads to the corners of the underside of the base.

PLATFORM

The platform is made of 3/4" x 2" x 14" wood. Shape the ends, as shown. Drill a 1-3/8" diameter hole for the connecting rod and make a 1/4" x 2" slot for the vane. Attach a 1/2" x 3/4" x 1-1/4" base block for the teeter-totter posts to the platform in the position shown with glue and finishing nails.

The propeller shaft and pivot block is shaped from 3/4" x 2-1/2" x 3-1/2" wood to the pattern shown. Drill 1/4" holes for the propeller shaft tube and the pivot tube, as shown. The holes must be accurately centered and perpendicular to the wood surfaces for the whirligig to work properly. I use a drill press and drill press vise for drilling these holes.

Glue and nail the wood propeller shaft and pivot block to the platform. Then install the brass shaft tube. The tube should fit tightly in the hole so that it will not turn. Next, install a 1/4" diameter steel ball in the pivot

KIDS ON TEETER-TOTTER

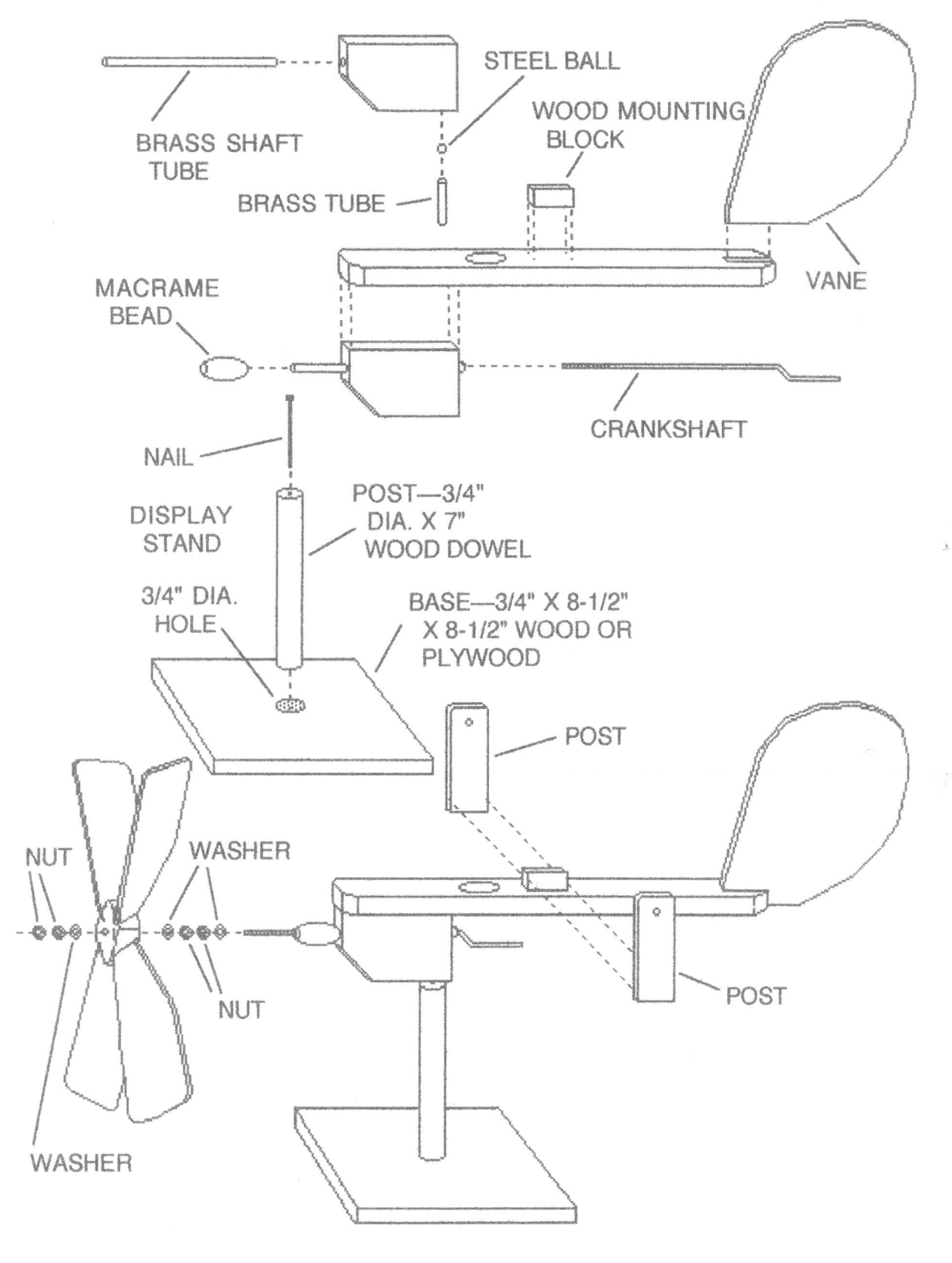

Platform and display stand assembly.

121

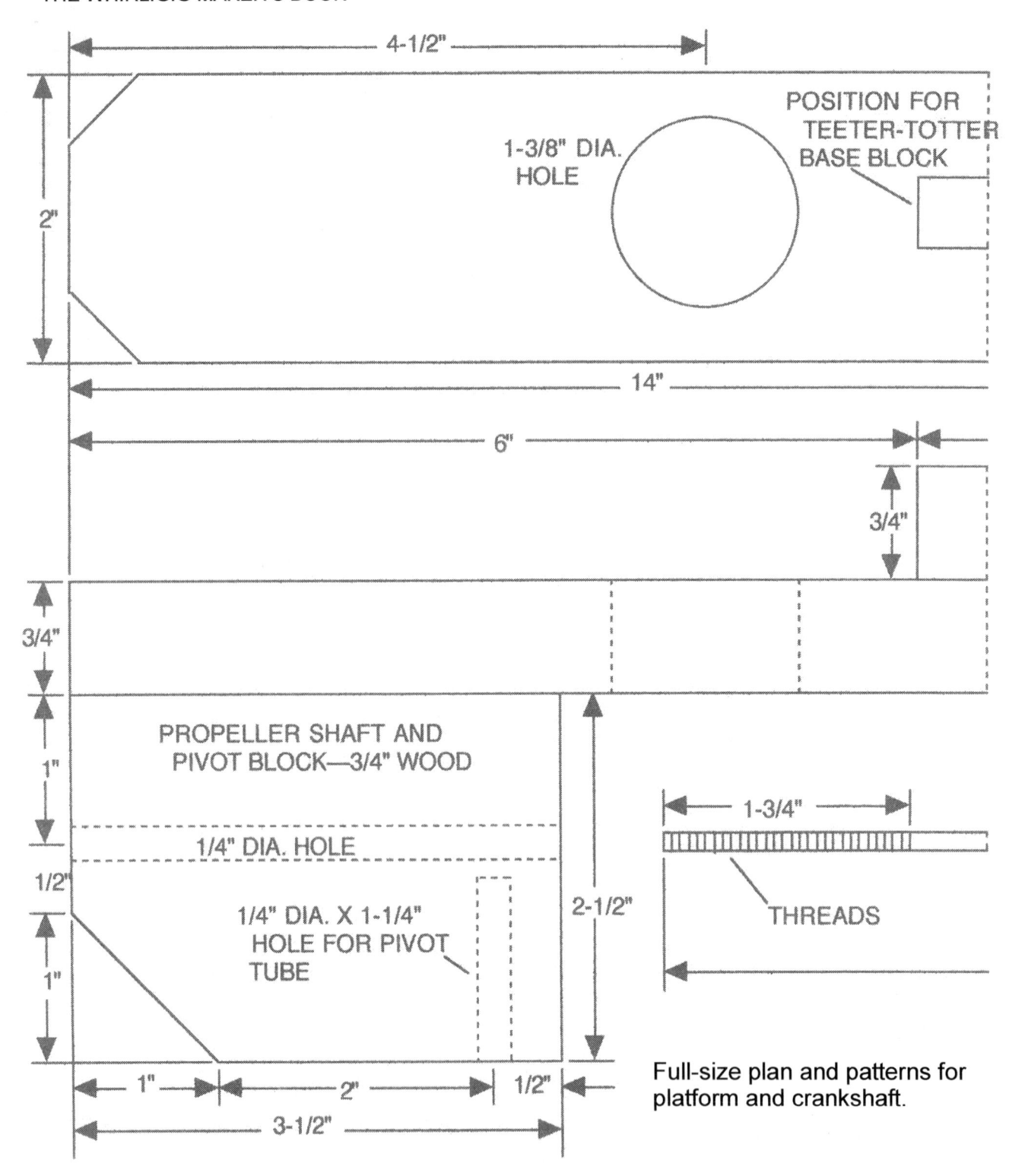

THE WHIRLIGIG MAKER'S BOOK

Full-size plan and patterns for platform and crankshaft.

hole. Then install the brass pivot tube, as shown.

Cut the vane from 1/4" plywood to the pattern shown. Glue the vane in the platform slot, as shown.

Sand the platform. The platform can be painted at this time, or you can wait until the assembly has been completed. The color scheme can be as desired.

KIDS ON TEETER-TOTTER

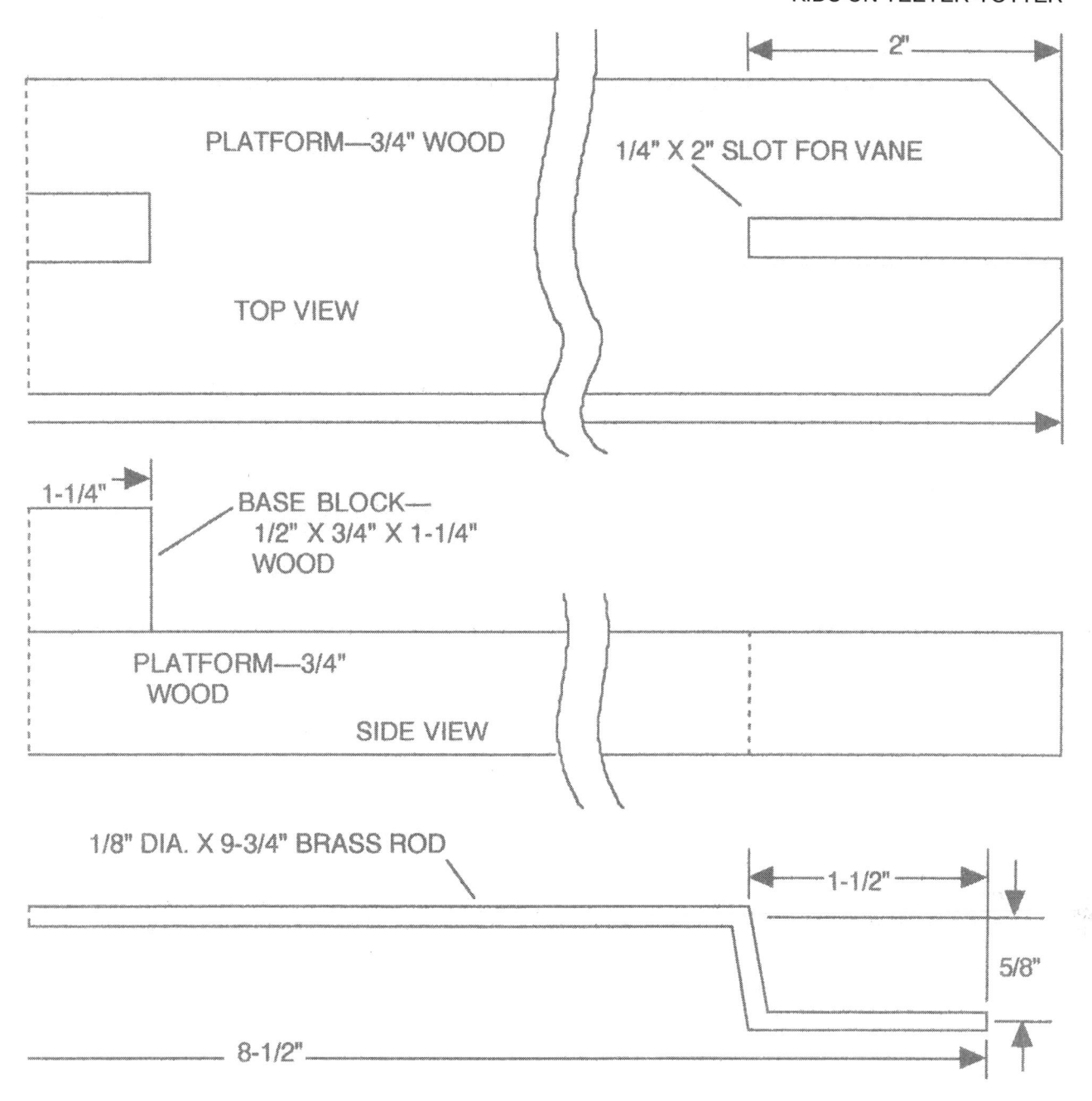

PROPELLER AND CRANKSHAFT

The crankshaft is made from 1/8" diameter x 9-3/4" brass rod. Make threads for 1-3/4" on one end of the rod using a 6-32 die. Bend the crank on the other end of the rod to the pattern shown. Slip the crankshaft into the shaft tube. The shaft should turn freely in the tube with no binding. Apply light oil to the shaft to further decrease friction.

The propeller hub is made from 3/4" x 1-1/2" x 1-1/2" wood. Drill a 1/8" shaft hole. Cut the 3/16" wide x 1/2" deep notches for the propeller blades at 45 degree angles to the face of the hub. A clockwise propeller is shown, but you can reverse the notches for a counterclockwise rotation if desired. The slots need to be made accurately for the whirligig to work properly.

Cut the propeller blades from 3/16" wood or plywood to the pattern shown.

Then glue the blades in the slots in the hub. Place the hub on a flat surface with the forward side down. The blades are then installed with the forward side flush with the flat surface.

123

THE WHIRLIGIG MAKER'S BOOK

PLATFORM

1/4" O.D. (9/64" I.D.) X 6-1/4" BRASS TUBING

SHAFT AND PIVOT BLOCK

1-1/2"

1/4" DIA. STEEL BALL

1/4" O.D. (9/64" I.D.) X 1-1/4" BRASS TUBING

Crankshaft and pivot tube assembly.

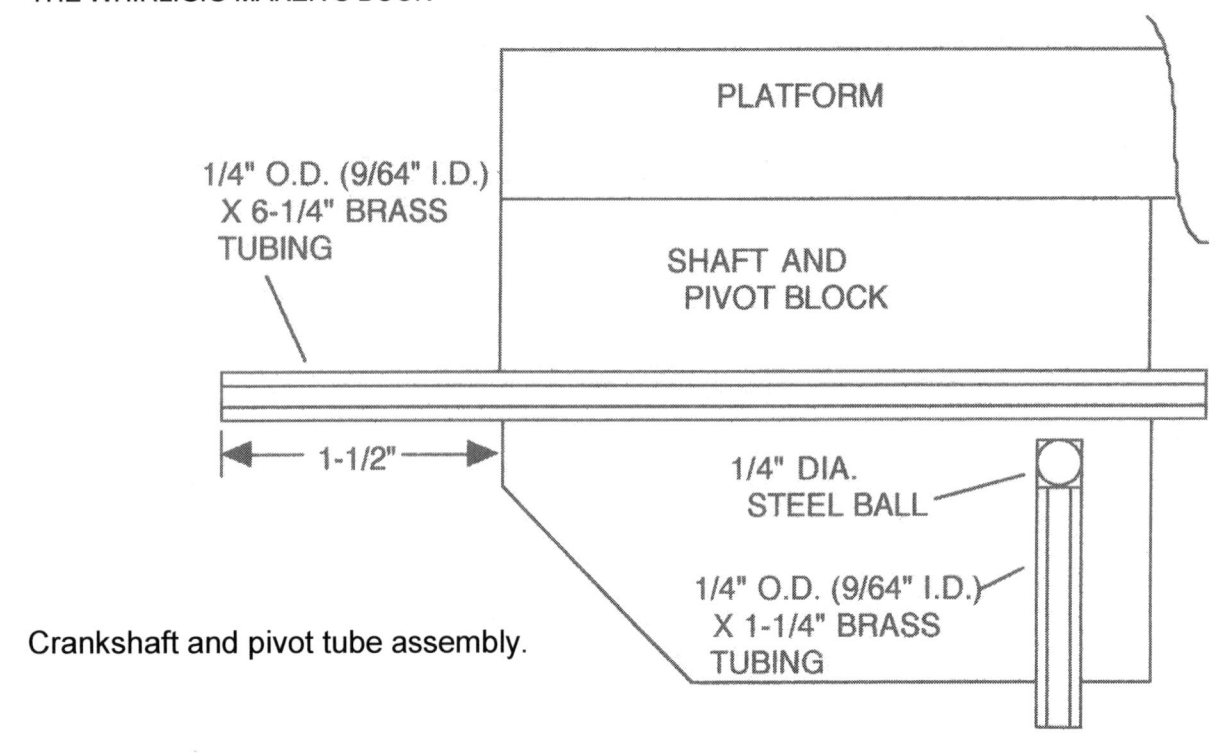

Install the macramé bead over the shaft tube. This is for decorative purposes only and can be omitted if desired. Install a washer and two nuts over the threaded end of the shaft, as shown. Then thread the propeller hub onto the shaft. Secure the propeller with a washer and two nuts.

Test the assembly in front of a fan to make certain that the propeller and shaft assembly works properly.

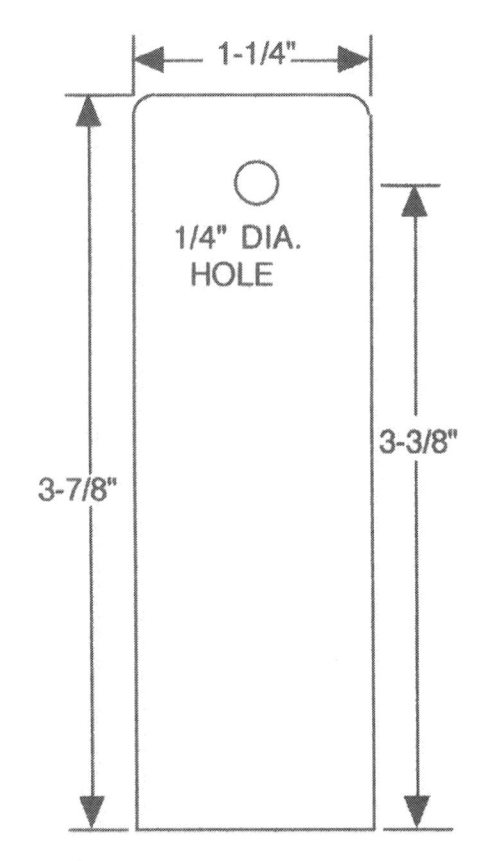

1-1/4"

1/4" DIA. HOLE

3-3/8"

3-7/8"

Pattern for teeter-totter posts.

KIDS ON TEETER-TOTTER

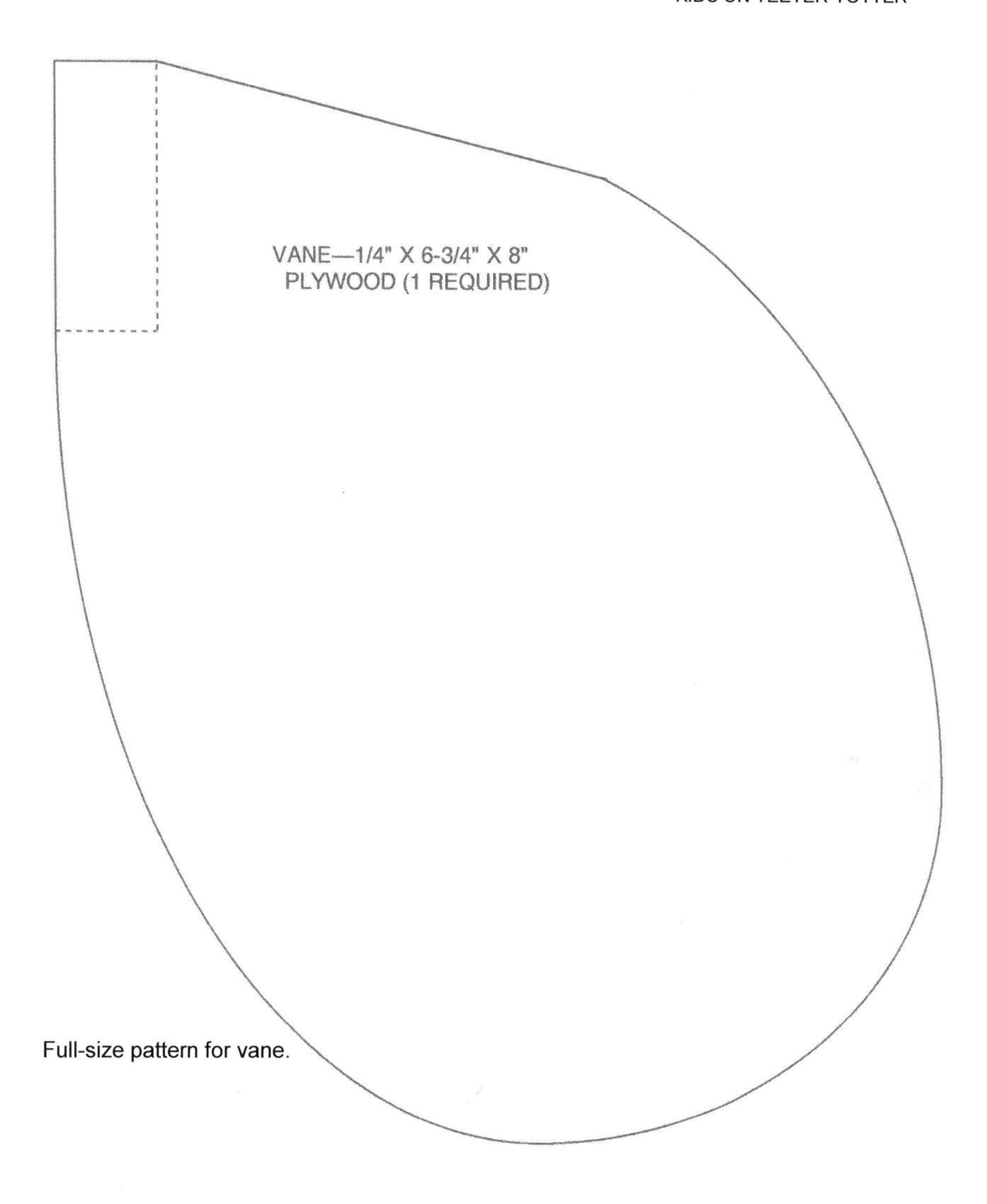

VANE—1/4" X 6-3/4" X 8"
PLYWOOD (1 REQUIRED)

Full-size pattern for vane.

THE WHIRLIGIG MAKER'S BOOK

ASSEMBLY OF PROPELLER

PROPELLER BLADE—
3/16" WOOD OR
PLYWOOD
(4 REQUIRED)

2-1/2"

3-1/2"

7"

1-1/4"

PROPELLER HUB—3/4"
WOOD (1 REQUIRED)

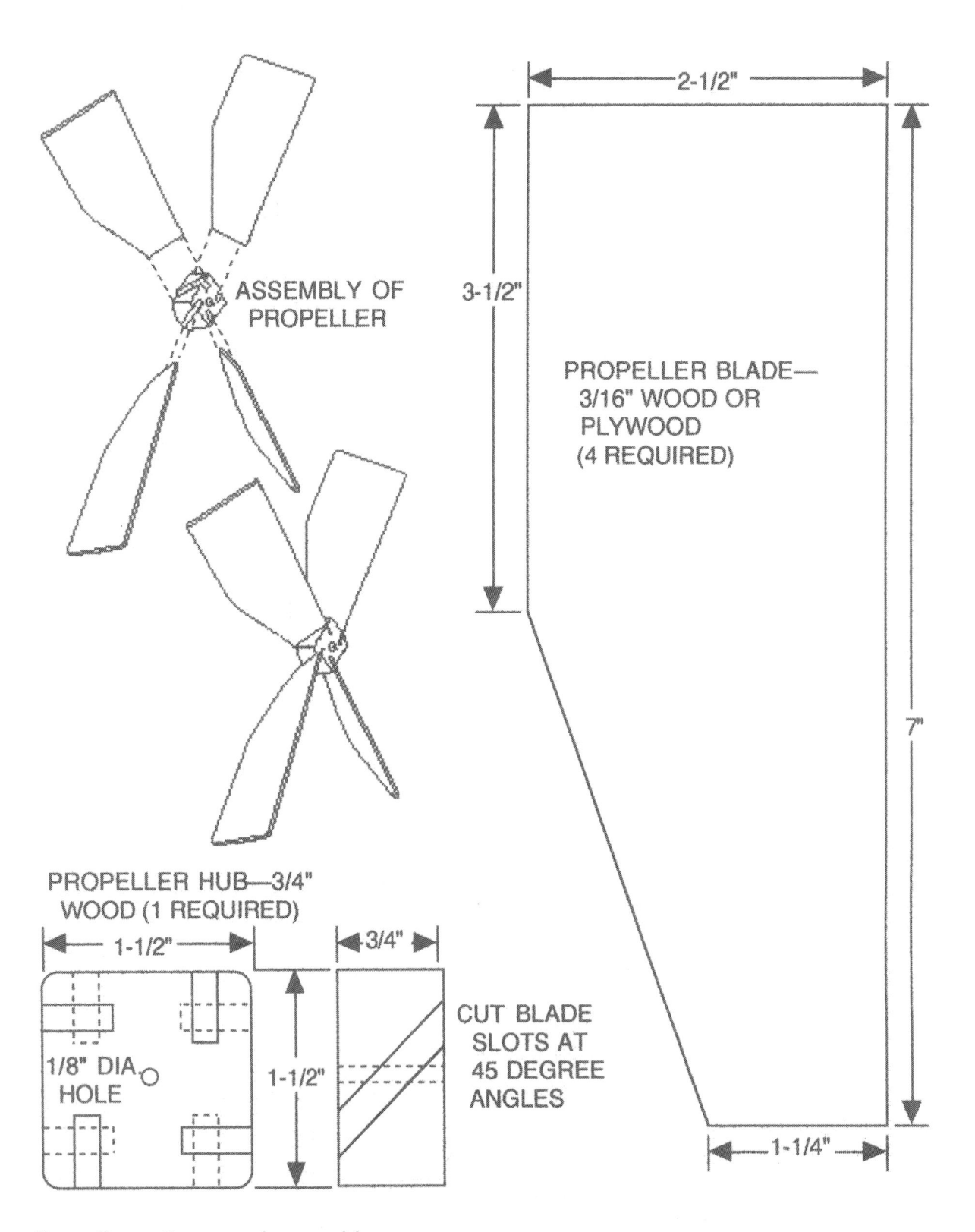

1-1/2"

1/8" DIA HOLE

1-1/2"

3/4"

CUT BLADE
SLOTS AT
45 DEGREE
ANGLES

Propeller patterns and assembly.

126

KIDS ON TEETER-TOTTER

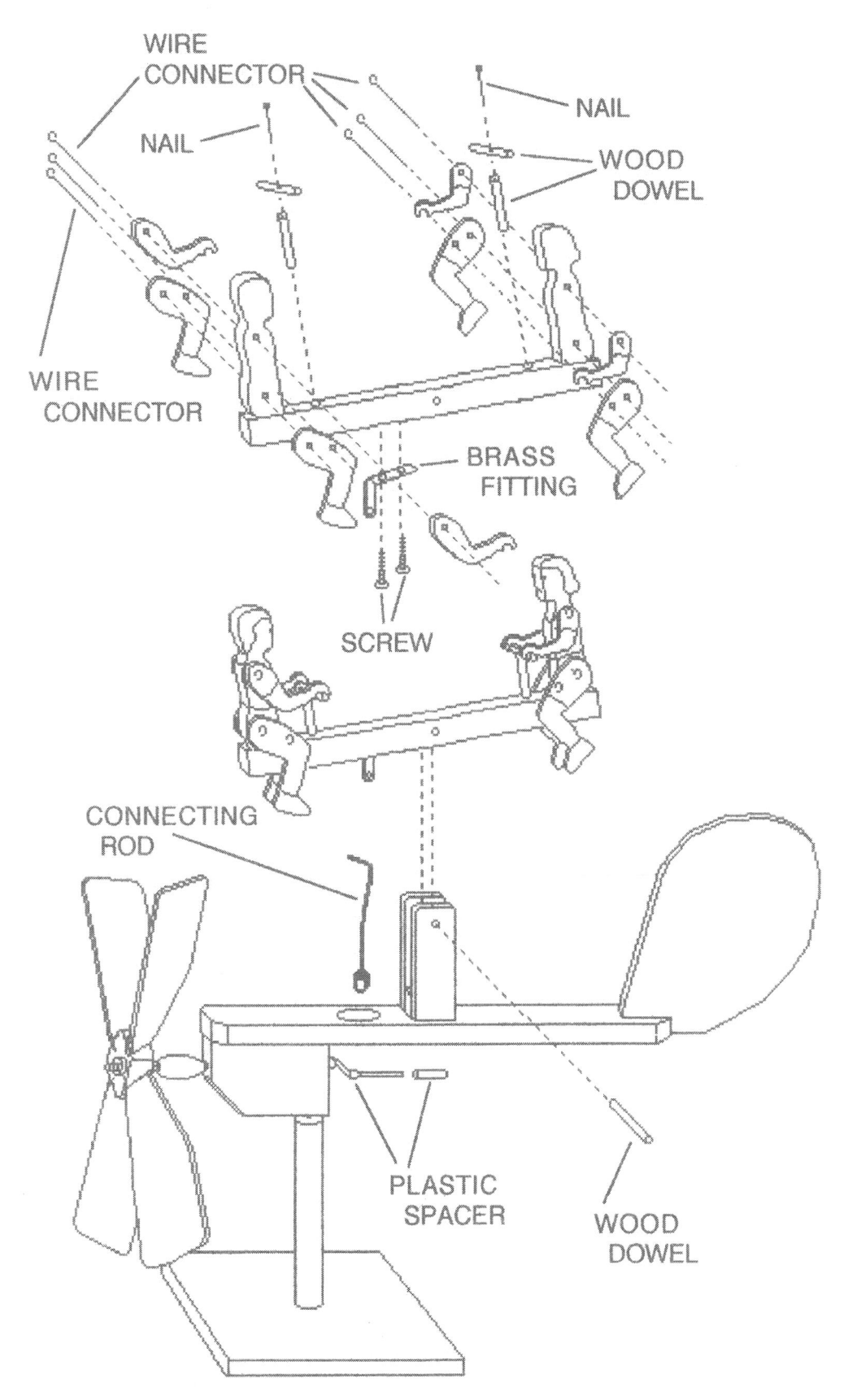

Assembly of children and teeter-totter.

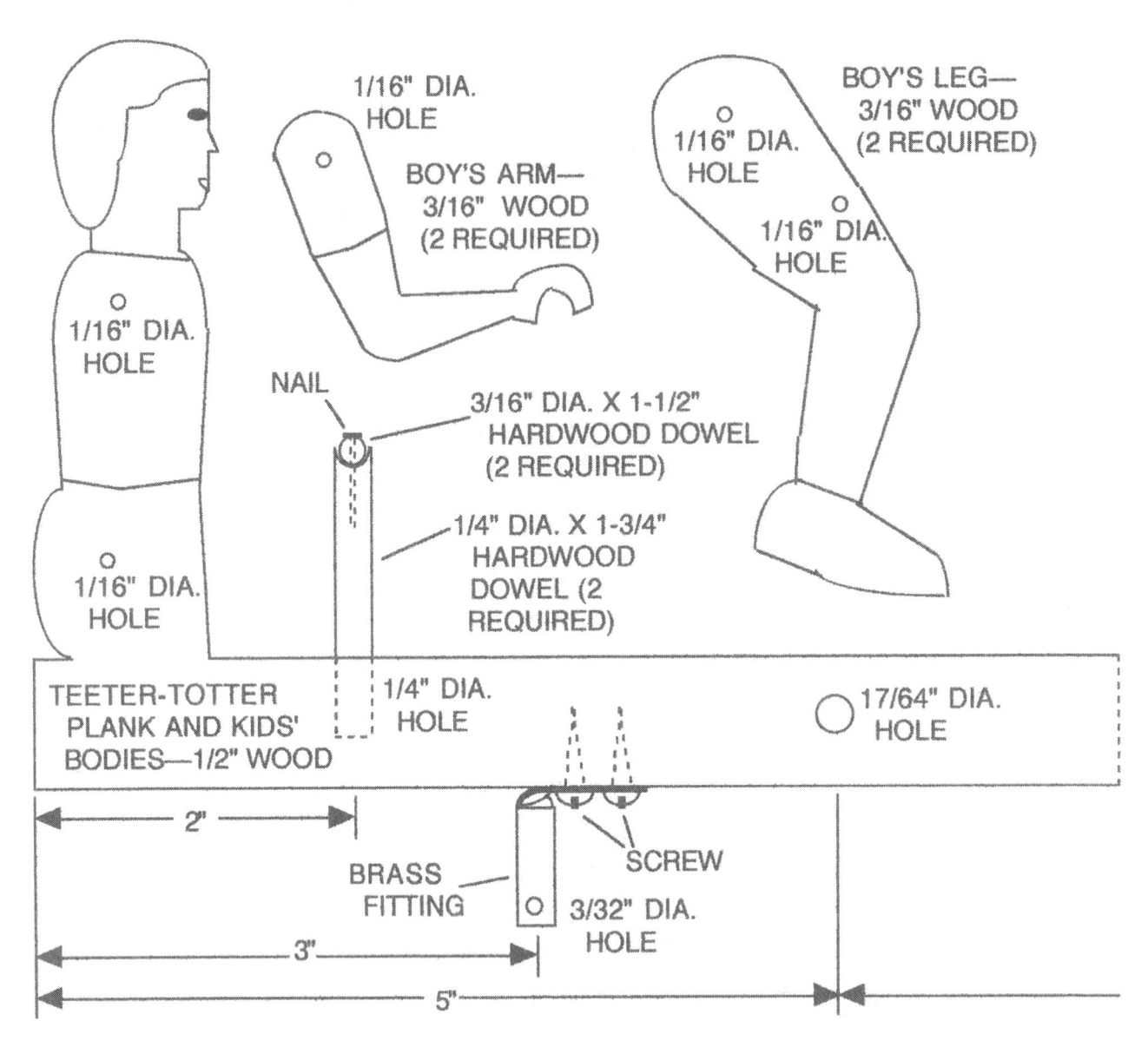

Full-size patterns for children and teeter-totter plank.

TEETER-TOTTER AND KIDS

Cut the teeter-totter posts to the patterns shown. Attach the posts to the mounting block with glue and finishing nails.

The teeter-totter plank and children's bodies are cut from 1/2" x 4-1/2" x 10" wood. Trace the pattern onto the wood. An alternate method is to use a 1/2" x 3/4" x 10" piece of wood for the plank. Then cut the children's bodies separately and attach them to the plank with glue and wood dowel pegs. Regardless of the method used, drill 1/16" wire holes in the bodies in the positions

shown. Drill a 17/64" hole in the center of the plank for the pivot dowel and 1/4" diameter holes for the hand-hold posts.

Assemble the hand-hold posts and rods as shown. Drill small pilot holes for the nails. Glue the posts in the mounting holes in the teeter-totter plank.

Shape a brass fitting for the connecting rod and attach it to the bottom of the teeter-totter plank, as shown. An alternate method is to use a small securely in the underside of the plank for the connecting rod attachment.

Connect the teeter-totter plank to the

KIDS ON TEETER-TOTTER

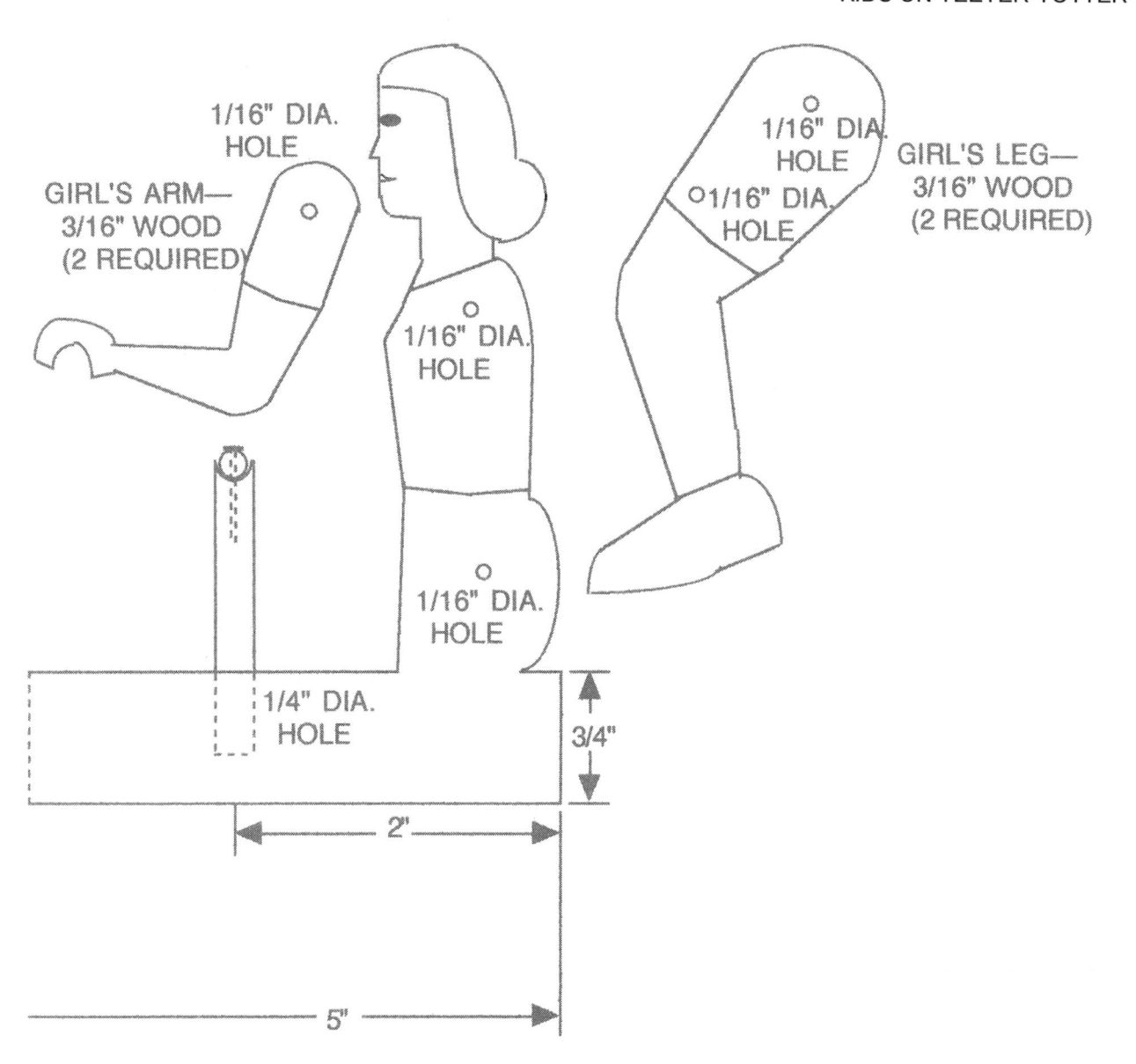

GIRL'S ARM—
3/16" WOOD
(2 REQUIRED)

1/16" DIA. HOLE

1/16" DIA. HOLE

1/16" DIA. HOLE

1/16" DIA. HOLE

GIRL'S LEG—
3/16" WOOD
(2 REQUIRED)

1/16" DIA. HOLE

1/4" DIA. HOLE

3/4"

2"

5"

posts with the wood dowel. The teeter-totter plank should pivot freely. If not, remove the wood dowel and sand areas that cause the binding. Apply paraffin wax to the center section of the hardwood dowel.

Cut the arms and legs to the patterns shown. Drill 1/16" diameter holes in the positions shown for the mounting wires. The painting can be done at this time, or you can do a trial assembly and then disassemble for painting later. The arms and legs are then attached to the children's bodies with wires. Bend loop rings in the ends of the wires.

The connecting rod is shaped from 15/64" diameter x 6" stiff wire. Bend a wire loop around a 1/8" diameter rod. Circle the rod twice, making a tight circle. The eye fits over the crankshaft between two plastic spacers. The wire connecting rod passes through the hole in the platform and is connected to the brass fitting (or eye screw) on the teeter-totter plank. Bend the wire so that the teeter-totter plank will be level when the crank is in a horizontal position to one side. Pass the wire through the eye and then secure it with a piece of plastic tubing that fits tightly over the end of the wire connecting rod, or bend a loop in the wire. The loop must be a fairly close fit, but not so tight that binding will occur.

Assembled whirligig.

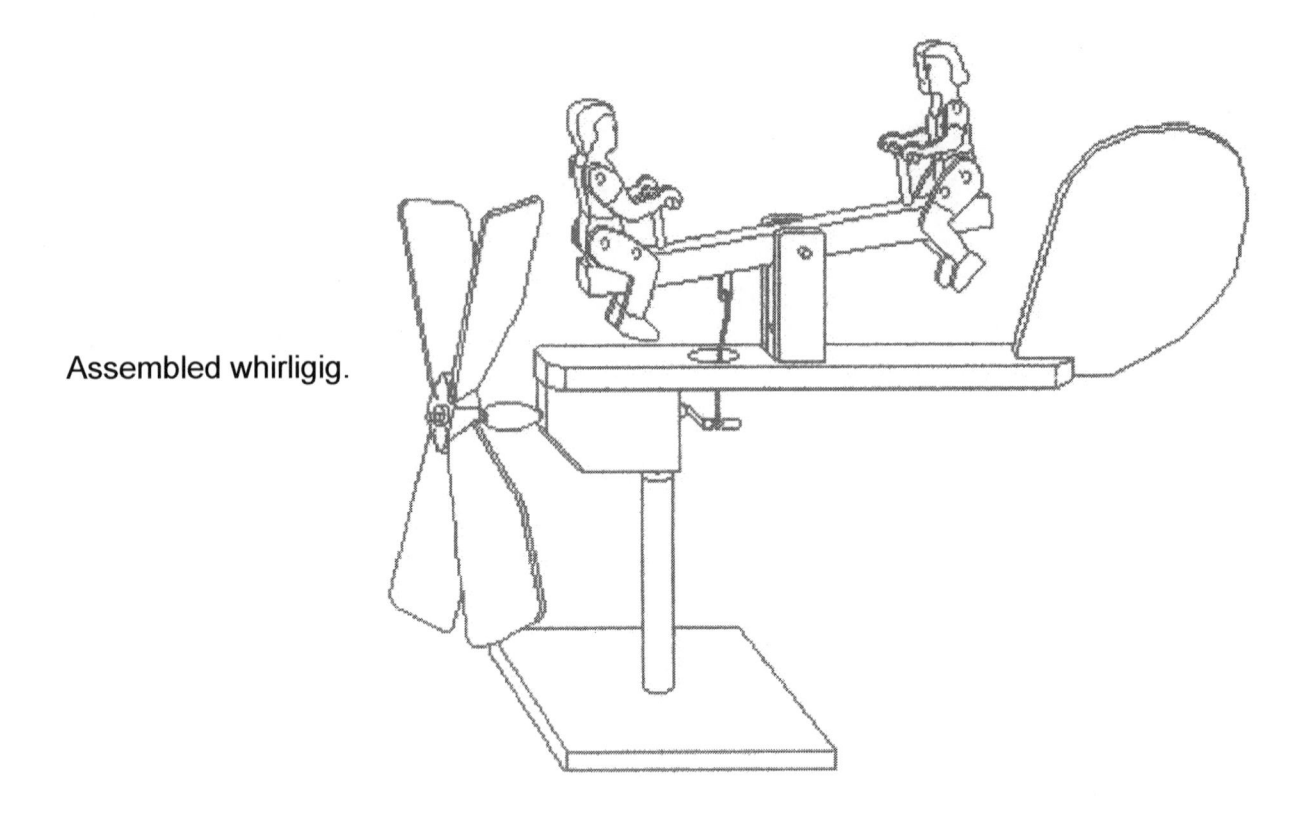

TESTING AND FINISHING

The whirligig is ready for testing. This can be inside with a fan or outdoors in a light wind. The whirligig should start easily if all of the parts turn properly. Make any necessary adjustments and add oil to friction areas of metal parts.

If sanding and painting was not done previously, disassemble as necessary and do the sanding and painting.

Chapter 12

TRAMPOLINE

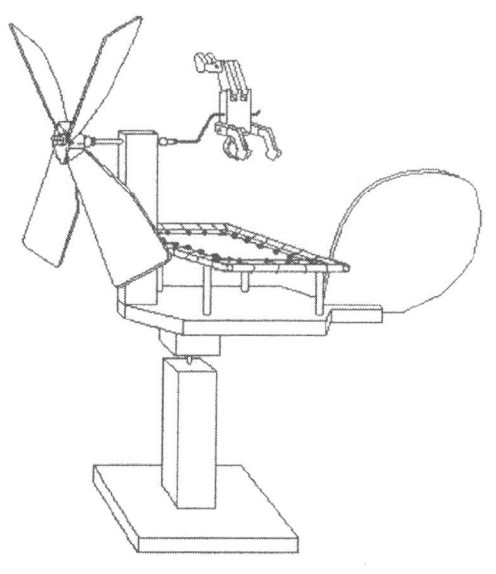

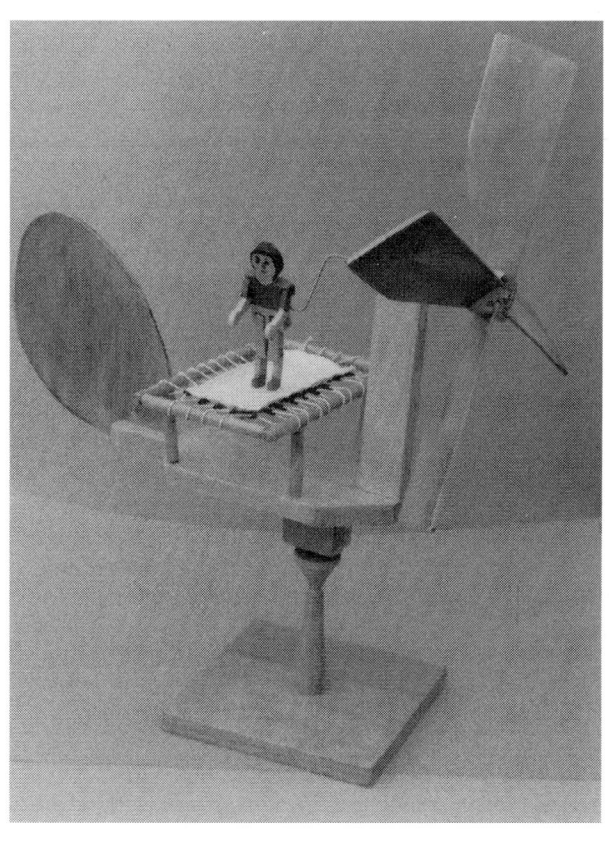

The Trampoline whirligig has a performer who does a realistic backward somersault on a trampoline that's fun to watch. The performer's body is fixed to the crankshaft, which creates the jumping and somersaulting action as the propeller turns. The unique pivoting action of the arms and legs adds to the total effect.

MATERIALS

- 3/4" x 8" x 8" wood or plywood for display base.
- 1-1/2" x 1-1/2" x 6" wood for display post.
- 3/4" x 1-1/2" x 8" wood for propeller shaft post.
- 3/4" x 5-1/2" x 12" wood for platform.
- 1/4" x 7" x 8" plywood for vane.
- 1-1/2" x 1-1/2" x 2" wood for pivot block.
- 3/16" x 6" x 15" wood or plywood for propeller blades.
- 3/4" x 1-1/2" x 1-1/2" wood for propeller hub.
- 1/2" x 1-1/4" x 4" wood for performer's body.
- 3/16" x 2" x 4" wood or plywood for arms.
- 3/8" x 1/2" x 3" wood for upper legs.
- 1/4" x 3/4" x 3" wood for lower legs.
- 1/16" x 2" x 5" plywood for covers for back, shoulders, and front of upper legs.
- 3/16" x 1" x 1" wood for propeller counterweight holder.
- 3/8" diameter x 44" hardwood dowel for trampoline frame.
- 3/16" outside diameter (7/64" inside diameter) x 3-1/8" brass tubing for shaft bearing.
- 3/32" diameter x 12" brass rod for crank shaft.
- 1/4" outside diameter (9/64" inside diameter) x 1-1/2" brass tube for pivot bearing.
- 1/32" diameter x 8" stiff wire for attaching arms to body and upper and lower legs together and to body.
- 1/4" diameter steel ball for pivot bearing.
- 4-40 nut (2 required) for attaching propeller hub to shaft.
- Washer (4 required) for use on propeller shaft.
- 1/8" diameter x 4" nail for pivot rod for display base.
- 3/32" inside diameter x 1/2" plastic tubing for crankshaft spacer.
- 3/8" diameter wood ball with 3/32" hole (2 required) for crankshaft spacers and decorations.
- Slug weight approximately 1/4" diameter x 3/16" thick (weight and size may vary depending on particular whirligig).
- 5" x 10" soft cloth for trampoline bed.
- Shoelace for trampoline bed loops.
- Round elastic cord for lacing trampoline bed to frame.
- Thread for sewing shoelace to cloth trampoline bed.
- Glue.
- Epoxy glue.
- Finishing nails.
- Small felt pad for display base (4 required).
- Paint.

DISPLAY STAND

The display stand is useful not only for displaying the finished whirligig indoors, but also for holding the whirligig during construction and for testing it in front of a fan. Construction is easy. The base is 3/4" x 8" x 8" wood or plywood. The 1-1/2" x 1-1/2" x 6" post is glued and nailed (use finishing nails from underside) to the center of one side of the base. A 1/8" diameter x 4" nail is driven 2" into the center of the top of the post for use as a pivot rod. Make certain that the nail is driven perpendicular to the top of the post. Cut the head off of the nail with a hacksaw. File the upper end of the nail smooth, rounding the corners slightly.

Sand and paint the display stand. A clear or color finish can be used.

Attach felt pads to the corners of the underside of the base.

TRAMPOLINE

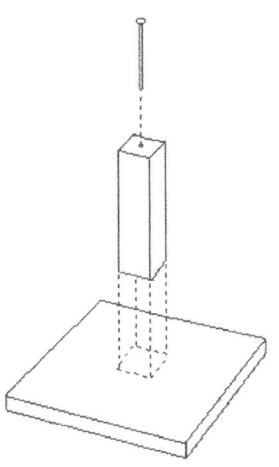

Assembly of display stand.

PLATFORM AND TRAMPOLINE FRAME

The platform is made of 3/4" x 5-1/2" x 12" wood. Mark the pattern shown on the wood. Drill the four 3/8" holes through the wood in the locations shown. Then cut the wood to the pattern. Make a 1/4" x 2-1/2" slot for the vane.

The pivot block is a separate piece of wood attached to the underside of the platform. Cut the block to the pattern shown and drill a 1/4" diameter x 1-1/4" hole for the steel ball and pivot bearing tube. The hole must be accurately centered and perpendicular to the wood surface for the whirligig to work properly. Glue and nail the block to the bottom of the platform in the position shown. Install the steel ball and bearing tube. The tube should fit tightly in the hole so it will not turn.

The propeller shaft post is made from 3/4" x 1-1/2" x 8" wood. Drill a 3/16" diameter hole for the propeller shaft tube, as shown. The hole must be accurately centered and perpendicular to the wood surface for the whirligig to work properly.

Glue and nail the wood propeller shaft post to the platform. Then install the brass shaft tube. The tube should fit tightly in the hole so that it will not turn.

Cut the vane from 1/4" plywood to the pattern shown. Glue the vane in the platform slot, as shown.

The trampoline frame is made from 3/8" diameter hardwood dowel. Cut the dowel to the lengths shown and glue and nail the frame parts together and glue the legs in the platform holes.

Sand the platform. I recommend painting the platform, vane, and trampoline before further assembly.

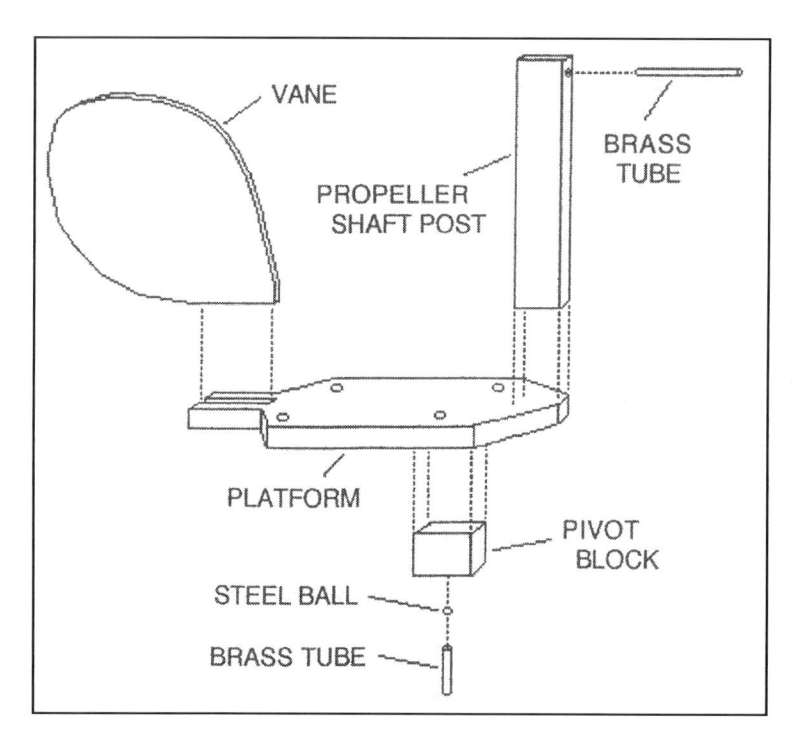

Assembly of platform.

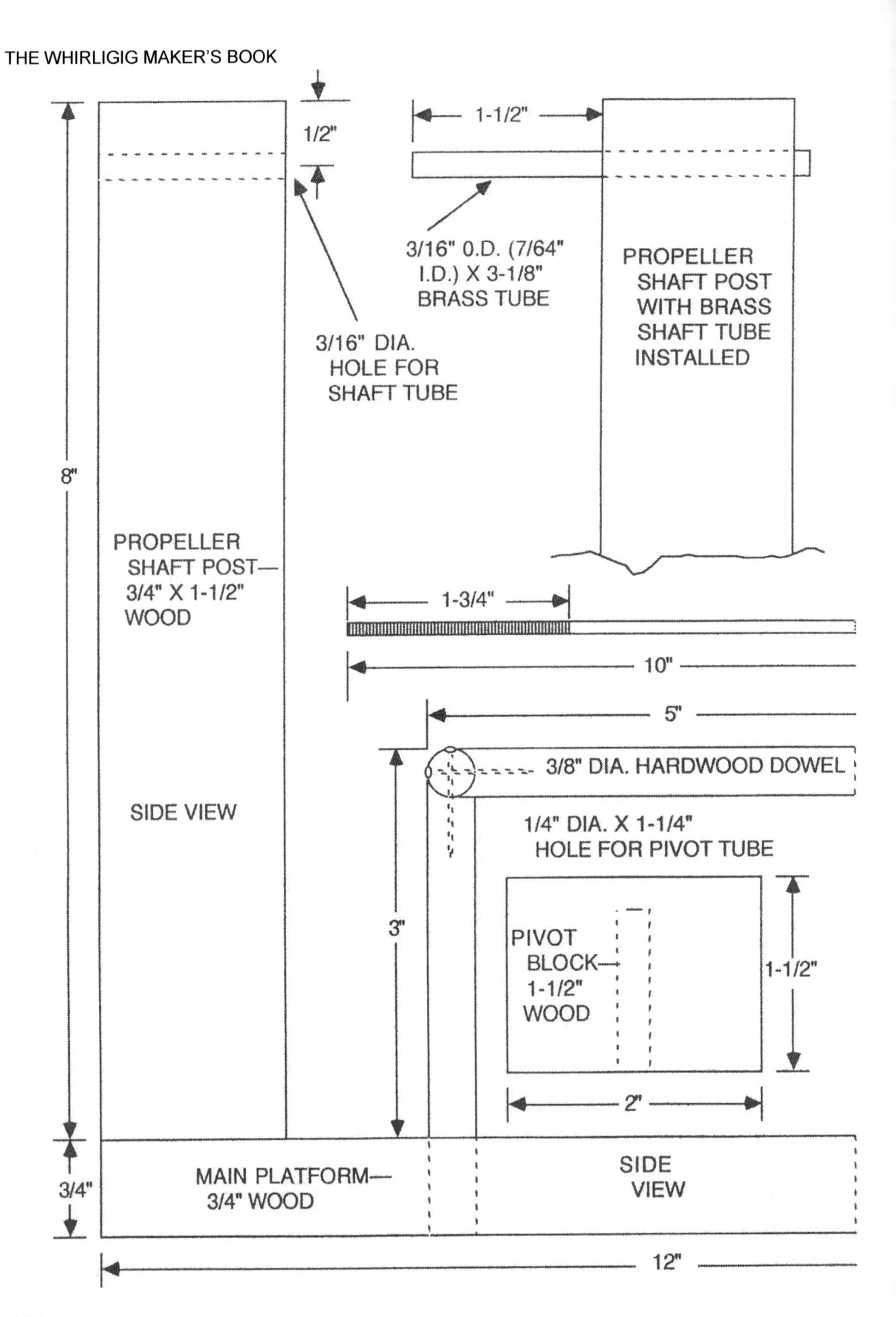

THE WHIRLIGIG MAKER'S BOOK

- 1/2"
- 1-1/2"
- 3/16" O.D. (7/64" I.D.) X 3-1/8" BRASS TUBE
- 3/16" DIA. HOLE FOR SHAFT TUBE
- PROPELLER SHAFT POST WITH BRASS SHAFT TUBE INSTALLED
- 8"
- PROPELLER SHAFT POST—3/4" X 1-1/2" WOOD
- SIDE VIEW
- 1-3/4"
- 10"
- 5"
- 3/8" DIA. HARDWOOD DOWEL
- 1/4" DIA. X 1-1/4" HOLE FOR PIVOT TUBE
- 3"
- PIVOT BLOCK—1-1/2" WOOD
- 1-1/2"
- 2"
- 3/4"
- MAIN PLATFORM—3/4" WOOD
- SIDE VIEW
- 12"

TRAMPOLINE

Side view plan and patterns for platform, trampoline frame, and crankshaft.

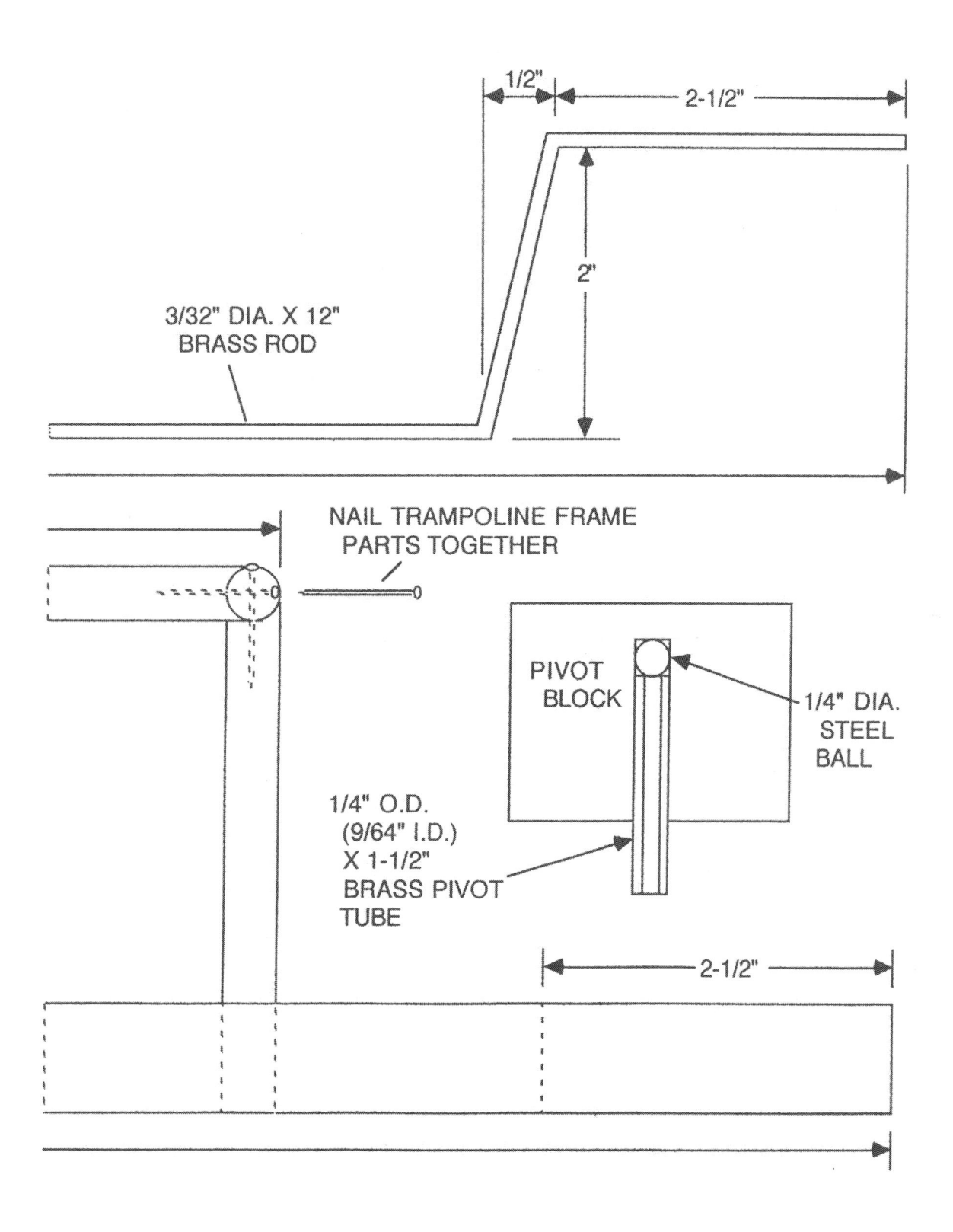

- 1/2"
- 2-1/2"
- 2"
- 3/32" DIA. X 12" BRASS ROD
- NAIL TRAMPOLINE FRAME PARTS TOGETHER
- PIVOT BLOCK
- 1/4" DIA. STEEL BALL
- 1/4" O.D. (9/64" I.D.) X 1-1/2" BRASS PIVOT TUBE
- 2-1/2"

135

Top view plan and patterns for platform and trampoline frame.

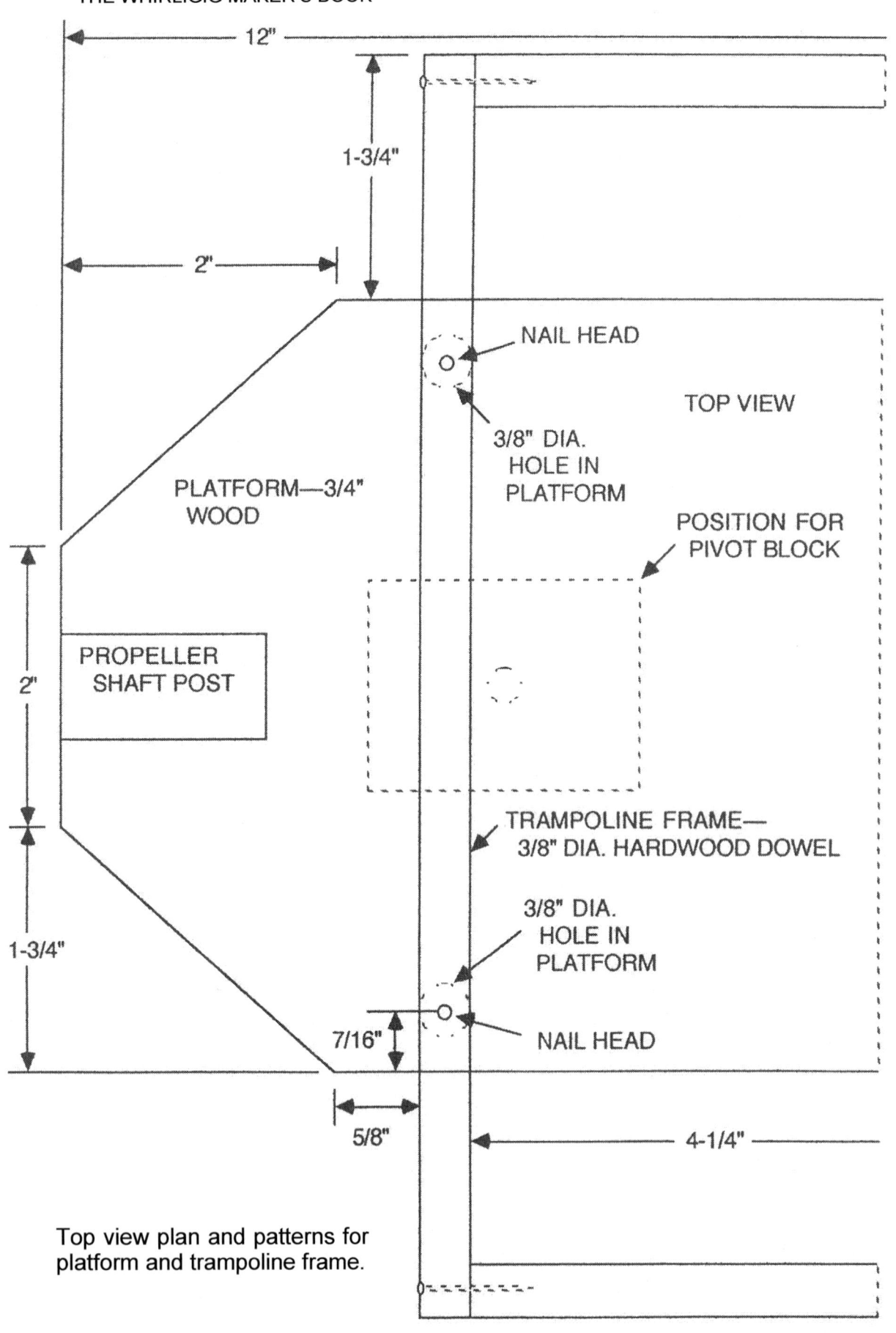

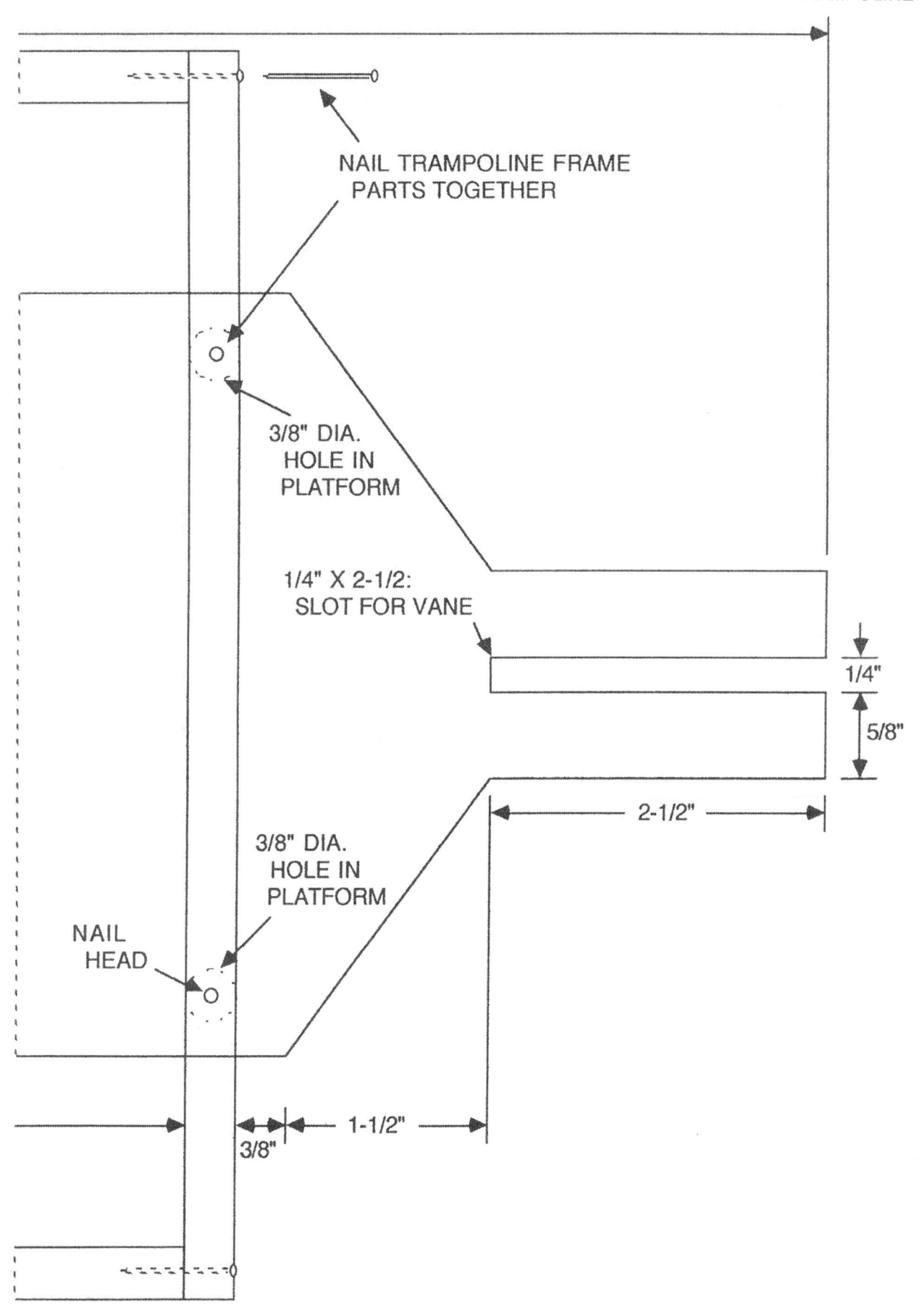

TRAMPOLINE

NAIL TRAMPOLINE FRAME PARTS TOGETHER

3/8" DIA. HOLE IN PLATFORM

1/4" X 2-1/2: SLOT FOR VANE

1/4"

5/8"

2-1/2"

3/8" DIA. HOLE IN PLATFORM

NAIL HEAD

1-1/2"

3/8"

THE WHIRLIGIG MAKER'S BOOK

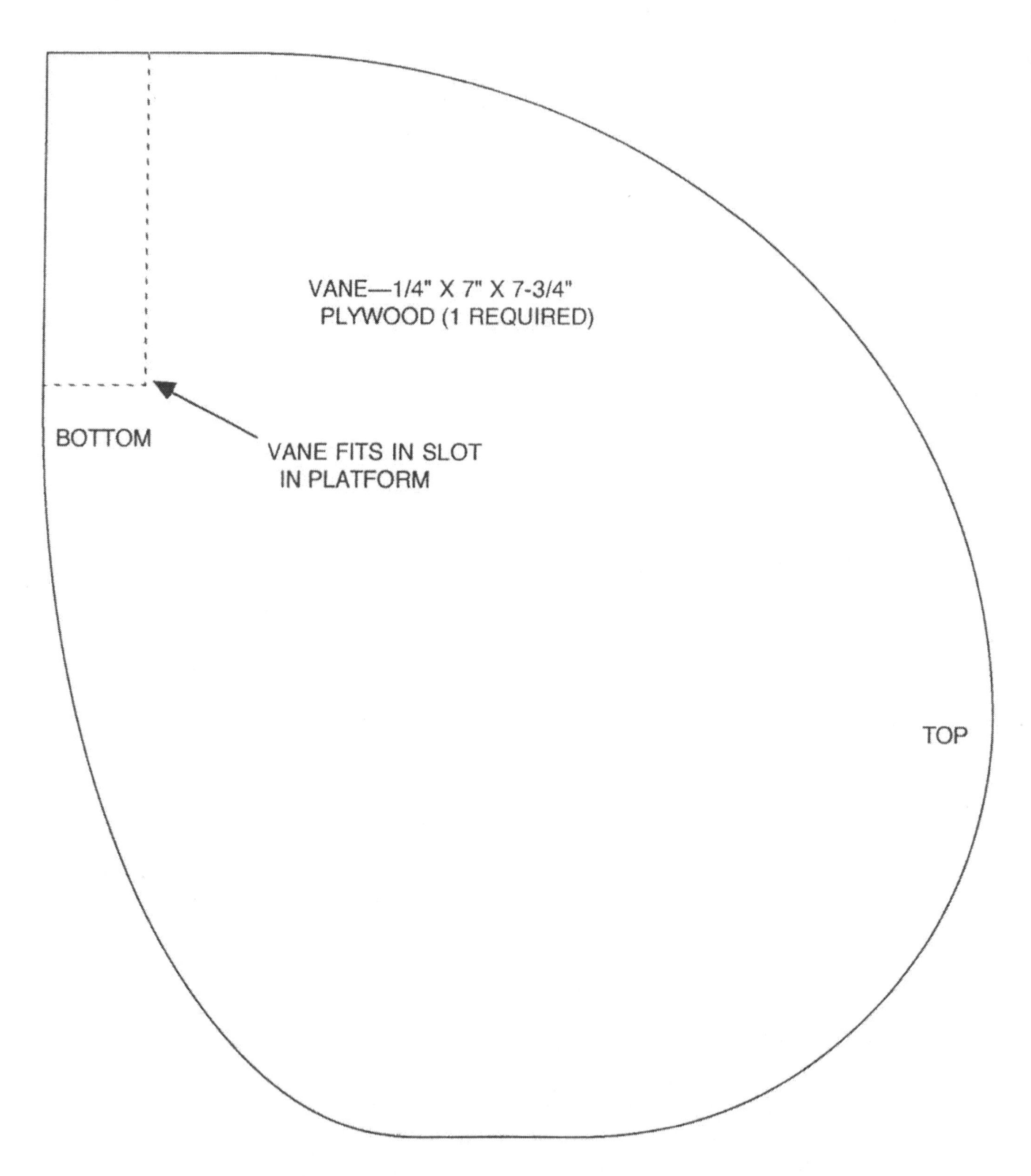

VANE—1/4" X 7" X 7-3/4" PLYWOOD (1 REQUIRED)

BOTTOM

VANE FITS IN SLOT IN PLATFORM

TOP

Full-size pattern for vane.

TRAMPOLINE

ASSEMBLY OF TRAMPOLINE FRAME

GLUE TRAMPOLINE FRAME IN PLATFORM HOLES

Trampoline frame assembly.

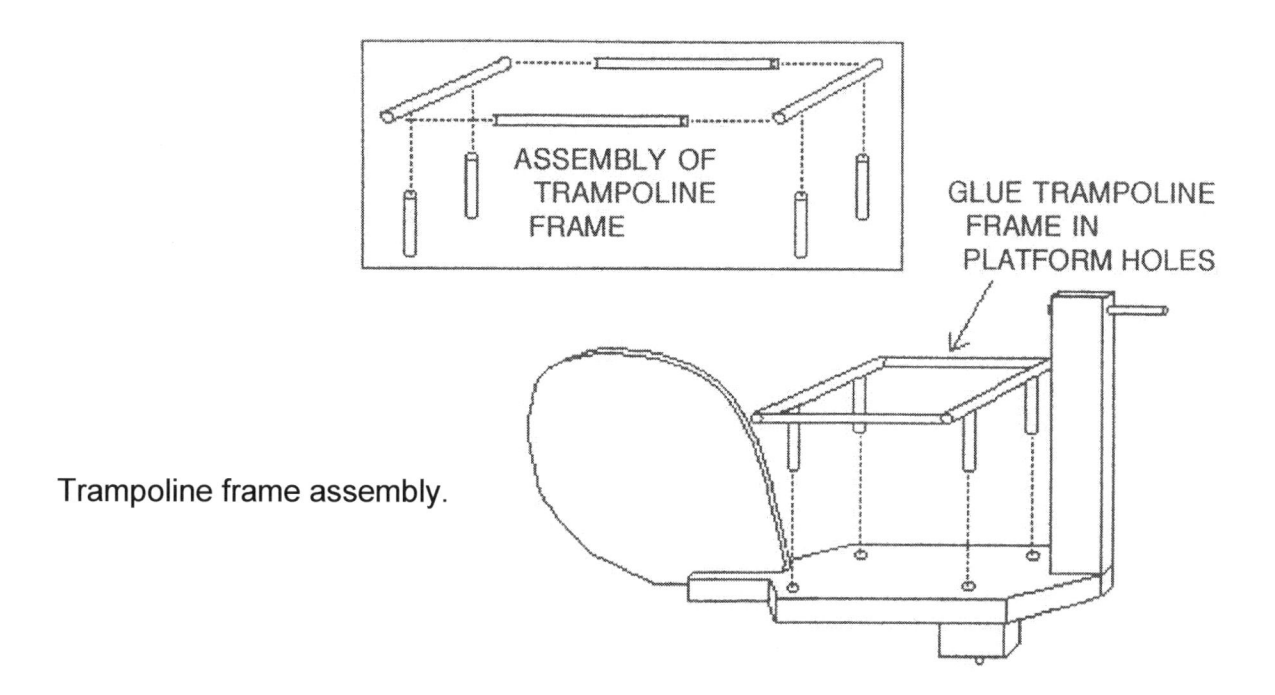

PROPELLER, CRANKSHAFT, TRAMPOLINE, AND PERFORMER

The crankshaft is made from 3/32" diameter x 12" brass rod. Make threads for 1-3/4" on one end of the rod using a 4-40 die. Bend the crank on the other end of the rod to the pattern shown. Install a wood ball and 1/2" long plastic spacer over the shaft 3-1/8" from the threads. The plastic spacer must fit tightly over the shaft to keep the shaft in position in the brass tube. Slip the crankshaft into the shaft tube. The shaft should turn freely in the tube with no binding. Apply light oil to the shaft to further decrease friction.

The propeller hub is made from 3/4" x 1-1/2" x 1-1/2" wood. Drill a 3/32" shaft hole. Cut the 3/16" wide x 1/2" deep notches for the propeller blades at 45 degree angles to the face of the hub. A clockwise propeller is used on the whirligig shown. This gives the correct direction for the backward somersault with the performer facing as shown. The slots need to be made accurately for the whirligig to work properly.

Cut the propeller blades from 3/16" wood or plywood to the pattern shown. Then glue them in the slots in the hub. Place the hub on a flat surface with the forward side down. The blades are then installed with the forward side flush with the flat surface.

Install a washer, nut, and 3/8" diameter wood ball over the threaded end of the shaft, as shown. Then thread the propeller hub onto the shaft. Secure the propeller with a washer and nut.

Test the assembly in front of a fan to make certain that the propeller and shaft assembly works properly.

The trampoline bed is made from a 5" x 10" piece of soft cloth. Sew a hem all the way around the material so that it has a 2-3/4" x 6-3/4" area after hemming. Then sew

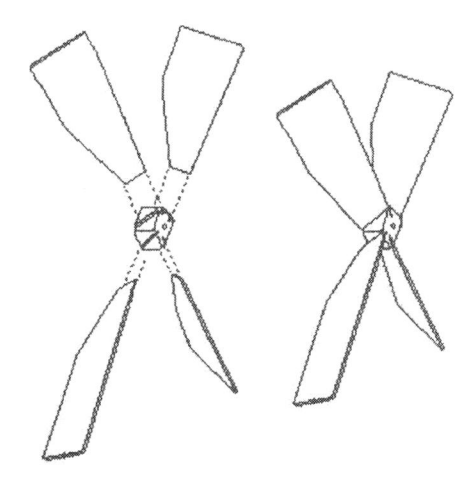

Assembly of propeller blades to hub.

139

THE WHIRLIGIG MAKER'S BOOK

Crankshaft assembly plan.

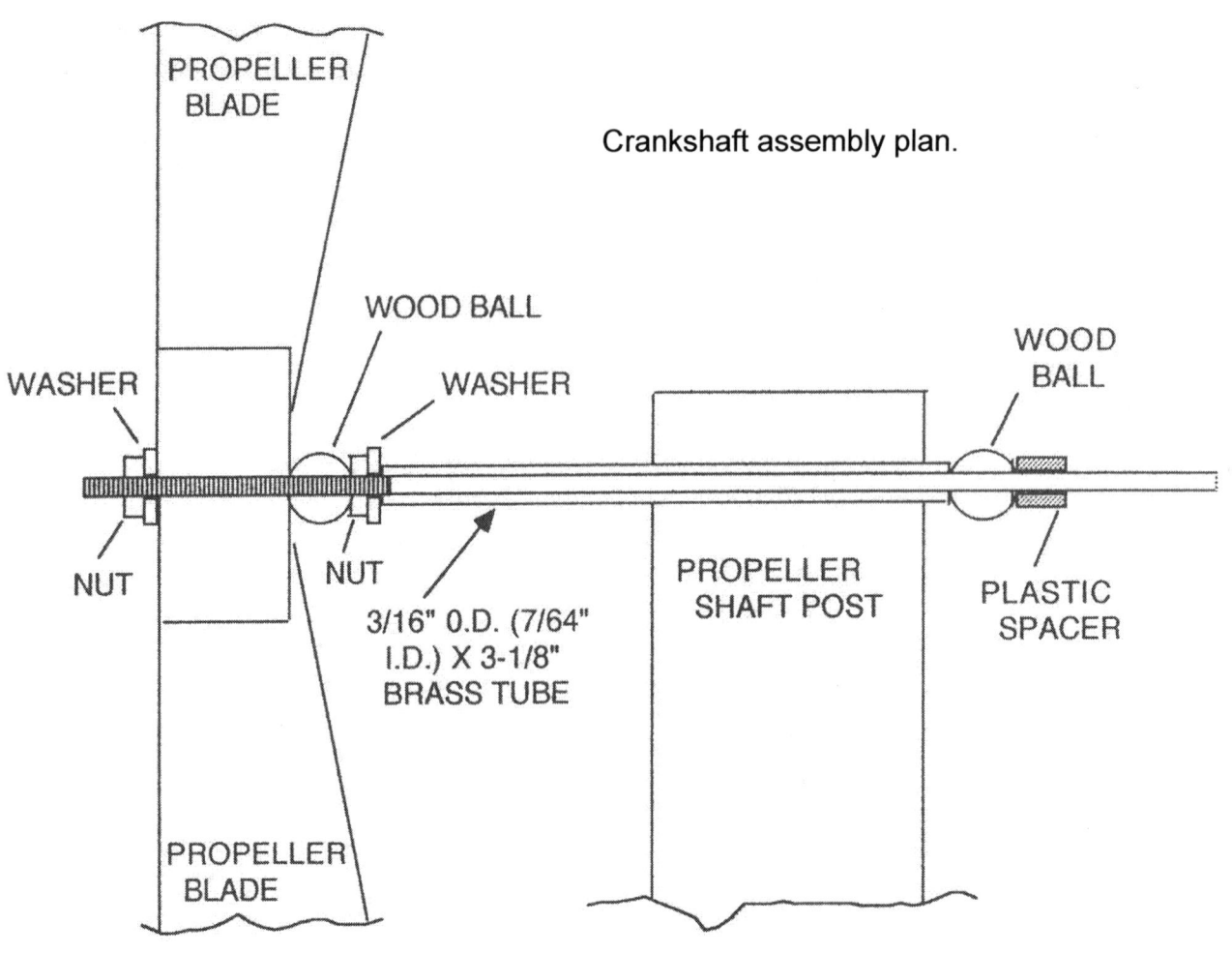

loops made from shoelace to the underside of the trampoline bed in the pattern shown.

The trampoline bed is then laced to the frame with round elastic cord. I used one long piece of cord. Start at one corner. Go through the first loop, then over and around the trampoline frame. Pass the elastic cord through the next loop. Continue this pattern all the way around and then tie the elastic cord together at the starting point.

Cut the trampoline performer parts to the patterns shown. Drill holes before sawing the parts to shape.

Shoulder, back, and upper leg covers are made from 1/16" plywood and glued to the body parts. These parts serve to limit the range and direction of motion of the arms and legs to give a realistic somersaulting action on the trampoline.

The trampoline performer parts are best sanded and painted before joining the parts together with the wires. If desired, however, you can do a trial assembly for testing the whirligig and then disassemble later for painting.

The arms and upper legs are attached to the body with 1/32" diameter stiff wire. Bend and loop one end of the wire. Pass the other end through the holes in the parts. Bend and loop the other end of the wire and cut off excess wire.

Attach the upper and lower leg parts together with wires in a similar manner.

The performer is fixed to the crankshaft. Slip the end of the crankshaft through the hole in the performer with the performer facing the direction shown in the illustrations. Position the performer in an upright standing position in the center of the trampoline bed with the crankshaft downward in the lowest position. Then move the performer forward, rotating the performer on the shaft slightly until the crankshaft is at about a 10 degree angle when the performer's body is vertical.

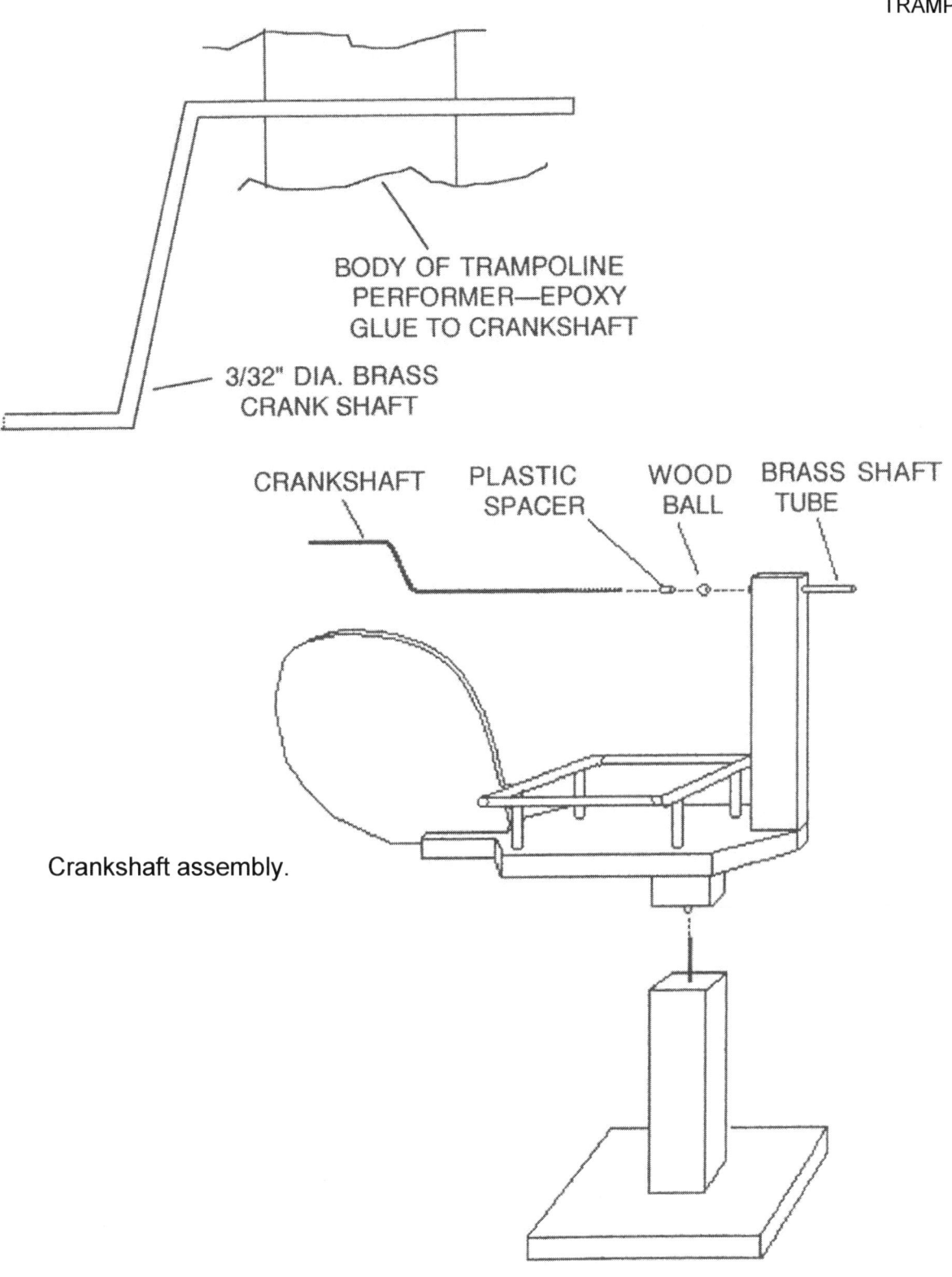

TRAMPOLINE

BODY OF TRAMPOLINE
PERFORMER—EPOXY
GLUE TO CRANKSHAFT

3/32" DIA. BRASS
CRANK SHAFT

CRANKSHAFT   PLASTIC   WOOD   BRASS SHAFT
             SPACER   BALL   TUBE

Crankshaft assembly.

If the crankshaft is a tight fit in the hole, it should be possible to try out the whirligig before epoxy gluing the body to the shaft. If the shaft fits extremely tight on the shaft, gluing may not be necessary.

THE WHIRLIGIG MAKER'S BOOK

SLUG COUNTERWEIGHT

RING FOR METAL COUNTERWEIGHT—3/16" PLYWOOD, 3/4" DIA. WITH 1/4" DIA. HOLE IN CENTER (1 REQUIRED)

PROPELLER BLADE—3/16" WOOD OR PLYWOOD (4 REQUIRED)

PROPELLER HUB—3/4" WOOD (1 REQUIRED)

3/32" DIA. HOLE

CUT BLADE SLOTS AT 45 DEGREE ANGLES

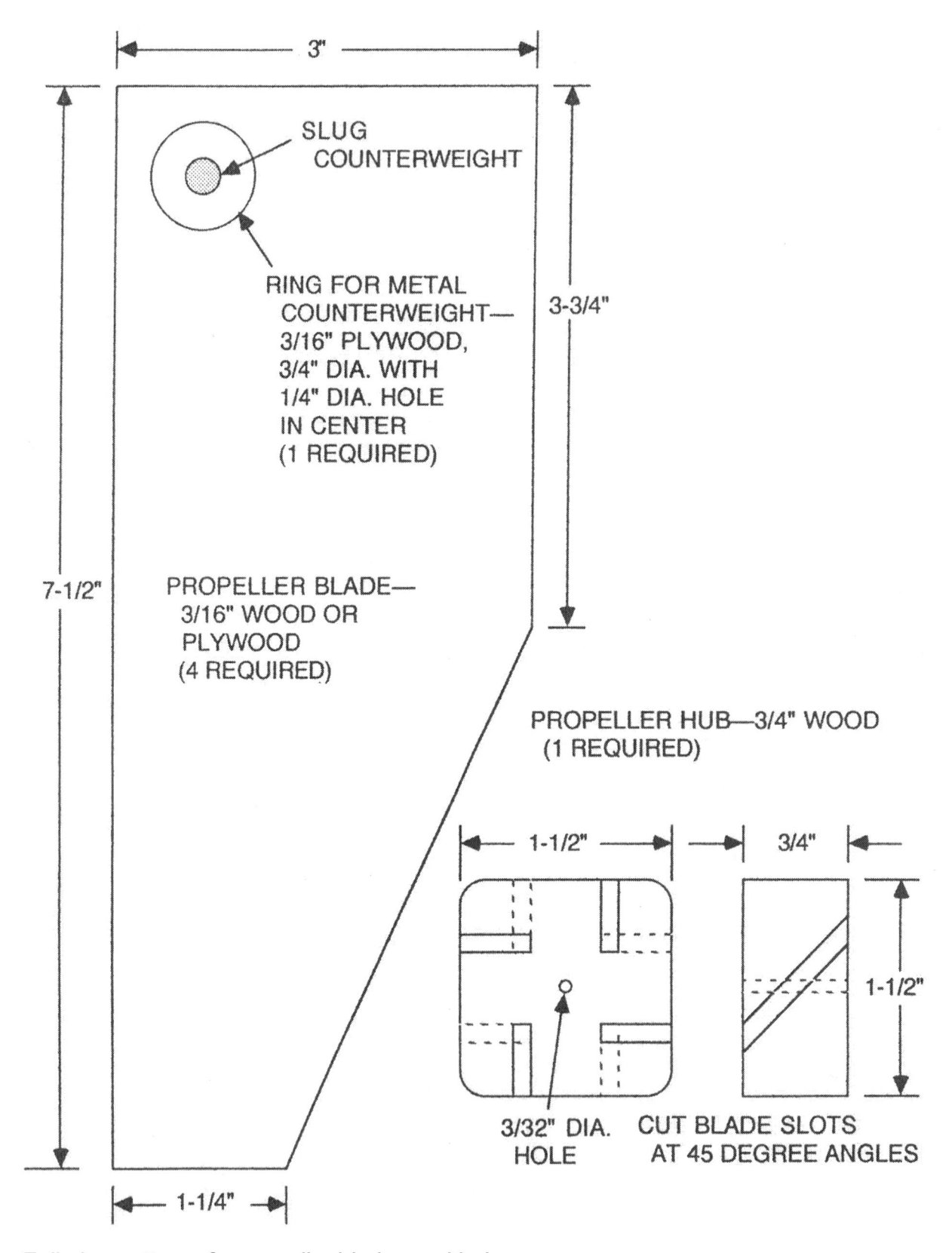

Full-size patterns for propeller blades and hub.

142

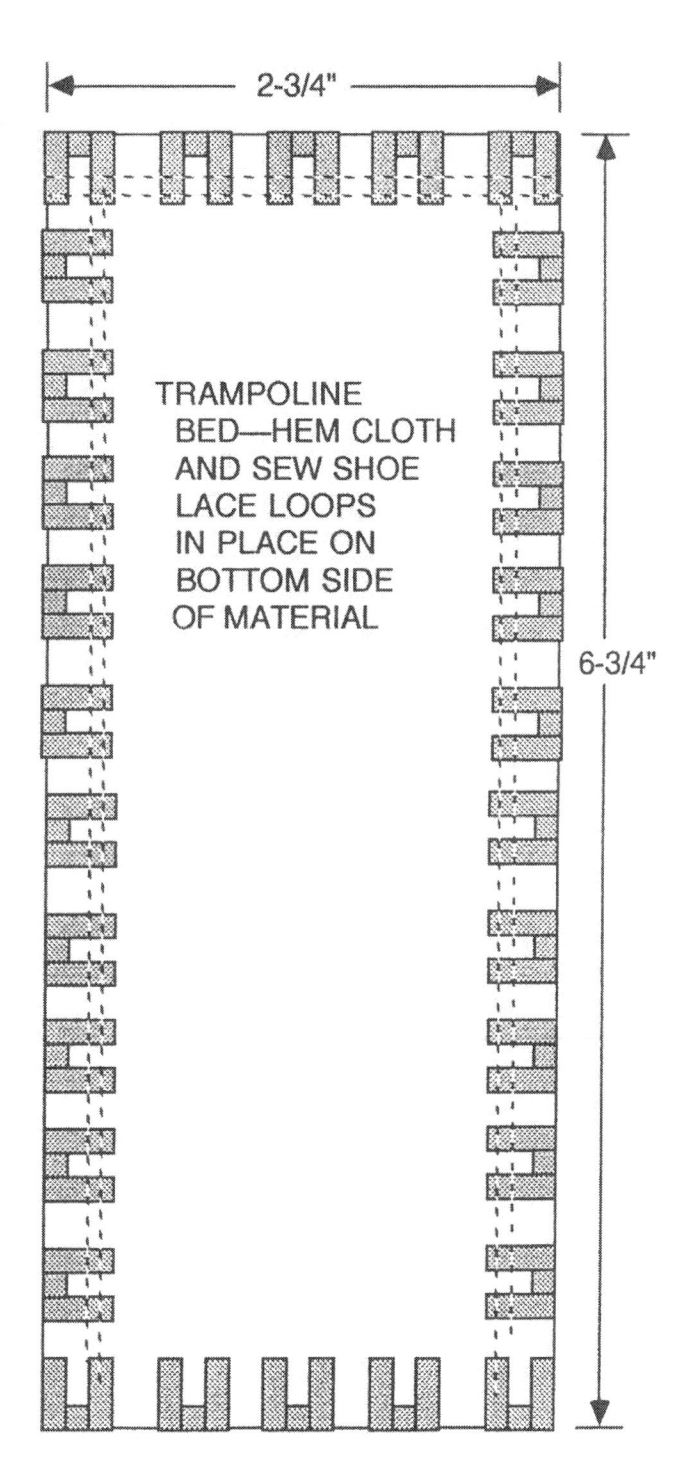

TRAMPOLINE BED—HEM CLOTH AND SEW SHOE LACE LOOPS IN PLACE ON BOTTOM SIDE OF MATERIAL

2-3/4"

6-3/4"

Full-size pattern for trampoline bed.

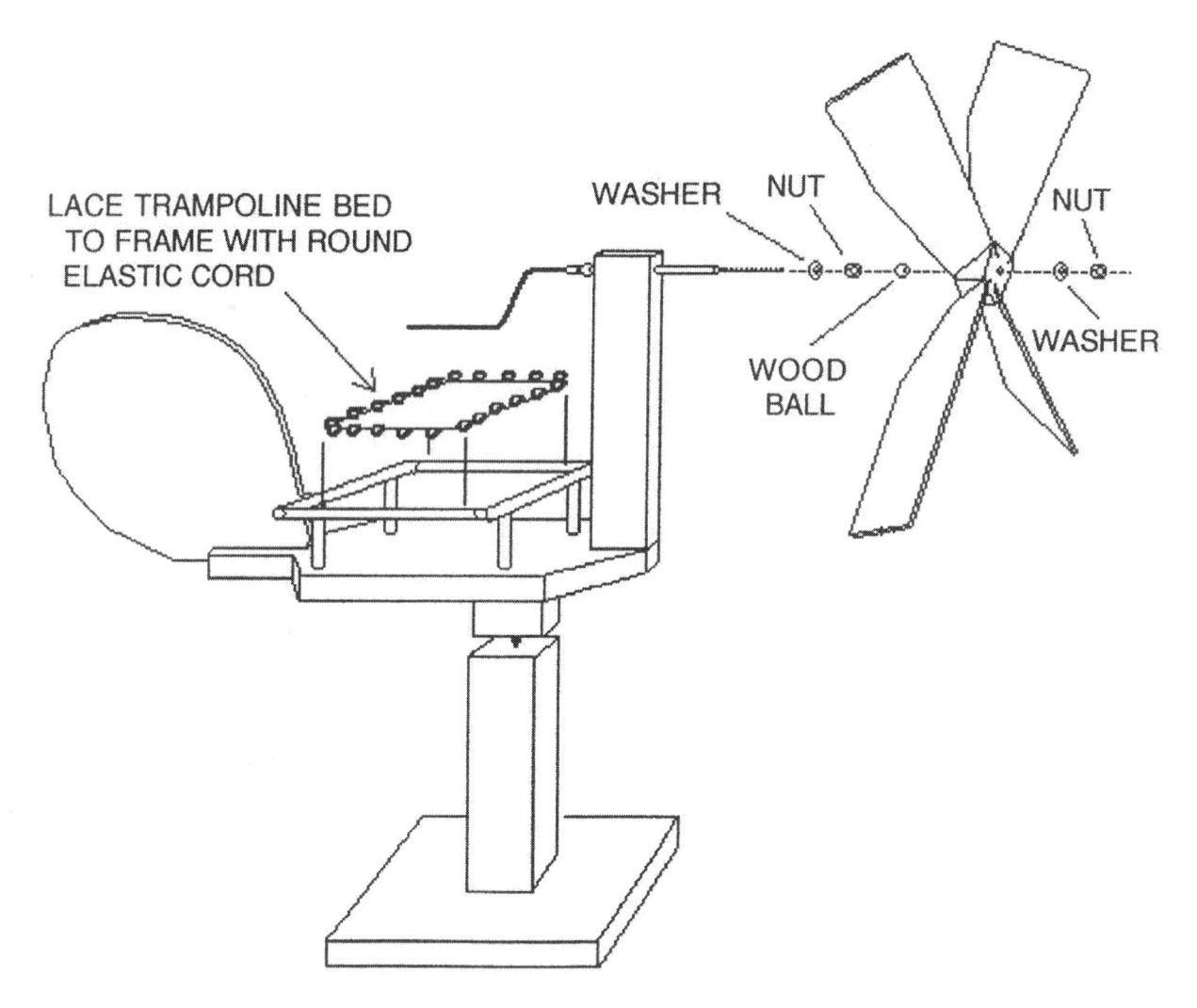

THE WHIRLIGIG MAKER'S BOOK

Assembly of propeller on crankshaft and trampoline bed to frame.

TRAMPOLINE

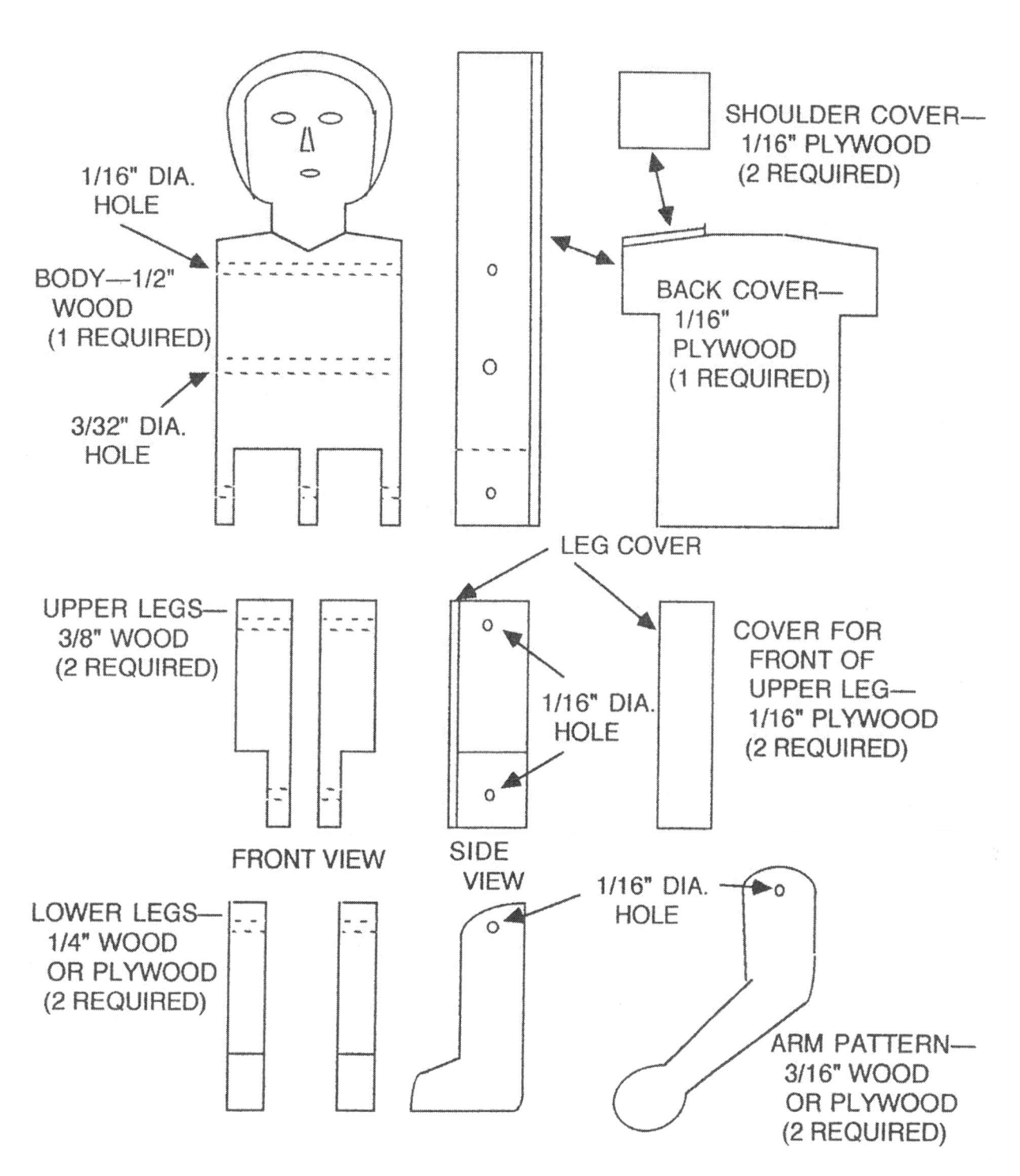

Full-size patterns for trampoline performer.

145

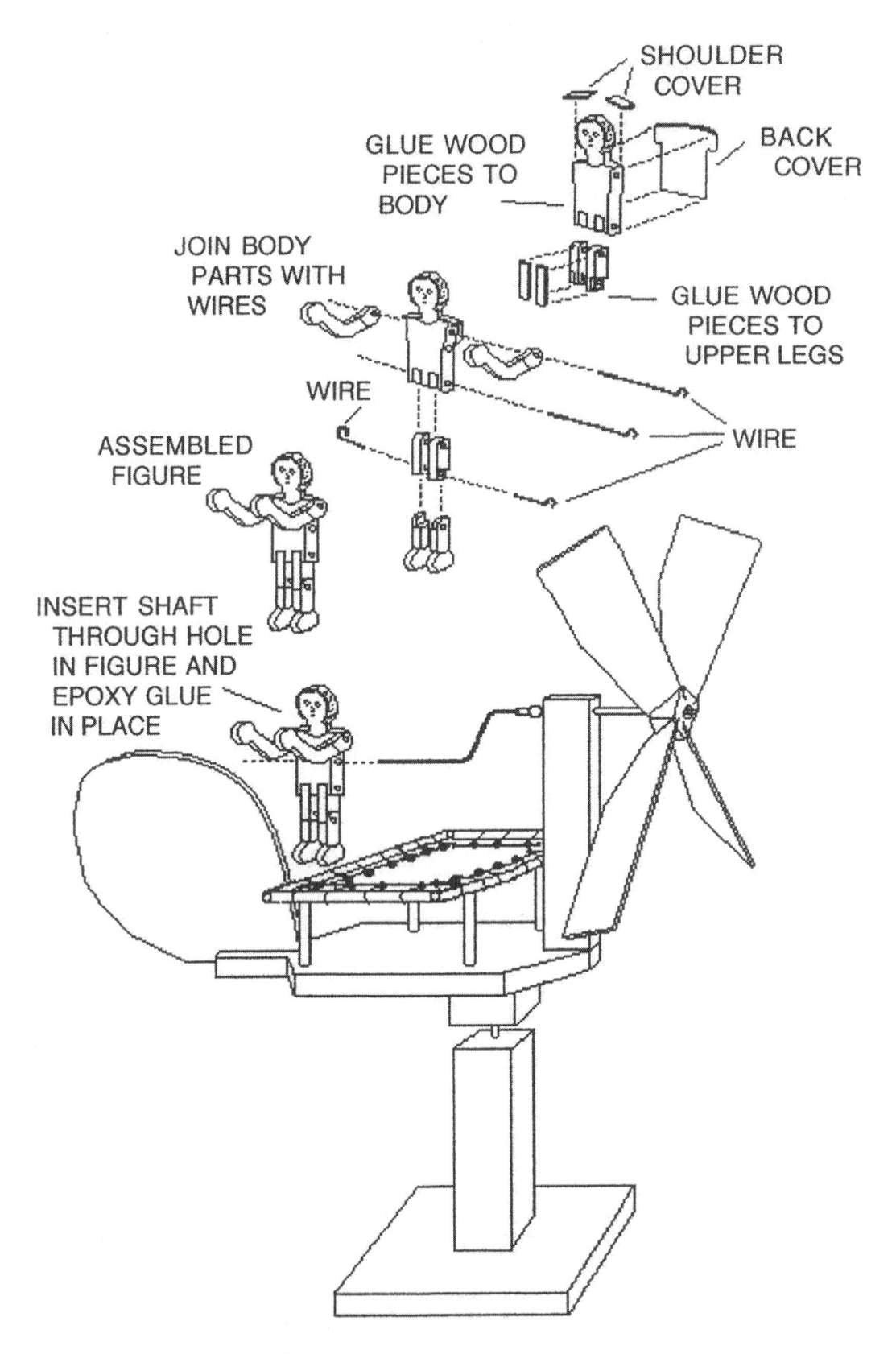

THE WHIRLIGIG MAKER'S BOOK

Assembly of trampoline performer.

TRAMPOLINE

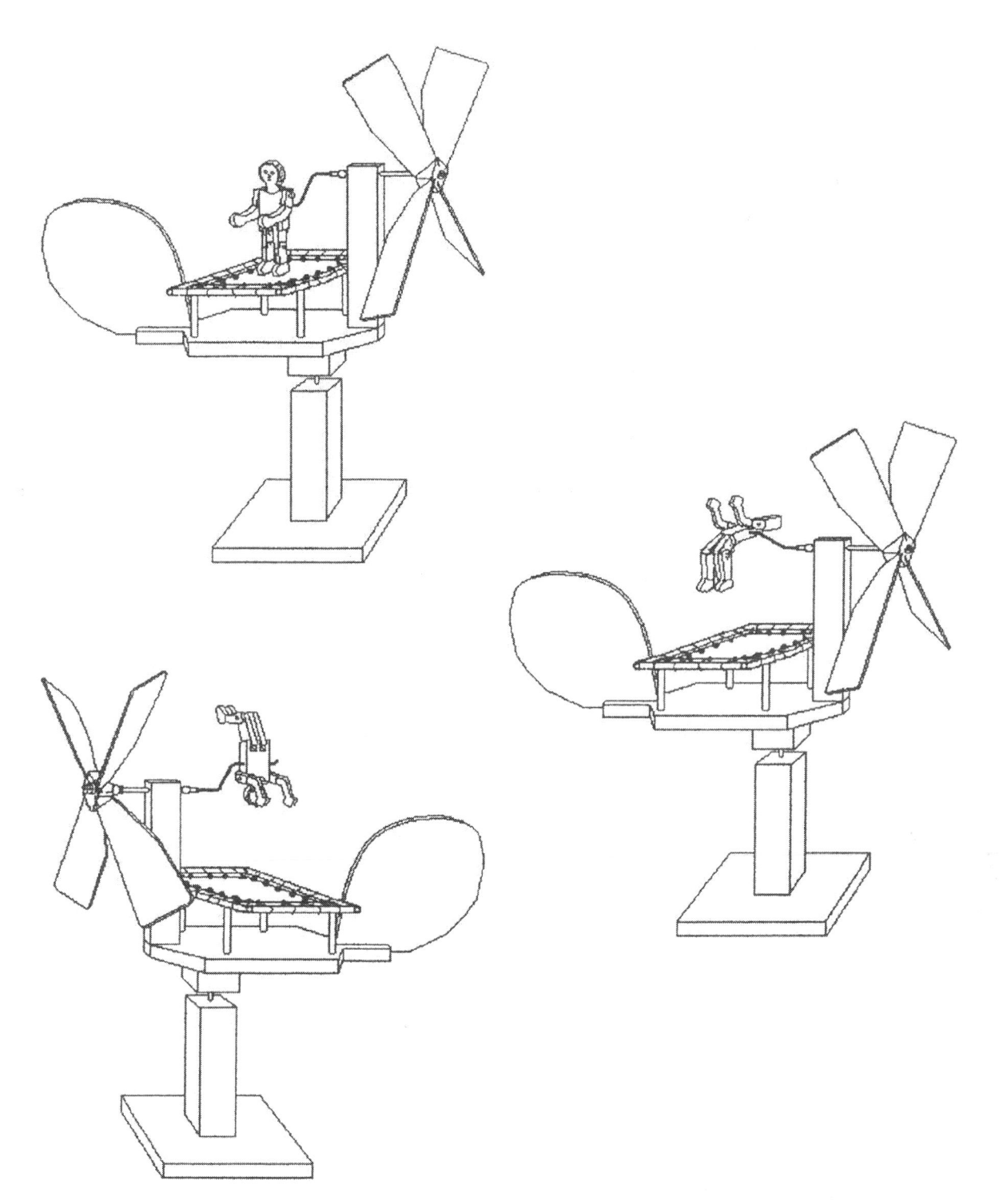

Assembled Trampoline whirligig.

147

TESTING AND ADDING COUNTERWEIGHT

The whirligig is ready for testing and adding a counterweight to propeller. The testing can be done inside with a fan or outdoors in a light wind. The whirligig should work without a counterweight on the propeller to balance the weight of the performer on the shaft, but will probably be difficult to get started.

To counterbalance, loosen the propeller nut and position two of the propeller blades in line with the crankshaft arm. Tighten the propeller nut with the propeller in this position. Then add a counterweight (about 1/8 to 1/4 ounce) to the propeller blade opposite the crank arm. The weight can be glued in a wood ring, as shown. It will take some experimenting to get the exact weight required to balance the performer on the shaft. When you have it exactly right, the propeller will remain in any position it is turned to. The closer you get to an exact balance, the easier and smoother the whirligig will start up and turn. The whirligig shown starts and works in a very light wind.

Make any necessary adjustments and add oil to friction areas of metal parts. The performer's feet should make firm contact with the trampoline bed. Make necessary adjustments in crankshaft to achieve desired action.

Chapter 13

FERRIS WHEEL

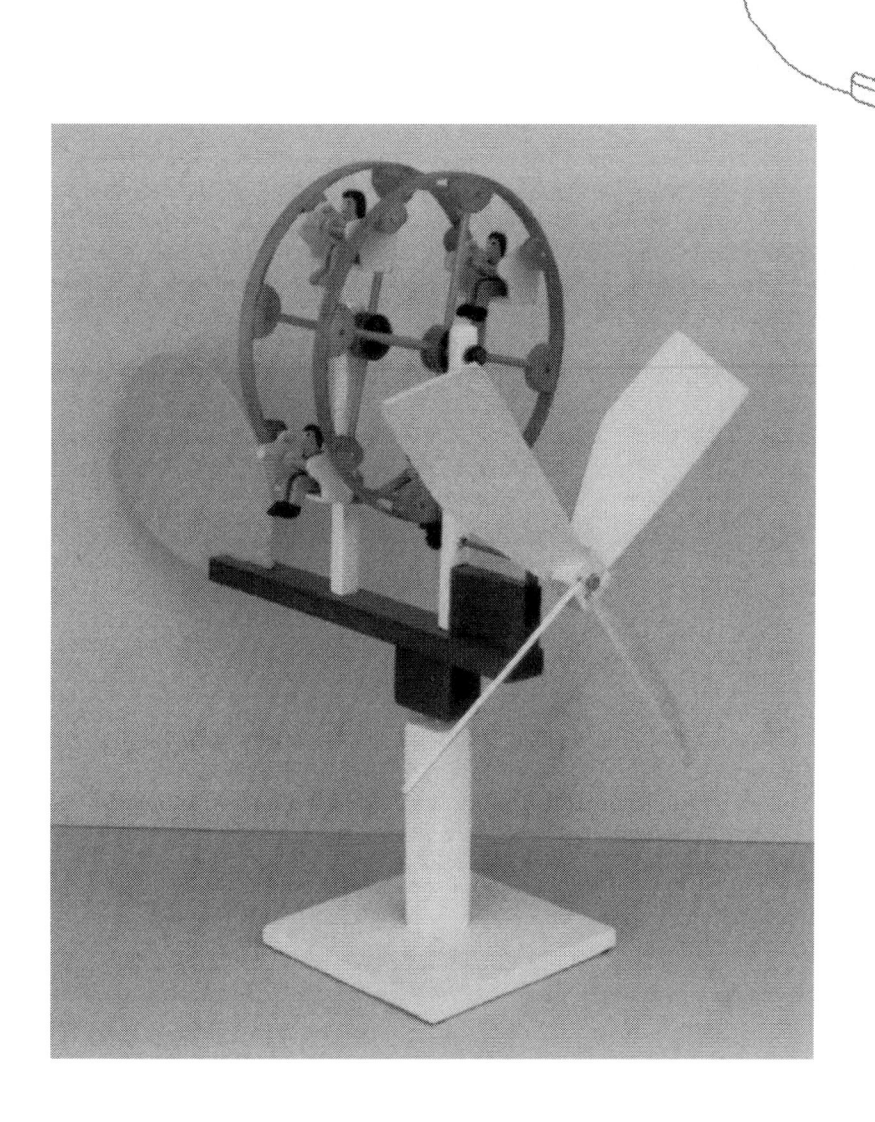

The Ferris Wheel whirligig is a fun project both to build and then watch perform after you have completed it.

MATERIALS

- 3/4" x 8" x 8" wood or plywood for display base.
- 1-1/2" x 1-1/2" x 7" wood for display post.
- 3/4" x 1-3/4" x 14" wood for platform.
- 1-1/2" x 2" x 2-1/4" wood for pivot block.
- 3/4" x 2" x 3" wood for propeller shaft block.
- 1/2" x 3/4" x 20" wood for Ferris wheel posts.
- 1/4" x 7" x 8" plywood for vane.
- 3/16" x 3" x 30" wood or plywood for propeller blades.
- 3/4" x 1-1/2" x 1-1/2" wood for propeller hub.
- 1/2" x 3" x 12" wood for wheel and chair mounting blocks.
- 3/4" x 1-1/2" x 3" wood or two Tinkertoy spools for Ferris wheel hub.
- 1/4" outside diameter (9/64" inside diameter) x 2" brass tubing for pivot bearing.
- 1/4" outside diameter (9/64" inside diameter) x 5/8" brass tubing for shaft bearing.
- 1/4" diameter steel ball for pivot bearing.
- 1/8" diameter x 6-3/4" brass rod for propeller shaft.
- 6-32 nut (7 required) for attaching propeller hub and drive wheel to shaft.
- Washer (6 required) for use on propeller shaft.
- 1/8" diameter x 5" nail for pivot rod for display base.
- 1/2" x 1" x 1" brass L-bracket (1 required) for mounting propeller shaft.
- Screw (2 required) for attaching brackets to platform.
- 3/8" outside diameter (1/8" inside diameter) x 1" plastic tube for propeller shaft spacer.
- 1" diameter rubber wheel with 1/8" diameter shaft hole.
- 5/8" diameter wood ball with 5/16" diameter hole (2 required) for use on Ferris wheel shaft.
- 10" diameter x 1/2" wide embroidery hoop (2 required) for Ferris wheel rings.
- 1/4" diameter x 28" hardwood dowel for Ferris wheel spokes.
- 3/16" x 24" hardwood dowel for Ferris wheel cross supports and chair mounting pegs.
- 1/8" x 1" x 2" wood for Ferris wheel axle spacers.
- 5/16" diameter x 6-1/2" hardwood dowel for Ferris wheel axle.
- 3/16" x 1-1/4" x 16" wood or plywood for chair boards.
- 1/8" x 2" x 16" wood or plywood for chair sides.
- 1/8" diameter x 16" hardwood dowel for hand rails.
- 1/4" x 6" x 12" wood or plywood for boy and girl riders.
- 3/8" outside diameter (3/16" inside diameter x 2" plastic tubing for chair mounting spacers.
- 1/32" diameter x 16" stiff wire for assembling figures.
- Glue.
- Finishing nails.
- Small felt pad for display base (4 required).
- Paint.

DISPLAY STAND

The display stand is useful not only for displaying the finished whirligig indoors, but also for holding the whirligig during construction and for testing it in front of a fan. Construction is easy. The base is 3/4" x 8" x 8" wood or plywood. The 1-1/2" x 1-1/2" x 7" post is glued and nailed to the center of the base. A 1/8" diameter x 5" nail is driven 2" into the center of the top of the post for use as a pivot rod. Drill a pilot hole perpendicular to the top of the post before driving the nail into the hole. Cut the head off of the nail with a hacksaw. File the upper end of the nail smooth, rounding the corners slightly.

Sand and paint the display stand. A clear or color finish can be used.

Attach felt pads to the corners of the underside of the base.

PLATFORM

The platform is made of 3/4" x 1-3/4" x 14" wood. Shape the ends, as shown. Make a 1/4" x 2-1/2" slot for the vane. Drill a 1/2" diameter holes for the Ferris wheel posts, as shown. Shape the propeller shaft block and Ferris wheel posts, as shown.

Glue the Ferris wheel posts in the mounting holes in the platform. Install brass shaft tube in hole in forward post.

Glue and nail the propeller shaft block in place. Use a 1/2" x 1" x 1" brass L-bracket with a 9/64" hole for the propeller shaft. Fasten the brass L-bracket to the platform with screws. Depending on the brackets selected, it may be necessary to expand hole sizes and/or drill additional holes.

The pivot block is shaped from 1-1/2" x 2" x 2-1/4" wood to the pattern shown. Drill a 1/4" hole for the pivot tube, as shown. The hole must be accurately centered and perpendicular to the wood surfaces for the whirligig to work properly.

Glue and nail the wood pivot block to the platform. Next, install a 1/4" diameter steel ball in the pivot hole. Then install the brass pivot tube, as shown.

Cut the vane from 1/4" plywood to the pattern shown. Glue the vane in the platform slot, as shown.

Sand the platform. The platform can be painted at this time, or you can wait until the assembly has been completed. The color scheme can be as desired.

PROPELLER AND SHAFT

The propeller shaft is made from 1/8" diameter x 6-3/4" brass rod. Make threads for 1-1/2" on one end of the rod and 3/4" on the other end using a 6-32 die. Slip the crankshaft into the holes in the mounting bracket and shaft tube. Install spacers, washers, nuts and drive wheel on shaft. The shaft should turn freely in the tube with no binding. Apply light oil to the shaft to further decrease friction.

The propeller hub is made from 3/4" x 1-1/2" x 1-1/2" wood. Drill a 1/8" shaft hole. Cut the 3/16" wide x 1/2" deep notches for the propeller blades at 45 degree angles to the face of the hub. Notice that a clockwise propeller is used so that the Ferris wheel riders will circle forward.

Cut the propeller blades from 3/16" wood or plywood to the pattern shown. Then glue the blades in the slots in the hub. Place the hub on a flat surface with the forward side down. The blades are then installed with the forward side flush with the flat surface.

Install the propeller on the shaft, as shown. Secure the propeller with a washer and two nuts.

Test the assembly in front of a fan to make certain that the propeller and shaft assembly works properly.

FERRIS WHEEL ASSEMBLY

Cut the chair mounting blocks and wheel blocks from 1/2" wood to the patterns shown. Drill holes as shown.

Cut the hub spools from 3/4" wood and drill the holes as shown. If desired, Tinkertoy spools can be substituted. Enlarge the axle hole in each spool to 21/64" diameter.

Assemble each wheel half to the pattern shown. For each wheel half, first install the four spokes in the hub spool, gluing them in place. Glue the wheel blocks to the spoke ends. Then glue the wheel blocks to the 10" diameter embroidery hoop. It is extremely important to have the hub spool hole in the exact center of the embroidery hoop.

Next, glue the chair mounting blocks to the hoop.

The two wheel halves should match each other exactly if properly assembled.

Join the two wheel halves with four 3/16" diameter x 3-1/2" hardwood dowels, gluing them to the wheel blocks with the ends of the dowels flush with the outside of the wheel blocks.

The wheel can be painted before further assembly.

Assemble the wheel to the posts as shown. The wheel must turn freely and the drive wheel must maintain contact with the wheel rim throughout the turning of the Ferris wheel. Make any required adjustments to maintain smooth even drive-wheel contact.

THE WHIRLIGIG MAKER'S BOOK

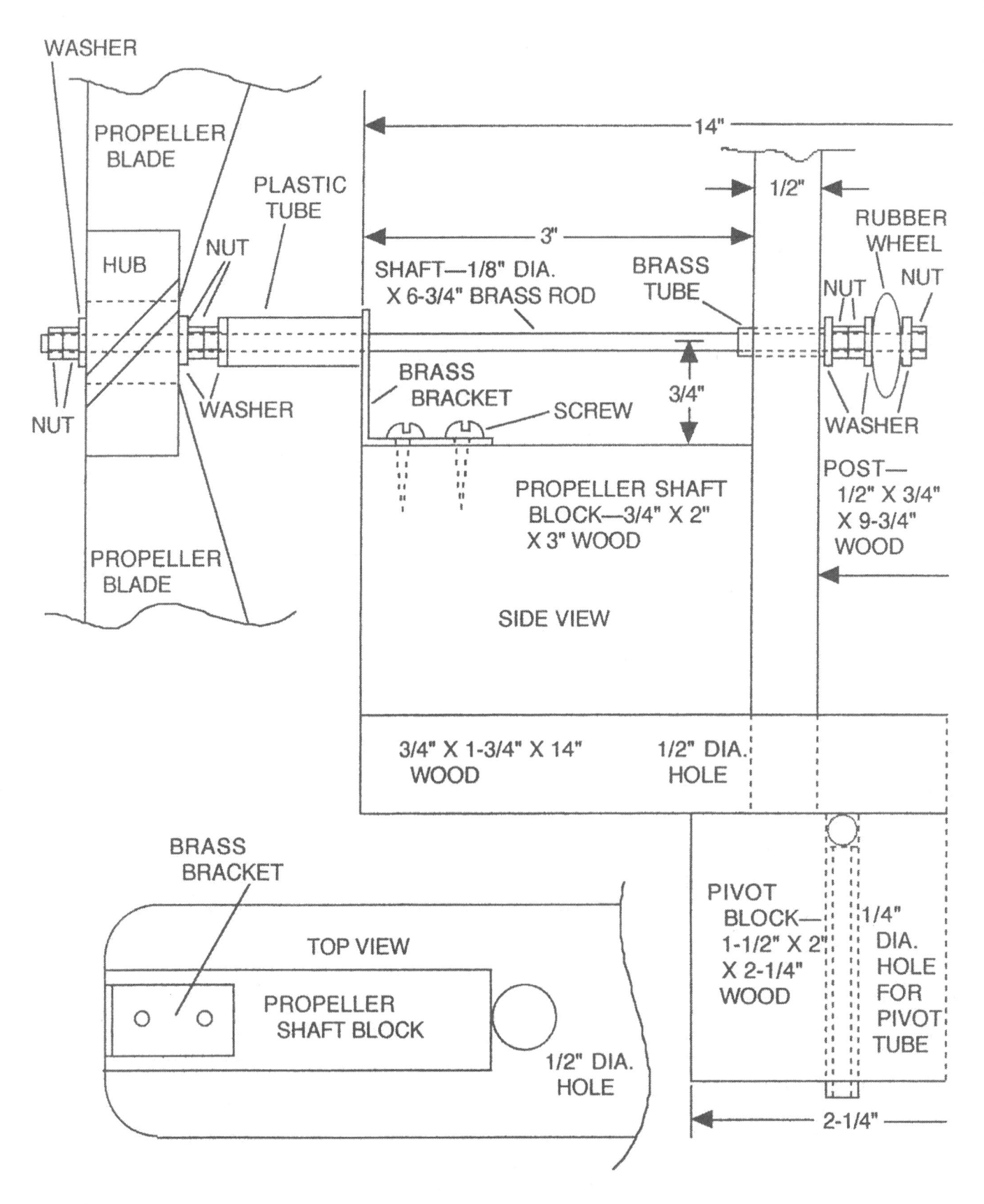

Full-size plan and patterns for platform and propeller shaft.

152

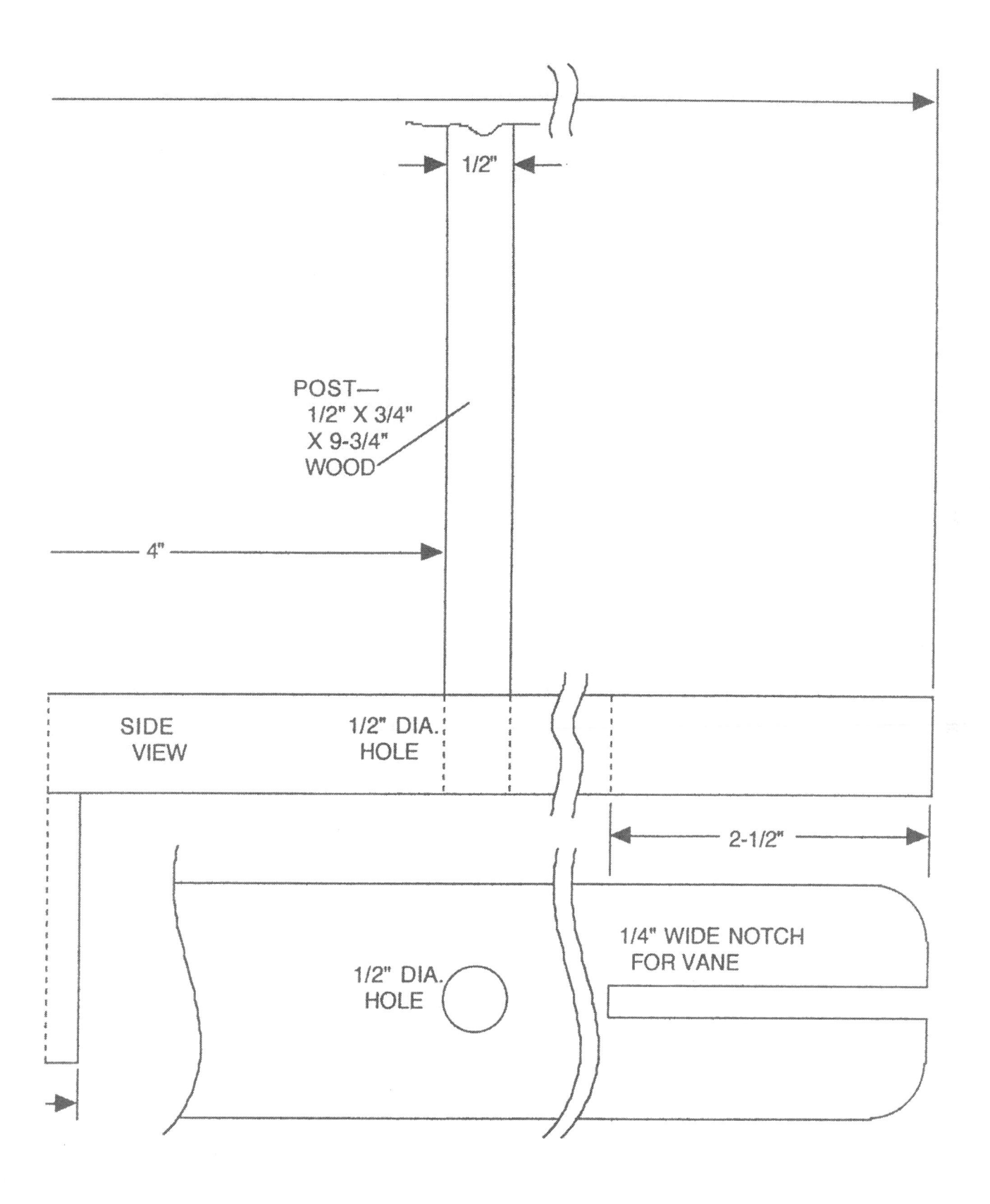

FERRIS WHEEL

1/2"

POST—
1/2" X 3/4"
X 9-3/4"
WOOD

4"

SIDE VIEW

1/2" DIA. HOLE

2-1/2"

1/2" DIA. HOLE

1/4" WIDE NOTCH FOR VANE

153

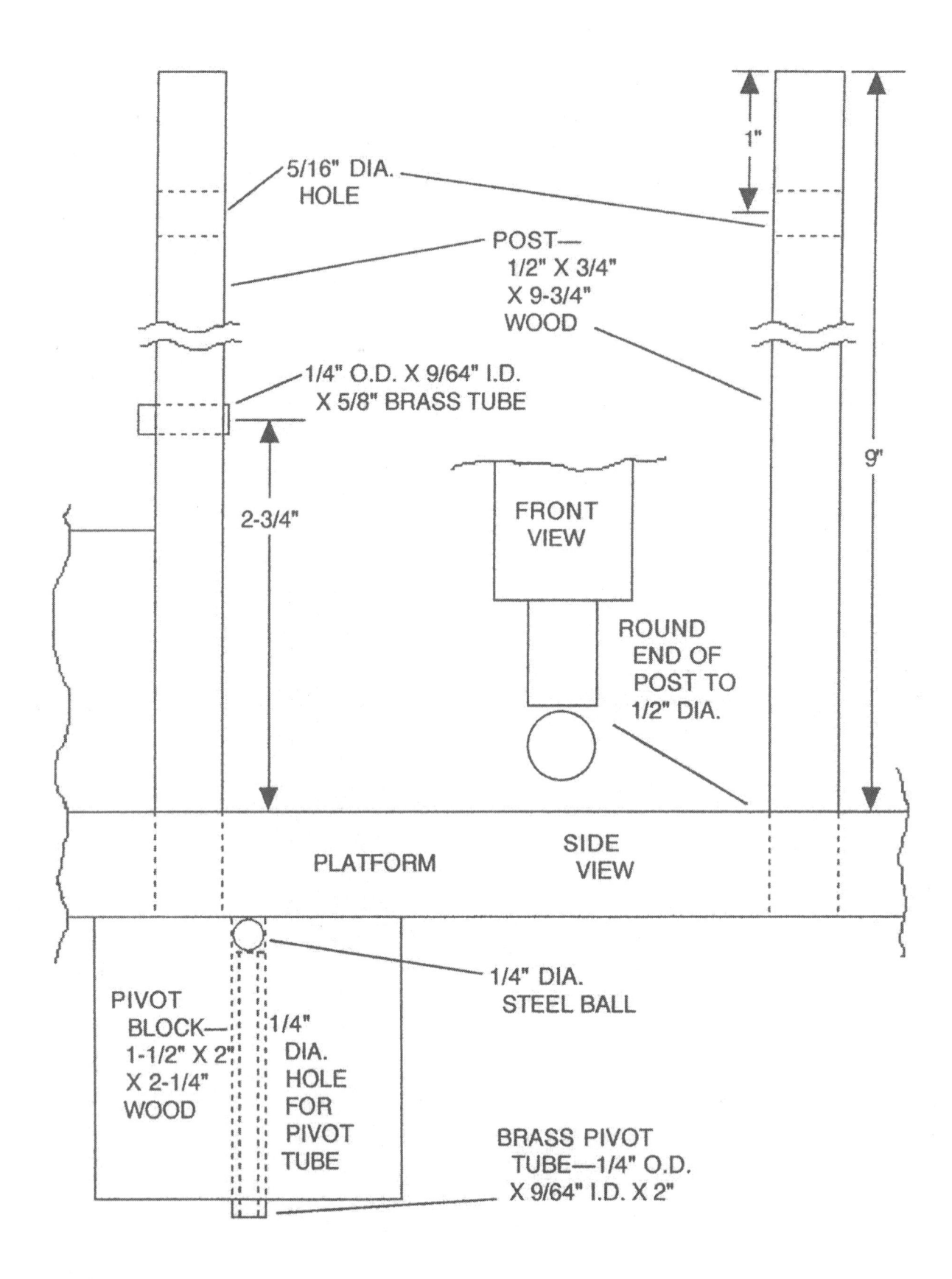

THE WHIRLIGIG MAKER'S BOOK

Plan and patterns for posts and pivot block.

154

FERRIS WHEEL

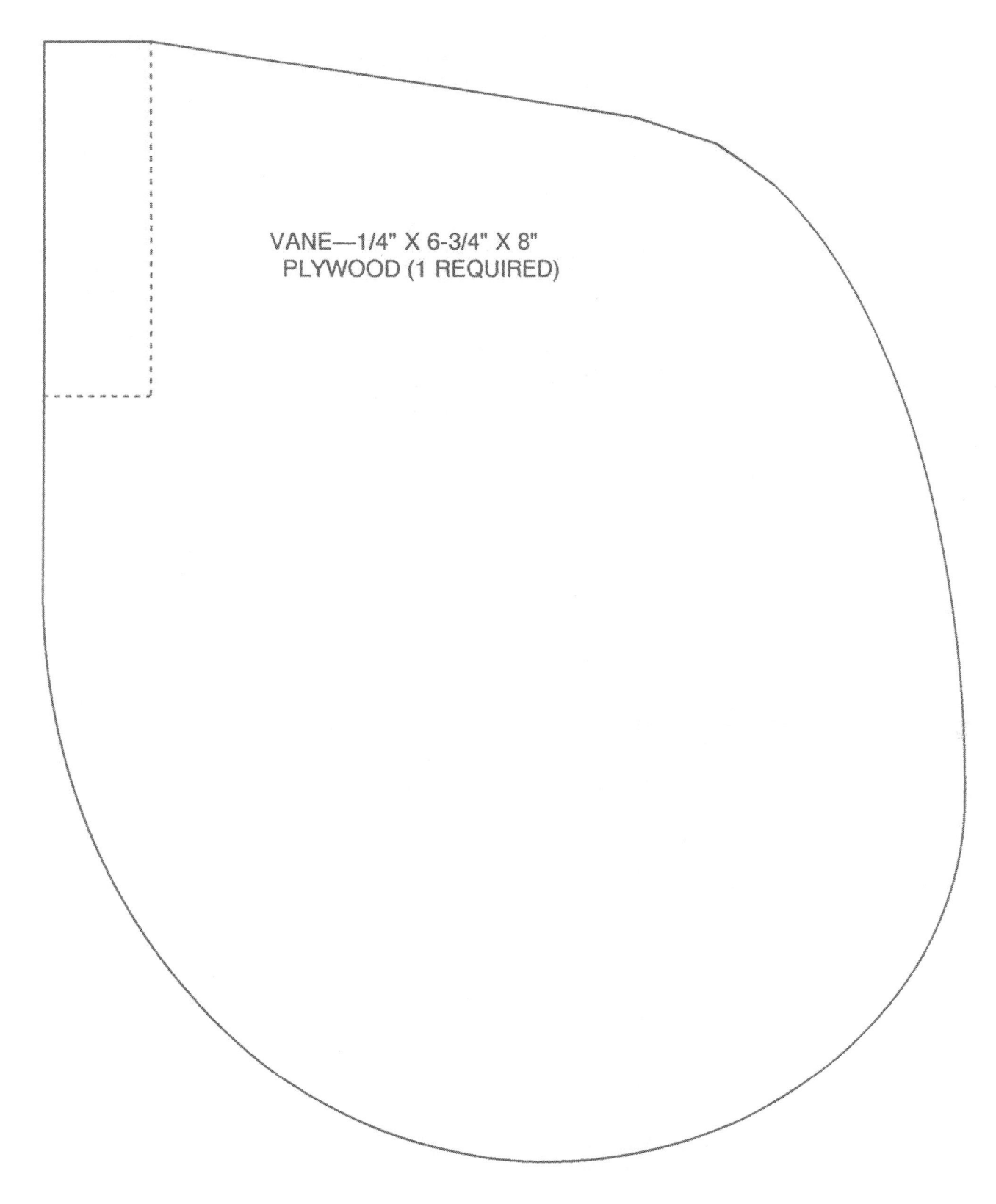

VANE—1/4" X 6-3/4" X 8"
PLYWOOD (1 REQUIRED)

Full-size pattern for vane.

155

THE WHIRLIGIG MAKER'S BOOK

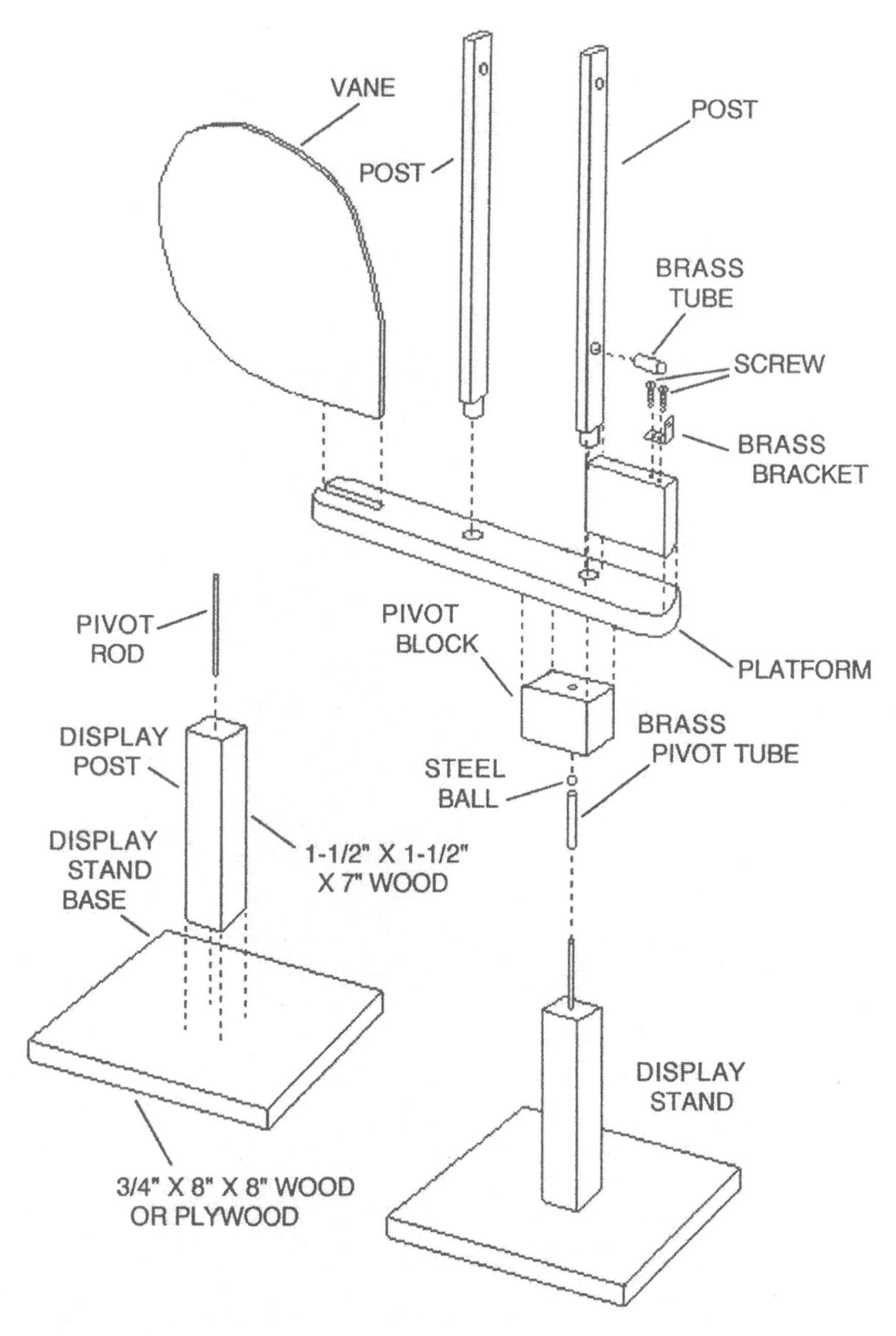

Assembly of base and platform.

FERRIS WHEEL

ASSEMBLY OF PROPELLER

PROPELLER BLADE—
3/16" WOOD OR PLYWOOD
(4 REQUIRED)

3"

3"

7-1/2"

1-1/4"

PROPELLER HUB—3/4" WOOD (1 REQUIRED)

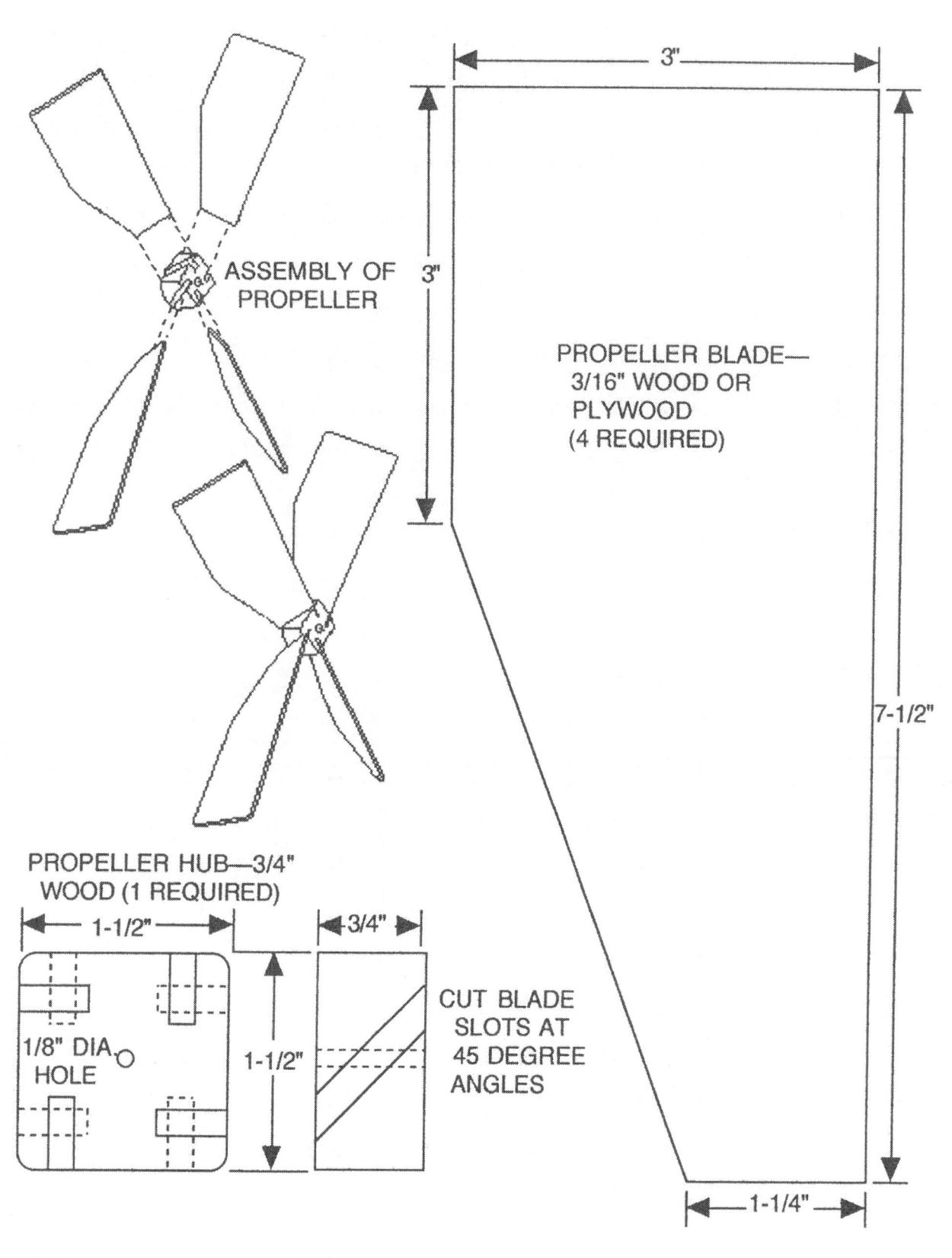

1-1/2"

3/4"

1-1/2"

1/8" DIA HOLE

CUT BLADE SLOTS AT 45 DEGREE ANGLES

Full-size patterns for propeller blades and hub.

157

THE WHIRLIGIG MAKER'S BOOK

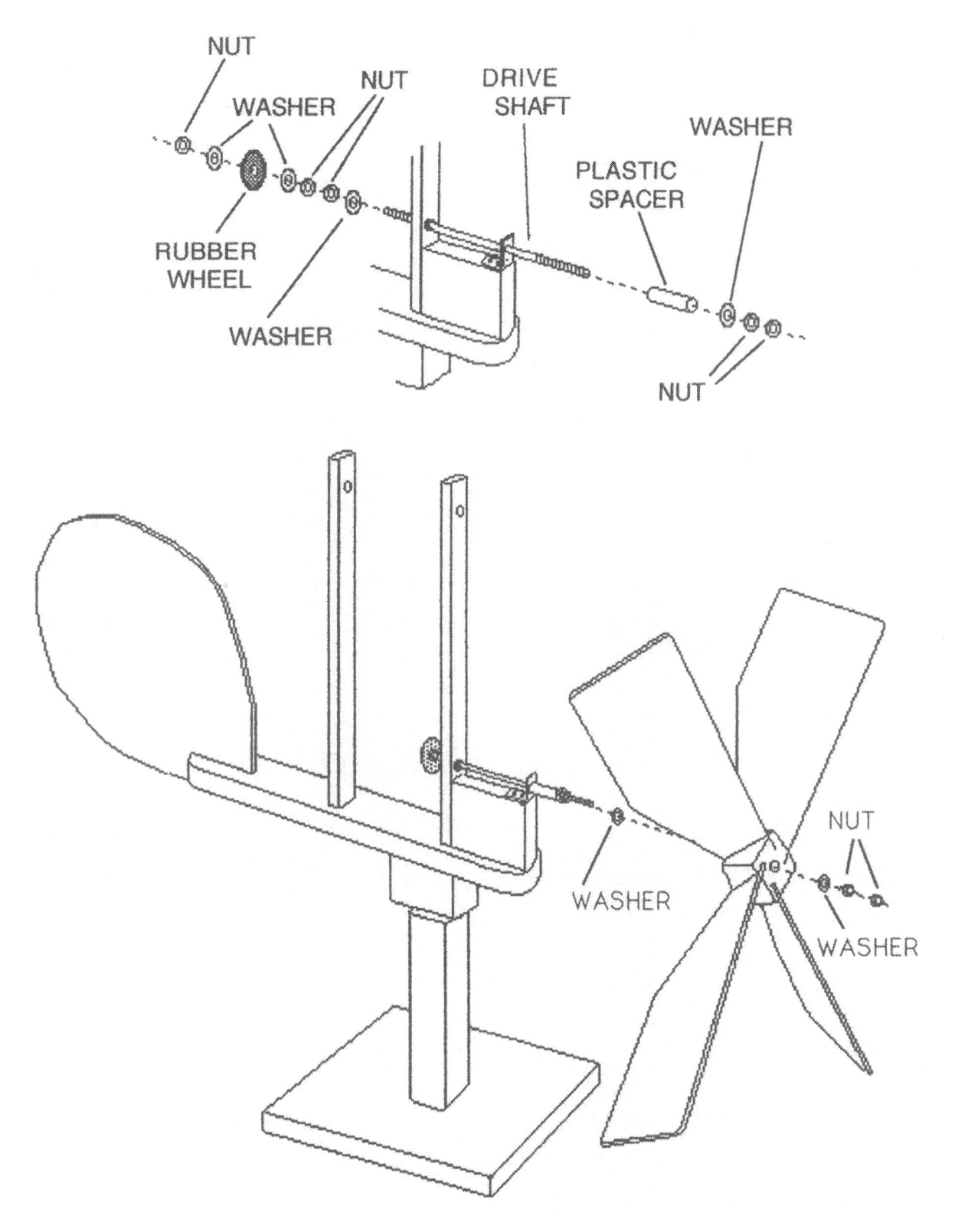

Assembly of propeller shaft.

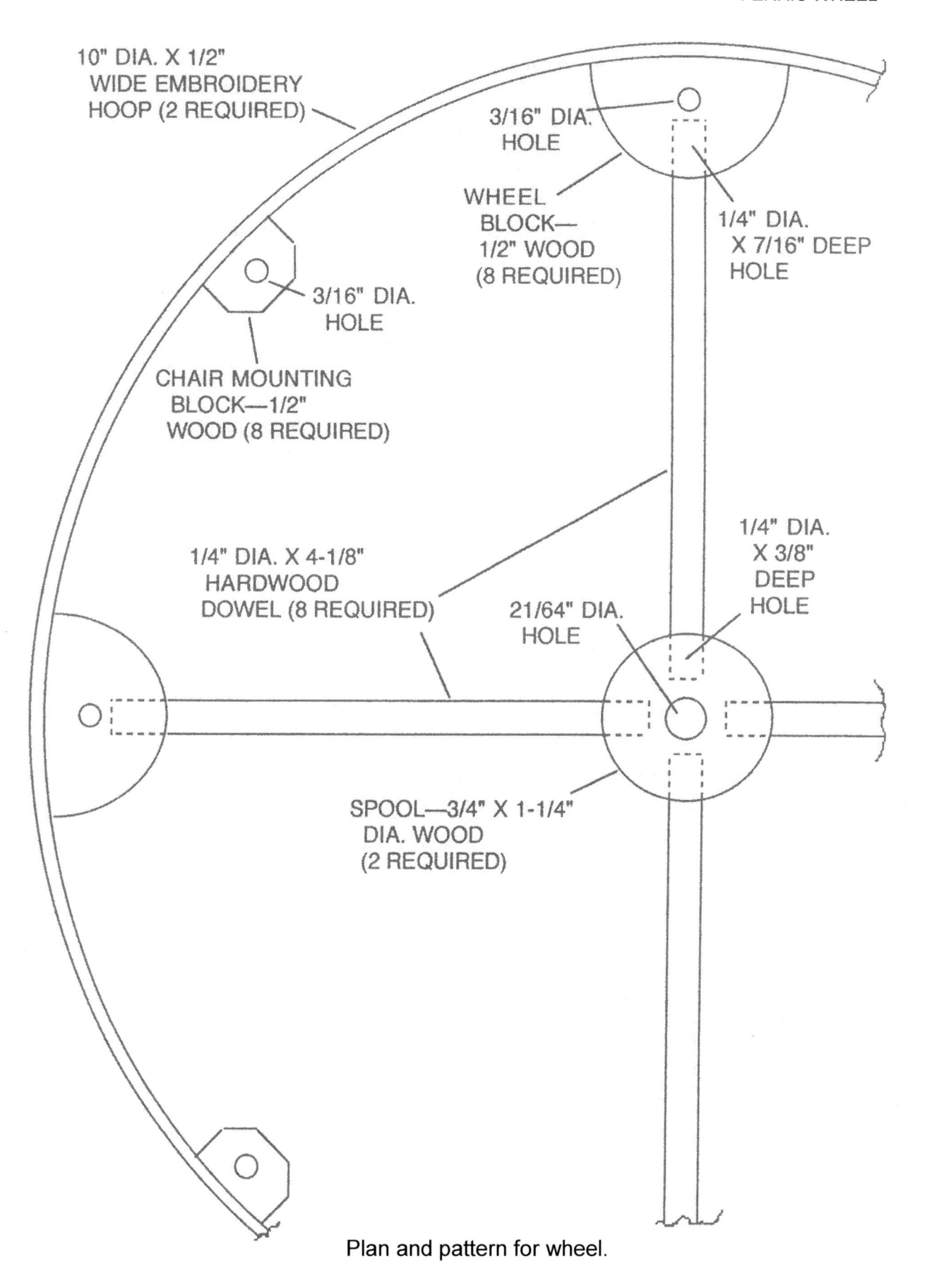

Plan and pattern for wheel.

CHAIRS AND RIDERS

The patterns for the chairs and riders for the Ferris wheel are shown. Assemble the four chairs, as shown, gluing the parts together.

Cut out the parts for the riders. Drill the holes, as shown. Paint the figures before further assembly. Then assemble the figures with glue and wires, as shown. Glue the riders to the chairs in the exact centers.

Assemble the chairs to the Ferris wheel with wood dowels and plastic tube spacers. The chairs must turn freely on the wood dowels if the whirligig is to work properly.

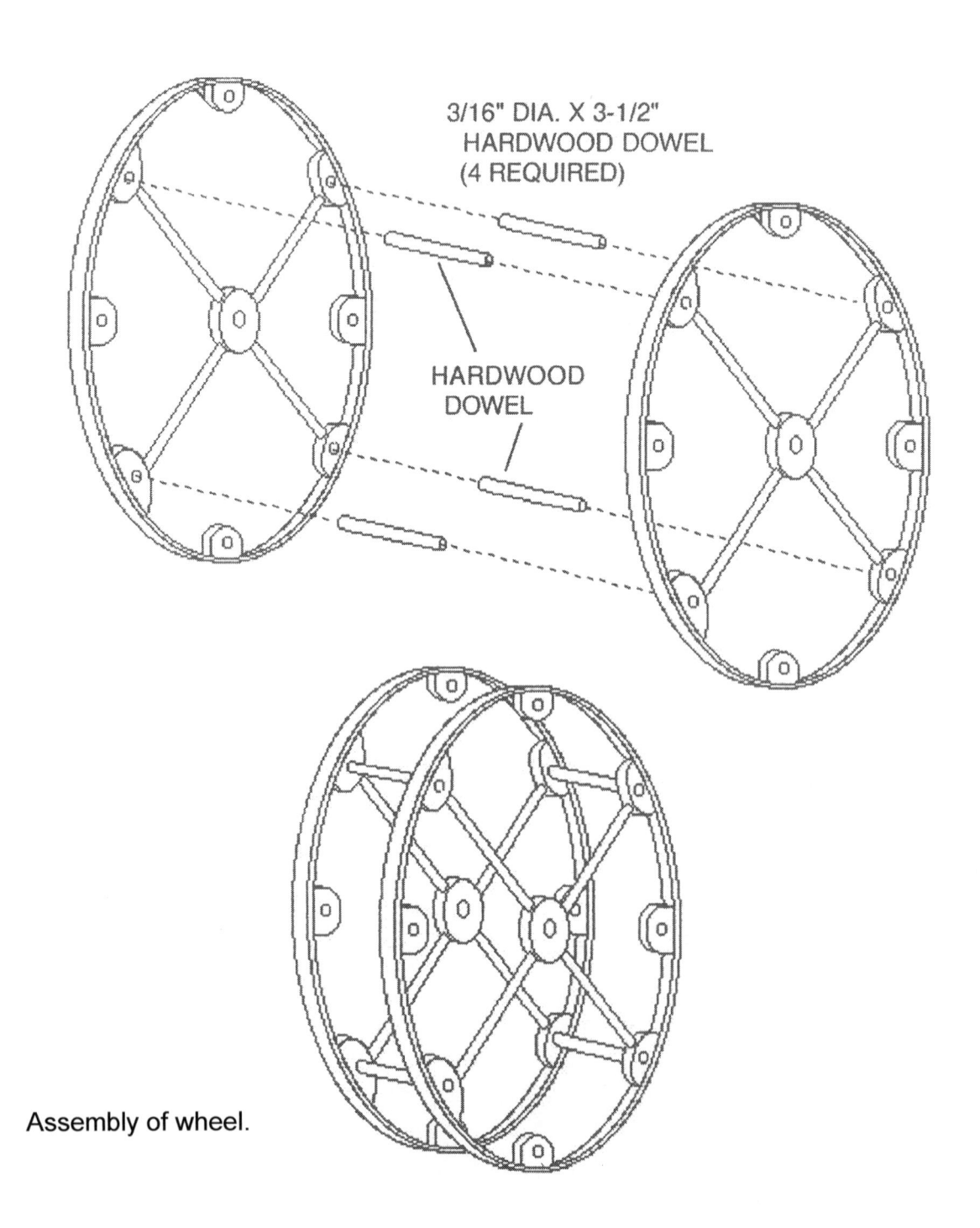

Assembly of wheel.

FERRIS WHEEL

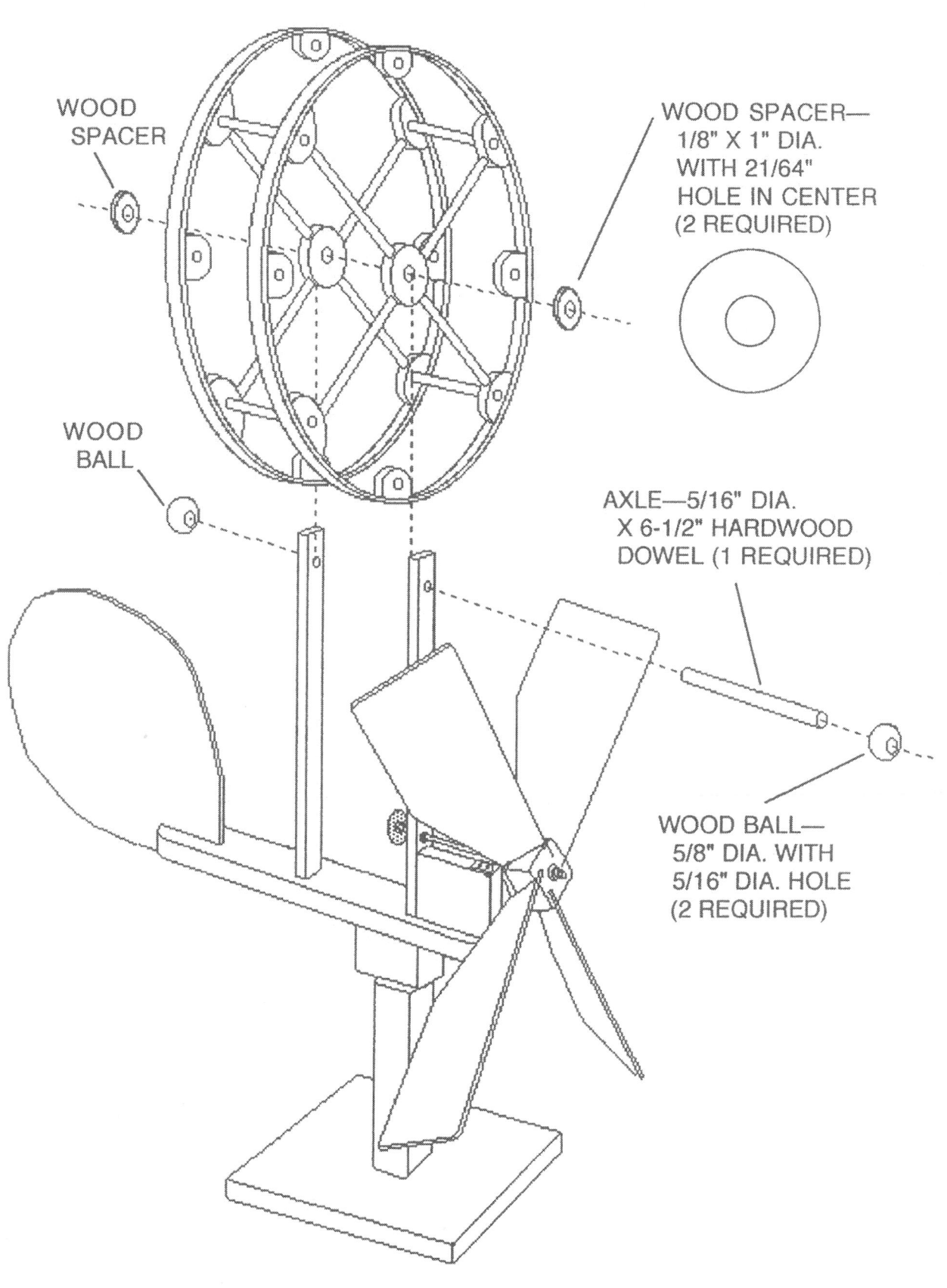

WOOD SPACER

WOOD SPACER—
1/8" X 1" DIA.
WITH 21/64"
HOLE IN CENTER
(2 REQUIRED)

WOOD BALL

AXLE—5/16" DIA.
X 6-1/2" HARDWOOD
DOWEL (1 REQUIRED)

WOOD BALL—
5/8" DIA. WITH
5/16" DIA. HOLE
(2 REQUIRED)

Assembly of wheel to posts.

161

THE WHIRLIGIG MAKER'S BOOK

TESTING AND FINISHING

The whirligig is ready for testing. This can be inside with a fan or outdoors in a light wind. The whirligig should start easily if all of the parts turn properly. Make any necessary adjustments and add oil to friction areas of metal parts.

If sanding and painting was not done previously, disassemble as necessary and do the sanding and painting.

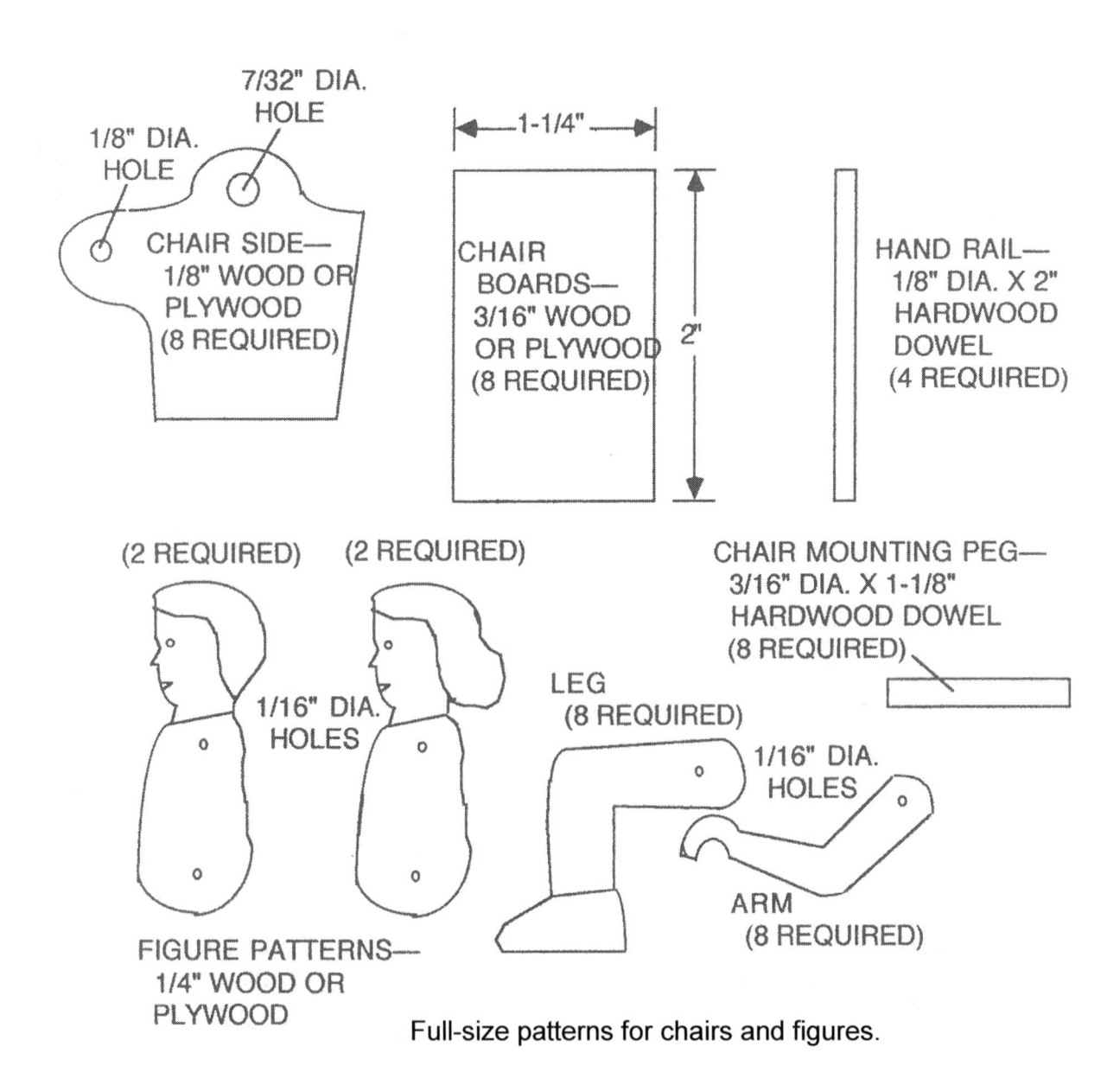

CHAIR SIDE— 1/8" WOOD OR PLYWOOD (8 REQUIRED), with 1/8" DIA. HOLE and 7/32" DIA. HOLE

CHAIR BOARDS— 3/16" WOOD OR PLYWOOD (8 REQUIRED), 1-1/4" × 2"

HAND RAIL— 1/8" DIA. × 2" HARDWOOD DOWEL (4 REQUIRED)

CHAIR MOUNTING PEG— 3/16" DIA. × 1-1/8" HARDWOOD DOWEL (8 REQUIRED)

FIGURE PATTERNS— 1/4" WOOD OR PLYWOOD (2 REQUIRED each), 1/16" DIA. HOLES

LEG (8 REQUIRED)

ARM (8 REQUIRED), 1/16" DIA. HOLES

Full-size patterns for chairs and figures.

FERRIS WHEEL

ASSEMBLY OF CHAIR

WIRE

ASSEMBLY OF FIGURES

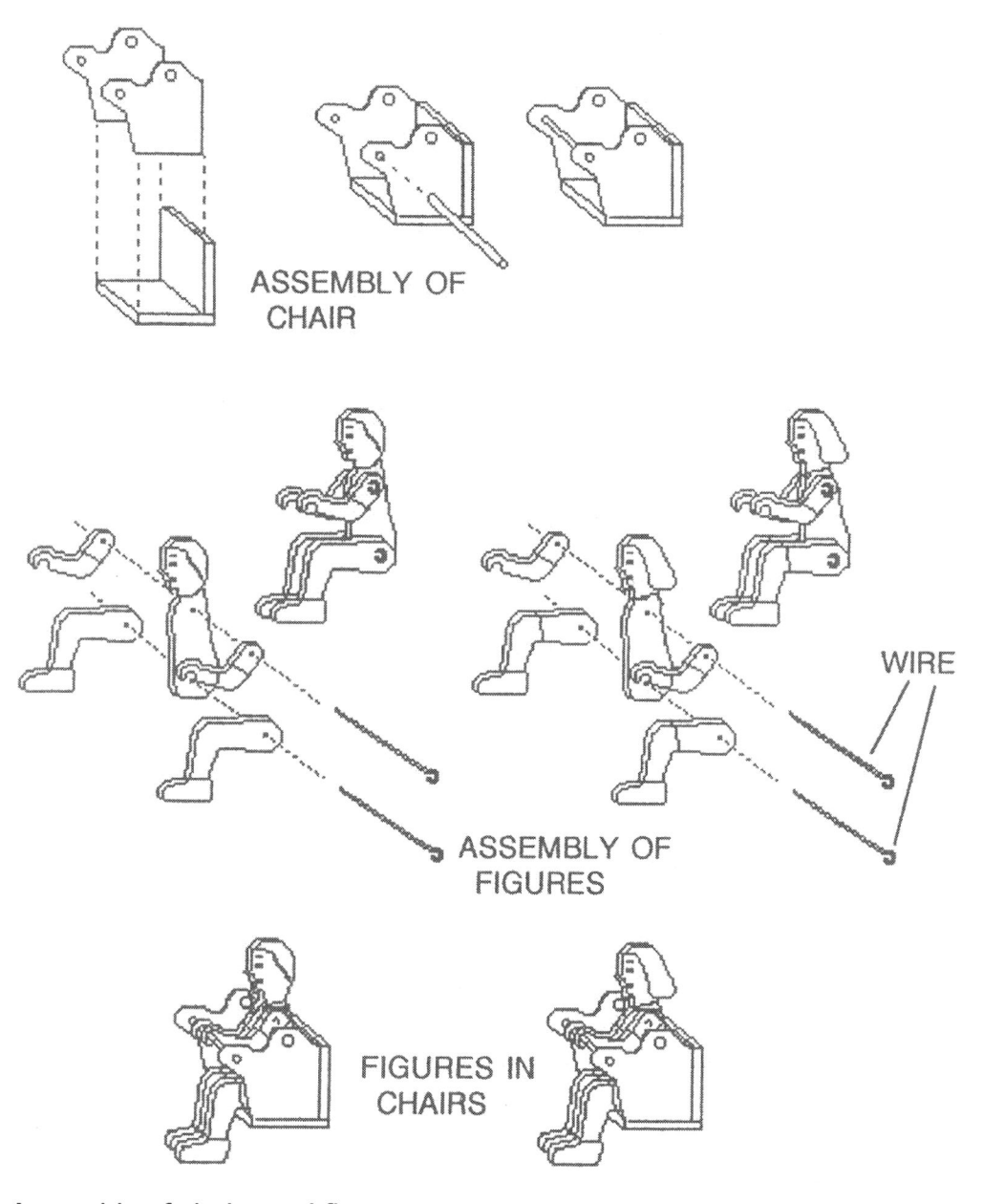

FIGURES IN CHAIRS

Assembly of chairs and figures.

163

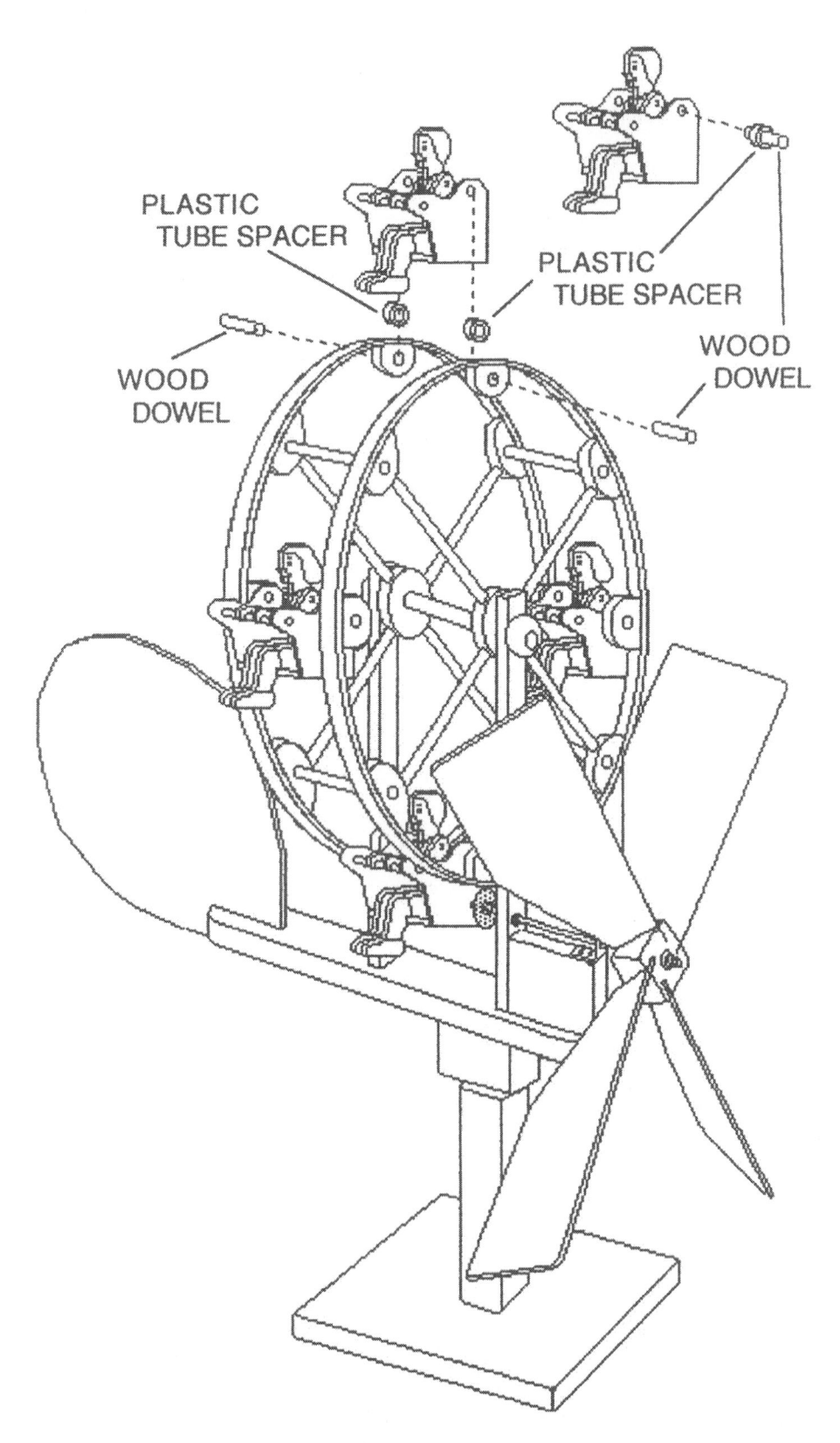

THE WHIRLIGIG MAKER'S BOOK

Assembly of chairs to Ferris wheel.

Chapter 14

UNICYCLIST

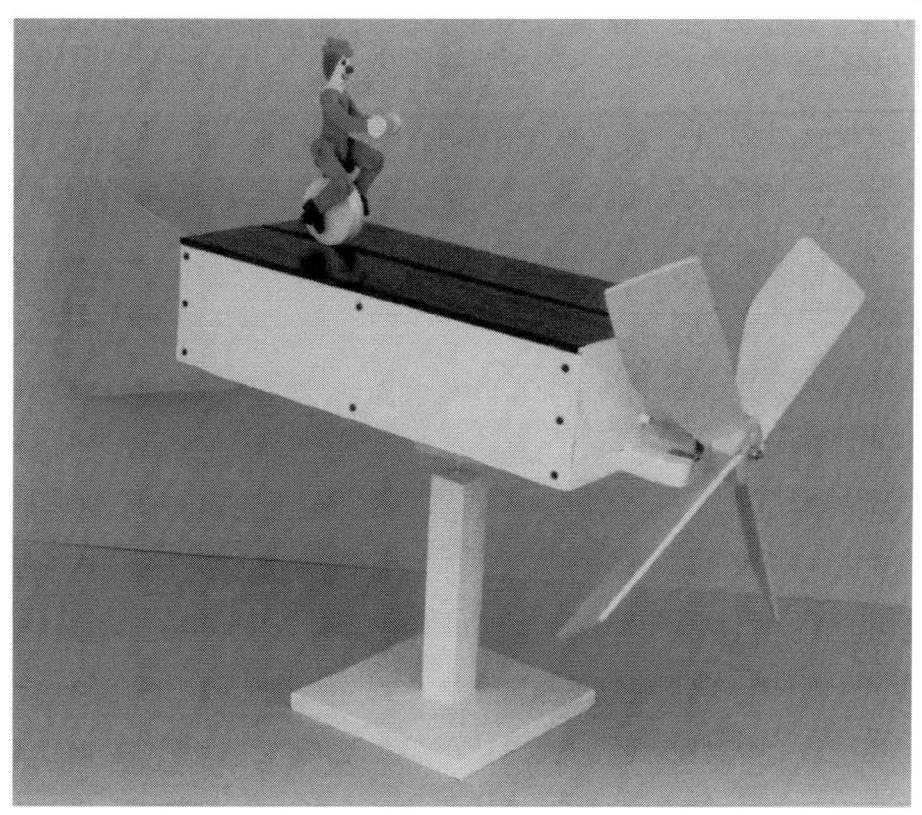

THE WHIRLIGIG MAKER'S BOOK

The Unicyclist whirligig is a fun project both to build and then watch perform after you have completed it. The back and forth riding of the unicycle without visible means of support is unique.

MATERIALS
- 3/4" x 8-1/2" x 8-1/2" wood or plywood for display base.
- 1-1/2" x 1-1/2" x 8" wood for display post.
- 1/8" diameter x 5" nail for pivot rod for display base.
- 3/4" x 7-1/2" x 22" wood for platform.
- 1/4" x 9" x 10" plywood for vane.
- 1/4" x 18" x 16-1/2" plywood for floor and side pieces.
- 3/4" x 3-1/2" x 15" wood for end pieces.
- 3/4" x 3/4" x 32" wood for side braces.
- 1-1/2" x 2" x 2-1/2" wood for pivot block.
- 1/4" x 7" x 7" plywood for driven wheel.
- 3/4" x 2" x 2" wood for wheel support block.
- 1/2" x 3/4" x 2" wood for connecting rod blocks.
- 3/16" x 3" x 30" wood or plywood for propeller blades.
- 3/4" x 1-1/2" x 1-1/2" wood for propeller hub.
- 1/4" x 6" x 10" plywood for unicycle rider body and wheel parts.
- 1/8" x 6" x 6" plywood for rider's arms and legs.
- 3/16" thick wood for arm spacers.
- 3/8" x 1" x 6" wood for leg spacers and cart wheels.
- 3/64" diameter stiff wire for arm and leg attachments.
- 1/8" diameter x 1" bolt (2 required) for attaching mounting block to unicycle support.
- Nut and washer (2 each required) for 1/8" diameter bolt.
- 1/4" diameter x 6" hardwood dowel for unicycle wheel axle and cart wheel axles.
- 1/2" diameter wood ball with 1/4" diameter hole (4 required) for mounting cart wheels.
- 1/8" diameter x 2" hardwood dowel for pedal axles.
- 1/4" diameter wood ball with 1/8" diameter hole (2 required) for mounting feet the pedal axle.
- Small plastic washer with 1/8" diameter hole (2 required) for pedal axle spacer.
- 1/4" outside diameter (9/64" inside diameter) x 2" brass tubing for pivot bearing.
- 1/8" diameter x 7" brass rod for crank shaft.
- 1" diameter rubber wheel with 1/8" diameter shaft hole for drive wheel.
- 3/8" diameter x 3" bolt with 1-1/2" of threads for axle for driven wheel.
- Nut and washer (2 each required) for 3/8" diameter axle bolt.
- 7/16" outside diameter (25/64" inside diameter) brass tube for driven wheel shaft bearing.
- 5/64" diameter x 8" stiff wire for connecting rod.
- 1/4" diameter steel ball for pivot bearing.
- 6-32 nut (7 required) for attaching propeller hub and drive wheel to shaft.
- Washer (6 required) for use on propeller shaft.
- 1" long plastic tubing with 1/8" diameter hole for crankshaft spacer.
- 1/2" x 1" x 1" brass L-bracket for propeller shaft mounting.
- 1/4" outside diameter (9/64" inside diameter) brass tubing for propeller shaft bearing.
- Screw (2 required) for mounting L-bracket.
- Wood screw and two washers for attaching connecting rod wire to driven wheel.
- Small wood screw (16 required) for mounting side pieces to platform box.
- Glue.
- Finishing nails.
- Small felt pad for display base (4 required).
- Paint.

DISPLAY STAND
The display stand is useful not only for displaying the finished whirligig indoors, but also for holding the whirligig during construction and for testing it in front of a fan.

UNICYCLIST

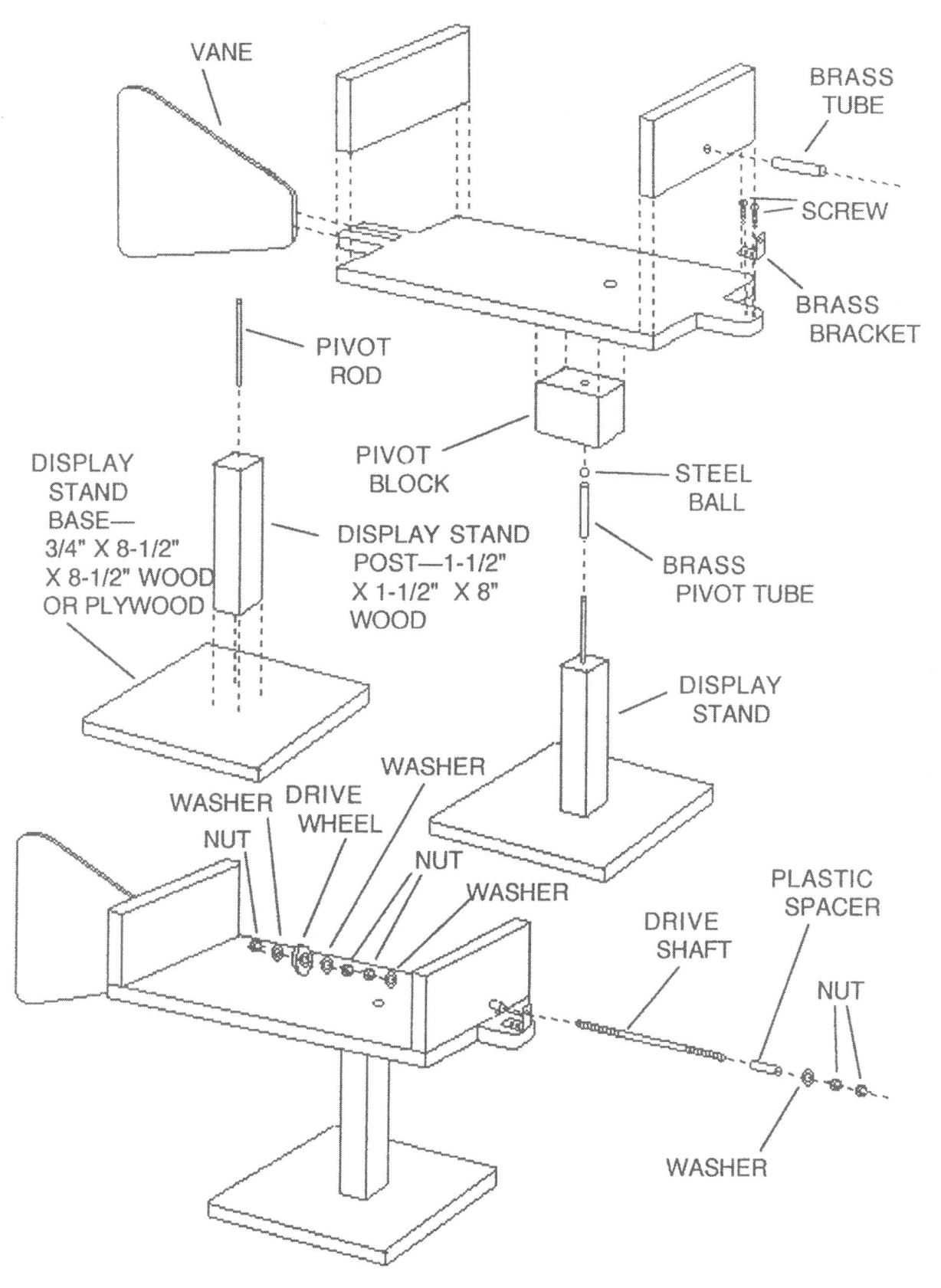

Assembly of base and platform.

167

THE WHIRLIGIG MAKER'S BOOK

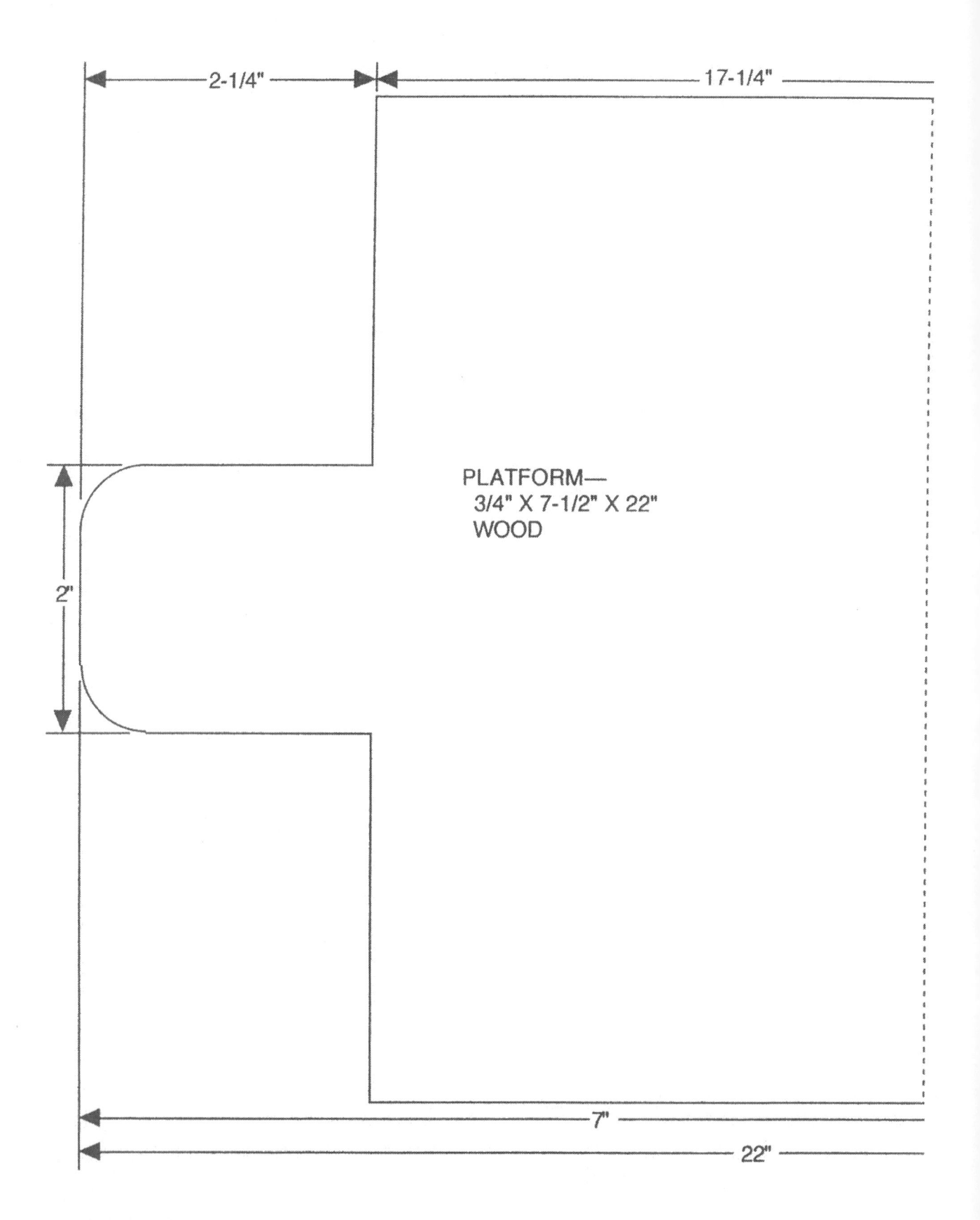

PLATFORM—
3/4" X 7-1/2" X 22"
WOOD

Full-size pattern for platform.

UNICYCLIST

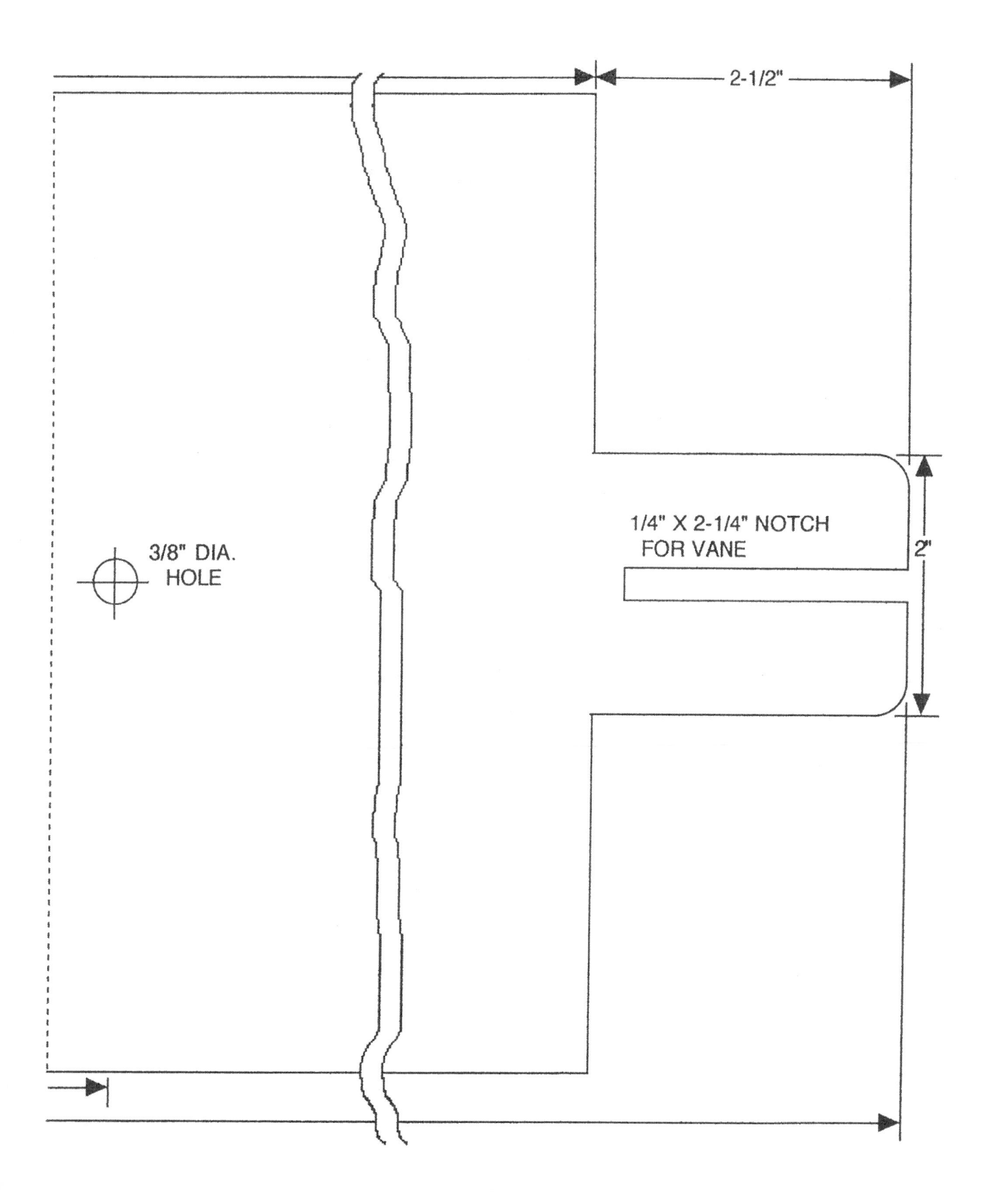

2-1/2"

3/8" DIA.
HOLE

1/4" X 2-1/4" NOTCH
FOR VANE

2"

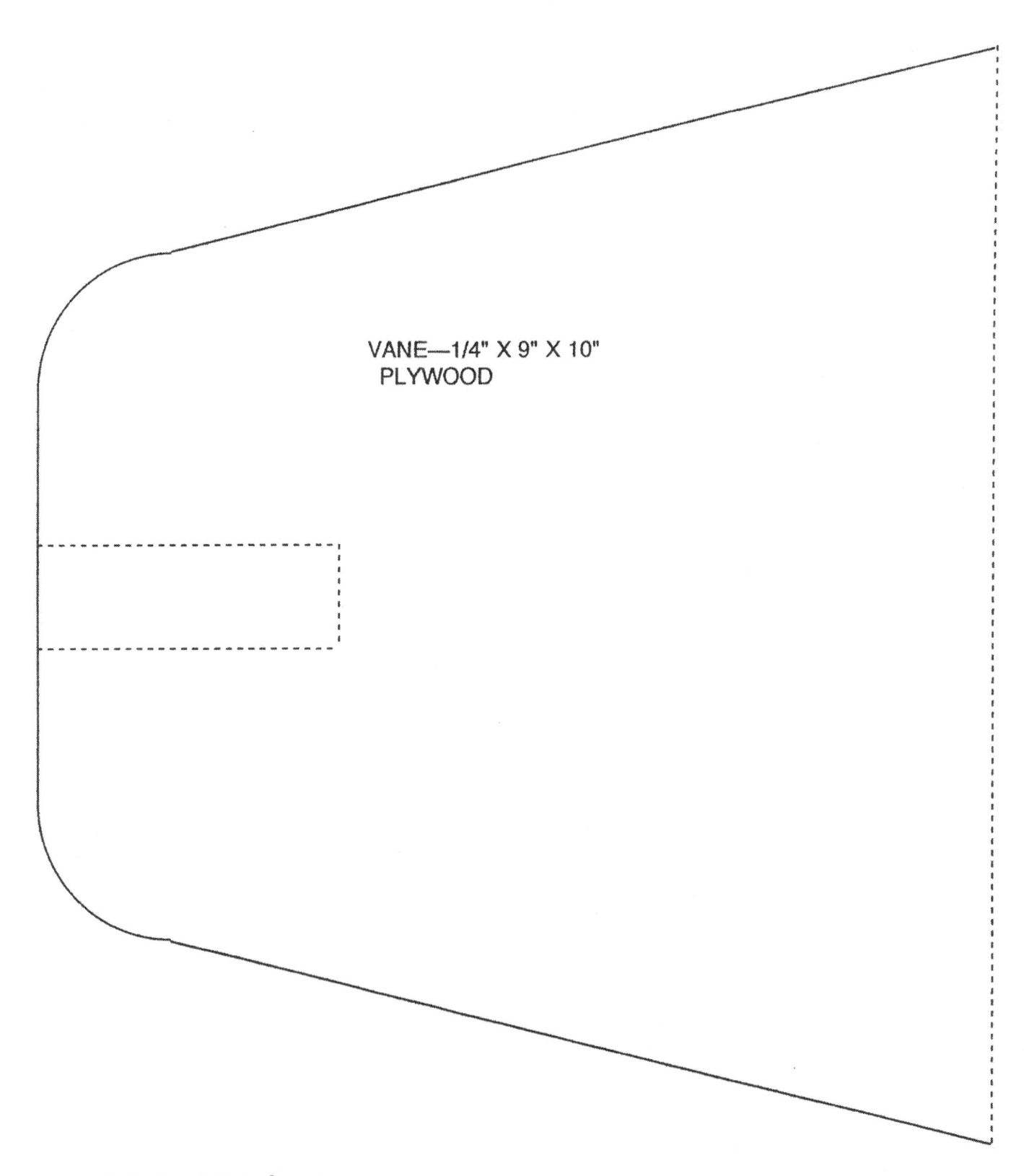

THE WHIRLIGIG MAKER'S BOOK

VANE—1/4" X 9" X 10" PLYWOOD

Full-size pattern for vane.

UNICYCLIST

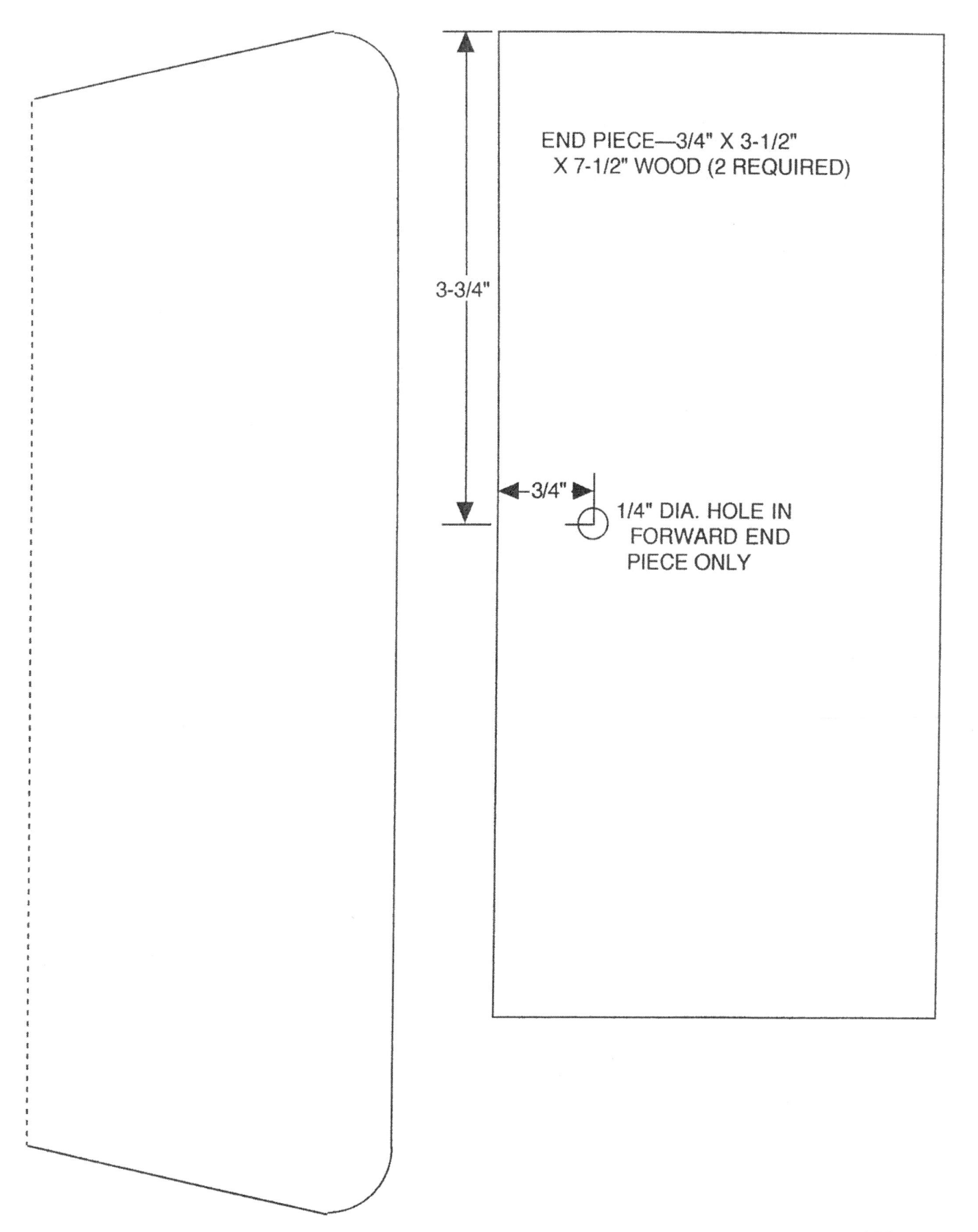

END PIECE—3/4" X 3-1/2"
X 7-1/2" WOOD (2 REQUIRED)

3-3/4"

←3/4"→

1/4" DIA. HOLE IN
FORWARD END
PIECE ONLY

THE WHIRLIGIG MAKER'S BOOK

Full-size plan and patterns for platform and propeller shaft.

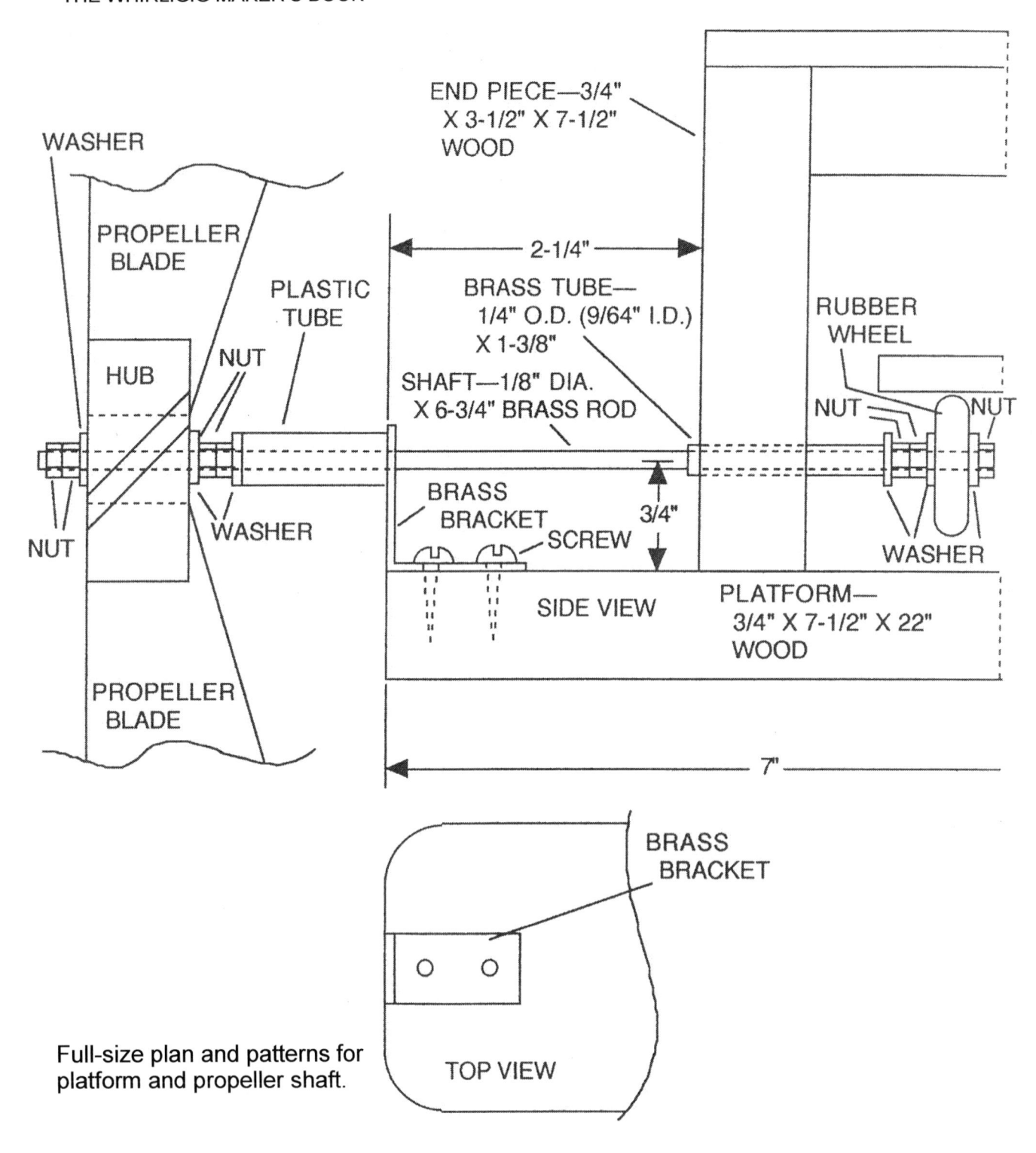

Construction is easy. The base is 3/4" x 8-1/2" x 8-1/2" wood or plywood. The 1-1/2" x 1-1/2" x 8" post is glued in the center of the base. Use nails from underside of base for added support. A 1/8" diameter x 5" nail is driven 2" into the center of the top of the post for use as a pivot rod. Drill a pilot hole perpendicular to the top of the post before driving the nail into the hole. Cut the head off of the nail with a hacksaw. File the upper end of the nail smooth, rounding the corners slightly.

UNICYCLIST

FLOOR

SIDE BRACE—3/4" X 3/4" X 15-3/4" WOOD (2 REQUIRED)

BOLT—3/8" DIA. X 3"

SCREW

WASHER

BRASS TUBE— 7/16" O.D. (25/64" I.D.) X 1-1/8"

MOUNTING BLOCK— 1/2" X 3/4" X 3/4" WOOD

WOOD—3/4" X 2" DIA. WITH 7/16" DIA. HOLE IN CENTER

DRIVEN WHEEL— 1/4" X 7" DIA. PLYWOOD WITH 7/16" DIA. HOLE IN CENTER

WASHER

NUT

WASHER

NUT

PIVOT BLOCK— 1-1/2" X 2" X 2-1/2" WOOD

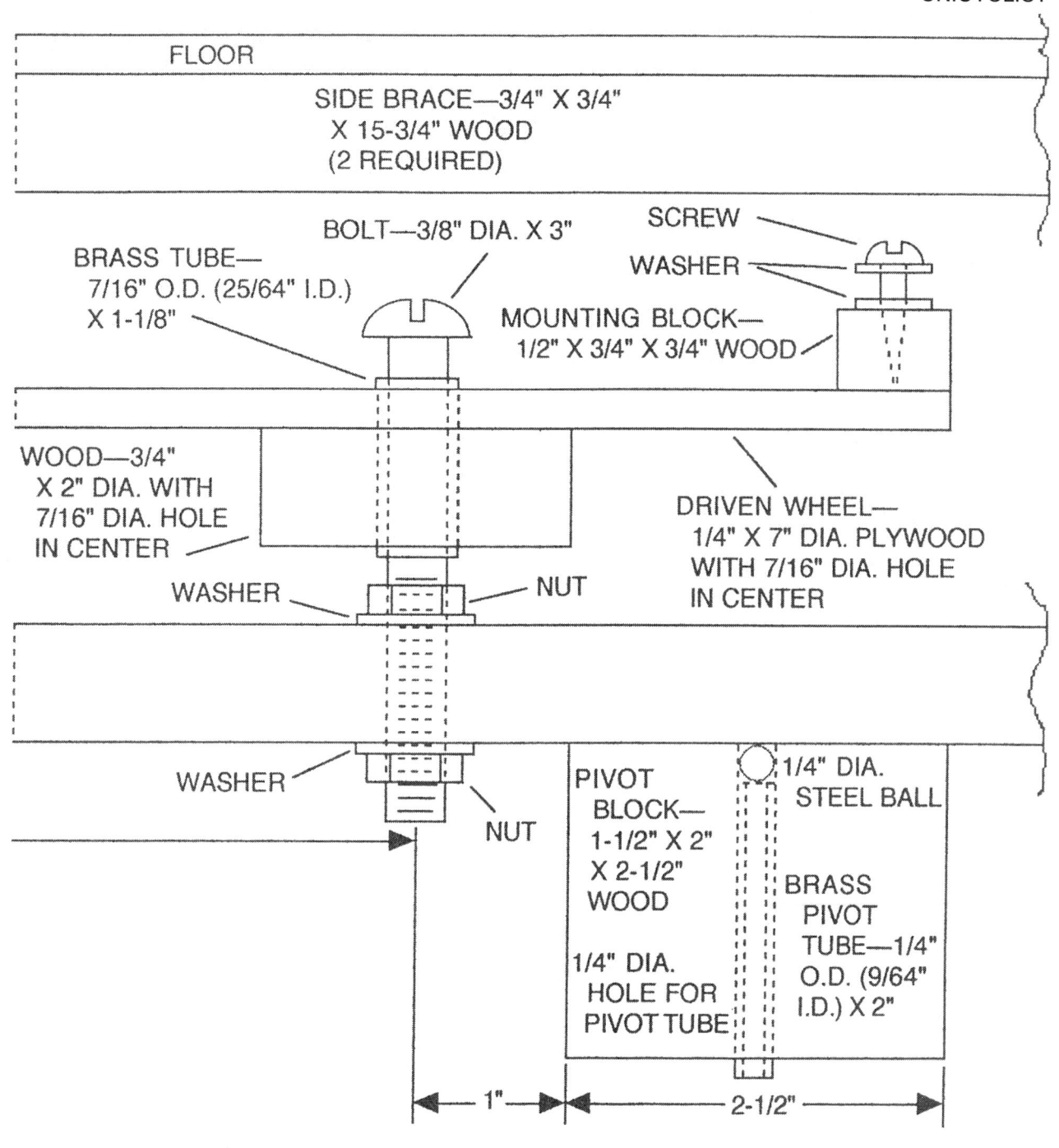

1/4" DIA. HOLE FOR PIVOT TUBE

1/4" DIA. STEEL BALL

BRASS PIVOT TUBE—1/4" O.D. (9/64" I.D.) X 2"

1" 2-1/2"

Sand and paint the display stand. A clear or color finish can be used.

Attach felt pads to the corners of the underside of the base.

173

PLATFORM AND PROPELLER

The platform is made of 3/4" x 7-1/2" x 22" wood. Shape the ends, as shown. Make a 1/4" x 2-1/4" slot for the vane. Drill a 3/8" diameter hole for the driven wheel shaft bolt, as shown.

Cut the end pieces to the pattern shown. Drill a 1/4" diameter hole in the forward end piece for the brass tube, as shown. Glue and nail the end pieces to the platform.

Use a 1/2" x 1" x 1" brass L-bracket with 9/64" diameter hole for the propeller shaft. Fasten the brass L-bracket to the platform with screws. Depending on the bracket selected, it may be necessary to expand hole sizes and/or drill additional holes. Install the brass shaft tube in the hole in the forward end piece. The tube should fit tightly in the hole so it will not slip or turn.

The pivot block is shaped from 1-1/2" x 2" x 2-1/2" wood to the pattern shown. Drill a 1/4" hole for the pivot tube, as shown. The hole must be accurately centered and perpendicular to the wood surfaces for the whirligig to work properly. I use a drill press and drill press vise for drilling this hole.

Glue and nail the wood pivot block to the platform. Next, install a 1/4" diameter steel ball in the pivot hole. Then install the brass pivot tube, as shown.

Cut the vane from 1/4" plywood to the pattern shown. Glue the vane in the platform slot, as shown.

The propeller shaft is made from 1/8" diameter x 6-3/4" brass rod. Make threads for 1-3/4" on one end of the rod and 1" on the other end using a 6-32 die. Slip the crankshaft into the shaft holes. Install spacers, washers, nuts and drive wheel on shaft. The shaft should turn freely in the tube with no binding. Apply light oil to the shaft to further decrease friction.

Cut the driven wheel, wheel support block, and connecting rod blocks to the patterns shown. Drill holes in positions shown.

Glue and nail the support block and connecting rod block to the driven wheel. Install the brass shaft tube in the hole in the center of the driven wheel and wheel support block. The tube must fit tightly in the hole so that it will not slip or turn.

Shape the wire connecting rod to the pattern shown. Attach the loop end to the driven wheel mounting block with a screw and two washers, as shown. The other end of the wire passes through the connecting wire mounting block. Bend the end of the wire so that it will not slip out of the hole in the mounting block.

Cut the floor and side braces to the patterns shown. Install the side braces and floor pieces to the platform with glue and nails. Leave a 9/64" space between the two floor sections. The floor pieces should extend beyond the end pieces 1/4" on each side of the platform.

The platform can be sanded and painted at this time. I paint the floor, including inside the notch, black and the unicycle wheel white for maximum contrast, but you can use any desired colors.

The propeller hub is made from 3/4" x 1-1/2" x 1-1/2" wood. Drill a 1/8" shaft hole. Cut the 3/16" wide x 1/2" deep notches for the propeller blades at 45 degree angles to the face of the hub. Notice that a clockwise propeller is shown. If desired, a counterclockwise propeller can be substituted.

Cut the propeller blades from 3/16" wood or plywood to the pattern shown. Then glue the blades in the slots in the hub. Place the hub on a flat surface with the forward side down. The blades are then installed with the forward side flush with the flat surface.

Paint the propeller at this time.

Install the propeller on the shaft, as shown. Secure the propeller with a washer and two nuts.

Test the assembly in front of a fan to make certain that the propeller and shaft assembly works properly.

UNICYCLIST

1/8" DIA. HOLE

UNICYCLE CONNECTING ROD BLOCK—1/2" X 1/2" X 3/4" WOOD (1 REQUIRED)

3/32" DIA. HOLE

SIDE VIEW

TOP VIEW

PATTERN FOR CONNECTING ROD WIRE

CONNECTING ROD BLOCK— 1/2" X 3/4" X 3/4" WOOD

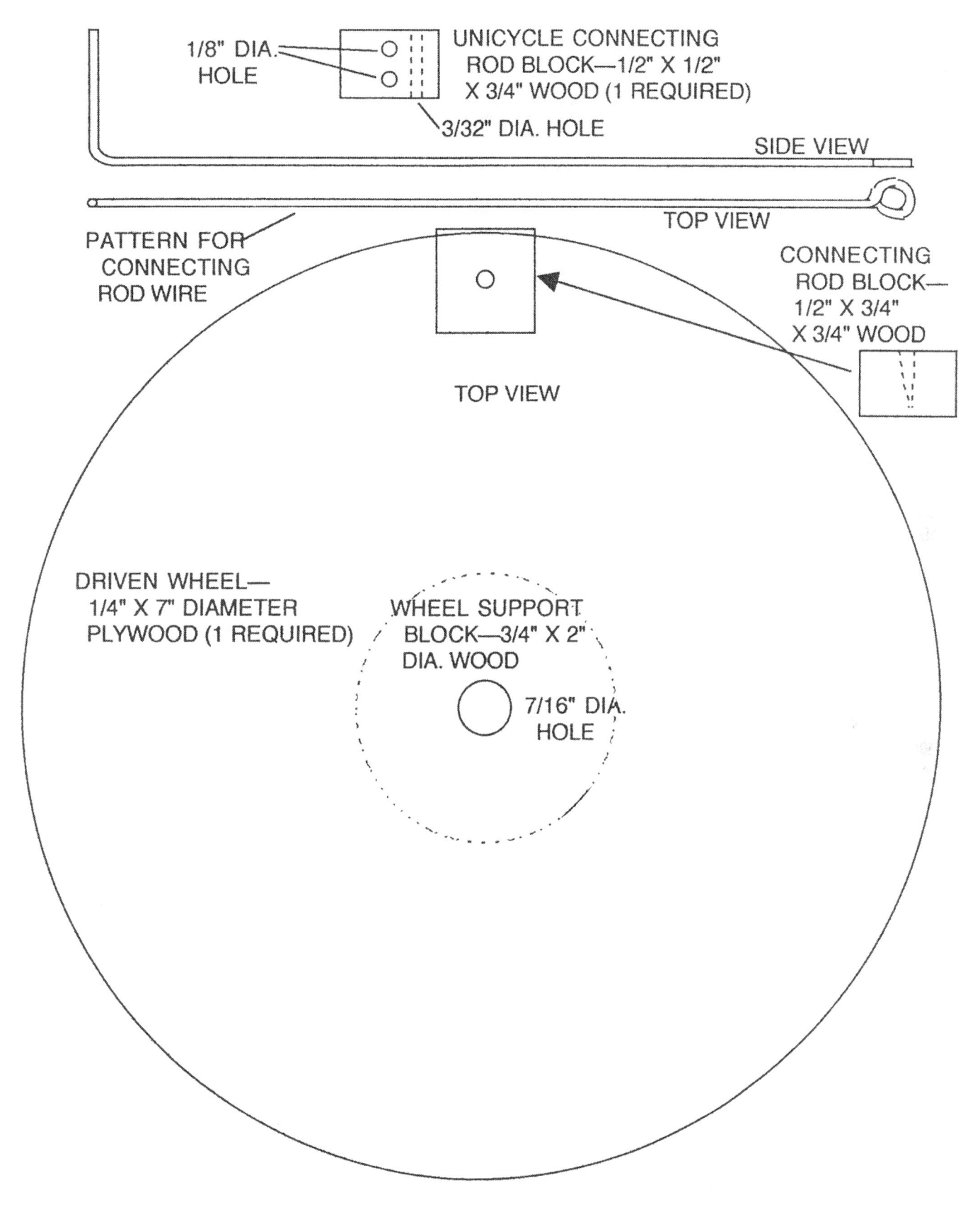

TOP VIEW

DRIVEN WHEEL— 1/4" X 7" DIAMETER PLYWOOD (1 REQUIRED)

WHEEL SUPPORT BLOCK—3/4" X 2" DIA. WOOD

7/16" DIA. HOLE

Full-size patterns for driven wheel and connecting rod and blocks.

175

THE WHIRLIGIG MAKER'S BOOK

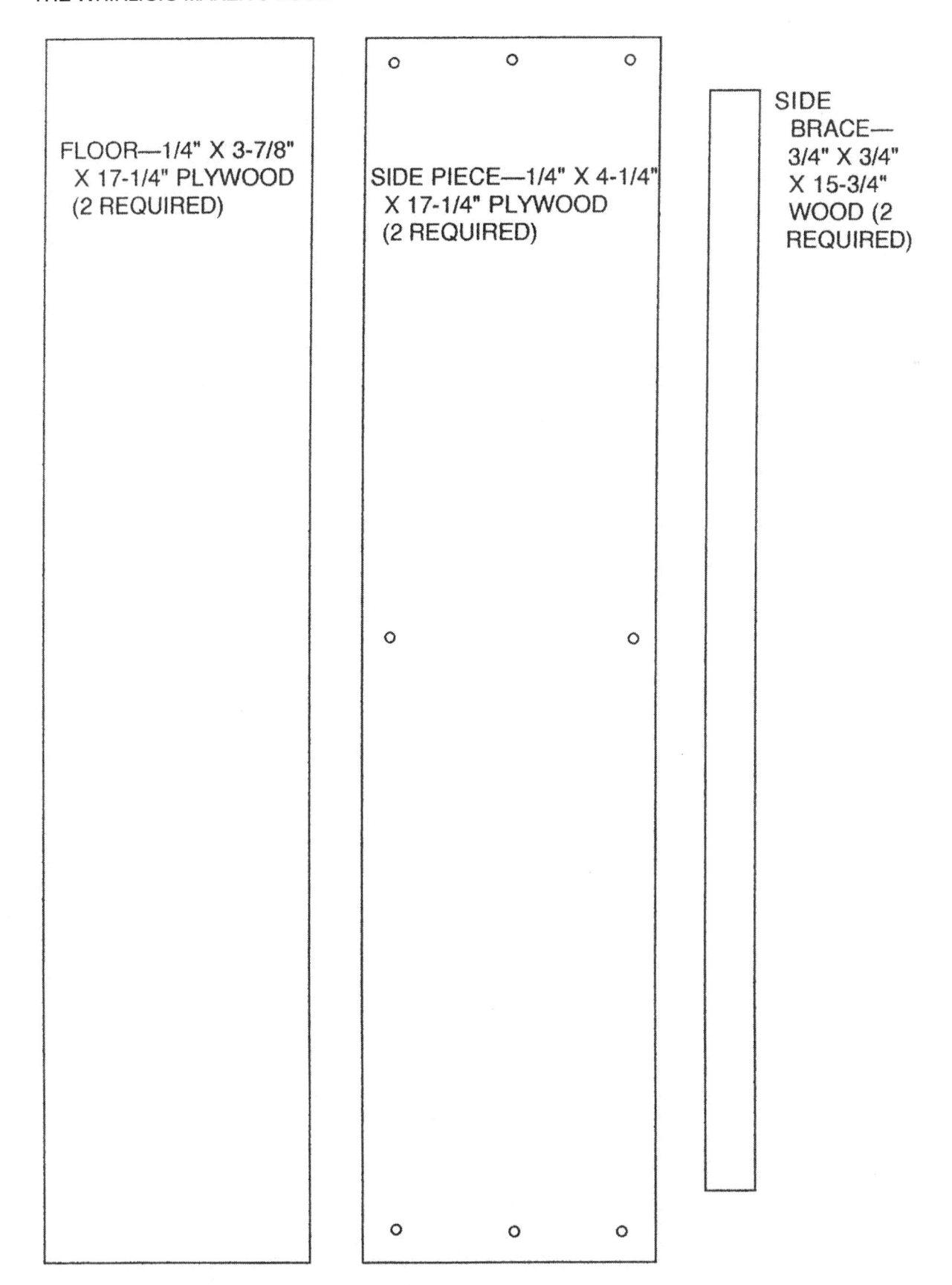

FLOOR—1/4" X 3-7/8" X 17-1/4" PLYWOOD (2 REQUIRED)

SIDE PIECE—1/4" X 4-1/4" X 17-1/4" PLYWOOD (2 REQUIRED)

SIDE BRACE— 3/4" X 3/4" X 15-3/4" WOOD (2 REQUIRED)

Patterns for floor and side pieces and braces (reduced to fit page, use dimensions shown).

UNICYCLIST

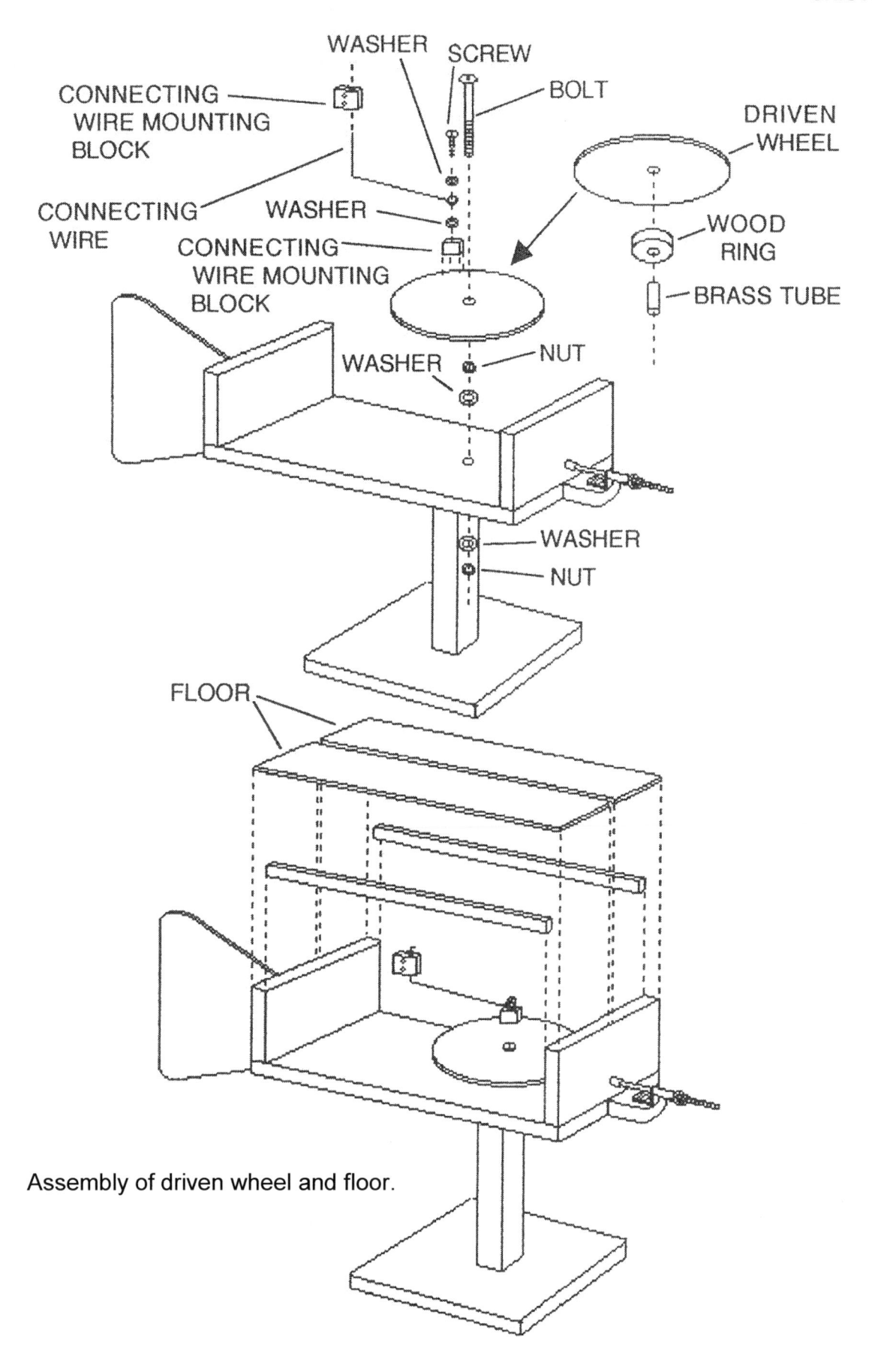

WASHER SCREW
CONNECTING WIRE MOUNTING BLOCK
BOLT
DRIVEN WHEEL
CONNECTING WIRE
WASHER
CONNECTING WIRE MOUNTING BLOCK
WOOD RING
BRASS TUBE
WASHER — NUT
WASHER
NUT
FLOOR

Assembly of driven wheel and floor.

177

THE WHIRLIGIG MAKER'S BOOK

ASSEMBLY OF PROPELLER

PROPELLER BLADE—
3/16" WOOD OR
PLYWOOD
(4 REQUIRED)

3"

3-3/4"

7-1/2"

1-1/4"

PROPELLER HUB—3/4"
WOOD (1 REQUIRED)

1-1/2"

1/8" DIA HOLE

3/4"

1-1/2"

CUT BLADE
SLOTS AT
45 DEGREE
ANGLES

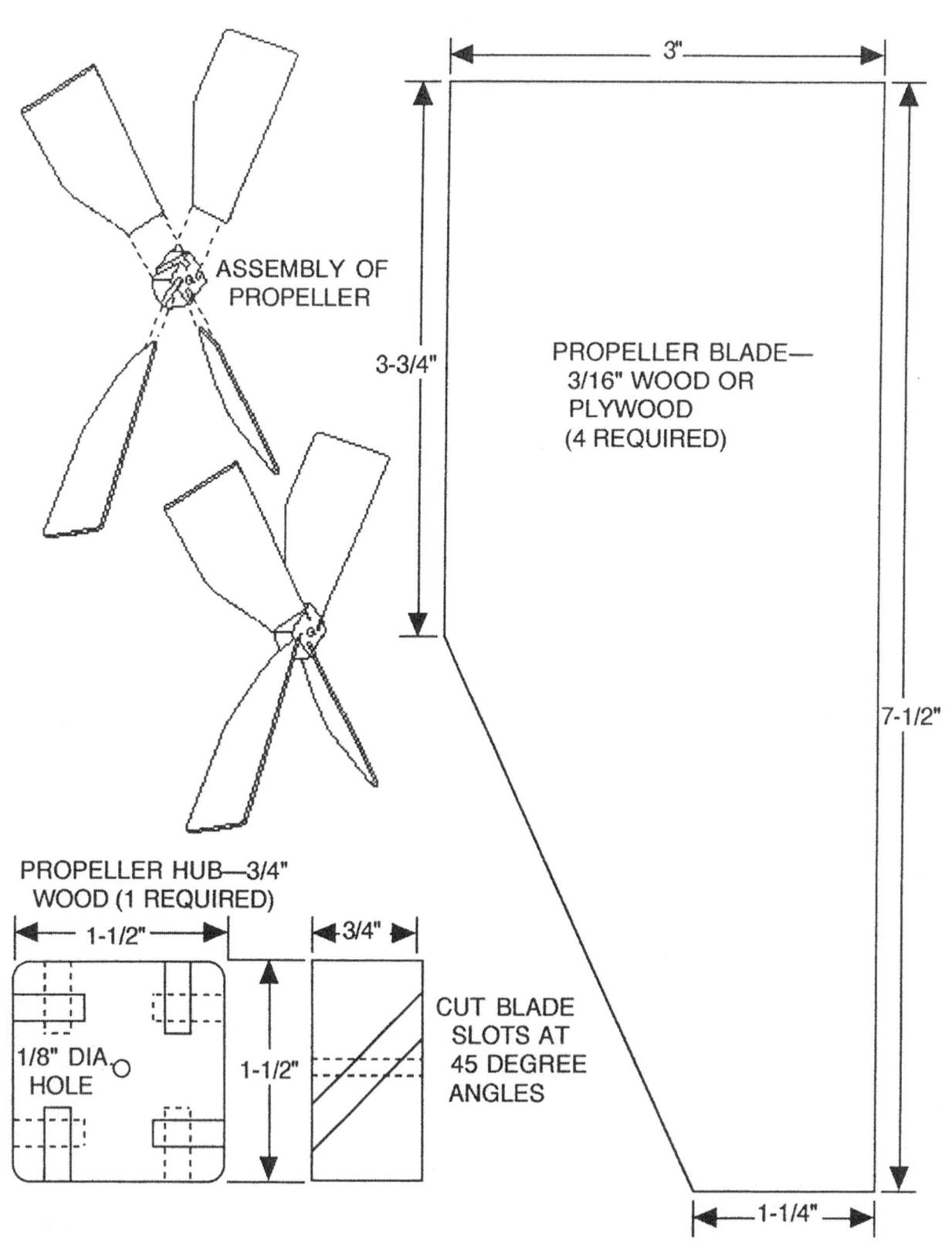

Full-size patterns for propeller blades and hub.

178

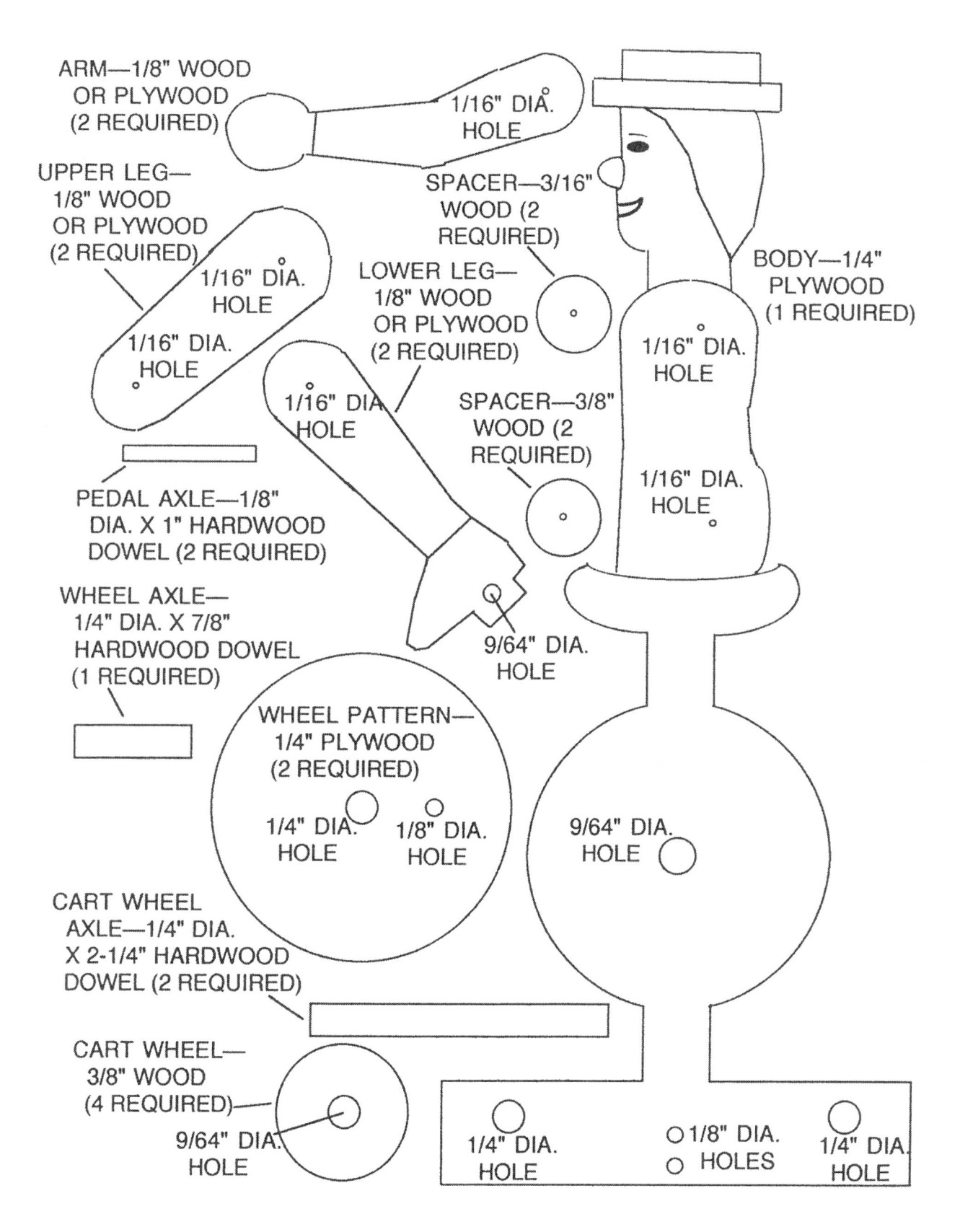

UNICYCLIST

ARM—1/8" WOOD OR PLYWOOD (2 REQUIRED)

1/16" DIA. HOLE

UPPER LEG—1/8" WOOD OR PLYWOOD (2 REQUIRED)

SPACER—3/16" WOOD (2 REQUIRED)

LOWER LEG—1/8" WOOD OR PLYWOOD (2 REQUIRED)

1/16" DIA. HOLE

1/16" DIA. HOLE

BODY—1/4" PLYWOOD (1 REQUIRED)

1/16" DIA. HOLE

1/16" DIA. HOLE

SPACER—3/8" WOOD (2 REQUIRED)

1/16" DIA. HOLE

PEDAL AXLE—1/8" DIA. X 1" HARDWOOD DOWEL (2 REQUIRED)

WHEEL AXLE—1/4" DIA. X 7/8" HARDWOOD DOWEL (1 REQUIRED)

9/64" DIA. HOLE

WHEEL PATTERN—1/4" PLYWOOD (2 REQUIRED)

1/4" DIA. HOLE

1/8" DIA. HOLE

9/64" DIA. HOLE

CART WHEEL AXLE—1/4" DIA. X 2-1/4" HARDWOOD DOWEL (2 REQUIRED)

CART WHEEL—3/8" WOOD (4 REQUIRED)

9/64" DIA. HOLE

1/4" DIA. HOLE

1/8" DIA. HOLES

1/4" DIA. HOLE

Full-size patterns for unicycle and rider.

179

FINAL CONSTRUCTION STEPS

The patterns for the wooden parts for the unicycle, rider, and cart are shown. Mark the patterns on the wood, drill the holes, and then cut out the patterns. Sand the parts.

Glue the two outside wheel section to the wood dowel axle, with the axle passing through the hole in the center piece. The pedal axle holes must be diametrically opposite each other so that one pedal axle will be down when the other is up. Leave enough space between wheel parts so that the outside wheel sections turn freely together on the fixed axle. Glue the pedal axles in the pedal axle holes.

Glue the wood arm and leg spacers to the body with the wire holes lined up.

Install the arms in place with glue and wire. Loop the wire ends on each side.

The painting is easiest if done before further assembly.

Assembly the legs by first installing a plastic washer on each pedal axle. Fasten the upper and lower legs together with wire, looping the ends on each side. Slip the feet over the pedal axles. Wood balls are slipped over the ends of the pedal axles to hold the feet in place. The legs are then mounted to the body at the hips with a wire looped on each side. The unicyclist should now pedal when the unicycle wheel is turned.

Slip the base of the unicycle through the notch in the floor and then install cart wheels, as shown. Bolt the connecting rod block to the base of the unicycle.

Test the whirligig before installing the side pieces. This can be inside with a fan or outdoors in a light wind. The whirligig should start easily if all of the parts turn properly. Make any necessary adjustments and add oil to friction areas of metal parts.

Cut the side pieces to the pattern shown and drill mounting holes for screws. Paint the side pieces and then fasten them to the platform with screws, as shown.

If sanding and painting was not done previously, disassemble as necessary and do the sanding and painting.

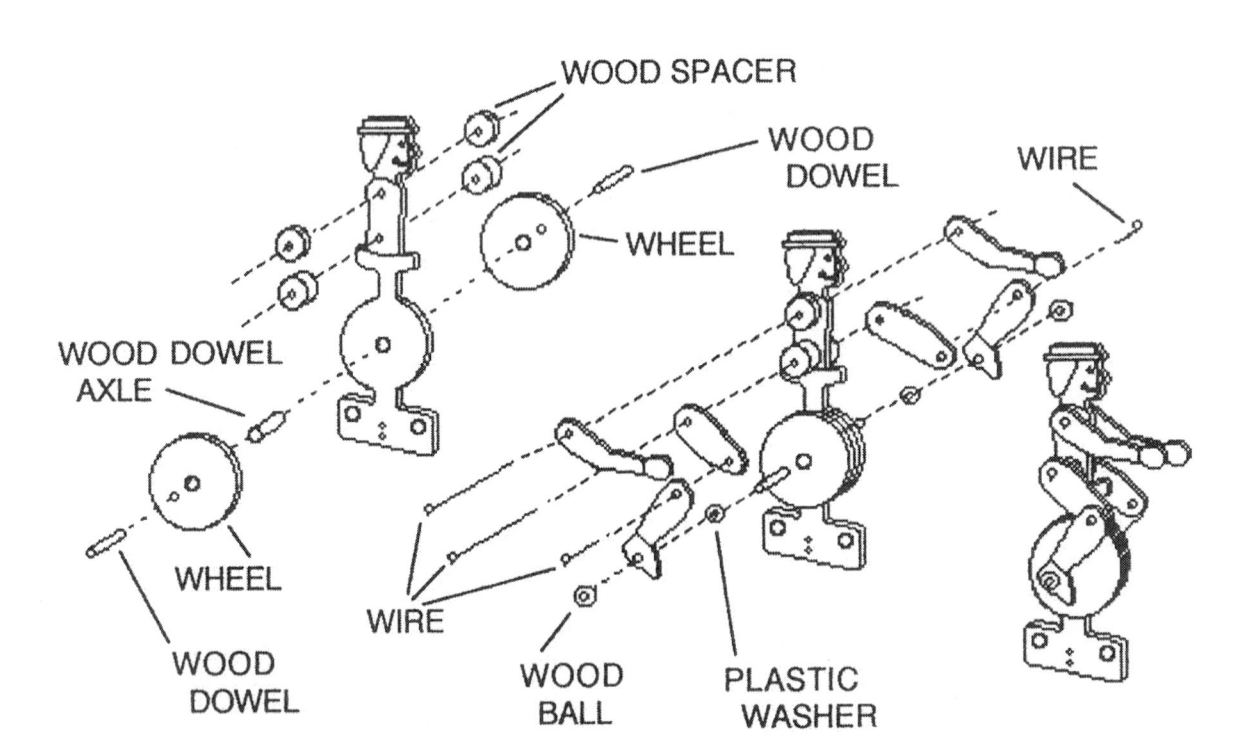

Assembly of unicycle and rider.

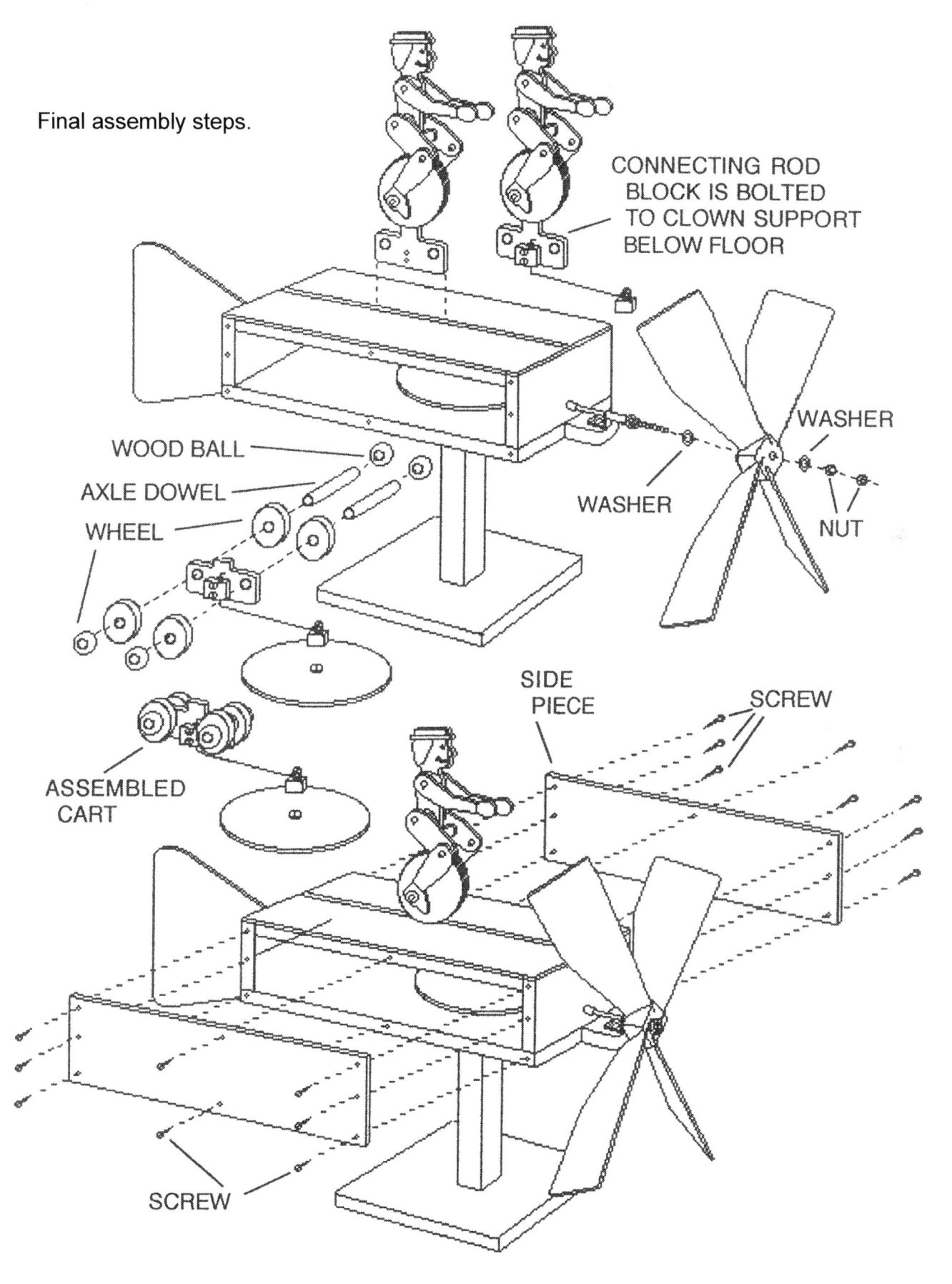

UNICYCLIST

Final assembly steps.

CONNECTING ROD BLOCK IS BOLTED TO CLOWN SUPPORT BELOW FLOOR

WOOD BALL
AXLE DOWEL
WHEEL
WASHER
WASHER
NUT
ASSEMBLED CART
SIDE PIECE
SCREW
SCREW

181

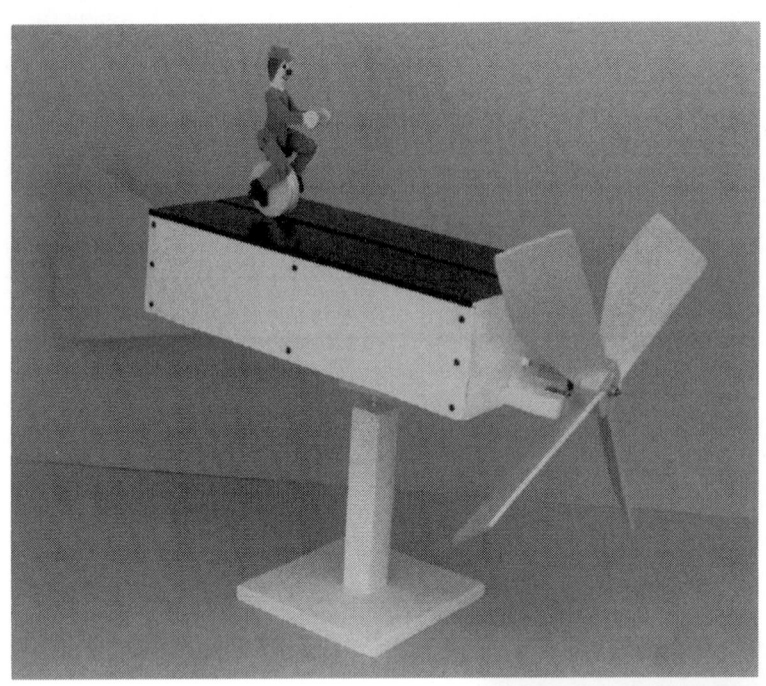

The Unicyclist whirligig in action.

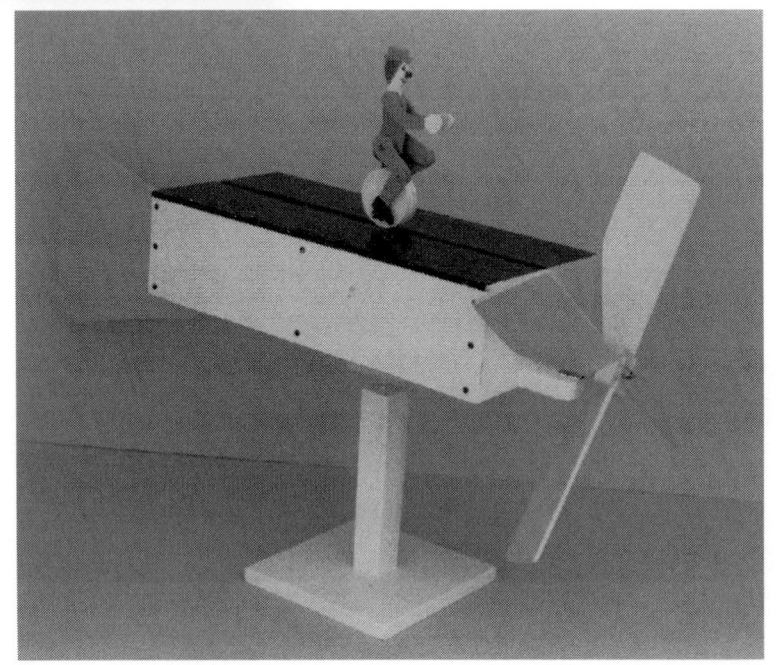

Chapter 15

FLYING DUCK

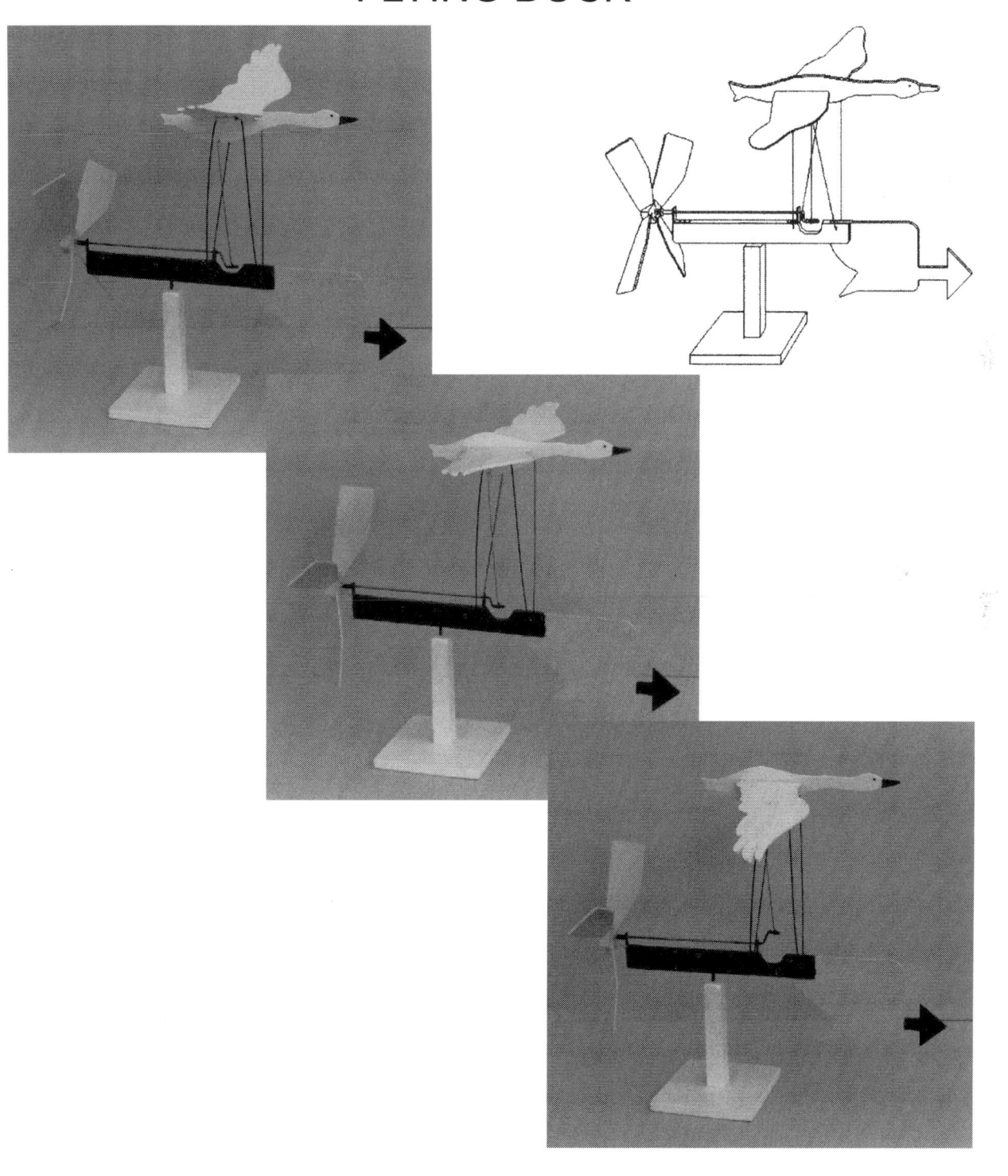

183

The Flying Duck whirligig is a fun project both to build and then watch perform after you have completed it.

MATERIALS

- 3/4" x 8-1/2" x 8-1/2" wood or plywood for display base.
- 1-1/2" x 1-1/2" x 8-1/2" wood for display post.
- 3/4" x 1-3/4" x 14" wood for platform.
- 1/4" x 7" x 12" plywood for vane.
- 1/4" x 14" x 16" plywood for duck body and wings.
- 1/2" x 1/2" x 3" wood for wing blocks.
- 3/16" x 2-3/4" x 28" wood or plywood for propeller blades.
- 3/4" x 1-1/2" x 1-1/2" wood for propeller hub.
- 1/4" outside diameter (9/64" inside diameter) x 1-3/4" brass tubing for pivot bearing.
- 1/8" diameter x 15" brass rod for crank shaft.
- 3/32" diameter x 14" stiff wire for connecting rod.
- 3/32" diameter x 28" piano wire or other stiff wire (2 required) for wing support wires.
- 1/4" diameter steel ball for pivot bearing.
- 6-32 nut (4 required) for attaching propeller hub to shaft.
- Washer (3 required) for use on propeller shaft.
- 3" long plastic tubing with 1/8" diameter hole for crankshaft spacers.
- 1/8" diameter x 4" nail for pivot rod for display base.
- 1/2" x 1" x 1" brass L-bracket (2 required) for crankshaft mounting.
- Screw (4 required) for mounting L-brackets.
- Glue.
- Finishing nails.
- Small felt pad for display base (4 required).
- Paint.

DISPLAY STAND

The display stand is useful not only for displaying the finished whirligig indoors, but also for holding the whirligig during construction and for testing it in front of a fan. Construction is easy. The base is 3/4" x 8-1/2" x 8-1/2" wood or plywood. The 1-1/2" x 1-1/2" x 8-1/2" post is glued in the center of the base. Use nails from underside of base for added support. A 1/8" diameter x 4" nail is driven 2" into the center of the top of the post for use as a pivot rod. Drill a pilot hole that is perpendicular to the top of the post before driving the nail into the hole. Cut the head off of the nail with a hacksaw. File the upper end of the nail smooth, rounding the corners slightly.

Sand and paint the display stand. A clear or color finish can be used.

Attach felt pads to the corners of the underside of the base.

PLATFORM

The platform is made of 3/4" x 1-3/4" x 14" wood. Drill holes as shown and make a 1/4" x 2" slot for the vane. The pivot hole must be accurately centered and perpendicular to the wood surfaces for the whirligig to work properly. I use a drill press and drill press vise for drilling these holes.

Use 1/2" x 1" x 1" brass L-brackets with 9/64" holes for the crankshaft. Fasten the brass L-brackets to the platform with screws. Depending on the brackets selected, it may be necessary to expand sizes of the holes and/or drill additional holes.

Cut the vane from 1/4" plywood to the pattern shown. Glue the vane in the platform slot, as shown.

Sand the platform. The platform can be painted at this time, or you can wait until the assembly has been completed. The color scheme can be as desired.

PROPELLER AND CRANKSHAFT

The crankshaft is made from 1/8" diameter x 15" brass rod. Make threads for 1-3/4" on one end of the rod using a 6-32 die. Install the crankshaft in the L-bracket holes with plastic spacers and washer and two nuts, as shown. The shaft should turn freely in the holders with no binding. Apply light oil to the shaft to further decrease friction.

The propeller hub is made from 3/4" x 1-1/2" x 1-1/2" wood. Drill a 1/8" shaft hole. Cut the 3/16" wide x 1/2" deep notches for the propeller blades at 45 degree angles to the face of the hub. A clockwise propeller is shown, but you can reverse the notches for a counterclockwise rotation if desired. The slots need to be made accurately for the whirligig to work properly.

Cut the propeller blades from 3/16" wood or plywood to the pattern shown.

Then glue the blades in the slots in the hub. Place the hub on a flat surface with the forward side down. The blades are then installed with the forward side flush with the flat surface.

Install the completed propeller on the threaded end of the crankshaft with washers and nuts, as shown.

Test the assembly in front of a fan to make certain that the propeller and crankshaft assembly works properly.

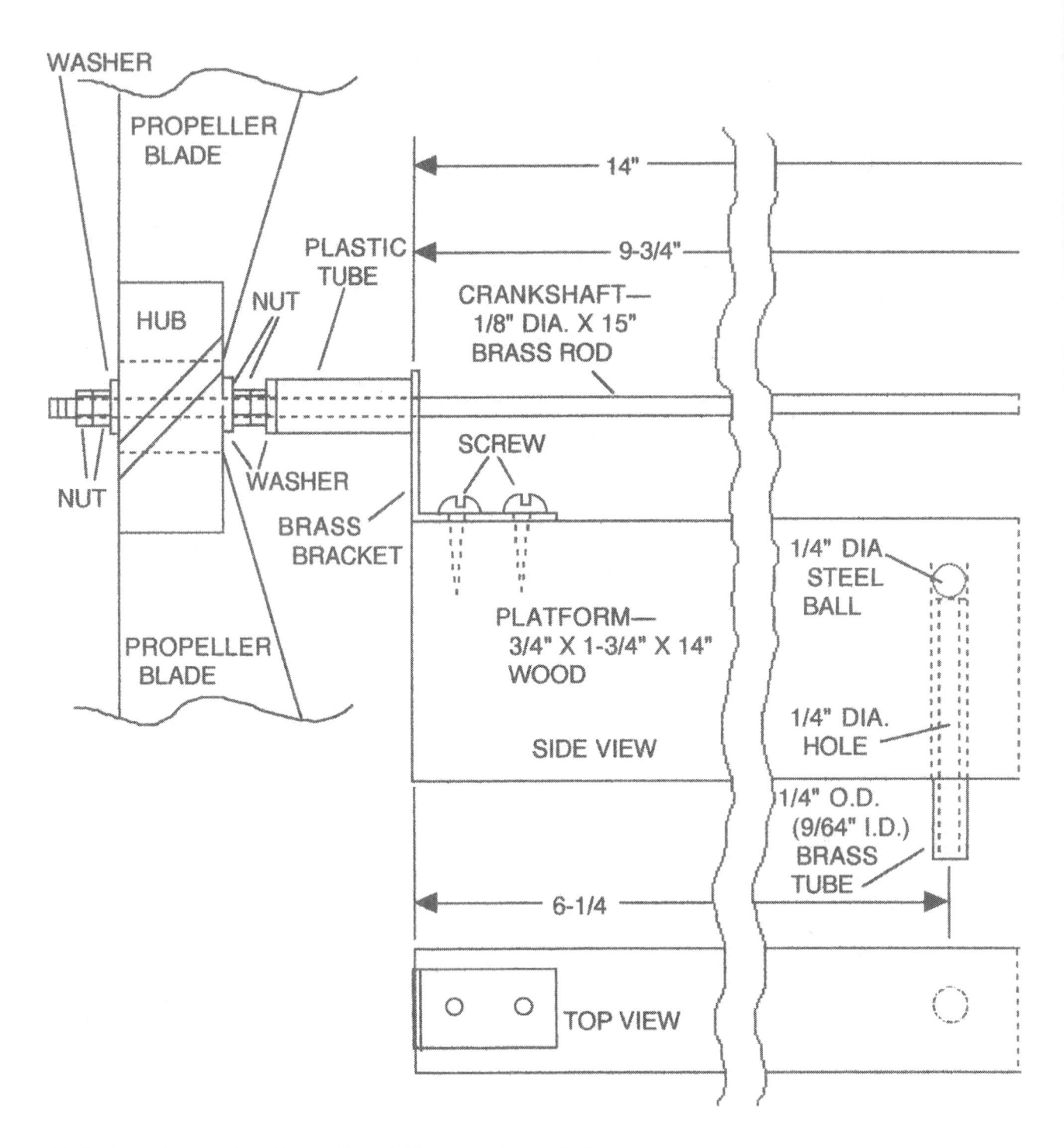

Full-size plan and patterns for platform and crankshaft.

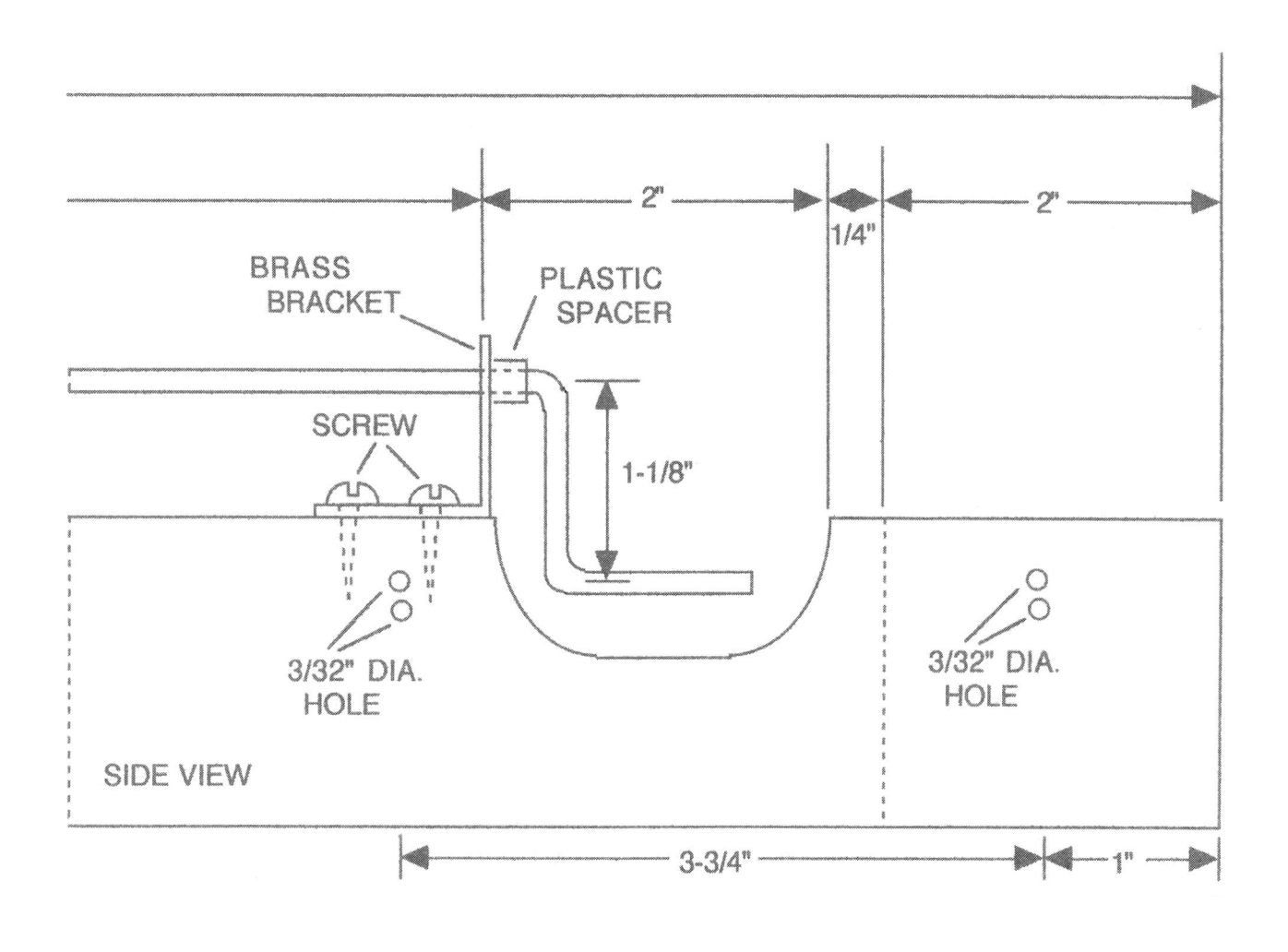

FLYING DUCK

├─────────── 2" ───────────┤ 1/4" ├───── 2" ─────┤

BRASS BRACKET
PLASTIC SPACER
SCREW
1-1/8"
3/32" DIA. HOLE
3/32" DIA. HOLE
SIDE VIEW

├────────── 3-3/4" ──────────┤ ├── 1" ──┤

TOP VIEW   NOTCH FOR VANE

187

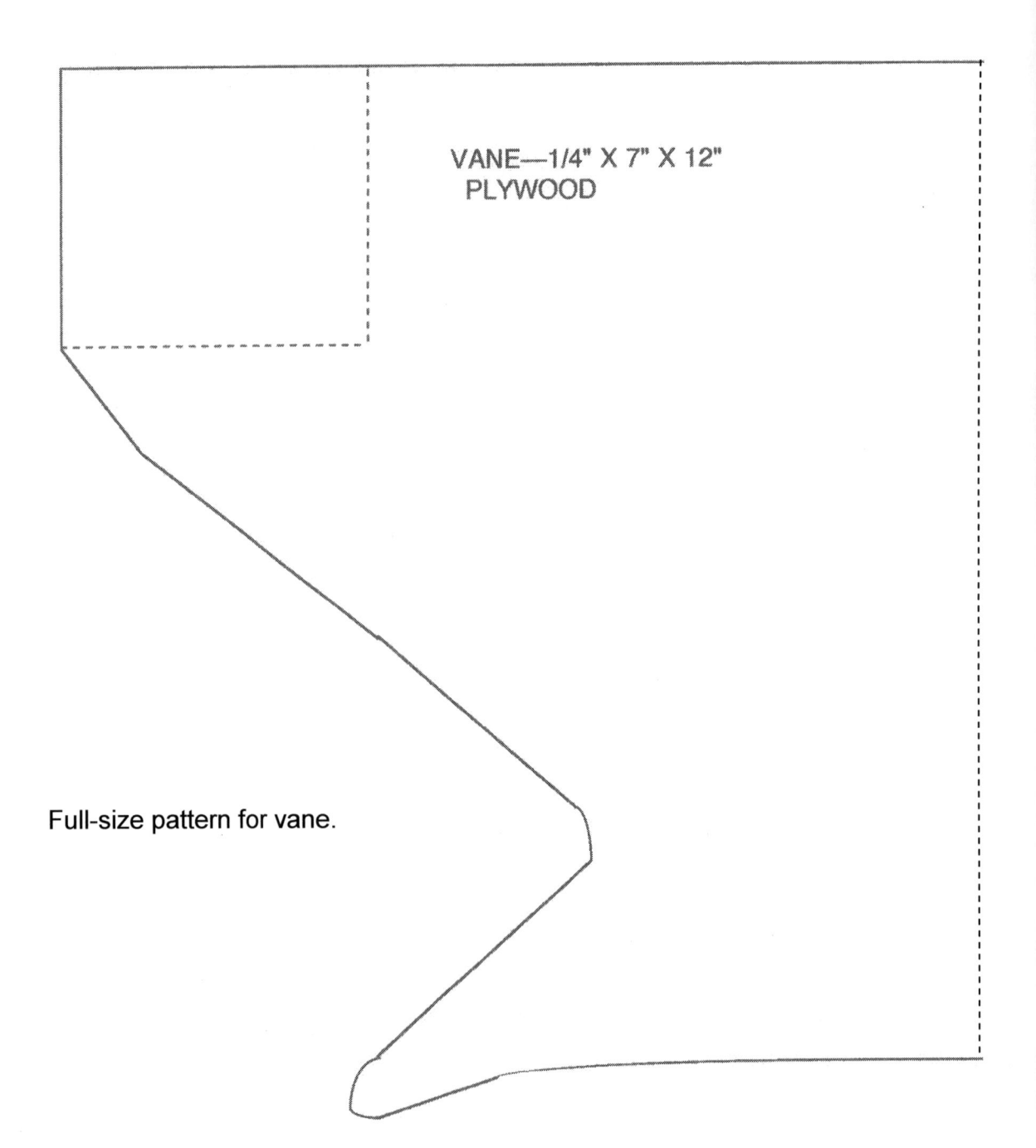

THE WHIRLIGIG MAKER'S BOOK

VANE—1/4" X 7" X 12"
PLYWOOD

Full-size pattern for vane.

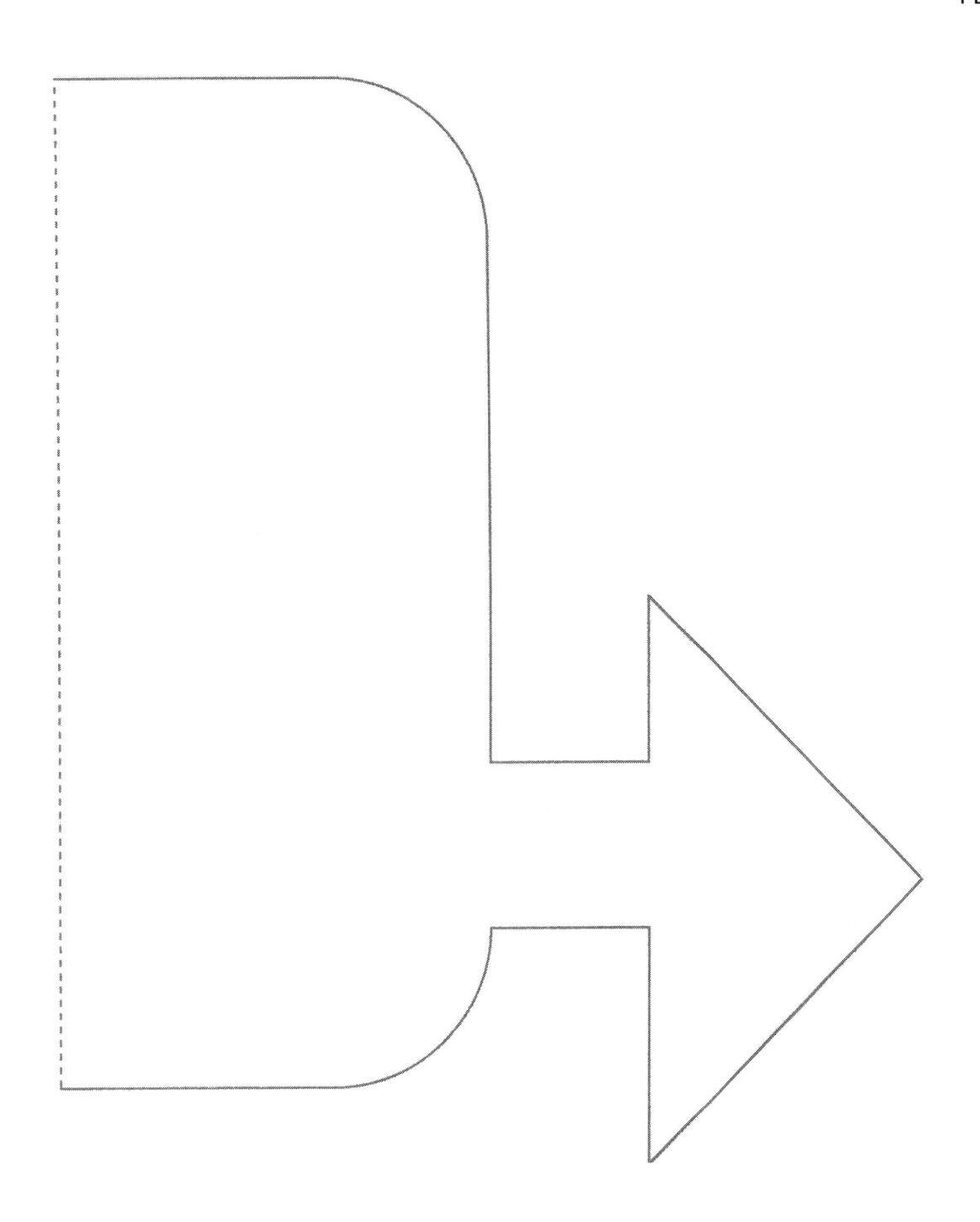

FLYING DUCK

189

THE WHIRLIGIG MAKER'S BOOK

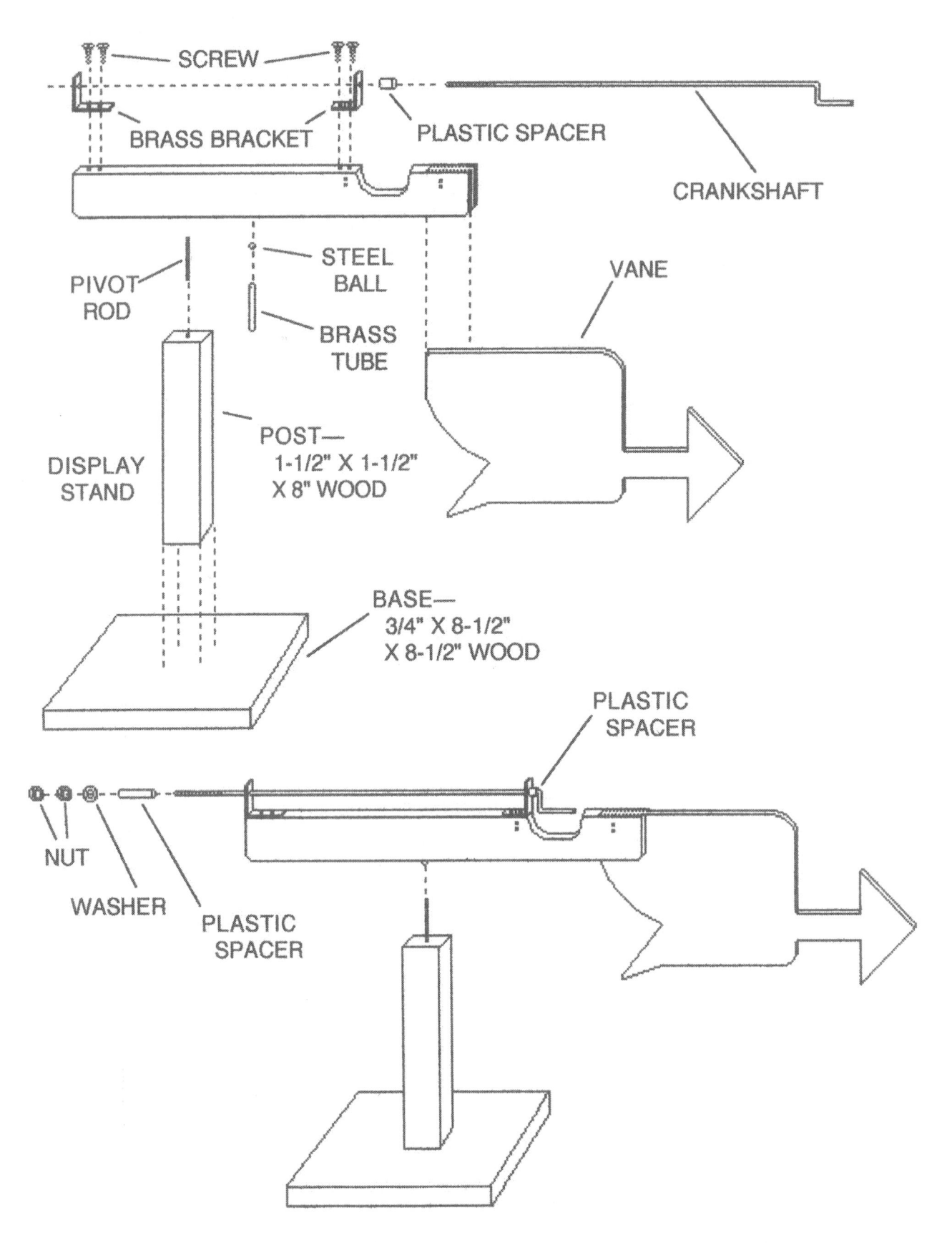

Assembly of display stand and platform.

FLYING DUCK

ASSEMBLY OF PROPELLER

PROPELLER BLADE—
3/16" WOOD OR
PLYWOOD
(4 REQUIRED)

2-3/4"

3-1/2"

7"

1-1/4"

PROPELLER HUB—3/4"
WOOD (1 REQUIRED)

1-1/2"

1-1/2"

3/4"

1/8" DIA HOLE

CUT BLADE SLOTS AT 45 DEGREE ANGLES

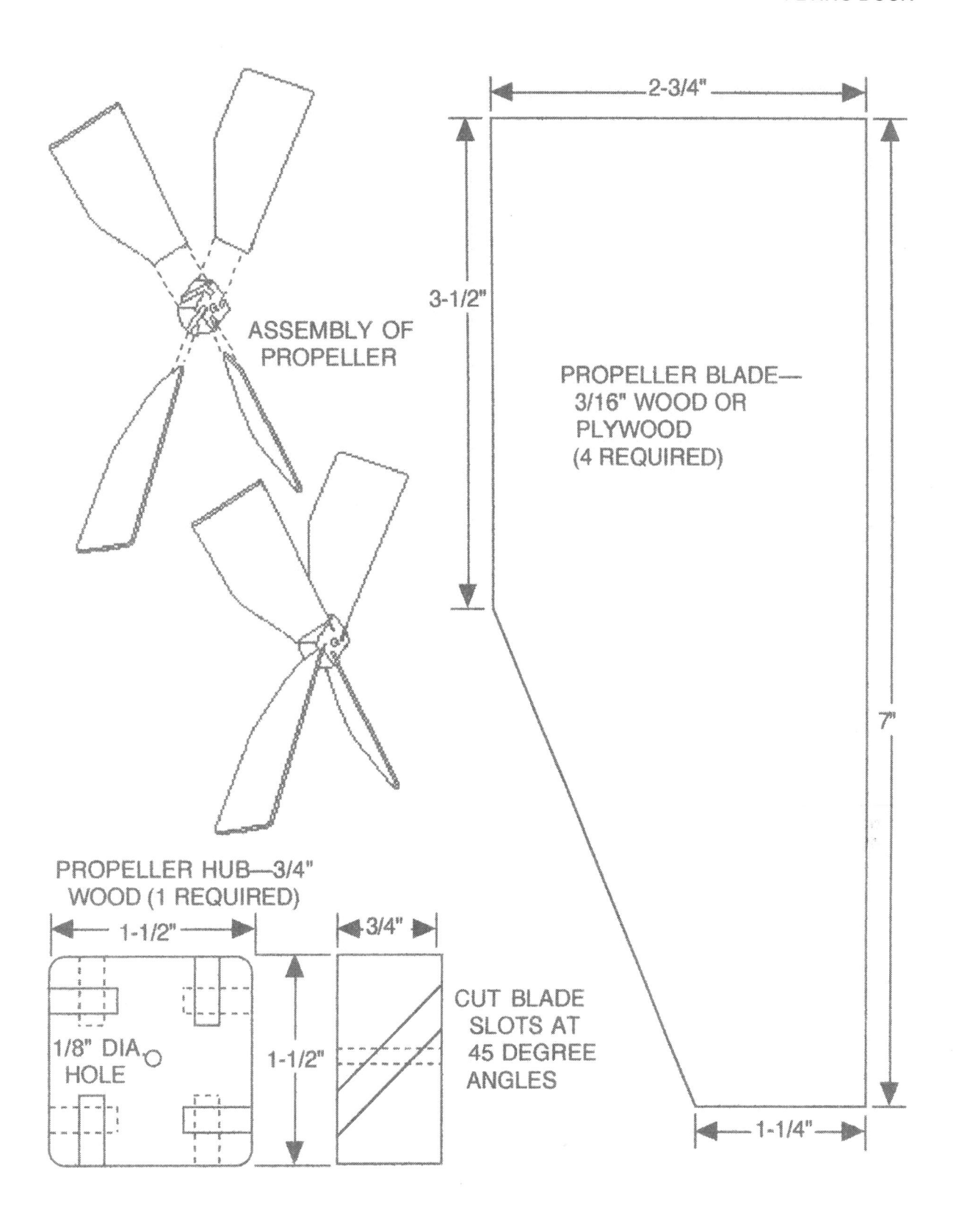

Full-size patterns for propeller blades and hub.

191

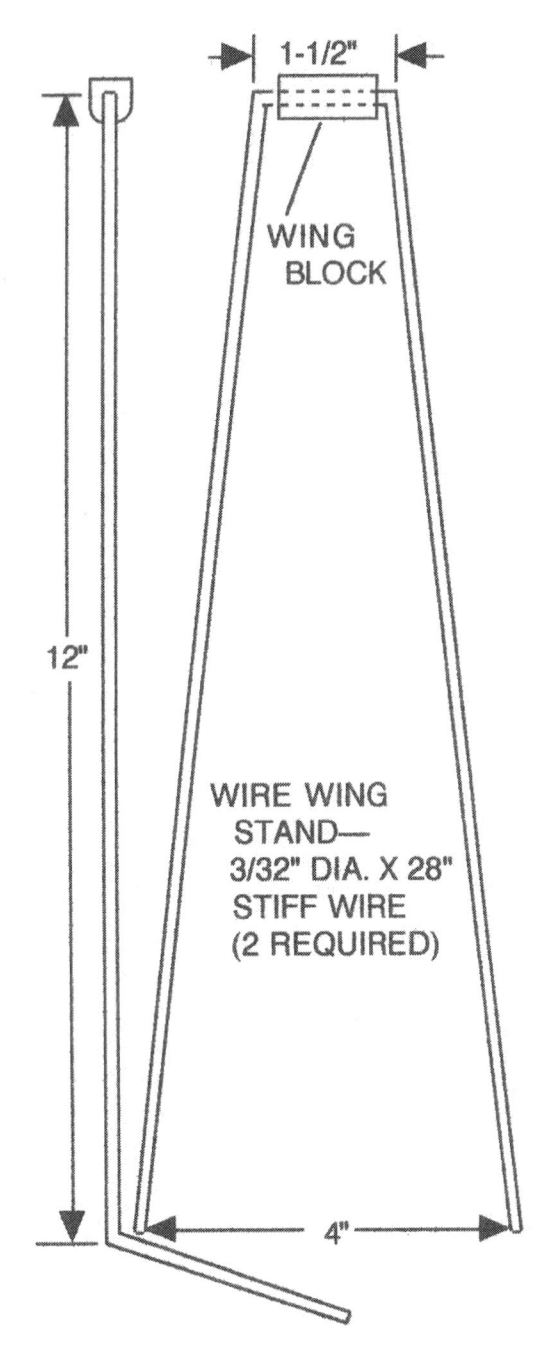

Pattern for wing stand.

FLYING DUCK

Shape the wing mounting blocks to the pattern shown. Drill 7/64" diameter holes for the wing mounting wires.

The wing mounting wires are bent to the pattern shown with the wing mounting blocks in place over the wire. The lower ends of the wires then pass through mounting holes in the platform. Cut the ends of the wires off 1/2" from the platform and bend loops in the wire and drive the free ends back into the wood.

Cut the duck body and wings from 1/4" plywood to the patterns shown. Drill holes as shown. It is easiest to paint the duck before further assembly, except leave unpainted areas for gluing the wing mounting blocks in place.

Lace the wings to the body with strong thread. Then glue the wings to the wing mounting blocks.

The connecting rod is shaped from 3/32" diameter x 14" stiff wire. Bend a wire loop around a 1/8" diameter rod. Circle the rod twice, making a tight circle. The eye fits over the crankshaft between two plastic spacers. Bend the wire to pass through the hole in the duck's body so that the wings will be level when the crank is in a horizontal position to one side. Pass the wire through the hole and then bend it downward and back to the original wire.

TESTING AND FINISHING

The whirligig is ready for testing. This can be inside with a fan or outdoors in a light wind. The whirligig should start easily if all of the parts turn properly. Make any necessary adjustments and add oil to friction areas of metal parts.

If sanding and painting was not done previously, disassemble as necessary and do the sanding and painting.

FLYING DUCK

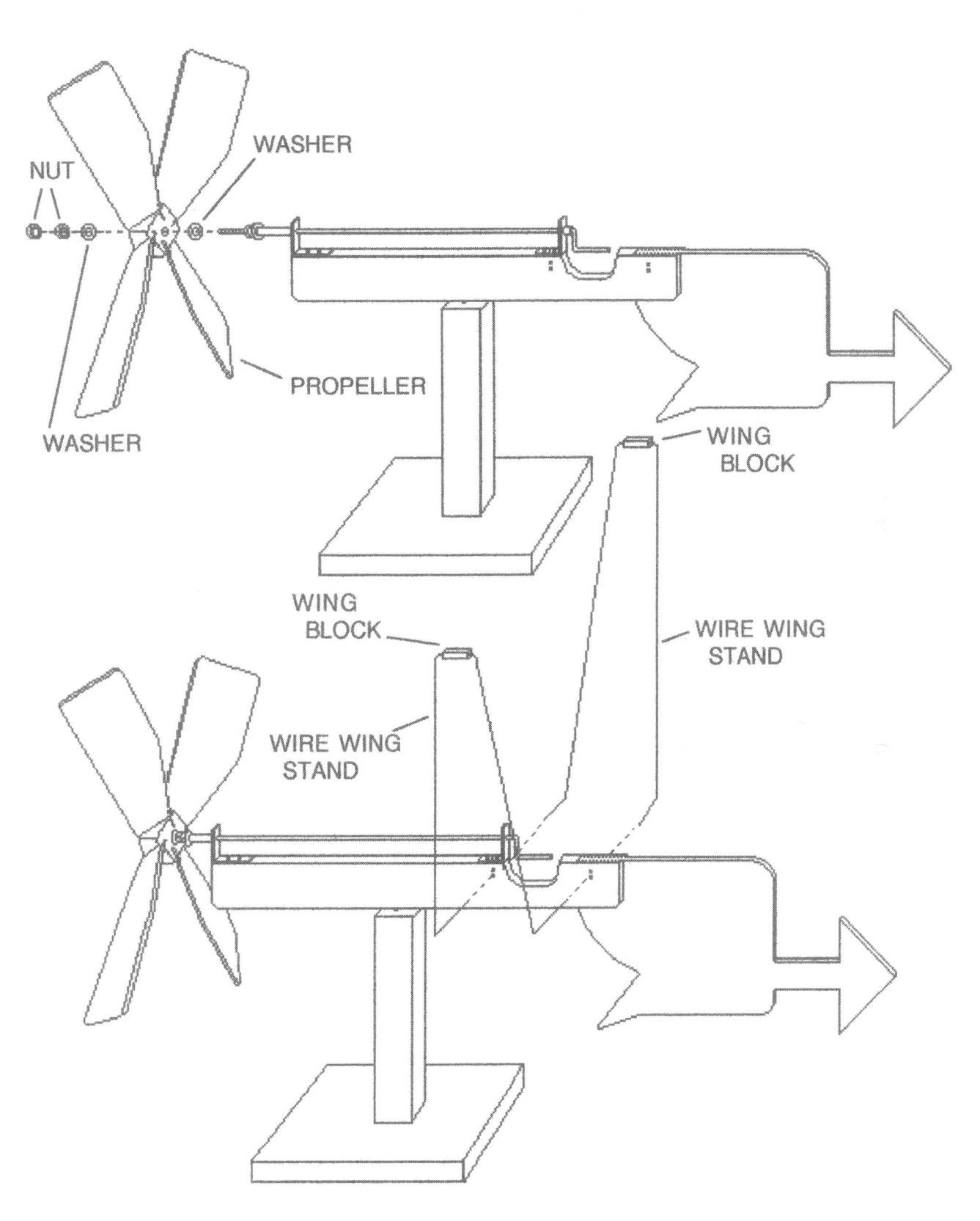

- NUT
- WASHER
- WASHER
- PROPELLER
- WING BLOCK
- WING BLOCK
- WIRE WING STAND
- WIRE WING STAND

Assembly of propeller to crankshaft and wire wing stand to platform.

THE WHIRLIGIG MAKER'S BOOK

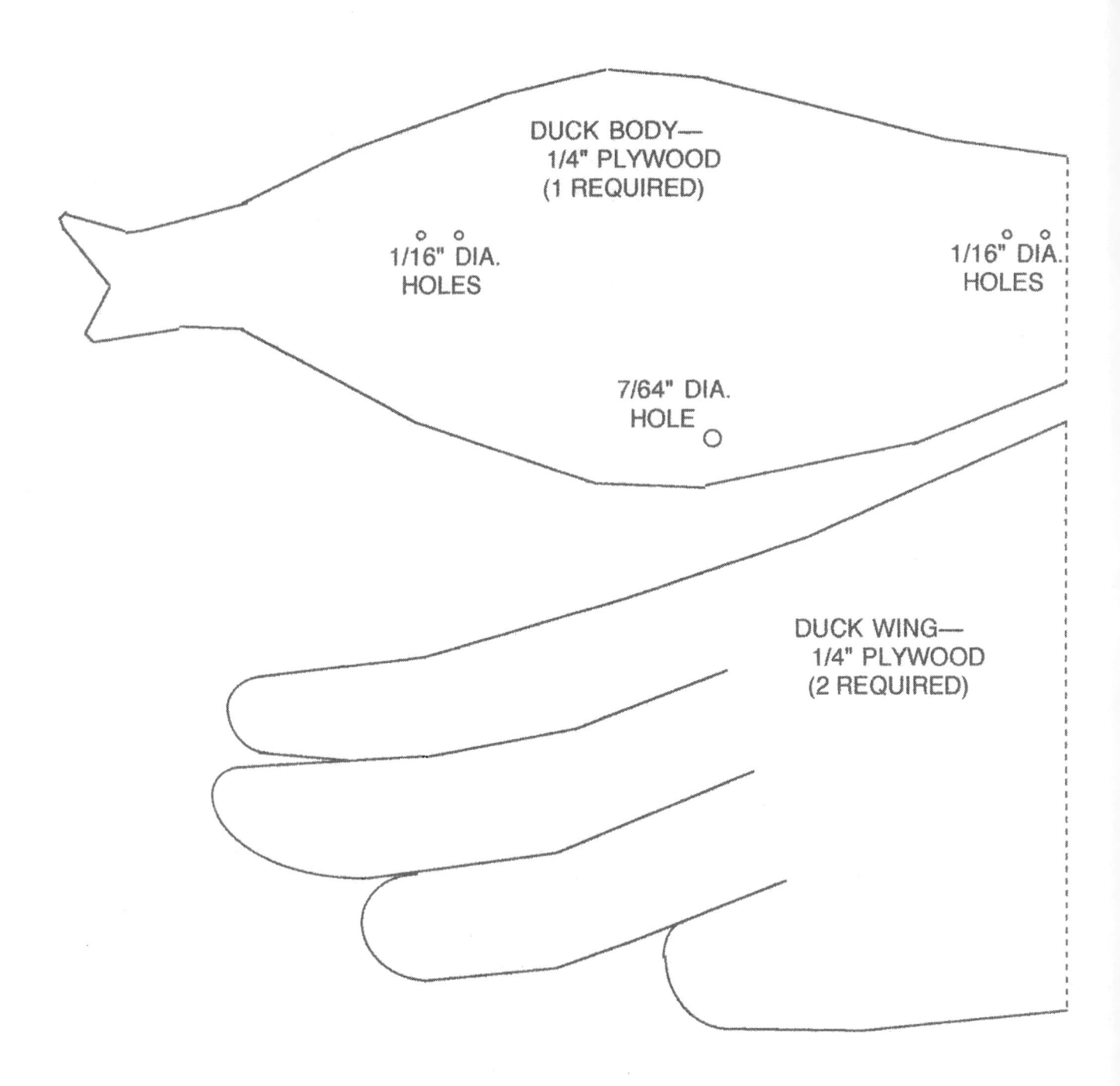

DUCK BODY—
1/4" PLYWOOD
(1 REQUIRED)

1/16" DIA. HOLES

1/16" DIA. HOLES

7/64" DIA. HOLE

DUCK WING—
1/4" PLYWOOD
(2 REQUIRED)

Full-size patterns for duck body, wings and wing blocks.

FLYING DUCK

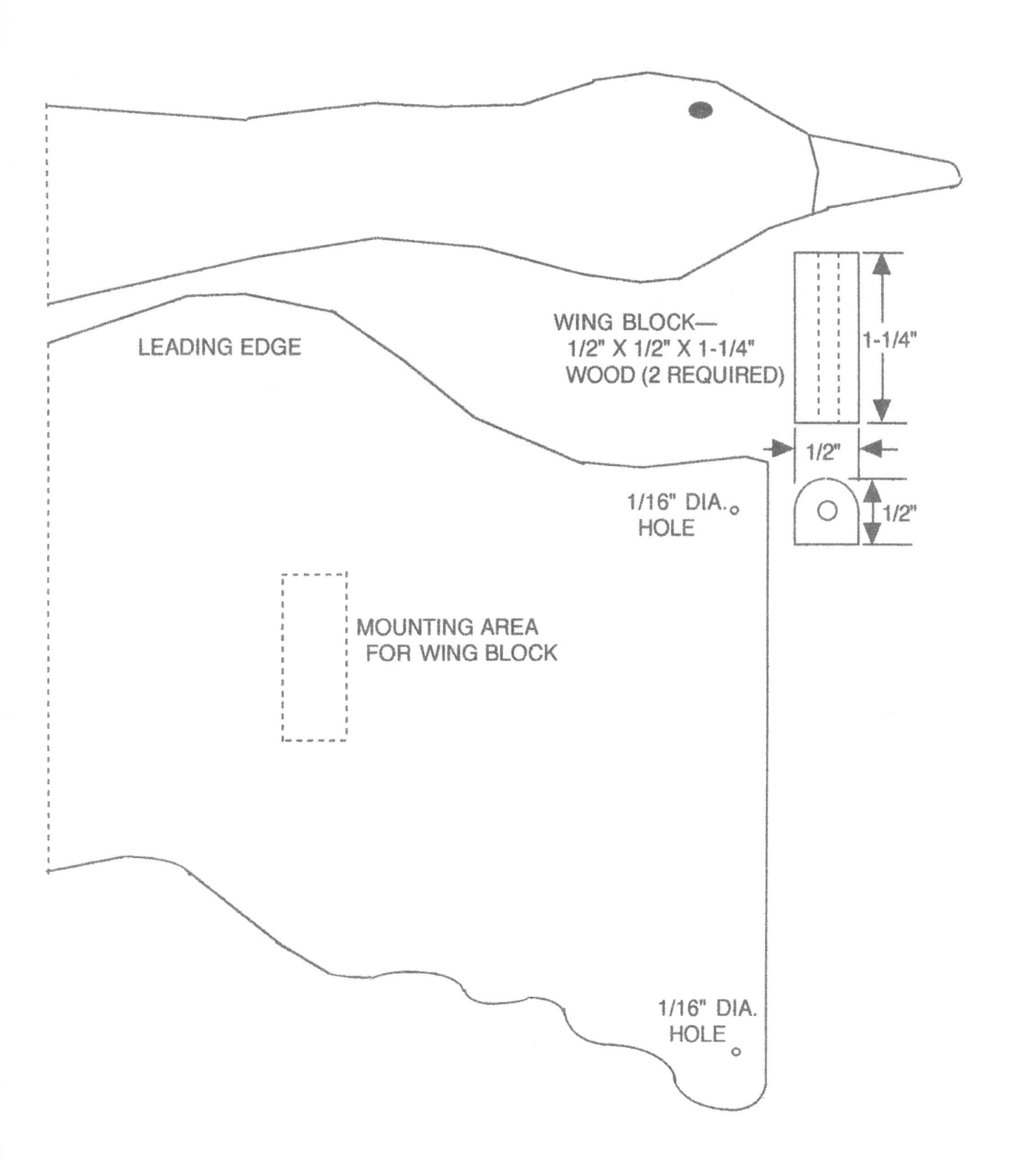

LEADING EDGE

WING BLOCK—
1/2" X 1/2" X 1-1/4"
WOOD (2 REQUIRED)

1-1/4"

1/2"

1/2"

1/16" DIA. HOLE

MOUNTING AREA
FOR WING BLOCK

1/16" DIA.
HOLE

195

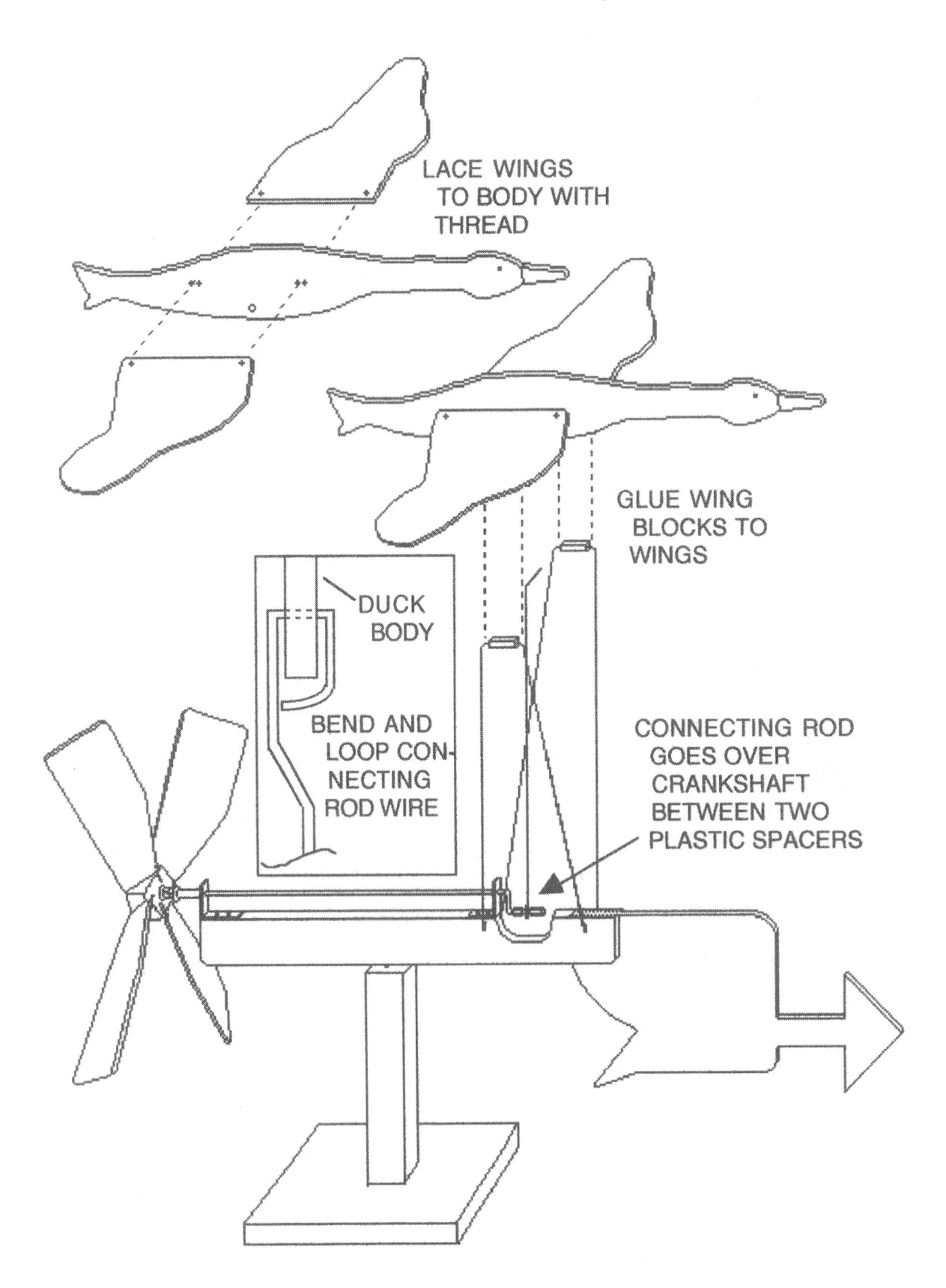

THE WHIRLIGIG MAKER'S BOOK

LACE WINGS TO BODY WITH THREAD

GLUE WING BLOCKS TO WINGS

DUCK BODY

BEND AND LOOP CONNECTING ROD WIRE

CONNECTING ROD GOES OVER CRANKSHAFT BETWEEN TWO PLASTIC SPACERS

Assembly of duck.

Chapter 16

ACROBATS

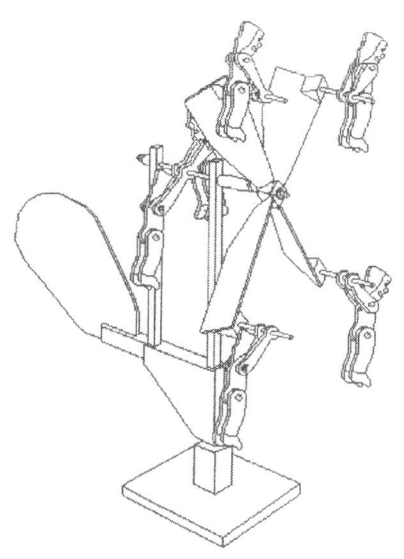

THE WHIRLIGIG MAKER'S BOOK

The Clown Acrobats whirligig has a unique action. Not only do the clown acrobats perform on the propeller shaft, but also from pegs connected directly to the tips of the propeller blades. The clown acrobats perform a variety of antics, depending on wind conditions and other factors.

MATERIALS
- 3/4" x 8" x 8" wood or plywood for display base.
- 1-1/2" x 1-1/2" x 4" wood for display post.
- 3/4" x 1" x 7-1/2" wood for platform.
- 3/4" x 1-1/2" x 3" wood for platform post.
- 1/2" x 3/4" x 23" wood for propeller shaft posts.
- 1/4" x 9" x 10" plywood for vane.
- 3/16" x 5" x 8" plywood for platform side pieces.
- 3/16" x 6" x 22" wood or plywood for clown acrobats.
- 3/16" x 5" x 15" wood or plywood for propeller blades.
- 3/4" x 2" x 2" wood for propeller hub.
- 1" x 1" x 5" wood peg mounting blocks.
- 1/4" diameter x 12" hardwood dowel acrobat pegs.
- 5/8" diameter wood ball with 1/4" diameter hole (2 required) for propeller shaft spacers.
- Wood macramé bead with 5/16" diameter hole x 1-7/8" long for shaft tube decoration (can be omitted if desired).
- 5/16" outside diameter (17/64" inside diameter) x 3-1/8" brass tubing for propeller shaft bearings.
- 1/4" outside diameter (9/64" inside diameter) x 2" brass tube for pivot bearing.
- 1/4" diameter x 9-3/4" brass rod for crank shaft.
- 1/32" diameter x 24" stiff wire for connecting arms and legs to clown bodies.
- 1/4" diameter steel ball for pivot bearing.
- 1/4" nut (4 required) for use on propeller shaft.
- 1/4" washer (3 required) for use on propeller shaft.
- 1/8" diameter x 5" nail for pivot rod for display base.
- Glue.
- Epoxy glue.
- Finishing nails.
- Small felt pad for display base (4 required).
- Paint.

DISPLAY STAND
The display stand is useful not only for displaying the finished whirligig indoors, but also for holding the whirligig during construction and for testing it in front of a fan. Construction is easy. The base is 3/4" x 8" x 8" wood or plywood. The 1-1/2" x 1-1/2" x 4" post is glued and nailed (use finishing nails from underside) to the center of one side of the base. A 1/8" diameter x 5" nail is driven 2-1/2" into the center of the top of the post for use as a pivot rod. Make certain that the nail is driven perpendicular to the top of the post. Cut the head off of the nail with a hacksaw. File the upper end of the nail smooth, rounding the corners slightly.

Sand and paint the display stand. A clear or color finish can be used.

Attach felt pads to the corners of the underside of the base.

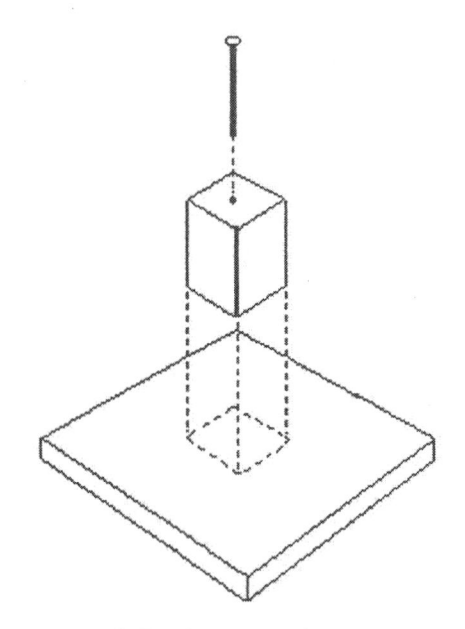

Assembly of display stand.

PLATFORM

The platform is made of 3/4" x 1" x 7-1/2" wood. Shape the ends, as shown. Drill 3/8" diameter x 1/2" deep holes for mounting the propeller shaft posts in the positions shown. Make a 1/4" x 2-1/2" slot for the vane. Next, round the corners of the platform on the end by the slot for the vane.

The platform post is made from 3/4" x 1-1/2" x 3" wood. Drill a 1/4" diameter x 2" hole for the pivot bearing. Nail and glue the platform post to the platform. Cut the side pieces from 3/16" plywood to the pattern shown. Glue and nail these to the assembly.

The propeller shaft posts are made from 1/2" x 3/4" x 11-1/2" wood pieces to the pattern shown. Drill 5/16" holes for the propeller shaft tubes, as shown. The holes must be accurately centered and perpendicular to the wood surfaces for the whirligig to work properly. I use a drill press and drill press vise for drilling these holes. Round 1/2" on the lower ends of the posts to 3/8" diameter. Then glue the posts in the mounting holes in the platform.

Install the brass shaft tubes in the post holes, as shown. The tubes should fit tightly in the holes so they will not turn. Add the wood macramé bead to the shaft tubing (this is for decoration only and can be omitted if desired). It should fit tightly over the shaft. If necessary, glue it in place.

I install a 1/4" diameter steel ball in the pivot hole. Then install the brass pivot tube, as shown. The tube should fit tightly in the hole so it will not turn.

Cut the vane from 1/4" plywood to the pattern shown. Glue the vane in the platform slot.

Sand the platform assembly. I recommend painting at this time, before further assembly.

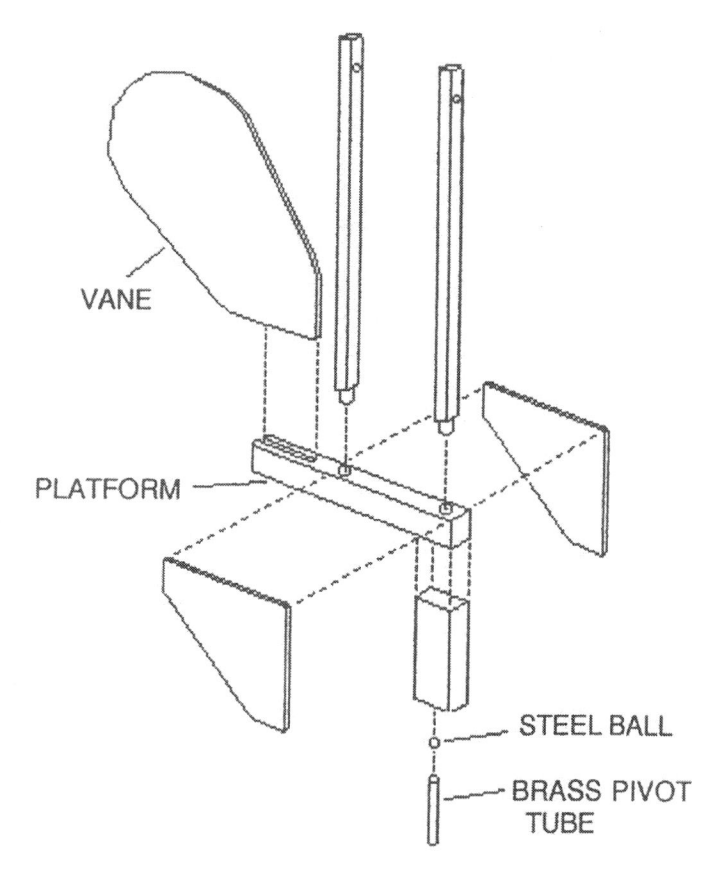

Assembly of platform.

THE WHIRLIGIG MAKER'S BOOK

WOOD MACRAME BEAD—
5/16" DIA. HOLE
X 1-7/8" LONG

5/16" O.D. (17/64" I.D.)
X 2-1/2" BRASS TUBE

5/16" O.D. (17/64" I.D.)
X 5/8" BRASS TUBE

3-1/4"

1/8"

3/8" DIA. X 1/2" DEEP HOLE

PLATFORM—3/4" X 1" X 7-1/2" WOOD

1/4" DIA. X 2" DEEP HOLE FOR PIVOT BEARING

PLATFORM POST—3/4" X 1-1/2" X 3" WOOD

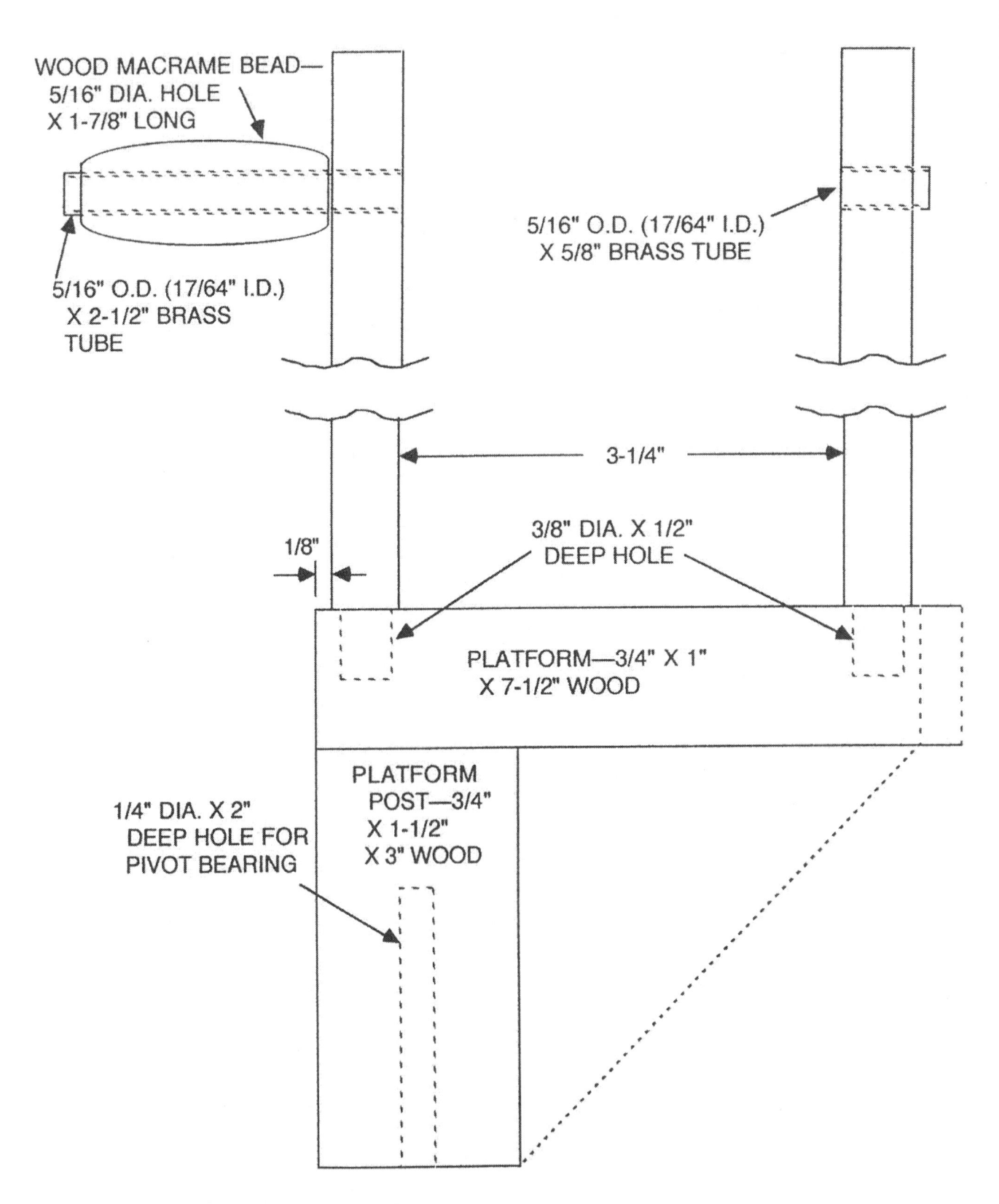

Full-size plan and patterns for platform.

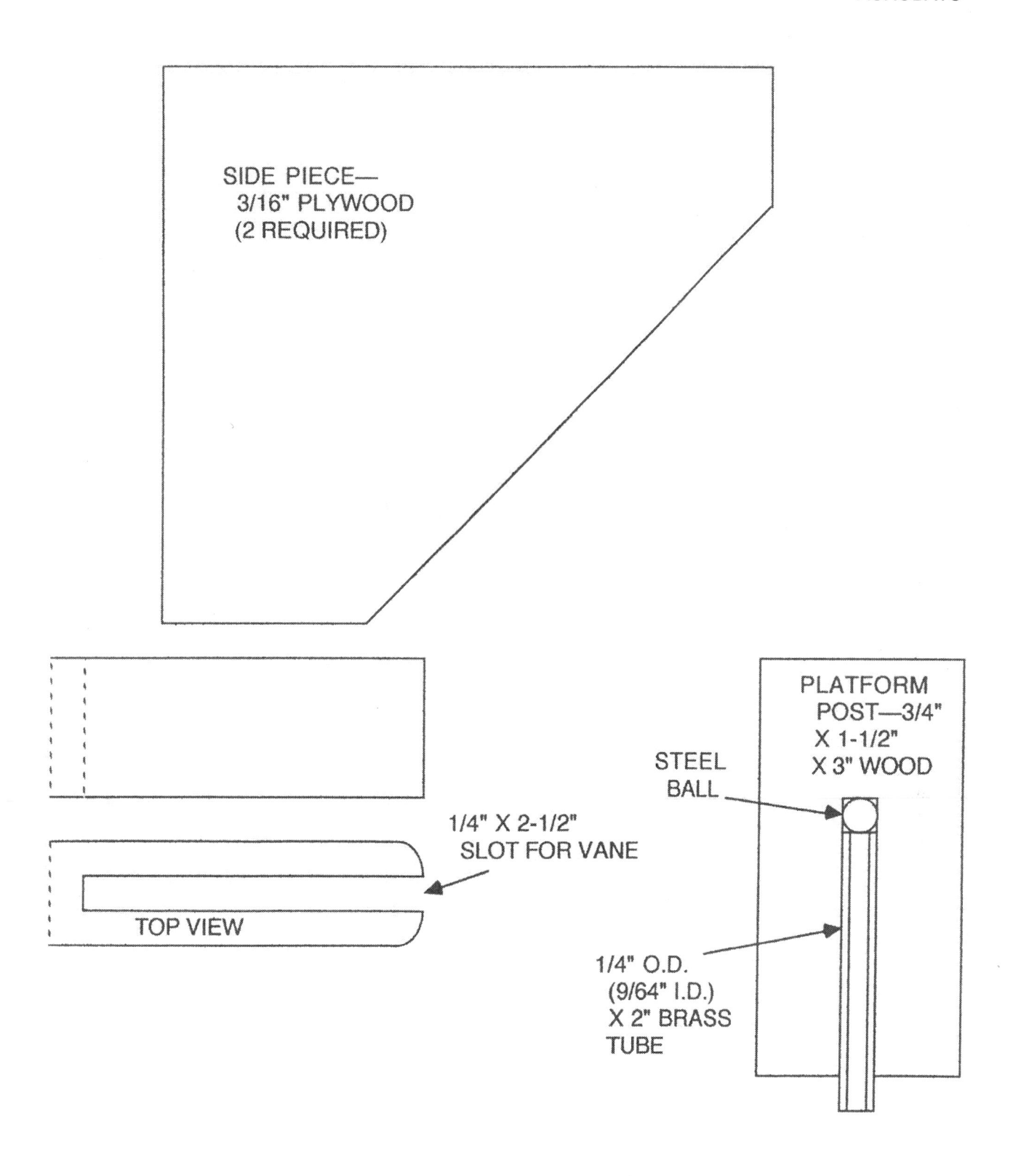

ACROBATS

SIDE PIECE—
3/16" PLYWOOD
(2 REQUIRED)

1/4" X 2-1/2" SLOT FOR VANE

TOP VIEW

PLATFORM POST—3/4" X 1-1/2" X 3" WOOD

STEEL BALL

1/4" O.D. (9/64" I.D.) X 2" BRASS TUBE

201

THE WHIRLIGIG MAKER'S BOOK

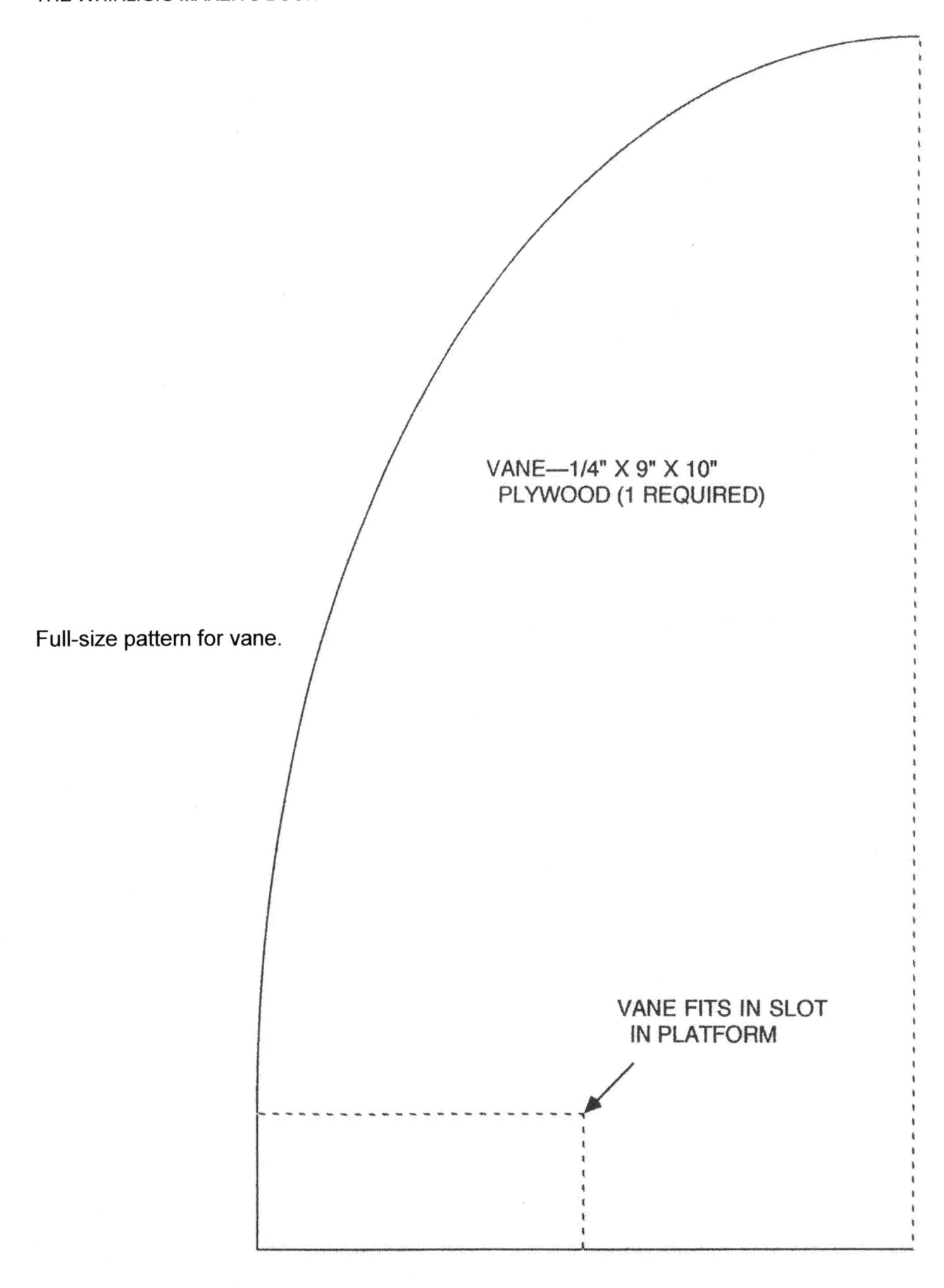

VANE—1/4" X 9" X 10"
PLYWOOD (1 REQUIRED)

Full-size pattern for vane.

VANE FITS IN SLOT
IN PLATFORM

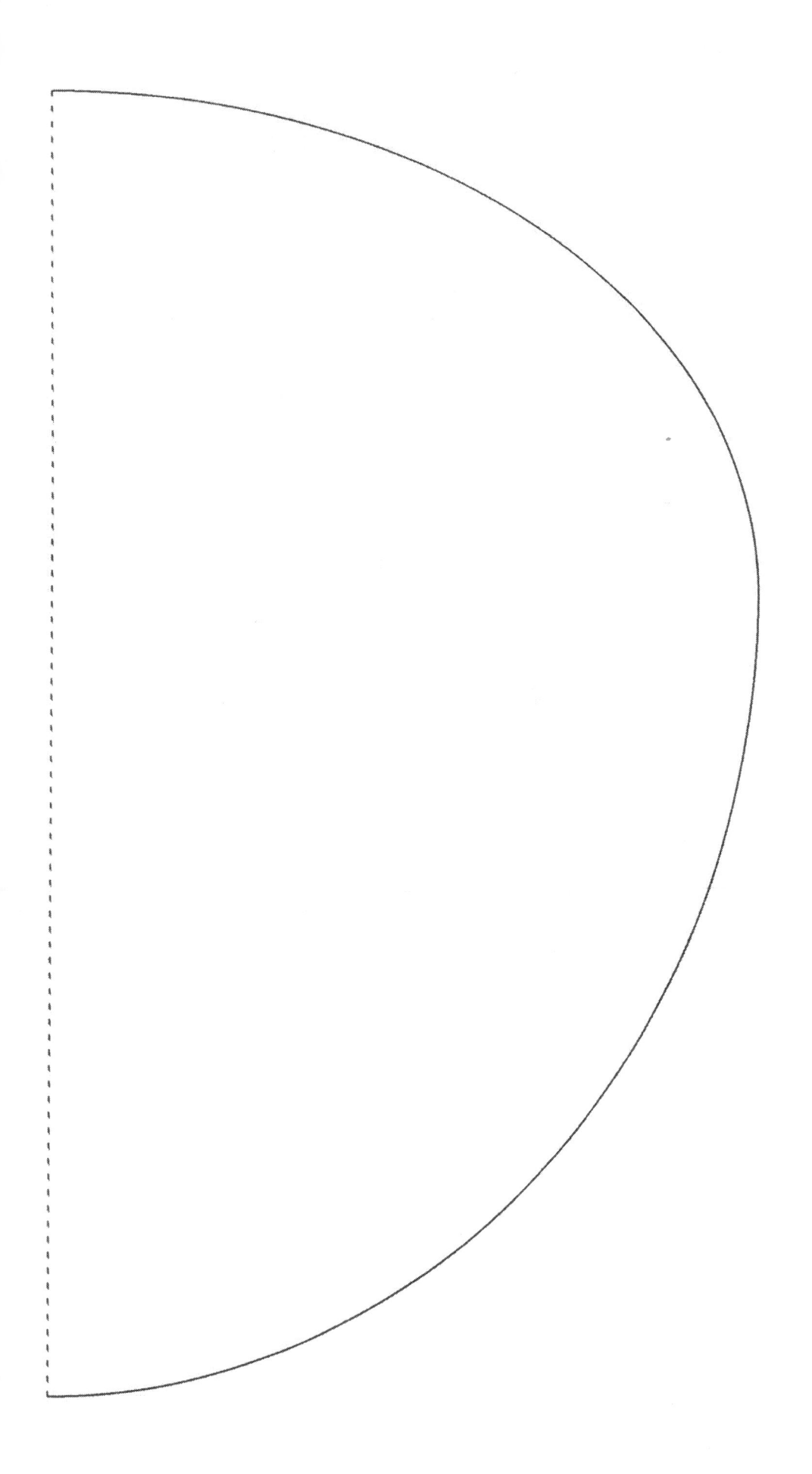

ACROBATS

203

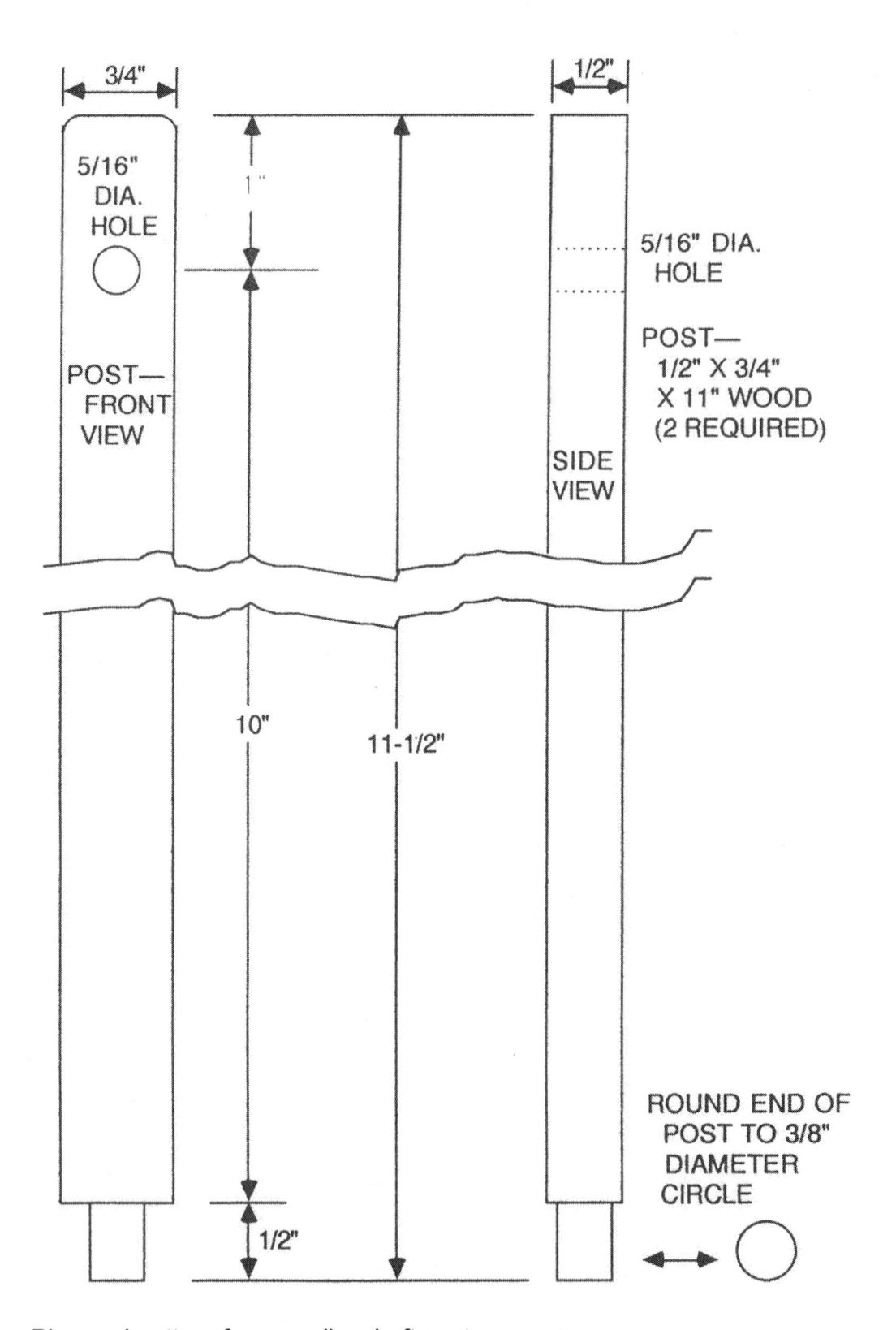

THE WHIRLIGIG MAKER'S BOOK

|← 3/4" →| |← 1/2" →|

5/16" DIA. HOLE

1"

POST— FRONT VIEW

5/16" DIA. HOLE

POST— 1/2" X 3/4" X 11" WOOD (2 REQUIRED)

SIDE VIEW

10"

11-1/2"

1/2"

ROUND END OF POST TO 3/8" DIAMETER CIRCLE

Plan and pattern for propeller shaft posts.

ACROBATS

5/16" O.D. (17/64" I.D.) X 5/8" BRASS TUBE

5/16" O.D. (17/64" I.D.) X 2-1/2" BRASS TUBE

Assembly of shaft tubes.

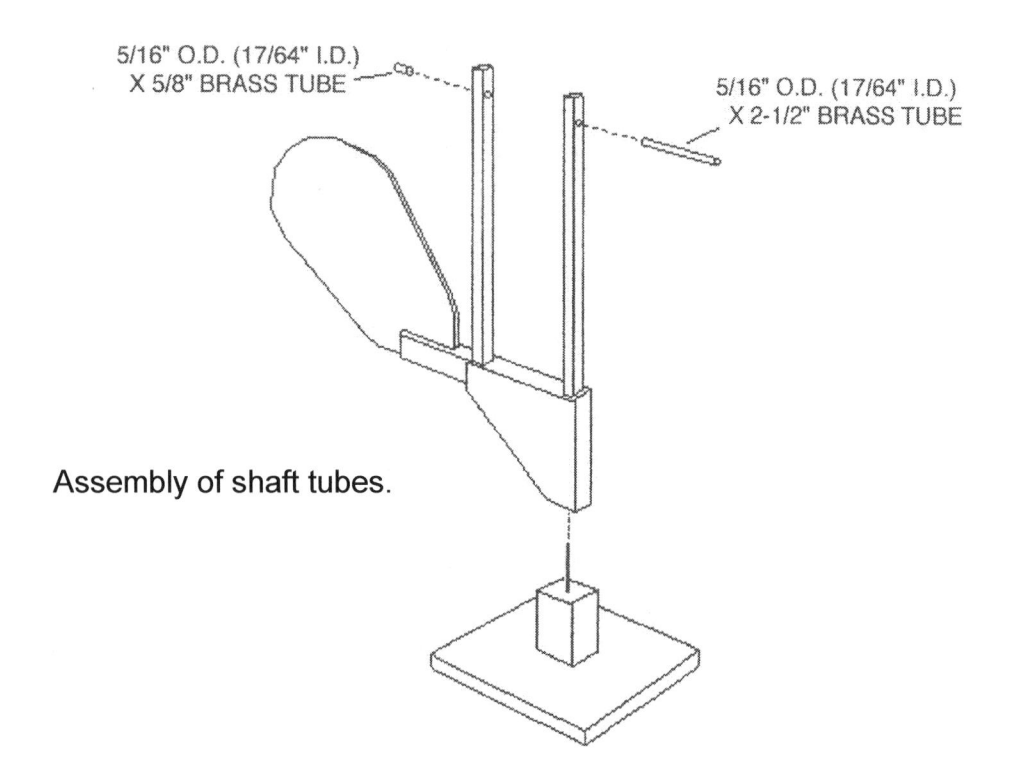

PROPELLER, CRANKSHAFT, AND CLOWN ACROBATS

The crankshaft is made from 1/4" diameter x 9-3/4" brass rod. Make threads for 2" on one end of the rod and 3/4" on the other end using a 1/4" die with standard threads. Slip the crankshaft into the shaft tubes for a trial fit. The shaft should turn freely in the tube with no binding.

The clown acrobats are made from 3/16" wood or plywood. There are six clown acrobats. Six bodies and twelve legs are required, plus eight single arms and a pair of the double arms.

Mark the patterns for the clown parts on the wood or plywood. Then drill all holes to the patterns shown before cutting out the parts. The hand holes should be drilled perpendicular to the wood surfaces, and accurately positioned so the holes in opposite hands will match.

Cut the parts to the patterns using a hand coping saw or power scroll or band saw. Sand the parts.

The clowns are best painted before assembly. As a general rule, use bright and contrasting colors and keep the details simple. You can paint all of the clowns the same color patterns, or use two or more patterns.

Assembly of the clown parts with wire is easy. The two clowns that connect to the double arms face each other. Use 1/32" diameter stiff wire. For each joint, bend and loop one end of the wire. Pass the other end through the holes in the parts. Bend and loop the other end of the wire and cut off excess wire. The arms and legs should rotate freely. When the hands are fixed to the bars, the arms will remain parallel to each other, but the legs can turn independently of each other.

Assembly the double clowns over the propeller shaft, as shown. The short threaded end of the shaft passes through the long shaft bearing tube, then through the clowns' hands. Work the hands over the shaft toward the center of the posts and pass the shaft on through the other post. Install the wood balls, washer, and nuts on the shaft, as shown. Center the arms between the posts and, leaving 1/4" space between arm pieces, epoxy glue the hand holes to the shaft.

THE WHIRLIGIG MAKER'S BOOK

DOUBLE ARM—
3/16" WOOD
OR PLYWOOD
(2 REQUIRED)

1/16" DIA. HOLE

SINGLE ARM—
3/16" WOOD
OR PLYWOOD
(8 REQUIRED)

1/16" DIA. HOLE

BODY—3/16"
WOOD OR
PLYWOOD
(6 REQUIRED)

1/16" DIA. HOLE

1/4" DIA. HOLE

1/4" DIA. HOLE

1/16" DIA. HOLE

LEG—3/16"
WOOD OR
PLYWOOD
(12 REQUIRED)

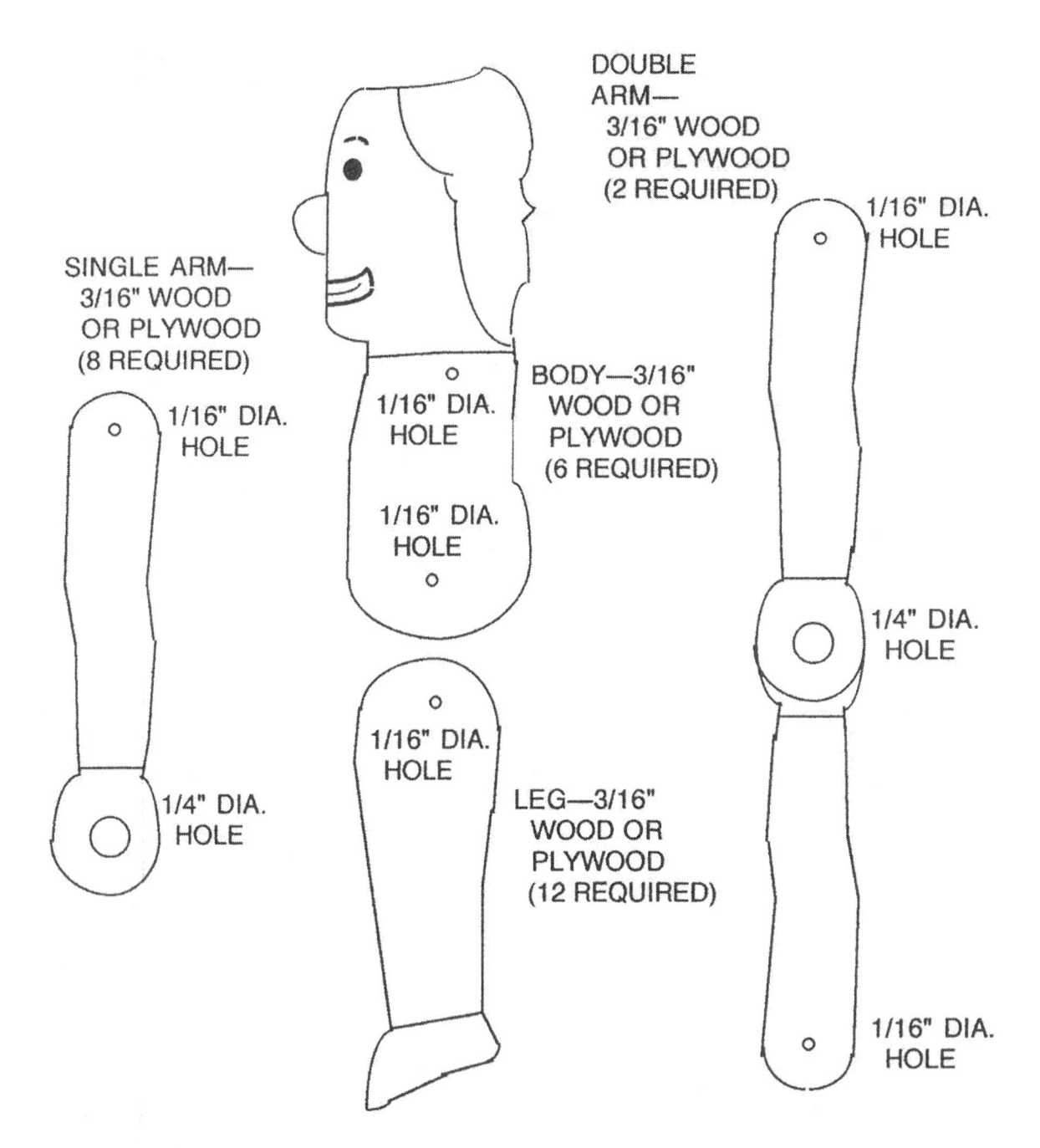

1/16" DIA. HOLE

Full-size patterns for clown acrobats.

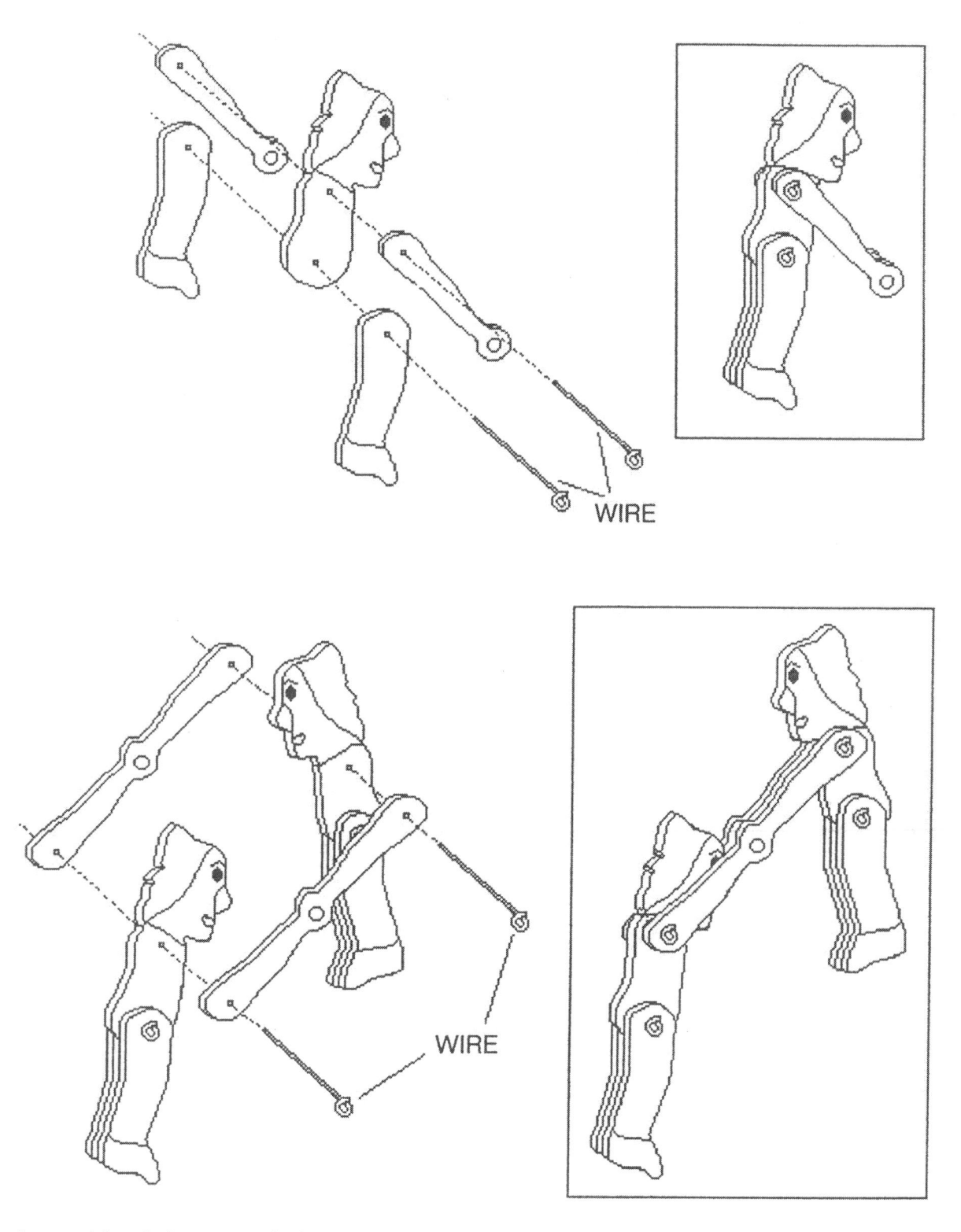

ACROBATS

WIRE

WIRE

Assembly of clown acrobats.

207

THE WHIRLIGIG MAKER'S BOOK

The propeller hub is made from 3/4" x 2" x 2" wood. Drill a 1/4" shaft hole. Cut the 3/16" wide x 3/4" deep notches for the propeller blades at 45 degree angles to the face of the hub. A clockwise propeller is shown, but you can reverse the notches for a counter-clockwise rotation if desired (this will also require reversing the direction of the clowns on the propeller pegs). The notches in the hub need to be made accurately for the whirligig to work properly.

Cut the propeller blades from 3/16" wood or plywood to the pattern shown. Then glue them in the slots in the hub. Place the hub on a flat surface with the forward side down. The blades are then installed with the forward side flush with the flat surface.

The peg mounting blocks are made from half sections of 1" x 1" wood. Drill the 1/4" peg holes before cutting the wood in half from corner to corner. If corner strips are used, place two together to form square piece for accurate drilling perpendicular to the face of the mounting blocks.

Glue the mounting blocks to the tips of the propeller blades, as shown. Then glue a peg dowel into the hole in each block. If everything was done properly, the pegs should be perpendicular to the face of the propeller.

I recommend painting the propeller unit before further assembly. However, leave the pegs unfinished until the hands have been installed over them.

Install a washer over the propeller end of the shaft. Then thread the propeller hub onto the shaft. Secure the propeller with a washer and nut.

Test the assembly in front of a fan to make certain that the propeller and shaft assembly with the double-clowns works properly.

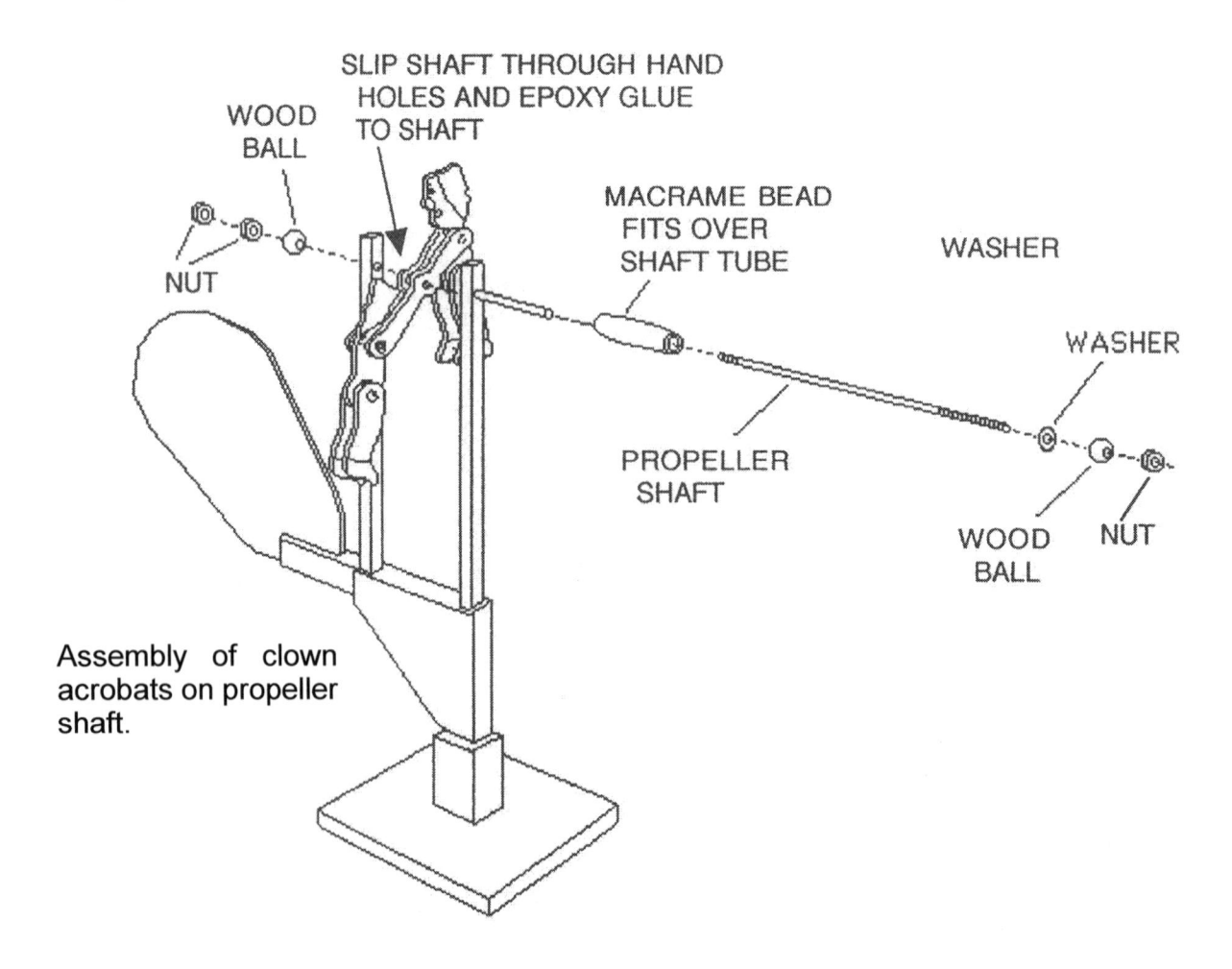

Assembly of clown acrobats on propeller shaft.

ACROBATS

PROPELLER BLADE

TOP VIEW

1/4" DIA. HOLE

MOUNTING BLOCK—HALF SECTION OF 1" X 1" WOOD 1-1/4" LONG (4 REQUIRED)

1/4" DIA. X 3" HARDWOOD DOWEL (4 REQUIRED)

PROPELLER HUB—3/4" WOOD (1 REQUIRED)

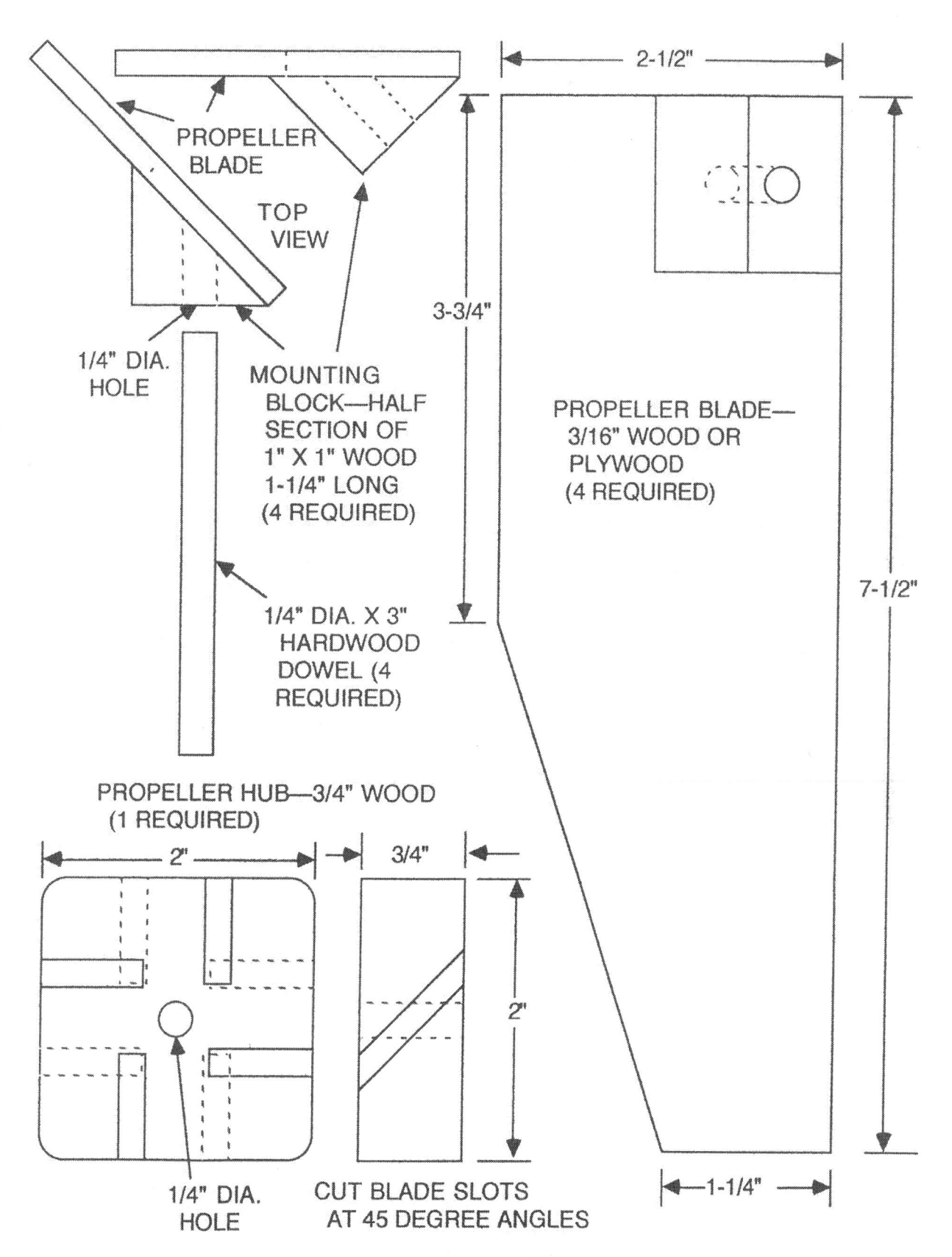

2"

3/4"

1/4" DIA. HOLE

CUT BLADE SLOTS AT 45 DEGREE ANGLES

2-1/2"

3-3/4"

PROPELLER BLADE— 3/16" WOOD OR PLYWOOD (4 REQUIRED)

7-1/2"

1-1/4"

2"

Full-size patterns for propeller hub, blades, and mounting blocks.

THE WHIRLIGIG MAKER'S BOOK

PROPELLER BLADE

WOOD MACRAME BEAD— 5/16" DIA. HOLE X 1-7/8" LONG

1/4" DIA. X 9-3/4" BRASS ROD— THREAD 2" FOR HUB AND 3/4" ON TAIL END

POST

WASHER

HUB

WASHER

NUT

5/16" O.D. (17/64" I.D.) X 2-1/2" BRASS TUBE

NUT

WOOD BALL

CLOWN ARMS— EPOXY GLUE TO HAND HOLES TO SHAFT

PROPELLER BLADE

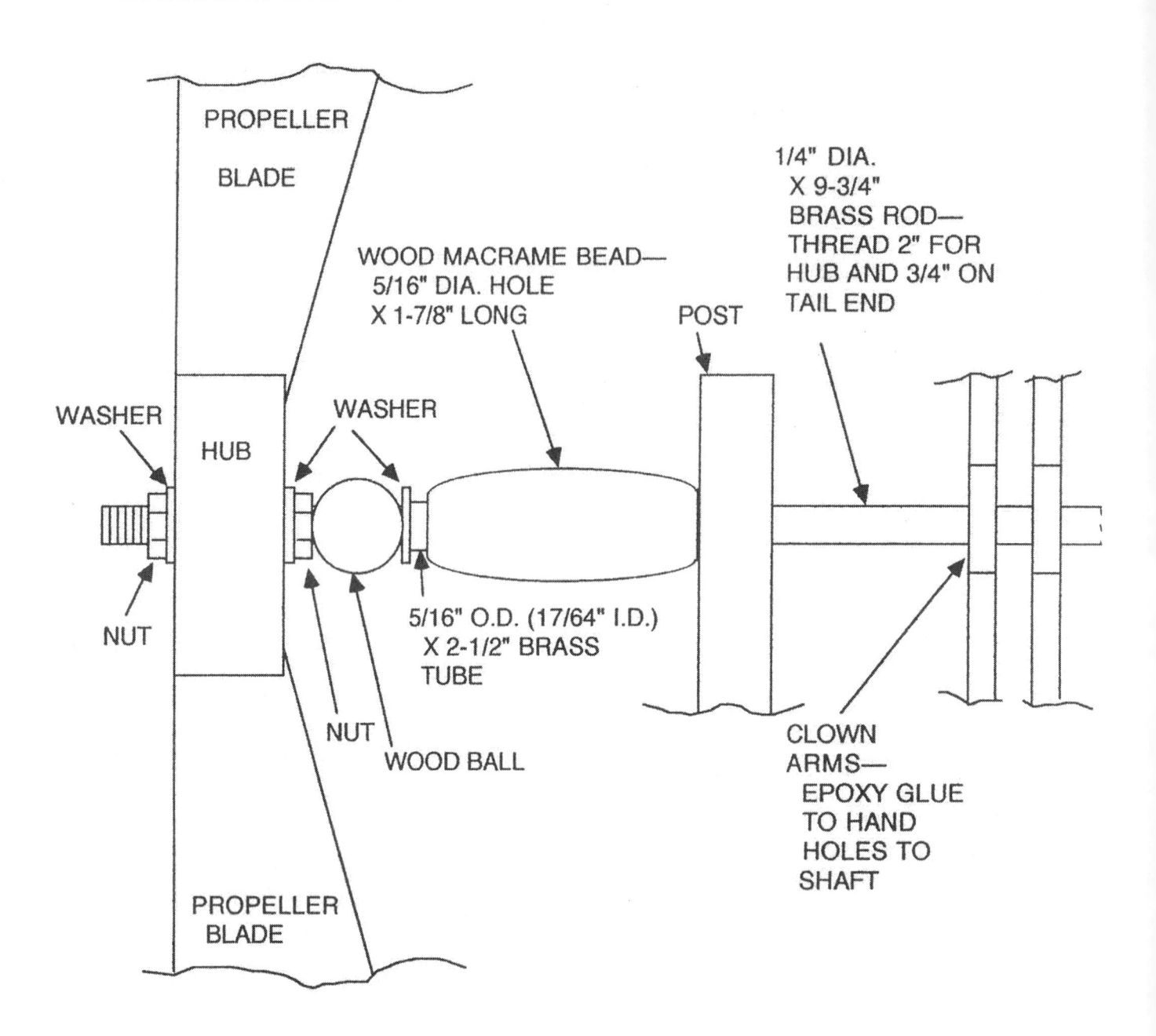

Propeller shaft assembly plan.

ACROBATS

POST

5/16" O.D. (17/64" I.D.) X 5/8" BRASS TUBE

NUT

WOOD BALL

GLUE BLOCK AND PEG TO PROPELLER BLOCK

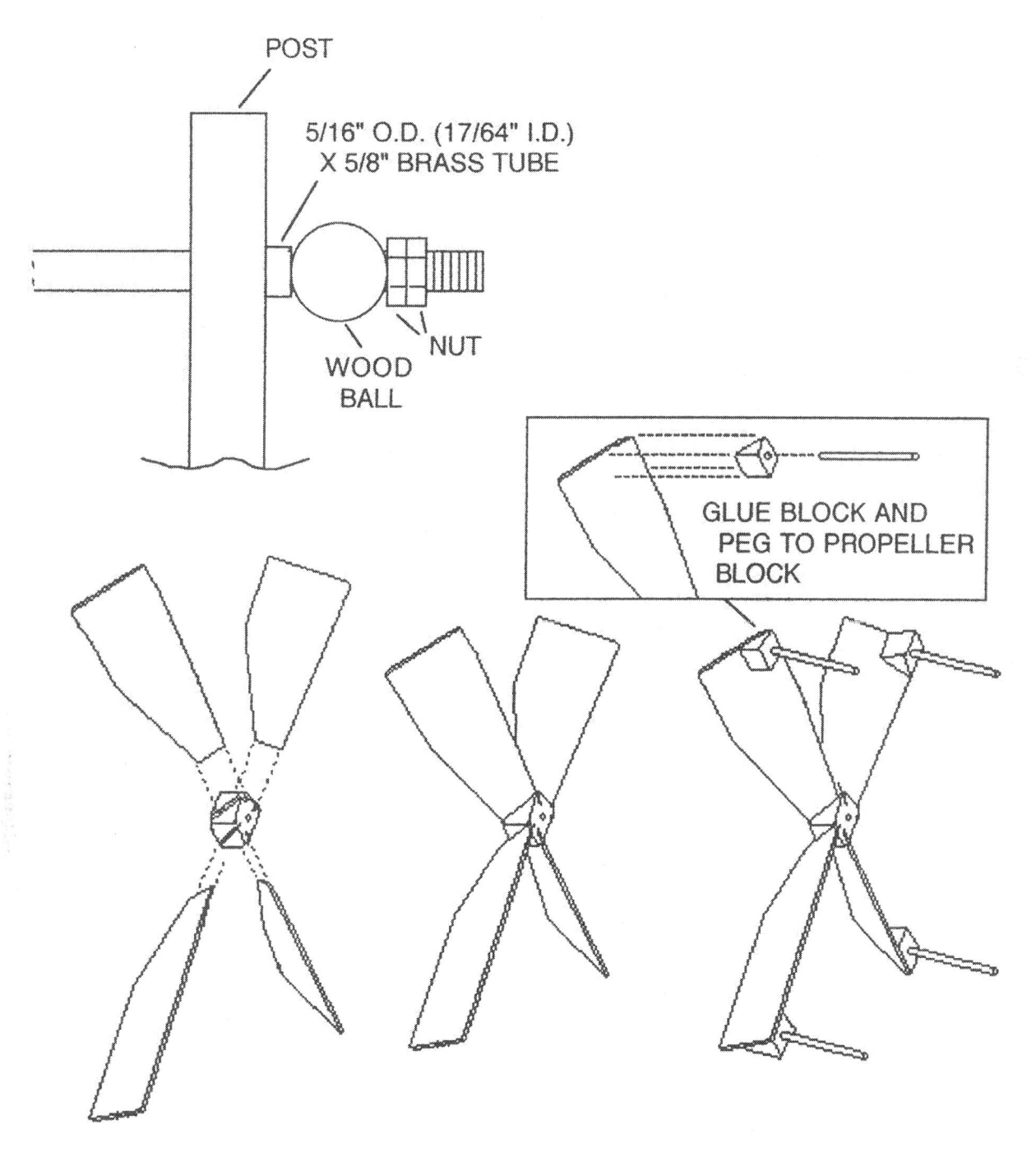

Assembly of propeller.

211

THE WHIRLIGIG MAKER'S BOOK

Next, install the single clowns over the pegs, centering the hands on the pegs with 1/4" space between hands. The arms should be positioned so that they extend outward from the blade tip and the hand and arm holes are in line with the forward edge of the propeller blades. Glue the hands to the pegs.

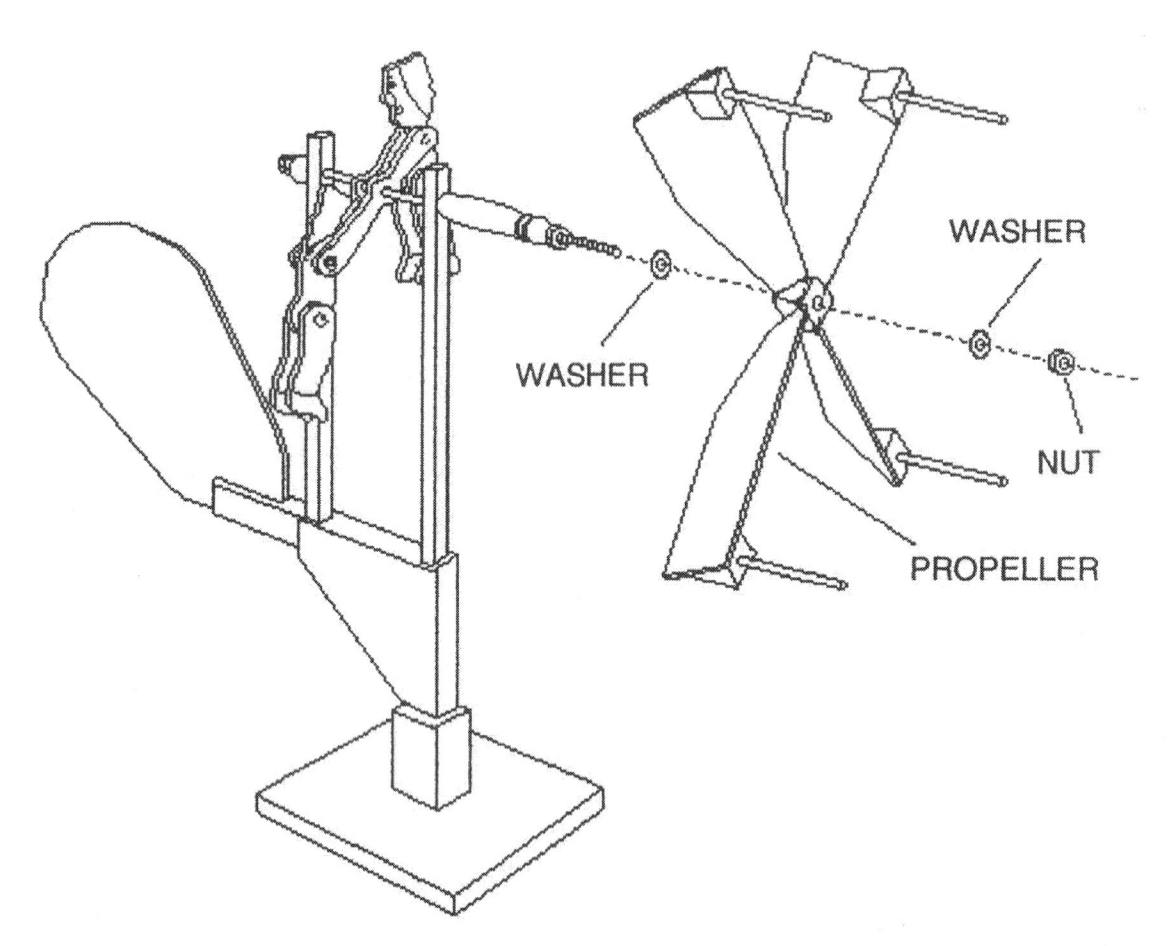

Assembly of propeller on shaft.

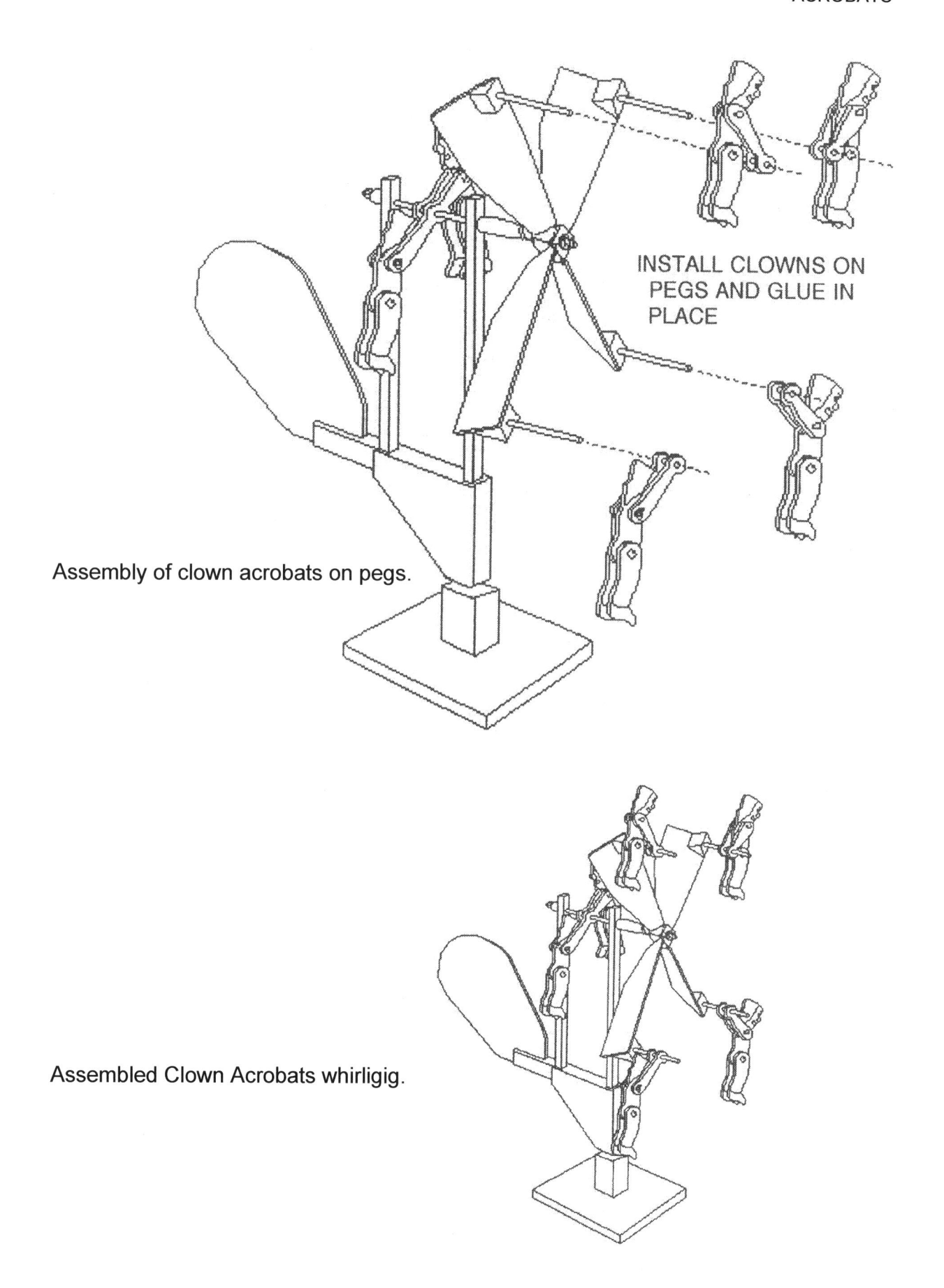

ACROBATS

INSTALL CLOWNS ON PEGS AND GLUE IN PLACE

Assembly of clown acrobats on pegs.

Assembled Clown Acrobats whirligig.

213

TESTING

The whirligig is ready for testing. This can be inside with a fan or outdoors in a light wind. The whirligig should start easily if all of the parts turn properly. Make any necessary adjustments and add oil to friction areas of metal parts.

You can create your own whirligigs using this same basic design. As a starter, you may want to replace the clowns with gymnasts or animal figures.

Chapter 17

CLOWN

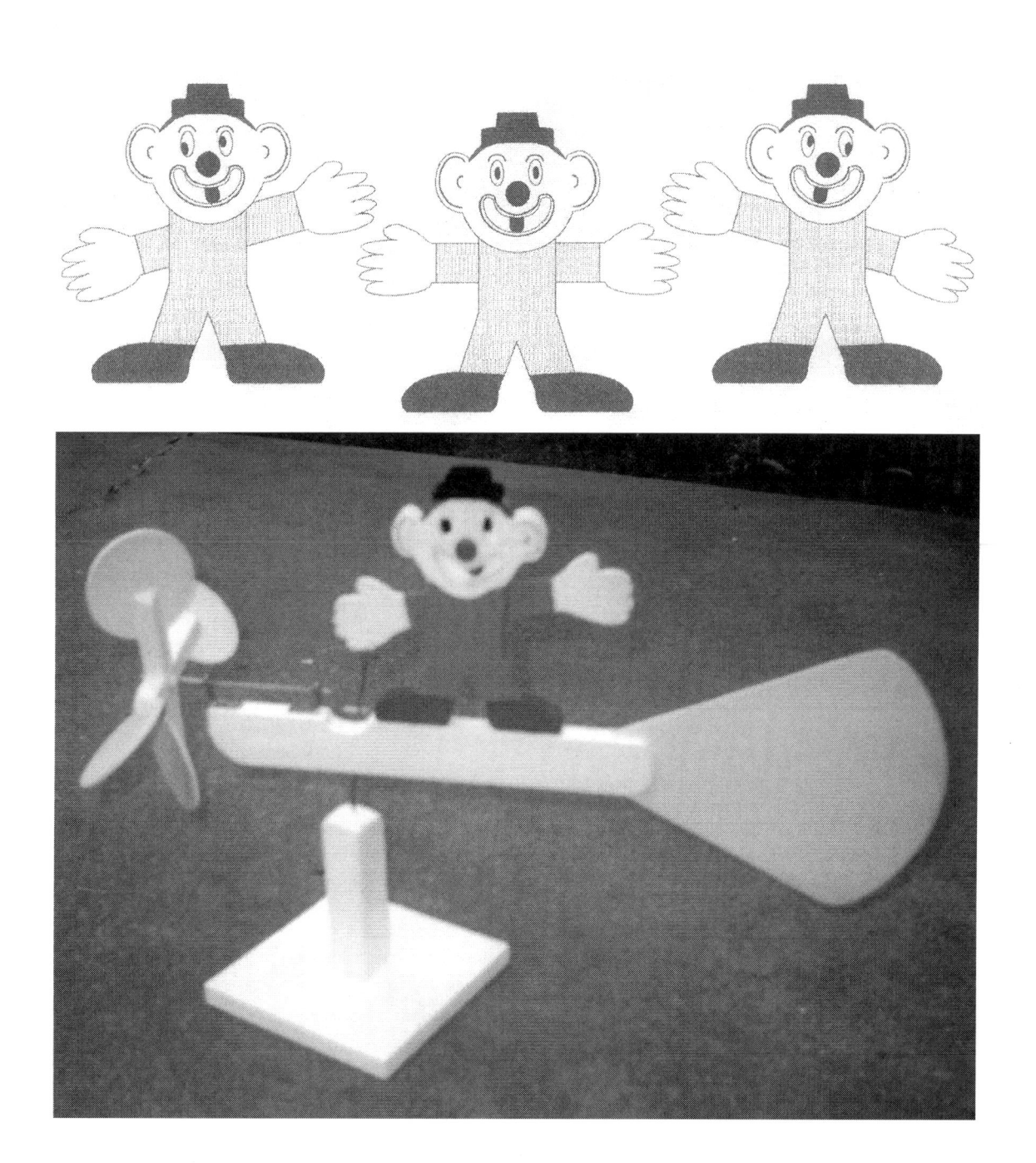

The Clown whirligig is a fun project both to build and then watch perform after you have completed it. When the wind turns the propeller, the clown rolls eyes and tongue back and forth and moves arms up and down.

MATERIALS

- 3/4" x 8" x 8" wood or plywood for display base.
- 1-1/2" x 1-1/2" x 6" wood for display post.
- 3/4" x 1-3/4" x 14" wood for platform.
- 1/8" x 8" x 10" plywood for vane.
- 3/8" x 3/4" x 6" wood for mounting blocks for clown.
- 1/4" x 10" x 18" plywood for clown body parts.
- 1/4" diameter x 2" hardwood dowel for clown nose axle.
- 5/8" diameter wood ball with 1/4" diameter axle hole for nose (2 required).
- 3/4" x 3/4" x 16" wood for propeller hub.
- 1/8" x 4" x 16" wood or plywood for propeller blades.
- 1/4" outside diameter (9/64" inside diameter) x 1" brass tubing for propeller-shaft spacer.
- 1/4" outside diameter (11/64" inside diameter) x 2" brass tubing for pivot tube.
- 1/8" diameter x 8" brass rod for crank shaft.
- 5/64" diameter x 4" stiff wire for connecting rod.
- 1/4" diameter steel ball for pivot bearing.
- 6-32 nut (4 required) for attaching propeller hub to shaft.
- Washer (3 required) for use on propeller shaft.
- 1" long plastic tubing with 1/8" diameter hole for crankshaft spacers.
- 4-40 x 1" round-head bolt (2 required) for attaching clown to platform.
- 4-40 x 1/2" round-head bolt (2 required) for attaching connecting rod plate to clown hand.
- 4-40 nut (4 required) and 4-40 washer (6 required).
- 1/16" x 1-1/2" brass strip for connecting rod plate.
- 5/32" diameter x 5" nail for pivot rod for display base.
- 1/2" x 1" x 1" brass L-bracket (2 required) for crankshaft mounting.
- Screw (4 required) for mounting L-brackets.
- 3/4" diameter plastic washer with 1/4" diameter hole (2 required) for clown nose axle spacers.
- Glue.
- Finishing nails.
- Small felt pad for display base (4 required).
- Paint.

DISPLAY STAND

The display stand is useful not only for displaying the finished whirligig indoors, but also for holding the whirligig during construction and for testing it in front of a fan. Construction is easy. The base is 3/4" x 8" x 8" wood or plywood. The 1-1/2" x 1-1/2" x 6" post is glued in the center of the base. Use nails from underside of base for added support. A 5/32" diameter x 5" nail is driven 2" into the center of the top of the post for use as a pivot rod. Drill a pilot hole that is perpendicular to the top of the post before driving the nail into the hole. Cut the head off of the nail with a hacksaw. File the upper end of the nail smooth, rounding the corners slightly.

Sand and paint the display stand. A clear or color finish can be used.

Attach felt pads to the corners of the underside of the base.

PLATFORM

The platform is made of 3/4" x 1-3/4" x 14" wood. Cut the wood to the pattern shown. Make a 1/8" x 1-1/2" slot for the vane. Drill 1/4" x 1-1/8" deep hole for pivot ball and tube. The pivot hole must be accurately centered and perpendicular to the wood surfaces for the whirligig to work properly. I use a drill press and drill press vise.

Use 1/2" x 1" x 1" brass L-brackets with 9/64" holes for the crankshaft. Fasten the brass L-brackets to the platform with screws. Depending on the brackets selected, it may be necessary to expand hole sizes and/or drill additional holes.

Cut the vane from 1/8" plywood to the pattern shown. Glue the vane in the platform slot, as shown.

Cut clown mounting blocks to the patterns shown and nail and glue them to the platform in the positions shown.

Install 1/4" diameter steel ball and 1/4" diameter x 2" brass tube in pivot hole.

Sand the platform. The platform can be painted at this time, or you can wait until the assembly has been completed. The color scheme can be as desired.

PROPELLER AND CRANKSHAFT

The crankshaft is made from 1/8" diameter x 8" brass rod. Make threads for 1-1/2" on one end of the rod using a 6-32 die. Bend crank in other end of shaft to the pattern shown. Install the crankshaft in the L-bracket holes. Use brass tube spacer and washer and two nuts on propeller end, as shown. Install short length of plastic tubing that fits snugly over tubing on other end. The shaft should turn freely in the holders with no binding. Apply light oil to the shaft to further decrease friction.

The propeller hub is made from two pieces of 3/4" x 3/4" x 8" wood. Cut 3/8" deep x 3/4" long notches in the wood pieces so that they fit together in a cross pattern. Glue pieces together. Drill a 1/8" shaft hole. Cut the ends of the wood pieces corner to corner for 2". Cut half the wood away in the same direction on each end of the propeller hub for

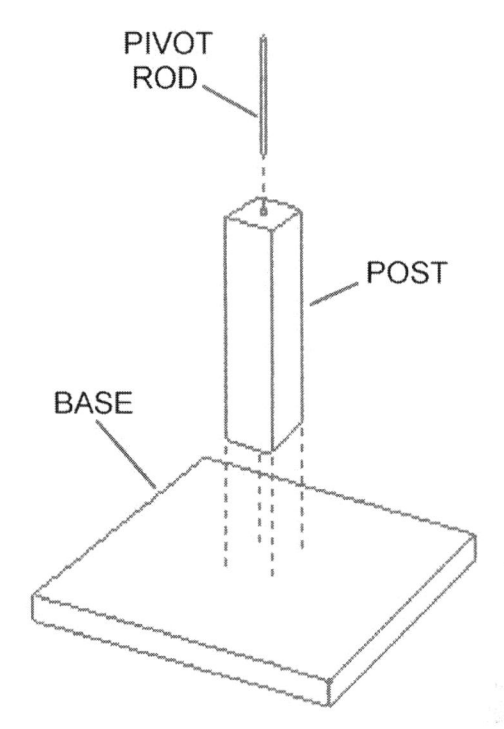

Assembly of display stand.

the propeller blades for a clockwise propeller, as shown. The cuts for the propeller blades need to be made accurately for the whirligig to work properly.

Cut the propeller blades from 1/8" wood or plywood to 4" diameter circles.

Then glue the blades to the hub. Position the blades carefully so they are centered on the hub. Use two small wire brads on each blade to reinforce joint and hold blades in position until the glue sets. Sand and paint the propeller.

Install the completed propeller on the threaded end of the crankshaft with washers and nuts, as shown.

Test the assembly in front of a fan to make certain that the propeller and crankshaft assembly works properly.

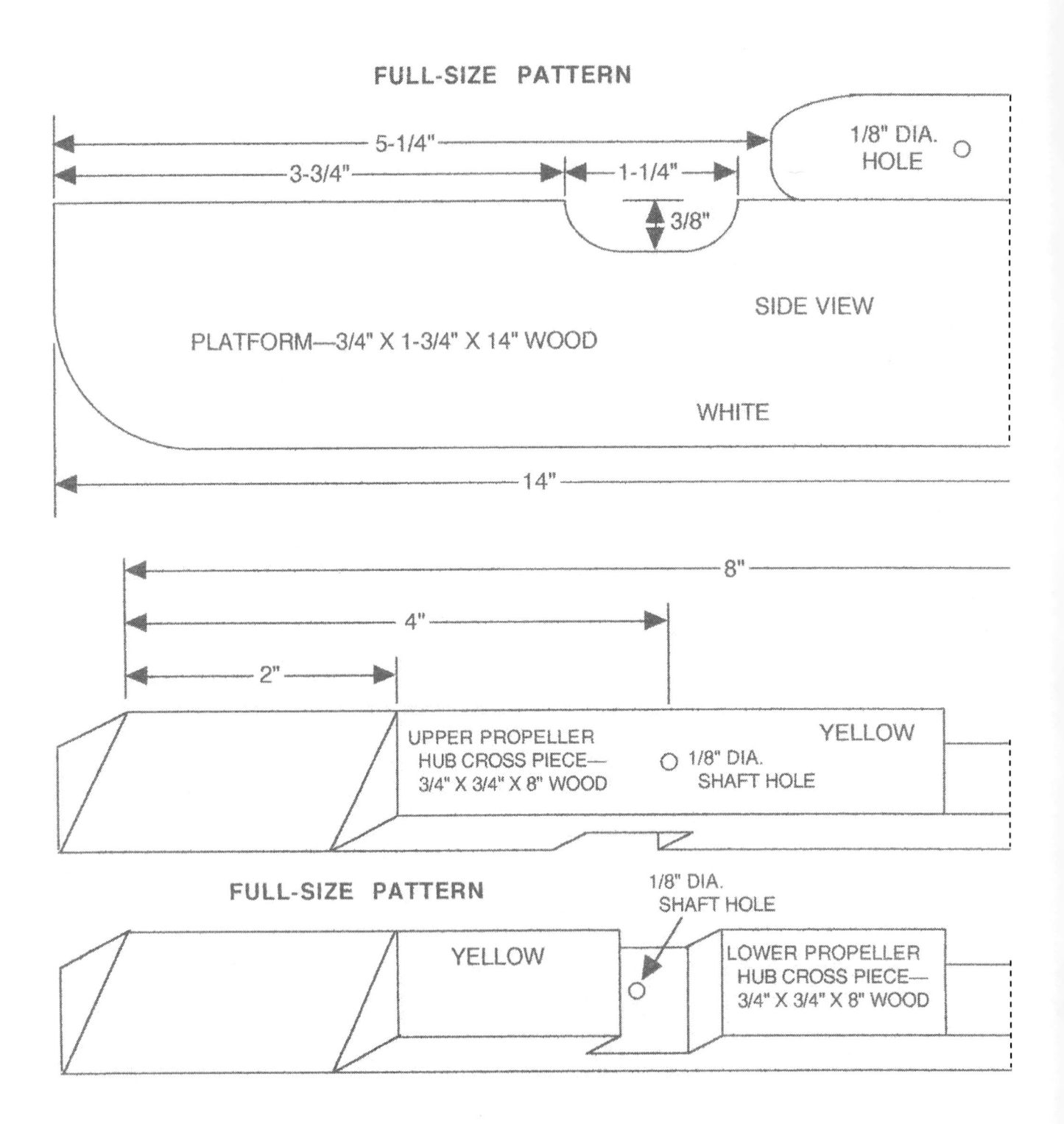

THE WHIRLIGIG MAKER'S BOOK

FULL-SIZE PATTERN

SIDE VIEW

PLATFORM—3/4" X 1-3/4" X 14" WOOD

WHITE

- 5-1/4"
- 3-3/4"
- 1-1/4"
- 3/8"
- 14"
- 1/8" DIA. HOLE

UPPER PROPELLER HUB CROSS PIECE— 3/4" X 3/4" X 8" WOOD

YELLOW

1/8" DIA. SHAFT HOLE

- 8"
- 4"
- 2"

FULL-SIZE PATTERN

YELLOW

LOWER PROPELLER HUB CROSS PIECE— 3/4" X 3/4" X 8" WOOD

1/8" DIA. SHAFT HOLE

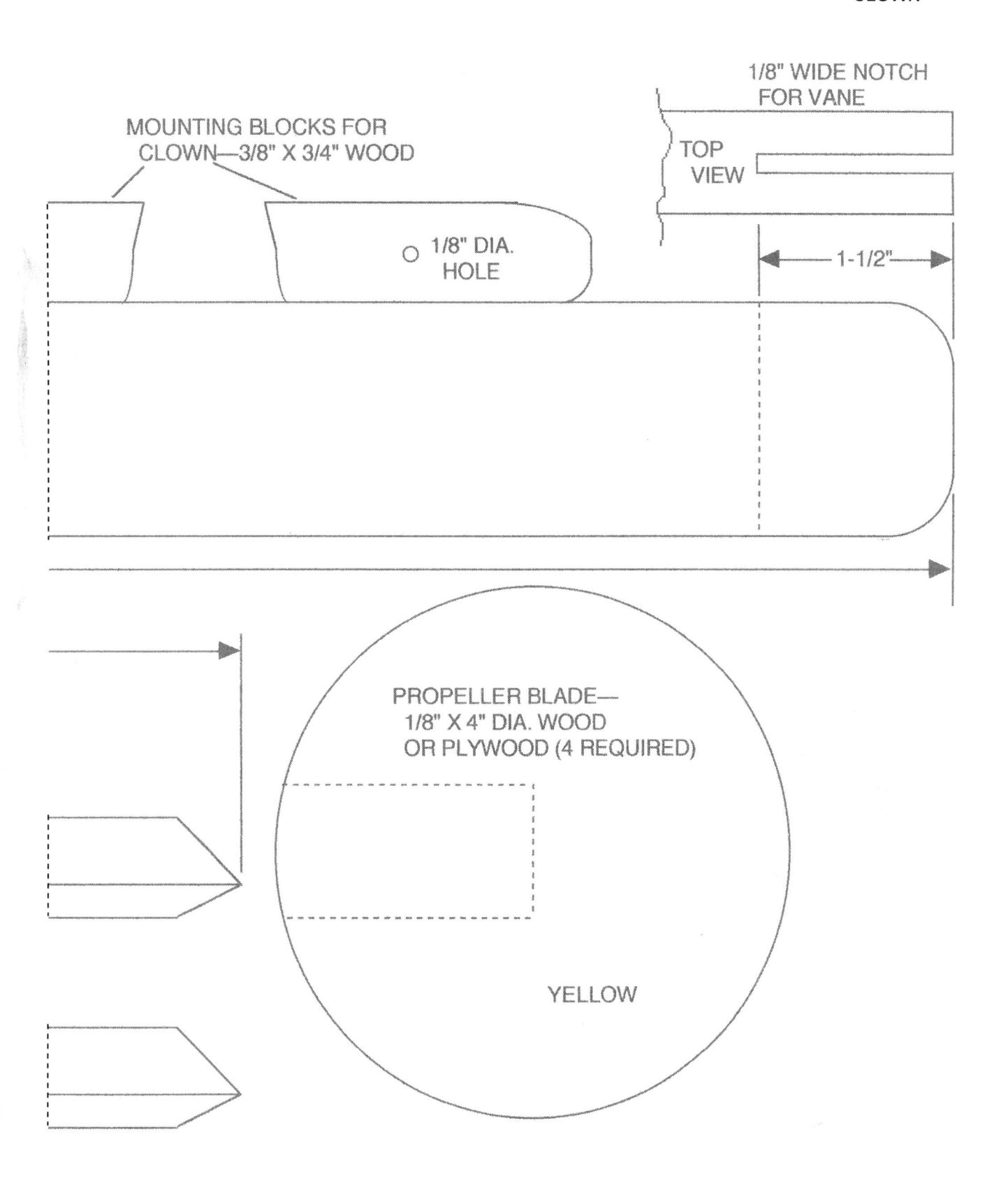

CLOWN

MOUNTING BLOCKS FOR
CLOWN—3/8" X 3/4" WOOD

1/8" DIA. HOLE

1/8" WIDE NOTCH
FOR VANE

TOP VIEW

1-1/2"

PROPELLER BLADE—
1/8" X 4" DIA. WOOD
OR PLYWOOD (4 REQUIRED)

YELLOW

219

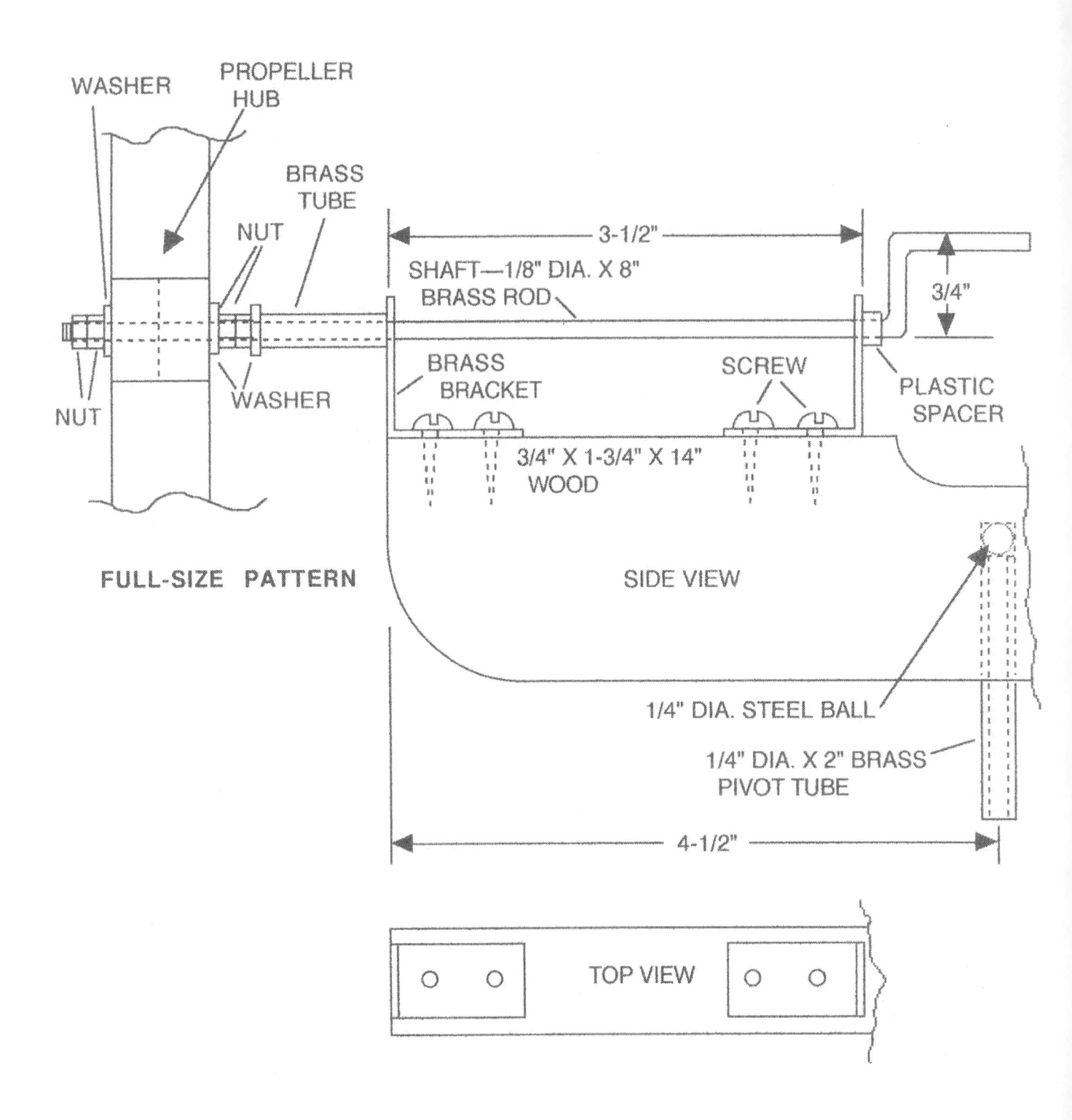

THE WHIRLIGIG MAKER'S BOOK

WASHER
PROPELLER HUB
BRASS TUBE
NUT
NUT
WASHER

SHAFT—1/8" DIA. X 8" BRASS ROD
3-1/2"
3/4"
BRASS BRACKET
SCREW
PLASTIC SPACER
3/4" X 1-3/4" X 14" WOOD

FULL-SIZE PATTERN

SIDE VIEW

1/4" DIA. STEEL BALL
1/4" DIA. X 2" BRASS PIVOT TUBE
4-1/2"

TOP VIEW

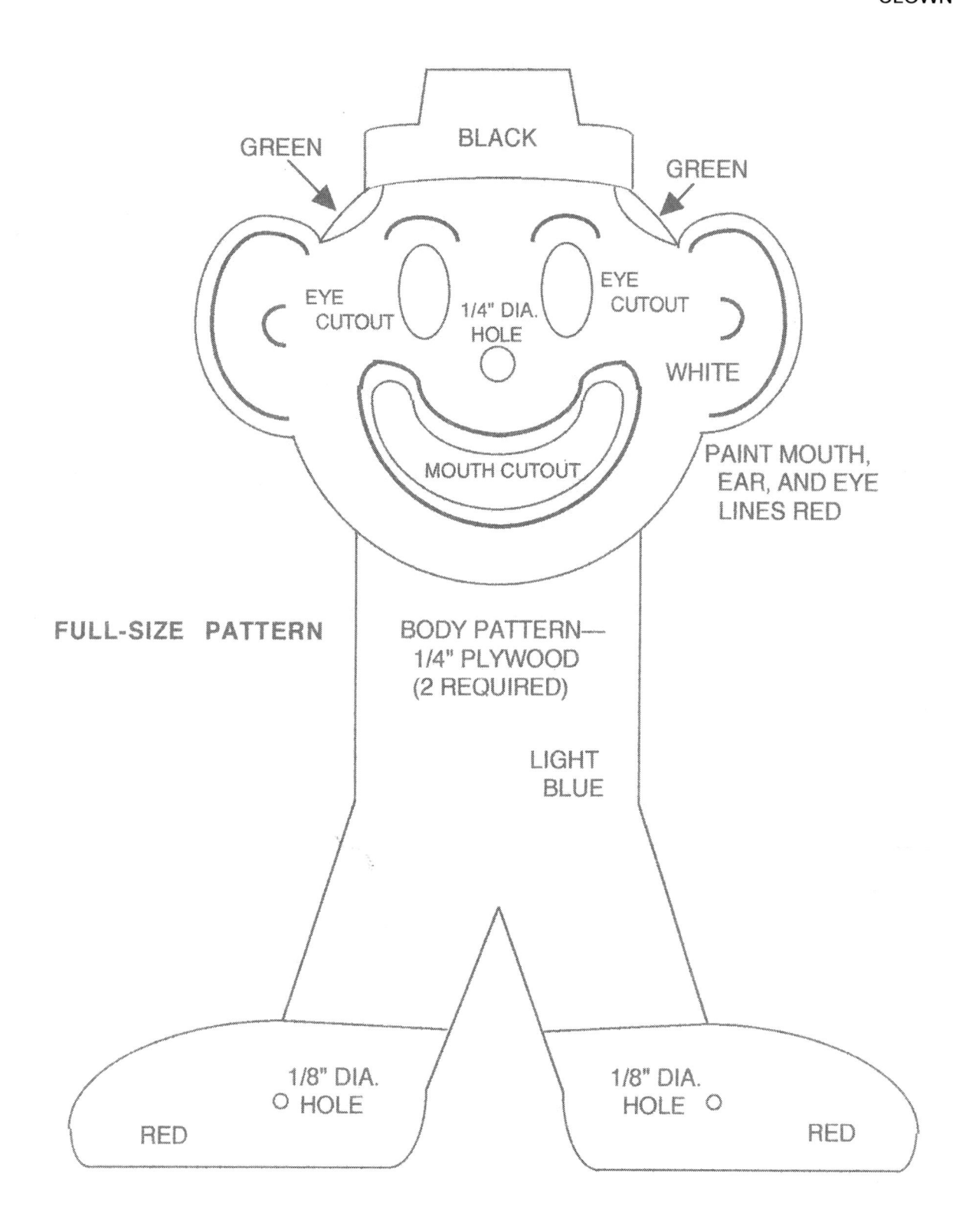

CLOWN

GREEN
BLACK
GREEN

EYE CUTOUT
1/4" DIA. HOLE
EYE CUTOUT

WHITE

MOUTH CUTOUT

PAINT MOUTH, EAR, AND EYE LINES RED

FULL-SIZE PATTERN

BODY PATTERN—
1/4" PLYWOOD
(2 REQUIRED)

LIGHT BLUE

1/8" DIA. HOLE
1/8" DIA. HOLE

RED
RED

221

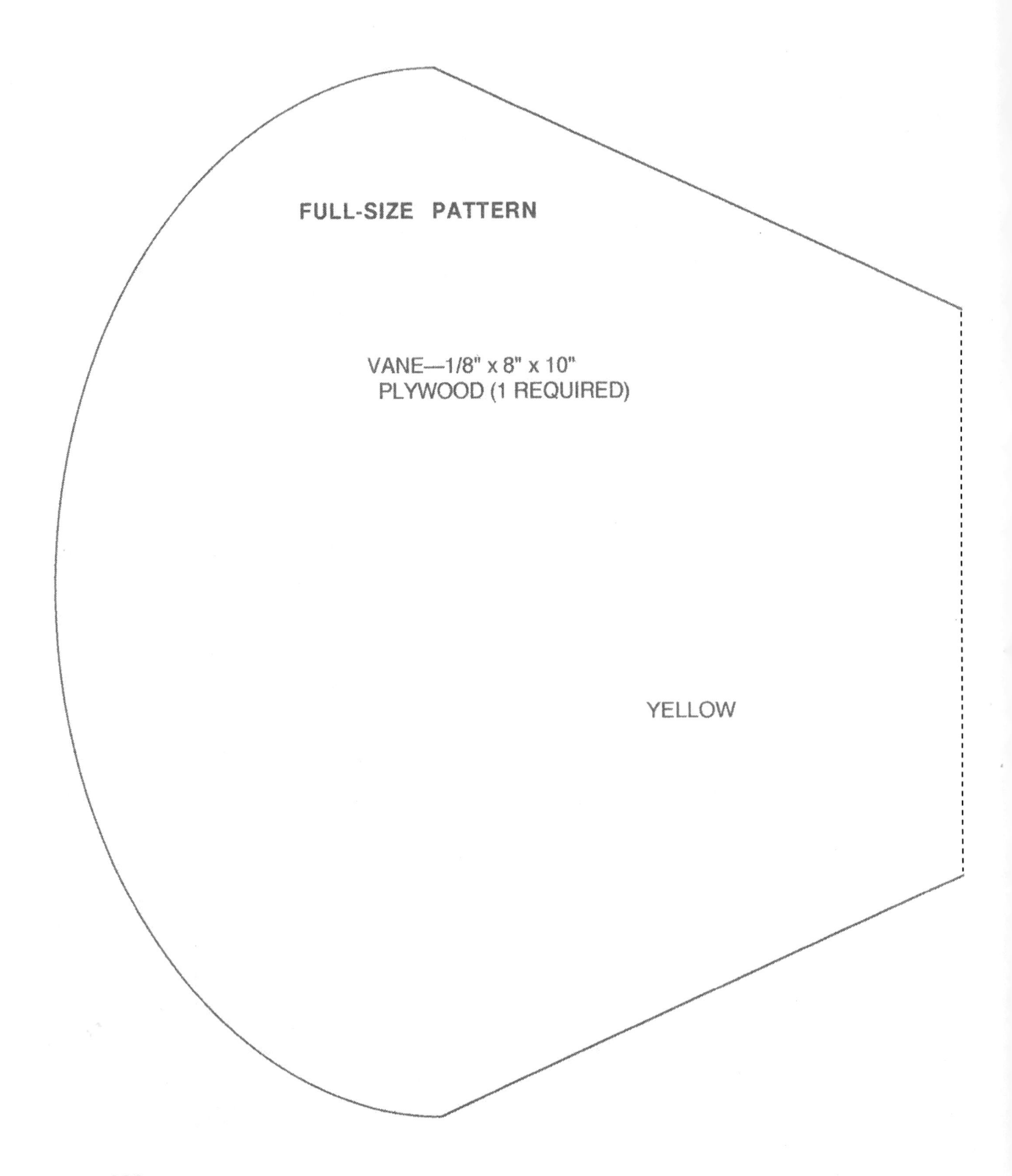

THE WHIRLIGIG MAKER'S BOOK

FULL-SIZE PATTERN

VANE—1/8" x 8" x 10"
PLYWOOD (1 REQUIRED)

YELLOW

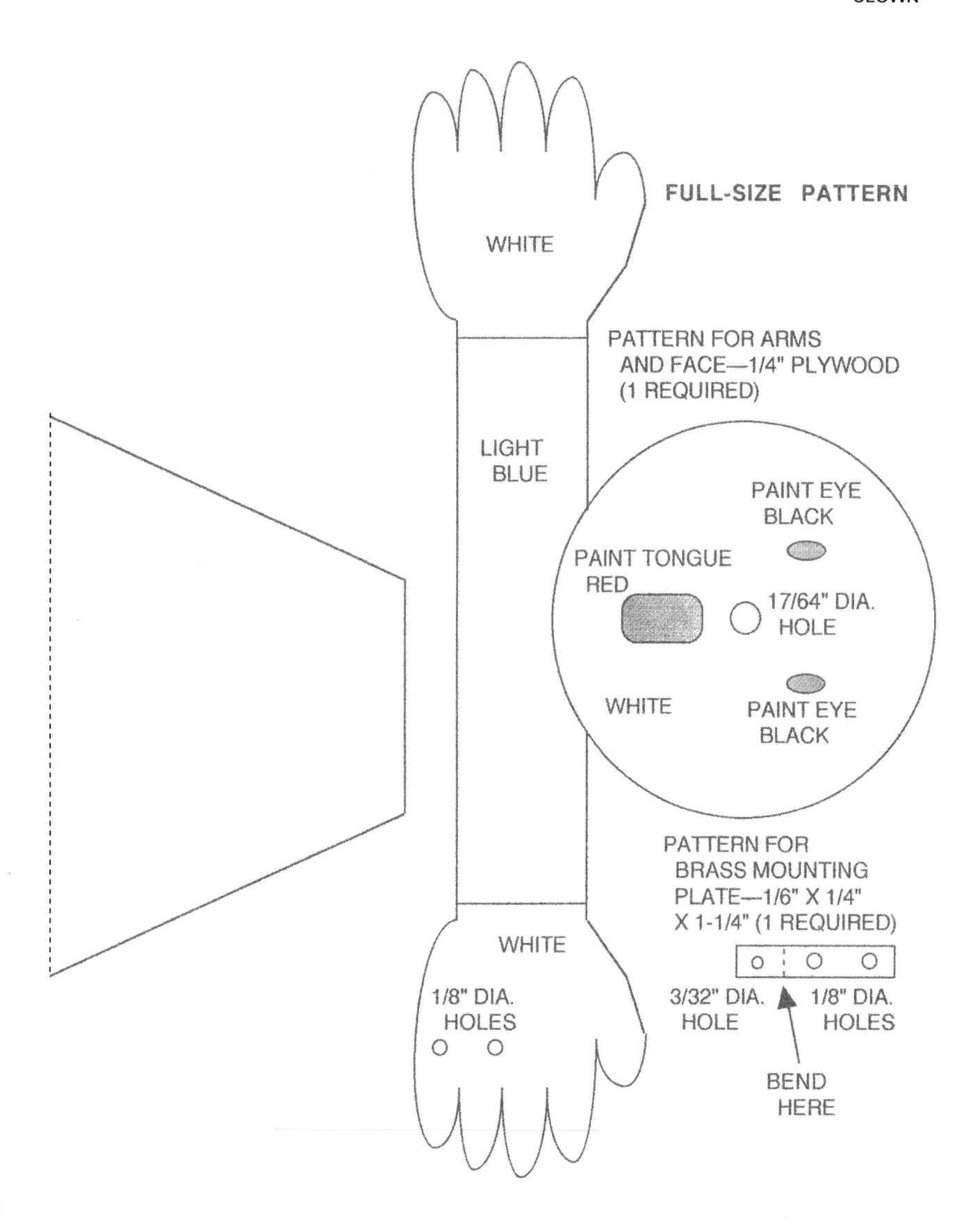

CLOWN

FULL-SIZE PATTERN

WHITE

PATTERN FOR ARMS
AND FACE—1/4" PLYWOOD
(1 REQUIRED)

LIGHT
BLUE

PAINT EYE
BLACK

PAINT TONGUE
RED

17/64" DIA.
HOLE

WHITE

PAINT EYE
BLACK

PATTERN FOR
BRASS MOUNTING
PLATE—1/6" X 1/4"
X 1-1/4" (1 REQUIRED)

WHITE

1/8" DIA.
HOLES

3/32" DIA.
HOLE

1/8" DIA.
HOLES

BEND
HERE

223

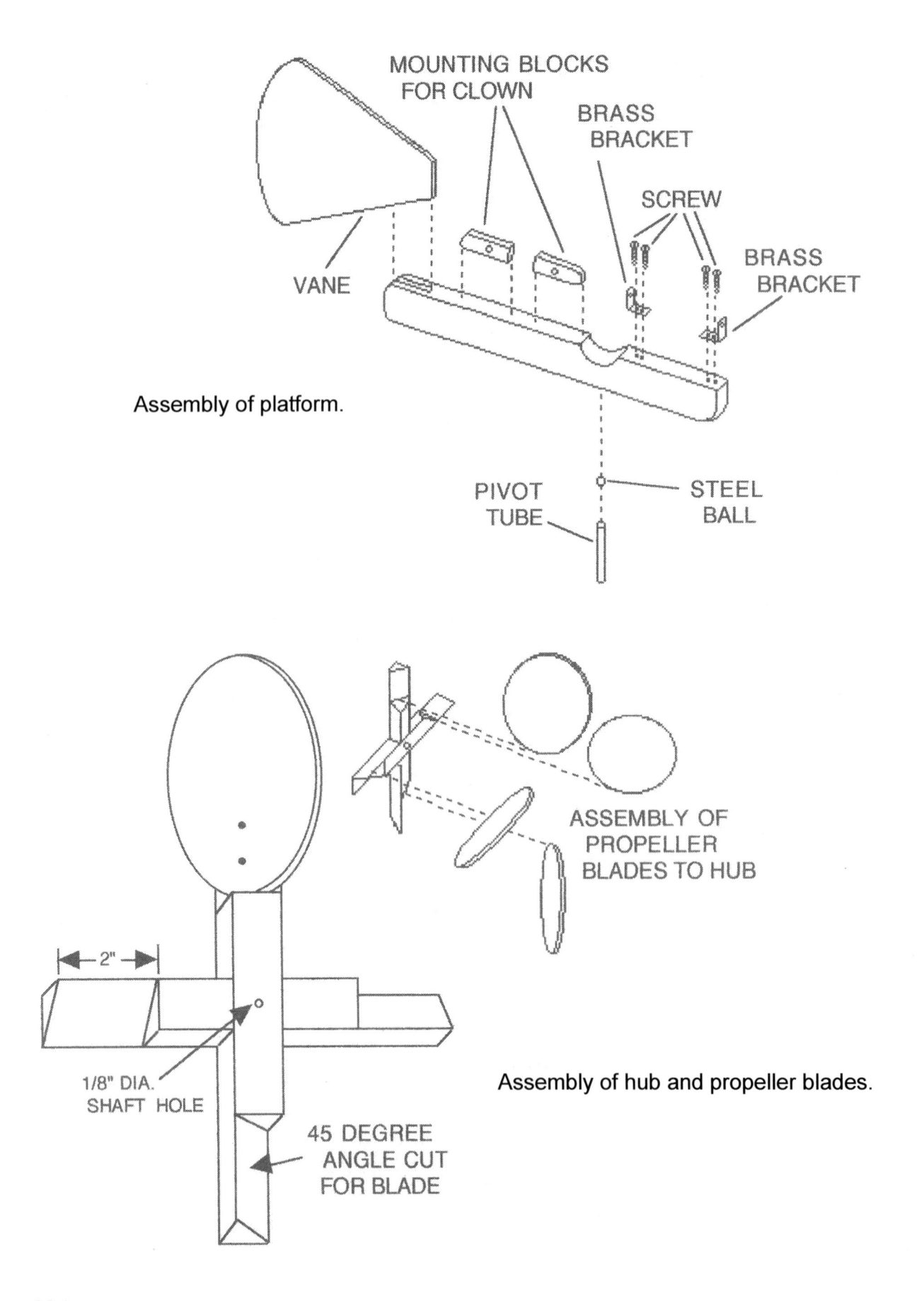

THE WHIRLIGIG MAKER'S BOOK

Assembly of platform.

- VANE
- MOUNTING BLOCKS FOR CLOWN
- BRASS BRACKET
- SCREW
- BRASS BRACKET
- PIVOT TUBE
- STEEL BALL

Assembly of hub and propeller blades.

- ASSEMBLY OF PROPELLER BLADES TO HUB
- 2"
- 1/8" DIA. SHAFT HOLE
- 45 DEGREE ANGLE CUT FOR BLADE

Assembly of crankshaft and propeller.

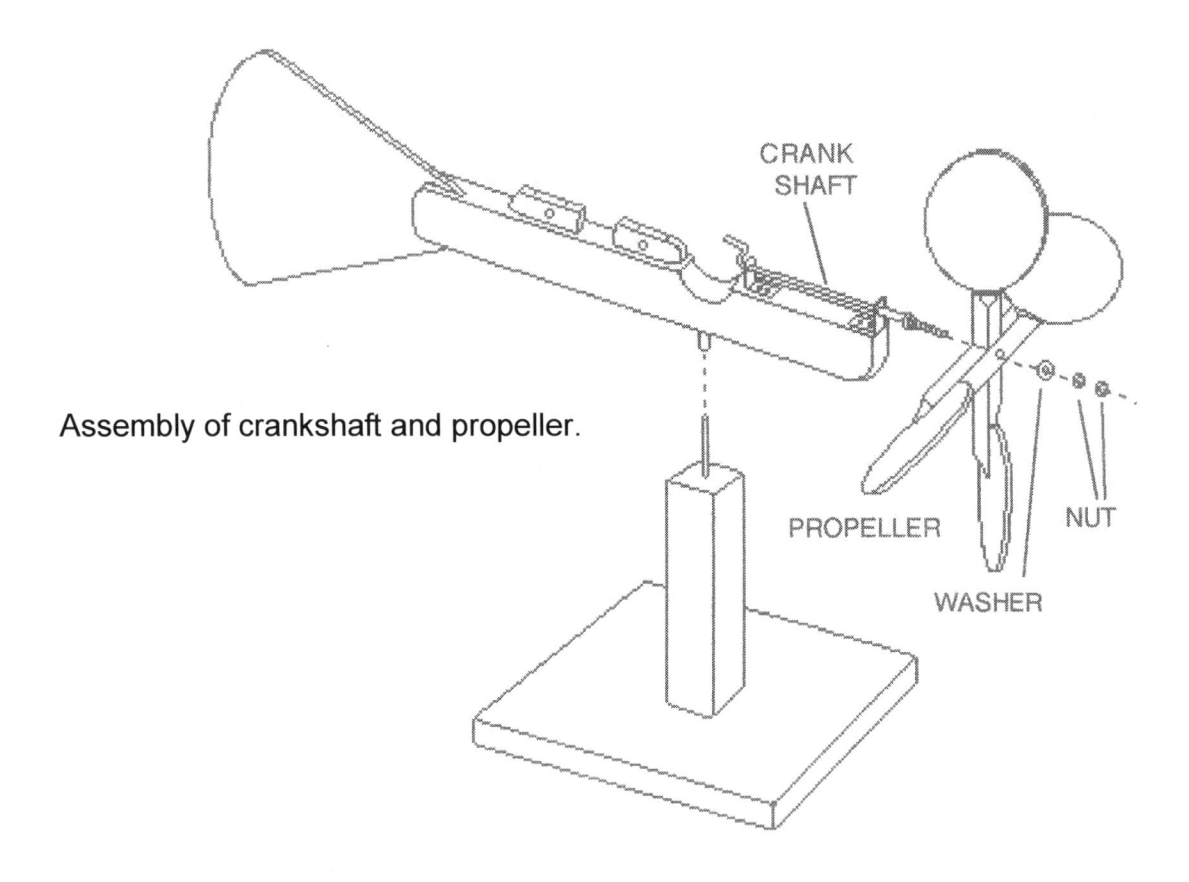

CLOWN

Cut the clown body parts from 1/4" plywood to the patterns shown. The two outside body parts should be back-to-back matches. Make eye and mouth cutouts to the patterns shown. Drill nose axle holes as shown. It is easiest to paint the body parts before further assembly. The black eyes and red tongue are painted to the patterns shown on the inside face piece on both sides. Drill and shape brass connecting rod plate and bolt this to clown hand in position shown.

Assemble the nose axle through the axle holes using plastic washers as spacers, as shown. Install the nose balls on each end of the axle. If the balls fit tightly over the ends of the axle, gluing will not be necessary. Leave enough space on the axle between the balls so that the arms rotate easily. Trim the ends of the axle off even with the tips of the nose balls.

Drill mounting holes and bolt the clown's feet to the mounting blocks.

The connecting rod is shaped from 5/64" diameter x 4" stiff wire. Bend a wire loop around a 1/8" diameter rod. Circle the rod twice, making a tight circle. The eye fits over the crankshaft between two plastic spacers. Bend the wire to pass through the hole in the mounting plate on the clown's hand so that the arms will be level when the crank is in a horizontal position to one side. Use tight fitting plastic spacers on each side of the connecting rod where it passes through the hole in the mounting plate.

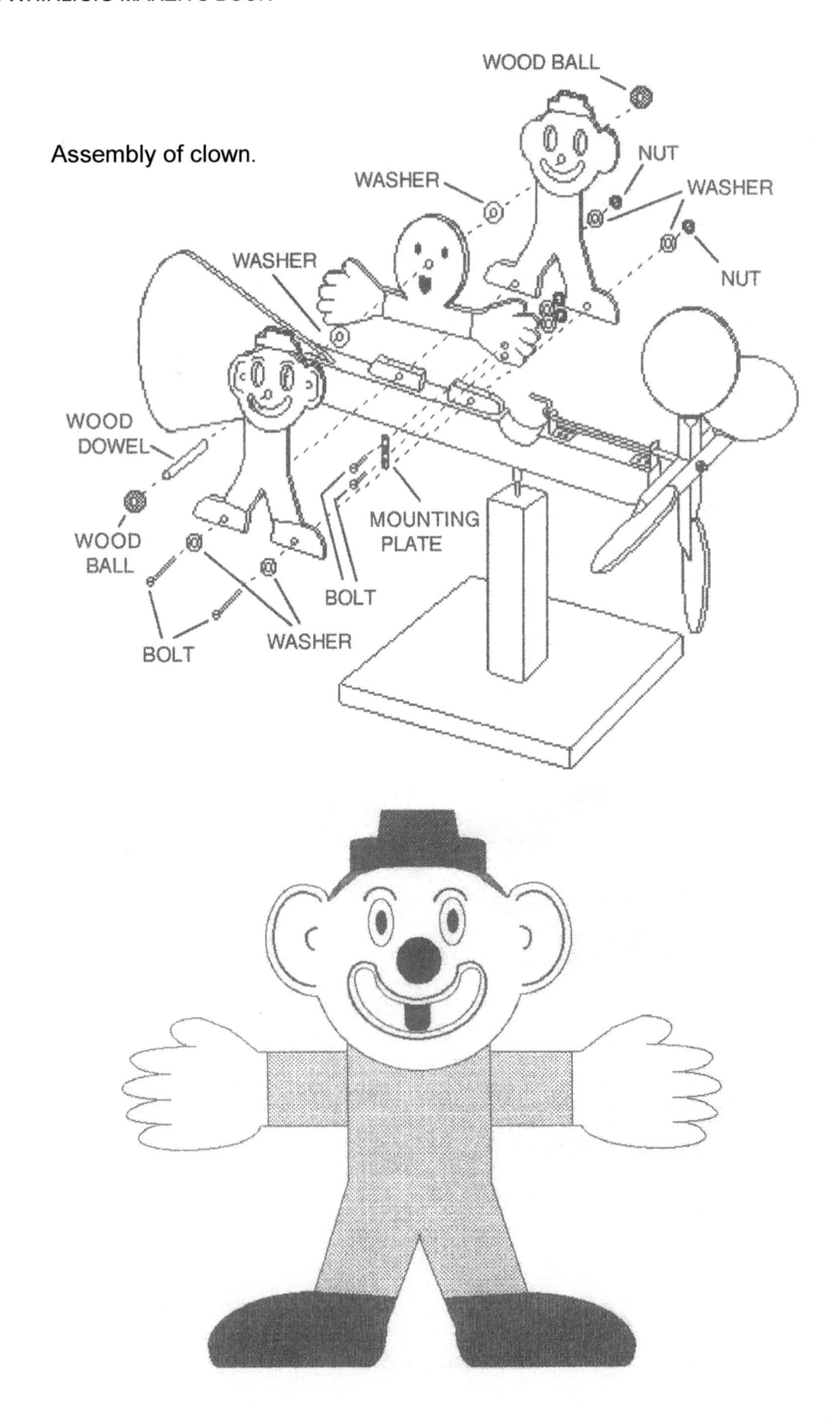

THE WHIRLIGIG MAKER'S BOOK

Assembly of clown.

TESTING AND FINISHING

The whirligig is ready for testing. This can be inside with a fan or outdoors in a light wind. The whirligig should start easily if all of the parts turn properly. Make any necessary adjustments and add oil to friction areas of metal parts.

If sanding and painting was not done previously, disassemble as necessary and do the sanding and painting.

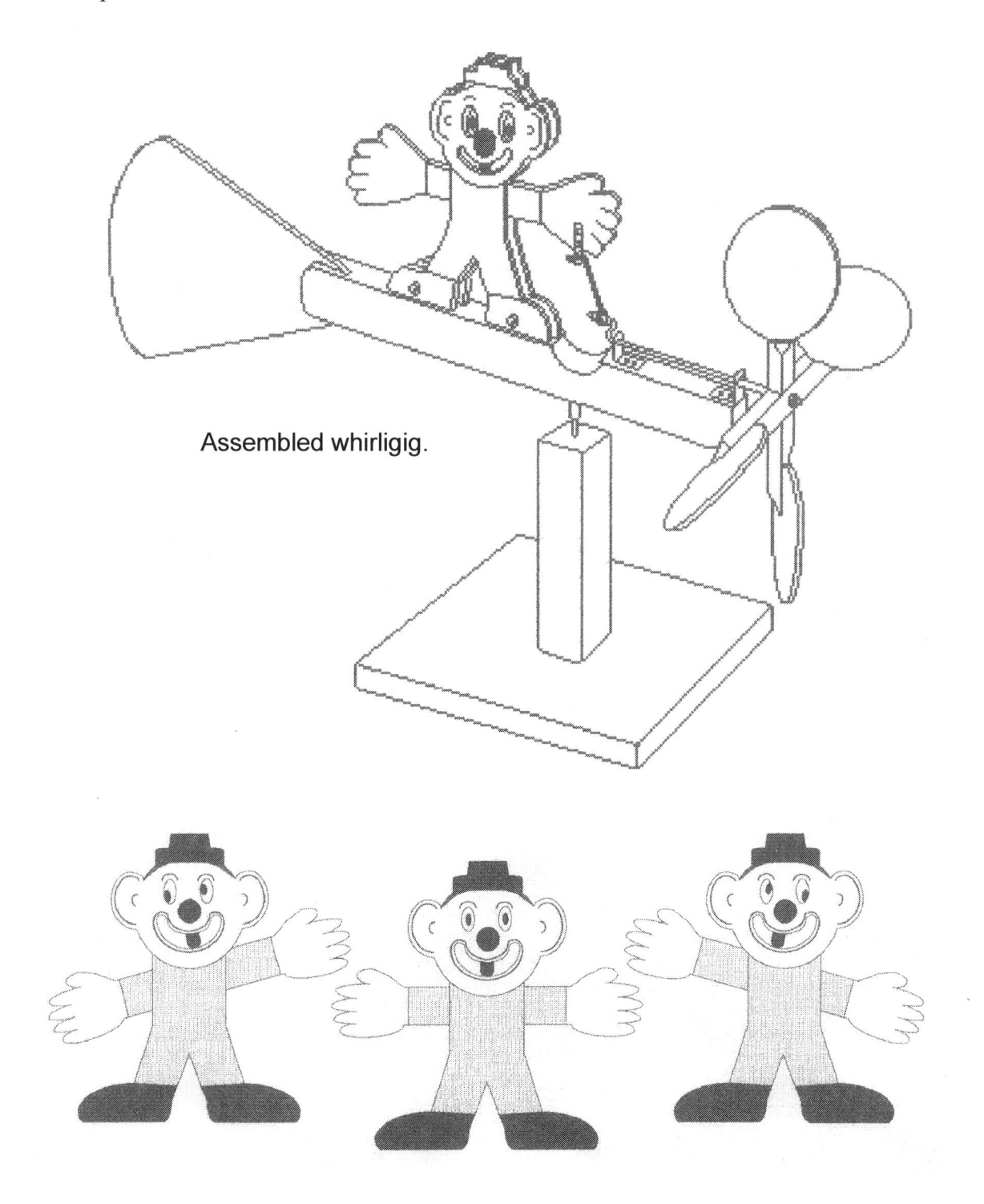

Assembled whirligig.

ABOUT THE AUTHOR

Jack Wiley is the author of fifty published books, including *How to Make Animated Toys and Whirligigs*, which may be of interest to readers of this book. For more information about the author and his books, go to: **http://www.amazon.com/author/jackwileypublications.**

Printed in Great Britain
by Amazon